EDI DEVELOPMENT STUDIES

Financial Regulation

Changing the Rules of the Game

Edited by
Dimitri Vittas

The World Bank
Washington, D. C.

The Economic Development Institute (EDI) was established by the World Bank in 1955 to train officials concerned with development planning, policymaking, investment analysis, and project implementation in member developing countries. At present the substance of the EDI's work emphasizes macroeconomic and sectoral economic policy analysis. Through a variety of courses, seminars, and workshops, most of which are given overseas in cooperation with local institutions, the EDI seeks to sharpen analytical skills used in policy analysis and to broaden understanding of the experience of individual countries with economic development. Although the EDI's publications are designed to support its training activities, many are of interest to a much broader audience. EDI materials, including any findings, interpretations, and conclusions, are entirely those of the authors and should not be attributed in any manner to the World Bank, to its affiliated organizations, or to members of its Board of Executive Directors or the countries they represent.

Because of the informality of this series and to make the publication available with the least possible delay, the manuscript has not been edited as fully as would be the case with a more formal document, and the World Bank accepts no responsibility for errors.

The material in this publication is copyrighted. Requests for permission to reproduce portions of it should be sent to the Office of the Publisher at the address shown in the copyright notice above. The World Bank encourages dissemination of its work and will normally give permission promptly and, when the reproduction is for noncommercial purposes, without asking a fee. Permission to copy portions for classroom use is granted through the Copyright Clearance Center, 27 Congress Street, Salem, Massachusetts 01970, U.S.A.

The backlist of publications by the World Bank is shown in the annual *Index of Publications*, which is available from Distribution Unit, Office of the Publisher, The World Bank, 1818 H Street, N.W., Washington, D.C. 20433, U.S.A., or from Publications, Banque mondiale, 66, avenue d'Iéna, 75116 Paris, France.

Dimitri Vittas is principal financial specialist with the Financial Policy and Systems Division of the World Bank's Country Economics Department.

Library of Congress Cataloging-in-Publication Data

Financial regulation : changing the rules of the game/edited by
    Dimitri Vittas.
        p.   cm.—(EDI development studies)
    Collection of papers mostly based on papers presented at a seminar held at Cambridge, Mass., June 10-15, 1990.
    Includes bibliographical references.
    ISBN 0-8213-2123-4
    1. Financial institutions—Law and legislation.   2. Finance—Law and legislation.
3. Banking law.   I. Vittas, Dimitri.   II. Series.
K1066. Z9F56   1992
346'.0821—dc20   92-14470
[342.6821]   CIP

EDI Catalog No. 340/059

CONTENTS

FOREWORD

EDI's Financial Sector Training Program focuses on the structure, reform, development and management of financial systems and institutions in developing countries through a systematic review of:

- the policies and mechanisms for reforming the structure of financial systems;
- the policies and regulations necessary to prevent and deal with systemic distress, as well as with insolvency and illiquidity of financial intermediaries;
- the development of markets for short- and long-term financial instruments;
- the role of institutional elements in the development of financial systems;
- the links between the financial sector and the real sectors, particularly in the case of the restructuring of financial institutions and industrial enterprises;
- the dynamics and management of financial systems during periods of stabilization and adjustment; and,
- the policies and mechanisms for facilitating access to international financial markets.

EDI's financial sector program covers each of these topics independently or in various combinations, designed to reach specific audiences based on specific needs. The program also offers specialized training activities developed in conjunction with the industrial sector program, which includes topics such as privatization and private sector development.

This collection of papers on financial regulation is mostly based on papers presented at a seminar on "Financial Sector Liberalization and Regulation" that was organized jointly by the Harvard Law School Program on International Financial Systems and the Economic Development Institute of The World Bank between June 10 and 15, 1990, at Cambridge, Massachusetts. The seminar was attended by senior policymakers from over 30 developing and developed countries. A number of additional papers are also included in this volume because of their relevance to the issues under discussion. The views presented in this volume are entirely those of the authors and do not necessarily reflect those of The World Bank or those of any of the other institutions with which the authors are affiliated.

Amnon Golan, Director
Economic Development Institute

ACKNOWLEDGMENTS

I am grateful to the co-directors of the 1990 Cambridge "Financial Sector Liberalization and Regulation" seminar: Philip Wellons of Harvard Law School and Hernan Cortés-Douglas, then of the Economic Development Institute (EDI) of the World Bank and currently with the International Monetary Fund. Many thanks are also due to Professor Hal S. Scott of Harvard Law School, Millard Long of the World Bank, and Xavier Simon of EDI for their support and guidance in organizing the seminar.

I am also grateful to Isabelle Bleas, Gail Taylor, Gwendolyn Junod, and Matthew Leger, all of EDI, for their contribution to the smooth functioning of the seminar and the production of this volume. The help provided by Susana Carey in editing some of the papers and the editorial guidance of John Didier of the Studies and Training Design Division of EDI are also acknowledged.

Finally, many thanks are due to the authors for their contributions to the seminar and to this volume, and to the participants at the seminar, especially the policymakers from developing and developed countries, who provided invaluable comments drawing on their practical experience in dealing with the many regulatory issues addressed in this volume.

Dimitri Vittas
Financial Policy and Systems Division
The World Bank

ABOUT THE CONTRIBUTORS

David C. Cole is with the Harvard Institute for International Development (HIID). He has been Director of several programs organized by HIID and has acted as Adviser to the Ministry of Finance in Indonesia. He has written extensively on financial reform in East Asian countries.

Hernan Cortes-Douglas is Senior Economist with the Central Banking Department of the International Monetary Fund. He was previously Senior Economist with the Economic Development Institute of the World Bank. He has written several articles on the Chilean economy and financial system.

Mario Draghi has been a Director General of the Italian Treasury since March 1991. Previously he was Adviser to the Bank of Italy, and between 1984 and 1990 he was Executive Director for Italy at the World Bank. He has written extensively on macroeconomic and financial issues.

Charles Freedman is Deputy Governor of the Bank of Canada. He joined the Research Department of the Bank of Canada in 1974, became Deputy Chief of the Department of Monetary and Financial Analysis in 1977, and was named Chief of the Department in 1979. He was appointed Adviser to the Governor in 1984 and named Deputy Governor in 1988. His principal interests are in the design of monetary policy and issues regarding financial institutions.

Akiyoshi Horiuchi is Professor of Economics at the University of Tokyo. He is an expert on monetary, banking, and financial issues in Japan and has written extensively on Japanese interest rate policy and on the main bank system.

Millard Long is Senior Adviser, Financial Systems, in the World Bank's Technical Department for Europe and Central Asia. He joined the World Bank in 1980 and was Chief of the Financial Policy and Systems Division between 1984 and 1991. He has played a leading role in policy, research, and operational support work dealing with all kinds of financial sector issues. In 1989 he was Director of the World Development Report on Financial Systems and Development.

Ignacio Mas is an investment officer with the International Finance Corporation. He was previously with the World Bank where he worked on financial sector issues and on treasury operations. He was also a research associate at the Harvard Institute for International Development and acted as resident representative in Bolivia for Professor Jeffrey Sachs during the 1985-86 Bolivian stabilization program.

Vincent Polizatto is Senior Financial Specialist with the Financial Policy and Systems Division at the World Bank. Prior to joining the World Bank in 1987, he worked for the Office of the Comptroller of the Currency in the United States, first as field examiner and then as Senior Adviser, International Relations and Financial Evaluation. He has advised many developing countries on issues of prudential regulation and banking supervision.

Thomas Rabe is consultant with the Treuhandstalt, the agency that is responsible for restructuring and privatizing the enterprise sector of the former East Germany. He was previously a consultant with the European Commission in Brussels, dealing with issues of insurance and pension fund regulation.

Andrew Sheng is Chief of the Financial Policy and Systems Division at the World Bank. Prior to joining the World Bank in 1989, he served as Adviser in the Bank Regulation Department of the Central Bank of Malaysia between 1984 and 1989 and as Chief Economist between 1981 and 1984. He was actively involved in the resolution of the Malaysian banking crisis of 1985-87. He has written extensively, and has advised many developing countries, on bank regulation and bank restructuring issues.

Dr. Betty Slade is with the Harvard Institute for International Development. She has been resident adviser to the Ministry of Finance in Indonesia since December 1987. She has worked with the Indonesian Government on stabilization policy and financial reform.

Jon A. Solheim is Alternate Executive Director of the International Monetary Fund, representing the Nordic countries. He was previously Director of the Financial Markets Department at the Bank of Norway. He also acted as secretary of the Government Bank Insurance Fund which was set up in 1991. At the Bank of Norway he was principally concerned with policy issues on the structure and regulation of financial markets.

Samuel H. Talley is a consultant in the Financial Policy and Systems Division at the World Bank. He specializes in policy issues relating to banking structure and regulation and deposit insurance. He was previously on the staff of the Federal Reserve Board, first as senior economist in the Research Division and later as assistant director in the Division of Banking Supervision and Regulation.

Dimitri Vittas is Principal Financial Specialist with the Financial Policy and Systems Division of the World Bank. Prior to joining the World Bank in 1986 he worked for the British Bankers Association in London and Citibank in Greece. His principal interests include financial regulation and structure, banking economics, and contractual savings. In 1989 he was a member of the team that produced the World Development Report on Financial Systems and Development.

Lawrence J. White is Professor of Economics at New York University's Stern School of Business. Between 1986 and 1989 he served as a Member of the Federal Home Loan Bank Board and between 1982 and 1983 he served as Director of the Economic Policy Office, Antitrust Division, U.S. Department of Justice. He is the author of several books and articles, including a book published in 1991 on the debacle of U.S. thrifts.

1

INTRODUCTION AND OVERVIEW

Dimitri Vittas

Introduction

The 1980s have witnessed major and fundamental changes in the scope and orientation of financial regulation. Governments in both developed and developing countries have engaged in an extensive rewriting of the rules of the game that govern the operations of financial institutions and markets. Credit and interest rate controls as well as restrictions on new entry and on the permissible activities of financial institutions have been removed or substantially relaxed. In their place, governments have established prudential and investor protection regulations that aim at safeguarding the soundness of the financial system and protecting the interests of users of financial services, especially the nonprofessional investors.

Regulatory reform has been associated with—in many cases it has been prompted by—major structural changes and innovations in financial markets. In many high income countries, there is a clear trend toward universal banking and a growing integration of banking and securities business. Integrated financial systems raise issues in financial regulation that cut across banking and nonbanking markets. Two major issues regard the structure of regulation and the role of market forces in monitoring and controlling the performance of individual institutions.

In developing countries, the dominant position of commercial banks, which are often state owned, has been challenged by the creation of nonbank financial intermediaries and the emergence of more active securities markets. This raises regulatory issues that go beyond traditional concerns with the performance and standing of commercial and development banks. However, commercial banks are likely to continue to play a central part in the financial systems of developing countries so that issues in bank regulation, including the role of prudential controls and supervision and the resolution of banking crises, will continue to be of prime concern to policymakers.

Whether financial systems are dominated by commercial banks or are based on a more diversified structure, an important ingredient that shapes the functioning and efficiency of financial institutions is the stance of macrofinancial policy. Failure to maintain macroeconomic stability has deleterious effects on the operations of financial institutions. This is true both at times of excessive (inflationary) expansion and at times of corrective contractions. Moreover, the pursuit of macroeconomic and financial stability may come into conflict with the process of financial innovation.

A related issue concerns the pace and implications of financial reform and the transition from a system subject to financial repression, limited competition, and directed allocation of resources to one based on competitive market forces operating in a stable and well-structured framework. The importance of sustaining macroeconomic and financial stability while implementing financial reform is now amply recognized by policymakers. However, questions regarding the pace and sequencing of reforms are still difficult to answer.

This volume of papers explores recent developments in financial regulation and addresses some of the issues highlighted above. The volume is divided into six parts: introduction and overview, general issues in regulatory reform, issues in financial liberalization, banking crises and restructuring, regulatory framework for banks and other financial institutions, and regulatory issues in integrated financial systems.

This introductory chapter provides an overview and summary of the papers that follow. Its purpose is to highlight the main issues addressed in each chapter and draw together the main lessons that emerge from the experience of different countries.

General Issues in Regulatory Reform

Rewriting the Rules of the Game

In the first paper on general issues in regulatory reform, **Millard Long** and **Dimitri Vittas** stress that the 1980s was not a decade of financial deregulation but a period when the rules of the game were substantially rewritten.

Long and Vittas note that the repressive regulations of the post World War II period were motivated by widespread dissatisfaction with the functioning and structure of the financial systems inherited from the colonial era and the Great Depression. Governments used finance as a tool of economic and industrial development by taking banks under public control, directing institutions to lend to selected industries on subsidized terms, and keeping interest rates low, usually below the rate of inflation. Although the policies met some of the government objectives, they failed to create robust financial systems. With the onset of the debt crisis in the 1980s and the ensuing economic recessions, firms in most developing countries, especially in Africa, Eastern Europe, and Latin America, were unable (or unwilling) to service their debts. Financial institutions became decapitalized and technically insolvent.

The failure of the traditional model of economic development fed disillusionment with government intervention in resource allocation. This has been reinforced by the recent collapse of centrally planned economies in Eastern Europe, the former Soviet Union, and other parts of the world. As a result, there is now growing emphasis on private sector development as an engine of stable and sustainable growth. However, to develop financial systems that can finance their private sectors efficiently, countries need to restore their financial institutions to vitality, achieve and sustain macroeconomic stability, and build their financial infrastructure by developing modern and effective information, legal, and regulatory systems.

In using regulatory reform for shaping the structure of the financial system, policymakers can choose between alternative models. The historical distinction between bank-based and securities-based systems is less relevant these days as internally generated funds have become the primary source of corporate finance in most countries. An important differentiation still exists between relationship-based and transaction-based systems, but in developing countries policymakers would be well advised to encourage, at least initially, the creation of simple structures that are more transparent and easier to manage and supervise.

Long and Vittas suggest three criteria for evaluating financial regulation and structure: stability, efficiency, and fairness.[1] Stability is important because unstable financial systems have a large adverse impact on economic activity. Financial stability can be enhanced by increasing capital requirements and strengthening financial supervision. But the stability of the financial system is also affected by its structure. Systems with "narrow" banks or "non-par" banks would be exposed to lower systemic risks.

The relationship between structure and efficiency is also complex. In the research literature the issues of economies of scale and scope in finance still seem unresolved. In developed countries, there is growing concentration and a spread of universal banking, suggesting economies of both scale and scope. Moreover, available evidence suggests that concentrated banking systems tend to have lower margins and operating costs as well as higher profits. But in developing countries, large banks tend to be inefficient. Their size is the result of controls and restrictions on competition and entry rather than superior efficiency. Allowing universal banking might exacerbate the dominant position of large banks with adverse effects on competition and efficiency.

Fairness covers many issues ranging from the protection of users of financial services to the creation of a level playing field for competing institutions and the resolution of problems caused by potential conflicts of interest. Fairness can be more easily achieved in systems with simple structures, but limits on the permissible range of activities of

---

1.   Key and Scott (1991) develop a "banking matrix" that lists four policy goals of regulation: promoting competitive markets, ensuring safety and soundness, avoiding systemic risk, and providing consumer protection. These are very similar to the three criteria of stability, efficiency, and fairness.

different types of institutions might undermine efficiency and, to a lesser extent, stability.

Long and Vittas emphasize that there are tradeoffs between the three criteria and suggest that there are no general answers to the questions posed by these tradeoffs. Answers must be sought in the context of particular countries on a case-by-case basis, although it is clear that extreme solutions that promote one criterion and totally disregard the others would not be optimal.

The Rationale, Objectives, and Impact of Financial Regulation

The impact of regulation on financial structure is the subject of the second paper in this volume. **Dimitri** notes that regulation is perhaps the most important determinant of differences in financial structure exhibited by countries at a similar level of development and with access to common technologies. He also notes that the main rationale for financial regulation is the existence of market failure arising from externalities, market power, and information problems (Kay and Vickers 1988). Market failure is a necessary but not a sufficient condition for regulation. The other condition is that regulation can correct market failure in an effective and efficient way. Much of the debate among alternative theories of regulation is about the cost and effectiveness of regulation rather than about its rationale.

Externalities include the risk of systemic failure (the risk of failure of one or more banks as a result of the actual or threatened failure of another), the infection effect (the general lowering of standards and prices caused by excessive competition), and network effects (the costs and benefits of linking together competing institutions to a common network). Other externalities include the achievement of macrostability (to avoid distortions in relative prices, incentives, and expectations caused by high and volatile inflation) and the enhancement of the allocative efficiency of the financial system (to ensure the financing of projects and sectors, including small firms, with high dynamic efficiency gains). Concern about market power stems from the fear that dominant firms may undermine both allocative and dynamic efficiency (the former by charging high prices and earning excessive profits, the latter by avoiding competitive pressures). Finally, information problems arise from poor price and product information, from the free rider problem, and from informational asymmetries between the suppliers and users of financial services.

Vittas classifies financial regulations by their primary objective into six types: macroeconomic, allocative, structural, prudential, organizational, and protective. There is a certain correspondence between types of regulations and different rationales, although most regulations have effects that cut across different purposes. For instance, bank-specific credit ceilings are mainly applied for macroeconomic purposes but they also restrain banks from engaging in an uncontrolled and imprudent expansion of credit and thus serve to fulfill a prudential objective.

Historical experience suggests that macroeconomic and allocative controls tend to be ineffective and inefficient. Macroeconomic controls are often justified by the paramount importance of controlling the expansion of credit and maintaining price stability and by the absence of active money and government bond markets that would allow the use of market-based mechanisms for monetary and credit control. But rather than relying on direct controls that stifle competition and inhibit innovation, governments should stimulate the development of money and bond markets.

Allocative controls are motivated by the need to finance sectors with dynamic efficiency gains but limited or insufficient access to credit facilities. Allocative controls are a prime example of the argument that market failure is a necessary but not sufficient condition for regulation. Because of poor design and deficient implementation, especially inadequate monitoring of privileged borrowers, allocative credit controls have failed in most countries to achieve their objectives.

In contrast to macroeconomic and allocative controls, prudential, organizational, and protective controls are necessary because financial systems suffer from moral hazard, adverse selection, and the free rider problem; are susceptible to imprudent and fraudulent behavior; and are prone to instability and crisis. The main policy issue with regard to these types of controls is how to devise measures that are effective without undermining competition and innovation in the financial system.

Structural controls are the most controversial type of financial regulation. Their main objectives are to prevent excessive concentration of market power, limit the potential for conflicts of interest, and discourage financial institutions from assuming excessive risks by expanding into areas that are remote from their main focus of operations and expertise. But structural controls are often motivated by political considerations, such as preserving the dominant position of domestic banks or protecting the turfs of different types of financial institutions.

Structural controls may cause a fragmentation of the financial system into a large number of small institutions with limited capital resources. This is likely to increase both the risk of systemic failure and the risk of infection. Perverse and politically motivated structural controls may undermine the effectiveness of other types of financial regulation.

Vittas emphasizes the importance of creating a sound and robust financial constitution that encourages financial institutions to build adequate capital reserves, diversify their risks, and exploit potential economies of scale and scope. Such a constitution should be complemented with a system of effective supervision, short-term financial accommodation, long-term financial restructuring, and financial compensation for customers of failed institutions. Deposit insurance, which is a special case of financial compensation, has a role to play in protecting the interests of small depositors, but if it is used to prevent runs on fragmented and fragile institutions, it is likely to distort incentives and suffer from problems of moral hazard. A sound financial constitution, which avoids the fragmentation and segmentation of the financial system and discourages the continuing existence of fragile and undercapitalized institutions, would contribute to higher efficiency and stability and would avoid the costs of later interventions.

For most of the post World War II period, financial regulation in developing countries emphasized macroeconomic, allocative, and structural objectives, while prudential, organizational, and protective controls were conspicuous by their absence. A similar pattern was observed in most developed countries, although some emphasis was placed on prudential considerations in a few countries. Among developed countries, the United States stands out for its limited use of macroeconomic and allocative controls but extensive reliance on structural controls. Vittas maintains that many of the problems facing the U.S. financial system, such as the fragmented and fragile banking system, the financial crisis of the thrift industry, and the segmentation of the financial system, can be attributed to the adverse effects of structural regulations.

The fragmentation of the banking and thrift industries reflects a strong tradition of localism in American banking and an emphasis on populist policies motivated by fear of the concentration of power that large banks from out-of-state centers might acquire.[2] Vittas argues that economists have undermined potential support for consolidation of the banking and thrift industries by downplaying the potential economies of scale and scope of large banks. By focusing on the production side of banking services and neglecting potential economies in risk and marketing, they have largely failed to establish a strong case for greater consolidation.[3]

Regulatory reform in both developed and developing countries has been motivated by macroeconomic pressures and by rapid technological advances. Reform has been easier to implement where it could be accomplished without the need for cumbersome legislative changes. In fact, the threat of regulation, when prompt action is feasible, may have been as effective as actual regulation in discouraging excesses and preventing abuses. Vittas concludes by emphasizing that political leadership has an important role to play in promoting higher stability, efficiency, and fairness in the financial system by removing distortionary, inefficient, and ineffective regulations and replacing them with regulations that are, as far as possible, neutral between different financial intermediaries and markets.

---

2.   This view is echoed by White (see chapter 9) and Polizatto (chapter 10).

3.   In recent years, academic and bank economists have started to underscore the regulation-induced fragmentation and fragility of the U.S. banking system (see, for instance, Berlin et al. 1991, Berger and Humphrey 1990, Shaffer 1989, and Udell 1990). But these views have yet to generate wide political support for an extensive consolidation of the industry. If anything, opposition to banking consolidation is still quite strong, not only among political circles, but also among bank and academic economists.

Issues in Financial Liberalization

Financial Liberalization in Japan

Japan represents an interesting example of a country with initially extensive financial regulations (covering credit ceilings, interest rate controls, directed credit programs, geographic and sectoral segmentation, and branching restrictions) that was able to achieve a high rate of growth and then proceeded to deregulate its financial system in a gradual and controlled fashion. **Akiyoshi Horiuchi** analyzes the process of financial liberalization in Japan since the end of World War II. He first examines the relationship between financial regulation and economic growth during the high growth era, specifically the period from 1960 to the early 1970s. He then considers the financial liberalization that started in the mid-1970s. Horiuchi emphasizes that financial liberalization was induced by the structural changes caused by the achievement of high growth and that it was not a cause but rather a consequence of economic development in Japan.

Horiuchi notes that the Japanese financial system was under comprehensive regulation during the high growth era, but argues that some regulations were circumvented, for instance loan rates were effectively raised through the use of compensating balances. He also argues that the level of interest rates was not low in either nominal or real terms.[4] However, an important feature of the regulatory regime was the support of high profits for banks and other financial institutions and the general discrimination against consumer credit and housing finance.

The success of the Japanese authorities in containing inflation and maintaining macroeconomic stability is credited as the main reason why financial repression did not prevent the achievement of economic growth. Horiuchi attributes this to the constraint imposed by the balance of payments and the decision of the Japanese authorities to discourage foreign capital inflows to relieve this constraint. Controls on capital inflows were also motivated by the desire to "protect" domes-

---

4. This argument is based on the use of producer price inflation for calculating the real rate of interest. If the consumer price index is used instead, then the real rate of interest was rather low in Japan, as Horiuchi acknowledges.

tic industries from falling under foreign ownership. He lists electrical appliances, radio sets, TV sets, plate glass, cameras, synthetic fibers, laundries, and shipbuilding as benefiting from such protection. He maintains that the controls on foreign capital inflows reinforced the dominant role played by Japanese banks in corporate finance.

The role of banks was also shaped by the weakness and underdevelopment of the securities markets. There was no money or bond market so that nonfinancial corporations and households could not place their financial savings in uncontrolled instruments. The corporate bond market was prevented from playing a more active part by the Kisaikai, an association of trust banks and securities companies that imposed unfavorable conditions on the issue of corporate bonds. Finally, the equity market suffered from structural weaknesses, such as the issue of new shares at par and the sharp decline of equity prices in the mid-1960s that caused financial distress among securities firms and scared investors away from the securities markets.

Horiuchi argues that in this context the banks became the main agents of financial intermediation. Their ability to allocate resources efficiently was facilitated by the development of close relationships with major borrowers. In fact, it could be argued that the close links between banks and industry proved more effective in overcoming problems of asymmetric information and free riding than has been the case in countries with active and well-developed securities markets.

Horiuchi concludes his analysis of financial regulation during the high growth era by emphasizing that the role of government financial institutions in stimulating economic growth is exaggerated by many commentators.[5] In his view (as in the opinion of several other leading Japanese economists, such as Aoki, Komiya, and Teranishi), government institutions mainly provided financial support to declining industries, such as coal mining and shipping. The rapidly growing dynamic sectors were mainly financed by private financial institutions, although government financial institutions may have played an important role by conveying valuable signals about the government's industrial policy to the private sector.

---

5.   A detailed discussion of different views on the effectiveness of credit policies in Japan and on the role of government financial institutions is contained in Vittas and Wang (1991).

The structural changes that occurred after the oil crisis in 1973 included a big increase in government borrowing, a sharp decline in the demand for funds for industrial investment, and a growing internationalization of the Japanese economy. A landmark in the process of liberalization, especially as it affected wholesale and corporate financial services, was the relaxation of foreign exchange controls in 1980. The rapidly growing government debt forced the authorities to encourage the development of a modern and efficient bond market. This provided alternative instruments for the financial savings of both nonfinancial corporations and households. Interest rate controls on large deposits and restrictions on new deposit instruments were then relaxed. The large corporations were able to raise funds on the domestic and international capital markets and stimulated the deregulation and modernization of the corporate bond and equity markets. Japanese banks expanded their operations in overseas markets, and this led to growing international pressures for opening the domestic markets to foreign entry and competition.

Horiuchi identifies three issues as meriting close policy consideration: the need to modify the safety net in the financial system to protect small investors and prevent bank panics; the need to create a robust system of regulation and supervision of the securities markets, including regulations on insider trading and promotion of credit rating agencies; and the need to increase the effectiveness of antitrust legislation. He concludes his paper by reiterating that high growth in Japan was achieved without a flexible market-oriented financial system, but the structural changes of the post–high growth era stimulated the gradual liberalization that has been under way since the early 1970s.

Financial Liberalization in Indonesia

In contrast to Japan, which maintained a closed capital account throughout its high growth era and proceeded to liberalize its controls on capital flows on a very gradual and cautious basis, Indonesia provides an example of substantial deregulation and financial sector development in the context of a very open foreign exchange market. **David C. Cole** and **Betty F. Slade** review the Indonesian experience between the mid-1960s and the late 1980s. They stress that contrary to the conventional wisdom that the capital account should be opened only after domestic investment, trade, and financial reforms are first implemented, Indonesia removed all foreign capital controls when its foreign exchange position was still precarious and the economy was subject to a wide array of controls. Cole and Slade argue that the main reason for taking this action at that time was that the government could not exert effective control over foreign capital movements.

The removal of foreign exchange controls was preceded by drastic macroeconomic adjustment to eliminate fiscal deficits, restrict domestic credit expansion, and counteract the hyperinflation and negative growth of the early to mid-1960s. However, the authorities imposed various financial controls after 1973 but without reversing the decision to keep an open capital account. The combination of credit ceilings on domestic banks with an open capital account caused a shift of much financial activity offshore. Domestic financial sector development stagnated and most industrial investment was financed in overseas markets.

Since 1983, the Indonesian authorities have pursued a policy of financial reform to stimulate the growth of the domestic financial system, still within the context of an open foreign exchange system. The program of reform involved the removal of credit ceilings and interest rate controls and was preceded by a major devaluation and fiscal retrenchment. The reform resulted in rapid growth of the banking system but exposed the economy to sudden shocks emanating from large falls of foreign exchange reserves and bouts of speculation about imminent devaluation. These were reinforced by a further major devaluation in 1986. However, the authorities took measures to stimulate the development of an active domestic money market to allow a more flexible response to changes in the financial position of the country. More recently the Indonesian authorities have taken steps to stimulate the growth of the capital markets and to open the financial system to greater competition from both domestic and foreign participants.

Cole and Slade note that the periods of high domestic financial growth were not correlated with the periods of high real growth. The initial period of financial growth between 1968 and 1972 occurred at a time when the economy was growing quite rapidly, but mainly due to recovery from a long period of mismanagement and deterioration.

Then during the decade of high economic growth and high investment deriving from the oil boom, the domestic financial system languished. Finally, after the decline in oil prices, and real growth became more erratic, domestic financial development accelerated. Domestic financial growth was influenced more by financial policy measures than by the overall growth of the economy.

A key question addressed by Cole and Slade is whether the Indonesian experience represents a special case of a country that had to follow a less than optimal sequence of reforms by force of circumstances and managed to succeed largely due to good luck, or whether it represents a reasonable, or even better, sequence of financial reform. In their view, the open capital account has imposed a healthy degree of restraint on both fiscal and monetary policy. They note that an open capital account both incites and requires good macroeconomic management. For countries that are capable of pursuing reasonably sound macro policies, the Indonesian approach may be worthy of consideration.

Financial Liberalization in Chile

The third paper on issues in financial liberalization focuses on the Chilean experience in the 1970s and early 1980s. **Hernan Cortés-Douglas** highlights the links between financial and other reforms in Chile, following the military coup in 1973 that overthrew the Allende government. Cortés-Douglas emphasizes the success of the reforms in the long run and the extensive transformation of the Chilean economy and financial system over the past twenty years or so. He also stresses, however, the mistakes of the authorities in pursuing financial reform in the 1970s and underscores the conflict between opposing groups of policymakers on the importance of prudential regulation.

At the time of the 1973 coup, the Chilean economy was characterized by an oversized public sector, a very high rate of monetary expansion and inflation, extensive price and exchange controls, and excessive protectionism and regulation of industry, commerce, transportation, and finance. The Pinochet regime proceeded to reduce public sector deficits and implement far-reaching reforms in trade, public enterprises, and finance. The reprivatization of firms taken under public ownership by the Allende administration was a key element of early reforms. The prevailing philosophy was one of free markets with a minimal amount of regulation.

Credit ceilings, directed credit programs, and interest rate controls were eliminated. Limits on foreign capital imports and foreign borrowing were also removed, and access to such borrowing was encouraged by repeated pronouncements of the commitment to a fixed nominal exchange rate. To facilitate the privatization process, the authorities encouraged access to bank credit by the new owners and allowed the formation of large conglomerates, or *grupos*, with interests in banking, insurance, industry, and commerce. The groups bought banks on credit and used bank loans to buy privatized firms and to finance important investment projects and restructuring expenditures as well as real estate development projects and shopping malls in later years. The result was the creation of an excessively indebted private sector dominated by a few large conglomerates.

Cortés-Douglas underscores the differences of opinion among three opposing views within government ranks on the issue of financial reform. The predominant view was the "free banking" approach that downplayed the importance of prudential regulation and was against any involvement by the government in preventing bank failures. A second view emphasized the importance of prudential regulation and argued that the government should guarantee bank liabilities and regulate banks and other financial institutions to reduce the risk of failures. The third view was in favor of continued financial repression on the grounds that depositors should be protected but banks were difficult to control in a nonrepressed environment.

Cortés-Douglas discusses three episodes of financial failure in the 1970s that exemplified the confusion and inconsistency of policies of financial reform. The first was the failure in 1975 of the Chilean savings and loan institutions. Following the free banking and minimalist approach, the government refused to cover their deposit liabilities, but forced their conversion into long-term bonds at less than par value. The second episode occurred in 1976 when in order to prevent a flight to quality by depositors, the government guaranteed the deposits of the Banco Osorno group. This represented a first but partial victory by advocates of prudential regulation. The third episode was that of Banco Español in 1980 when following the introduction of a loan classification system, auditors announced that on 37 percent of loans the bank lacked information to assess the borrowers' ability to repay their loans. Although Banco Español was originally rescued by a takeover from another large bank, it was one of four banks and four finance companies that were intervened in November 1981.

The financial crisis of 1982 was precipitated by a regulation that sought to drastically limit lending by group-owned banks to companies affiliated to the same group. The conglomerates were given no time to comply with the new rules, but were able to evade them by creating many shell affiliates, swapping loans with other *grupos,* and using mutual funds to replace bank loans. The crisis was triggered, however, by the rise in international real interest rates, and the massive withdrawal of foreign funds following the devaluation of June 1982. When the crisis erupted, the authorities were forced to intervene and take over 60 percent of the banking sector. They were also forced to radically change their approach and to make strong and effective prudential regulation the cornerstone of bank and financial regulation.

Since the 1982 crisis, the financial system has undergone major transformation and expansion. The banks have been successfully reprivatized and the insurance sector has been deregulated with a strong emphasis on solvency monitoring. The reform and replacement of the public pension system by a government-mandated but privately operated system of individual capitalization accounts has contributed to the generation of large long-term savings and has stimulated the growth of the capital markets. Draconian rules have been imposed on the private pension funds to ensure their safety and protect the interests of their members. The Chilean authorities appear to have learned well the lesson that economic and financial liberalization must be accompanied by the creation of a strong and effective infrastructure of prudential regulation and supervision.

Banking Crises and Restructuring

The Chilean experience shows that economic and financial liberalization without a proper framework of prudential regulation may lead to abuses of market power, conflicts of interest, and unsustainable and imprudent expansion. Such a process is bound to end in a major financial crisis that requires the intervention of the authorities to avert the complete collapse of the financial system. However, banking crises may also occur in countries that do not undergo major liberalization of their financial systems. The proximate causes of banking crisis may then be either a segment of the banking system that is not properly supervised and may engage in imprudent or fraudulent behavior or a segment that is subject to inconsistent regulations and to incentives that are incompatible with stable and sustained expansion. Another aspect of banking crises is the speed of reaction by the authorities to restructure ailing institutions, contain losses, and remove the causes that brought about the crisis in the first place. Effective and speedy resolution mechanisms are essential for limiting losses and for avoiding the prolongation of the adverse effects of banking crises on the real economy.

Banking Crisis in Malaysia

Andrew Sheng discusses the experience of Malaysia with banking crisis and restructuring in the mid-1980s. The Malaysian case is a prime example of decisive and effective action. In 1985 and 1986, the economy suffered from deflation as falling prices caused nominal GNP to decline more rapidly than real GNP. The financial system also suffered from steep falls in commodity, securities, and property prices that had reached unsustainable levels following a long period of expansion and speculative investments in property and equities. With property loans accounting for 36 percent of all bank loans in 1986, up from 26 percent in 1980, commercial banks incurred heavy losses. In addition, finance companies and deposit taking cooperatives (DTCs) were heavily exposed to property investments.

Faced with a potentially major financial crisis and loss of confidence in the stability of the financial system, the authorities took decisive action to stem the losses, recapitalize distressed banks, and intervene in institutions that were unable to inject new capital. Because the Malaysian monetary authorities had in place an effective system of banking supervision with stiff requirements for provisions against bad and doubtful debts and suspension of interest accrual, the impact of the recession and of the fall in commodity, securities, and property prices on the big banks, though large in terms of reported losses, was contained by injections of fresh capital. Worst hit by the recession were four medium-sized commercial banks that incurred heavy losses, particularly from their involvement in the property sector. The central bank intervened, replaced the management and board of directors of these banks, and made arrangements for fresh injection of capital, including direct capital from the central bank itself. The central bank also had to assume control of four finance companies, which were unable to inject new capital to cover their losses.

The impact of the recession was much greater on DTCs, a group of institutions that accepted deposits from the public but were not supervised by the central bank and did not have access to its lender of last resort facilities. The first step here was to undertake a detailed investigation of affected institutions to establish the extent of losses. As Sheng notes, seventeen accounting firms were employed to undertake, in conjunction with examiners from the central bank, detailed audits of twenty-four affected institutions. To assess public opinion on an appropriate rescue scheme, the government appointed a committee to find a restructuring plan that would be acceptable to all. The committee recommended that DTCs with small losses should be merged or taken over by financially strong banks and finance companies. For DTCs with large losses, the committee recommended that depositors should be offered a combination of cash and equity or convertible bonds. All DTCs were placed under central bank supervision, while to forestall lawsuits from jeopardizing the whole rescue package, receivers from accounting firms were appointed by the High Court to manage their assets.

Despite the long history of effective bank supervision, the authorities introduced key changes in banking laws and regulations to emphasize prudential safeguards, such as minimum capital requirements, dispersion of ownership, controls on connected lending, limits on risk concentrations, guidelines on provisions for loan losses and suspension of interest accrual on nonperforming loans, and improved statistical reporting to the central bank. In addition, the central bank was granted clearer intervention powers, including the right to enter and search offices, detain persons, impound passports, freeze property, issue cease and desist orders, and assume control of operations.

The Malaysian authorities were able to contain the banking crisis by taking prompt action to assess the extent of losses and address the problems of capital adequacy and competent management. With economic recovery resuming in 1987, the central bank was able to stabilize public confidence in the financial system and avoid the dangers of contagion spreading.

Banking Crisis in Norway

In contrast to Malaysia, the Norwegian experience with financial liberalization and banking crisis has been one of prolonged distress and repeated interventions that culminated in the effective "nationalization" of virtually the whole banking system in 1991. To be fair, the Norwegian authorities did not lack in decisive action. As noted by **Jon A. Solheim**, they intervened to replace the management and board of directors of the DnC Bank in the spring of 1988, following heavy losses suffered after the collapse of securities markets in October 1987. They also arranged for mergers of institutions in distress, for capital injections, and for extension of appropriate guarantees by the country's two bank guarantee funds, not to mention the provision of liquidity by the central bank. However, where the authorities proved lacking was perhaps in undertaking a thorough assessment of both the extent of losses suffered by banks and their exposure to firms in financial difficulty.

The problems faced by Norwegian banks have their roots in the extensive deregulation of Norwegian banking in the mid-1980s after a long period of tight restrictions, in the failure to introduce adequate prudential regulations, and in the unfortunate timing of deregulation with a period of strong, but unsustainable, expansion that was stimulated by large oil revenues. Macro policy failures, such as the reluctance to raise the level of nominal interest rates and the delayed reduction of the tax deductibility of loan interest payments, resulted in a negative real after-tax cost of borrowing that stimulated the demand for bank loans and induced banks to compete for market share and disregard the soundness and long-term profitability of their lending.

When oil prices fell in 1986, the Norwegian economy suffered a major economic recession from which it has still to emerge. The banks incurred loan losses amounting to between 1.5 and 2.5 percent of loans each year. As a result, their capital has been seriously eroded and in some cases completely wiped out. Assistance was initially provided by the two Guarantee Funds operated by the commercial and savings banks, respectively, but after the exhaustion of these funds, the government was forced to establish a government bank insurance fund to support the operations of ailing banks. The authorities are also encouraging an extensive process of consolidation and retrenchment and have created a new institution that will participate in new equity issues from private banks and help return sound banks to private ownership.

The Thrift Debacle in the United States

While the Malaysian and Norwegian cases differ in the degree of success of government intervention, they both represent cases where banking problems were immediately recognized and prompt action was taken to tackle them. There are, however, many countries where governments have refused to recognize the existence of nonperforming loans and the mounting losses of banks. Among developed countries, a prime example of such attitude is the United States, where the authorities have been very slow to appreciate the deteriorating financial condition of the savings and loan industry. As noted by **Lawrence White**, faced with large losses deriving from a negative interest margin in the early 1980s, savings and loan associations were authorized to diversify into other risky activities in the hope that profits from new activities could help rebuild their eroded capital.

White discusses the debacle of the U.S. thrift industry in the context of its regulation and especially the accounting rules that applied on the measurement of its equity. He emphasizes the point that institutions with high leverage are inclined to engage in risky activities. This inclination is strengthened if depositors are protected by credible deposit insurance while prudential regulation and supervision is weak and ineffective. White stresses that since net worth and solvency are important concepts for prudential regulation, accounting rules should be designed to yield market values for assets, liabilities, and off-balance sheet items. He notes that the accepted accounting framework is based on historic costs rather than current values, while special accounting rules were introduced for the thrifts that allowed them to overstate their net worth.[6]

The wider investment powers conferred on thrifts in combination with increased limits for deposit insurance, the use of brokered deposits, the overstatement of net worth, and weakened thrift supervision encouraged many thrifts to undertake massive growth drives that in some cases resulted in a doubling or even quadrupling of their size within the spate of three years. Many of the rapidly growing thrifts were controlled by new entrepreneurs, who were either inexperienced and overly aggressive or engaged in outright fraud. This unsustainable expansion was then made worse by the fall in oil prices that affected particular thrifts in oil producing states such as Texas, Oklahoma, and Colorado, and radical changes in tax laws that first made commercial real estate a tax-favored investment and then reversed course and subjected real estate to less favorable tax treatment.

Faced with massive and growing losses from thrift insolvencies, the authorities were forced to seek additional funding for the disposal of insolvent thrifts and to transfer responsibility for regulating, supervising, and disposing thrifts to three new federal agencies and the Federal Deposit Insurance Corporation that had previously provided deposit insurance for commercial banks. The U.S. experience shows that failure to perceive the extent of the thrift problem and a perverse regulatory reaction in the early 1980s caused what could have been a manageable loss to magnify into a major debacle that is likely to exceed $150 billion on a discounted present value basis.

---

6.   White places strong emphasis on the use of market-value accounting. This is a view that is espoused by a growing number of economists but has yet to receive official backing. There are two problems with market-value accounting. First, it is difficult to assign market values to a wide range of assets and liabilities of financial institutions. Second, market values fluctuate widely and are depressed when capital is needed most. To be effective, market-value accounting must be accompanied by minimum capital ratios that vary procyclically with market values. Perhaps, market-value accounting would not be necessary if financial institutions are allowed to diversify their risks and are not allowed to take excessive risks, especially interest rate risks.

Regulatory Framework for Banks and Other Financial Institutions

The experiences of Chile, Malaysia, Norway, and the United States, reviewed in this volume, underscores the importance of an effective framework of prudential regulation and banking supervision. This is a theme that has received growing acceptance among policymakers in both developed and developing countries over the past decade or so. However, accepting a principle is not easily translated to successful action without a clear understanding of the necessary preconditions for such a framework and the essential changes in laws, regulations, and procedures.

Prudential Regulation and Supervision of Banks

Vincent Polizatto discusses prudential regulation and banking supervision and reviews both alternative approaches used in different developed countries and the growing convergence toward a common system of prudential regulation and supervision. Polizatto states that prudential regulation is the codification of public policy for sound and stable banking systems, while banking supervision is the means of ensuring the banks' compliance with public policy. He emphasizes the importance of political independence of bank supervisors and the need for support from government officials at the highest levels.

The prudential rules that should apply to banks include clear rules on criteria for entry, capital adequacy standards, asset diversification, limits on loans to insiders, permissible range of activities, asset classification and provisioning, external audits, enforcement powers, and failure resolution mechanisms. Criteria for entry should cover the minimum capital requirement, the qualifications of management, the development of reasonable business plans and projections, and the financial strength of the proposed owners. Capital adequacy standards should ideally include risk-based capital ratios that take account of the riskiness of different assets, both on and off the balance sheet. The guidelines formulated by the Basle Committee of Bank Supervisors are increasingly adopted by developing countries. Capital adequacy standards should also include a clear definition of different components of capital and should impose limits on the distribution of dividends if minimum standards are not met.

Banks achieve a better combination of risk and return by diversifying their operations. Thus, blanket restrictions on geographic expansion and product diversification should not be condoned by prudential regulations. But lending, investment, and other exposure limits, which prevent the concentration of risk in a single borrower or a related group of borrowers, are necessary for prudential purposes. These limits should be expressed as a percentage of a bank's capital. A frequent cause of loan problems is credit granted to insiders and connected parties. Therefore, limits on loans to insiders, including large shareholders and related companies, should be established. These should not only limit the amount of credit extended, but should also require that such credit should not benefit from more favorable terms and conditions than credit to ordinary customers. Prudential regulations should also stipulate whether banks can engage in commercial, industrial, and nonbanking financial activities and whether they can own equity stakes in nonbanking firms. To discourage banks from assuming excessive risks, clear limits should be set on such activities, if they are permitted at all.

Polizatto argues that one of the most serious deficiencies of prudential regulation in developing countries is the failure to recognize problem assets through classification, provisioning, write-off, and interest suspension. Prudential regulations should require banks to classify assets according to specific criteria, define nonperforming assets, suspend interest accrual on nonperforming assets (and reverse previously accrued but uncollected interest), preclude the refinancing or capitalization of interest, and mandate minimum provisions to the reserves for possible losses based on the classification of assets. External audits serve as a means to independently verify and disclose the financial position of banks. However, external audits must follow clear rules and procedures established by bank regulators and should include an examination of asset portfolio quality, standards for valuing assets, adequacy of loan loss reserves, and treatment of interest on nonperforming assets. Regulators should also have the power to appoint or dismiss auditors and should be informed of any significant findings in a timely manner.

A crucial aspect of prudential regulation regards the enforcement powers given to bank supervisors to intervene to prevent losses from magnifying and to effect timely resolutions of bank failures. Polizatto stresses the importance of conferring to bank supervisors the right to issue "cease and desist" orders, impose fines, appoint receivers, merge or liquidate banks, and generally play an active direct or indirect part in the management of ailing institutions.

Polizatto also reviews alternative models of bank supervision. He compares the informal system based on consultation, personal contact, discretion, and moral suasion that traditionally prevailed in Britain in the past with the strongly populist and confrontational approach based on detailed "rules of the game" and intensive on-site examinations that prevailed in the United States. A third system, reflecting the experience of continental Europe, was based on a legalistic approach that stipulated various ratios but relied on external auditors for verifying compliance with the rules. Polizatto stresses the convergence in systems of prudential regulation (e.g., the adoption of the risk-weighted capital ratios based on the guidelines formulated by the Basle Committee) and in systems of bank supervision. Most countries now emphasize the complementary roles of off-site surveillance and on-site inspection. The former relies on the submission of regular reports, assessment of financial position, and performance and peer reviews, while the latter involves detailed periodic examinations of bank records and policy statements.

Polizatto highlights the importance of recruiting able staff and training them to become specialized examiners as well as retaining experienced officers through appropriate compensation packages. He concludes his paper by stressing that the first line of defense against bank insolvencies and financial system distress is the quality and character of management within the banks themselves. Therefore, efforts to strengthen the financial system must also focus on building strong management.

The Role of Deposit Insurance

Deposit insurance represents one of the most controversial elements of the prudential regulatory framework of banks. The greatest concern focuses on the risk of moral hazard that is inherent in almost any scheme of deposit insurance. There is much debate about the faults in the design of deposit insurance in the United States and its contribution to the debacle of the thrift industry and the current weakness of commercial banks. Many proposals have been made about the use of risk-based premiums, the effectiveness of supervision, and the streamlining of failure resolution mechanisms, although the predominant experience is one of excessive encouragement of risk-taking and excessive cost to taxpayers.

Deposit insurance may have four objectives: to protect small depositors, to avert generalized bank runs, to promote competition, and to act as a catalyst for strengthening bank supervision. The first objective is valid and widely accepted and is in fact applied to all kinds of financial institutions (life insurance companies, mutual funds, and even pension funds) and not just deposit institutions. The other three objectives are open to question. As discussed by Vittas, structural controls that do not inhibit consolidation and do not encourage the emergence of fragmented and fragile banking systems may be more effective than the offer of deposit insurance both in averting bank panics and in promoting effective competition.[7]

Samuel Talley and **Ignacio Mas** do not challenge the conventional wisdom on the objectives of deposit insurance. They argue, however, that the debate about the rationale for explicit deposit insurance misses the point that in most countries the real choice facing policymakers is not between explicit schemes and no protection but between explicit and implicit deposit protection schemes. Experience from most countries shows that except for very small banks, governments generally intervene to protect depositors in failed banks and prevent bank panics that might involve a flight to cash and real assets or a capital flight overseas.

Talley and Mas specify the features of two extreme types of deposit protection: an implicit protection system where there are no detailed rules and procedures, protection is completely discretionary, the amount of protection may vary from zero to total protection, there is no *ex ante* funding, and *ex post* funding is provided by the government; and an explicit insurance scheme where there are detailed rules

---

7. See chapter 3.

and procedures, there is a legal obligation for protection (with some discretionary element for noninsured depositors), the amount of protection may vary from limited to total protection, there is *ex ante* funding through premiums, and failures are covered by the fund, although additional assessments may be levied on banks, or government contributions may be made.

Talley and Mas stress that explicit schemes have both advantages and disadvantages over implicit ones. They constitute a better administrative process for resolving bank failures and are more effective in protecting small depositors. On the other hand, they are less flexible than implicit schemes, which enjoy greater degrees of freedom in terms of the amount, form, and timing of the protection offered. Talley and Mas note that both types of schemes are exposed to moral hazard, but they stress that explicit schemes presuppose stable banking systems, effective prudential regulation and banking supervision, and adequate funding sources. The treatment of banks varies between the two schemes. If the government (or the central bank) assumes the costs of bank failures under an implicit system, then the banking system derives a large subsidy. In practice, however, banks are made to pay either through increased taxes (e.g., increased reserve requirements) or through induced participation in takeovers of failed banks, where the costs are shared between the involved bank and the authorities.

Talley and Mas also examine a number of important features of explicit deposit insurance systems. These include the choice between public and private as well as between compulsory and voluntary systems, the amount of protection (which may vary from limited, total, and discretionary), the role of prefunding, the base of premium assessment and use of fixed or risk-based premiums, and the design of failure resolution mechanisms. In general, Talley and Mas favor compulsory public systems with limited but discretionary protection, adequate prefunding, risk-based premiums, and effective resolution mechanisms. However, they stress that the design of national deposit insurance schemes must be effected on a case-by-case basis to take account of local circumstances.

The Regulation of Life Insurance Companies

The financial systems of most developing countries continue to be dominated by commercial banks. With few exceptions, insurance companies and pension funds account for small and insignificant shares of total financial assets. The main reasons for the underdevelopment of contractual savings institutions are the low level of income, the existence of pay-as-you-go public pension systems, the imposition of repressive regulations, and the use of insurance and pension reserves for financing the public sector deficit at below market rates.

Contractual savings institutions are more developed in those countries that impose mandatory funded schemes for pensions such as Singapore, Malaysia, and Chile. In fact, the organization of a country's pension system is nowadays a major determinant of financial structure, not only in developing countries but also in developed ones.[8] However, the regulation of the insurance business, and especially life insurance, is also an important factor.

Insurance regulation has traditionally followed two distinct approaches. One approach has emphasized the fixing of premiums at levels that are adequate to pay future claims and avoid insolvencies. The other approach is based on solvency monitoring. It avoids tariff setting but requires the maintenance of adequate technical reserves and capital resources for ensuring the solvency of insurance companies. The two approaches are not mutually exclusive. For instance, solvency margins are emphasized in countries where premiums are fixed centrally, while solvency monitoring has implications for premium setting by insurance companies. It is generally agreed that the first system of regulation achieves greater stability, but at the cost of higher prices and limited innovation. However, both systems face difficult issues in regulating distribution networks and selling techniques.

Thomas Rabe discusses the regulation of life insurance companies in the United Kingdom and Germany. He notes that in Germany policy conditions are subject to approval by supervisory authorities in order to prevent the offer of "deceptive" packages. The supervisory authority also approves the basic elements of premium calculation, such as mortality tables, discount rates, and loadings. The result of this

---

8. For a brief discussion of these points, see Vittas (1992).

approach is to discourage innovation (unit-linked life policies account for a very small share of total business in Germany) and to encourage high initial premiums that are then partly rebated to policyholders. In contrast, U.K. life insurance companies enjoy considerable freedom in both product innovation and premium setting. It is generally claimed that life policies are cheaper in the United Kingdom, especially for shorter terms.

Rabe notes that there are also substantial differences in the regulation of investments. In Germany, regulations limit the freedom of investment by specifying the range of permitted assets. Although the German authorities avoid the use of investment regulations for directing insurance funds into low-yielding securities, the imposed limits discourage investments in corporate equities and overseas assets. In the United Kingdom, insurance companies are not subject to any regulations on their investments, except that valuation rules specify upper limits on assets that are admissible in calculating technical reserves and solvency margins.

There is a substantial difference in the valuation of assets. In Germany, companies must use, in most cases, the lower of cost or current value. Unrealized investment gains may not be taken into the profit and loss account and cannot be distributed. Thus, like banks, German insurance companies have considerable hidden reserves. In the United Kingdom, companies are free to use market value, historic cost, or a value between the two. However, in statutory returns, assets must be shown at market values. Unrealized gains are commonly taken into the profit and loss, although it is the responsibility of the appointed actuary to determine which portion of unrealized gains can be distributed.

With regard to distribution networks, Rabe notes that there is no regulation on the selling and marketing of life insurance in Germany. As a result, most selling is effected through tied agents, and companies tend to mount lavish and aggressive campaigns that raise commissions and other selling costs. In the United Kingdom, there is regulatory distinction between tied agents and independent brokers (polarization). Tied agents sell products of one life office. In contrast, independent brokers are required to offer best advice. Because of the stringent standards, 50 percent of independent brokers have decided to become tied agents. The sale of life insurance products is still a controversial issue in the United Kingdom, as in most other countries. Insurance companies emphasize that insurance business is not bought and has to be sold, but there is widespread concern that customers are pushed to buy policies they do not need. It is estimated that 40 percent of long-term life policies are allowed to lapse after two years, at great expense to policyholders. Rabe concludes the comparison of regulatory regimes between the two countries by noting that in Germany there are no compensation or guarantee funds on the grounds that the state ensures that no insurance insolvency will ever be allowed to take place. In the United Kingdom, where regulation is less pervasive, compensation funds cover up to 90 percent of insured amounts in cases of insolvency.

Rabe also discusses the trend toward deregulation that is under way in most continental European countries and the policy of the European Commission to create a single market in insurance. The objectives of the single market include freedom of establishment in any member country; freedom of cross-border operations; use of the same key supervisory rules regarding solvency, reserving, guarantee funds, investments, and policy design; and similar controls over selling methods and distribution networks. An important feature is the elimination of premium controls and their replacement with solvency margins that take account of both premium levels and loss experience. In this way, deceptive packages may be avoided without stringent controls on prices and product innovation.

The initiatives taken by member states of the European Community have had a tremendous impact on insurance regulation in many other countries. Not only other European countries, including those in Eastern Europe, but also countries in Latin America, North Africa, and Asia have reformed or are contemplating reforms of their insurance legislation in line with the main principles adopted at the EC level.

Regulatory Issues in Integrated Financial Systems

The financial systems of many countries have been characterized by a number of major trends that have been described by long and ugly words. These are difficult to pronounce, and even more difficult to spell, but the trends are no less real. The trends can be usefully classified into pairs:

- Liberalization and deregulation
- Internationalization and globalization
- Securitization and marketization
- Privatization and demutualization
- Universalization and institutionalization
- Decompartmentalization and integration.

These trends reflect changes in both structure and behavior and have far-reaching implications for the stability, efficiency, and fairness of financial systems. The trends have been accompanied by a development that can be described as paradoxical: growing concentration of markets through an extensive consolidation process, but also growing competition through the removal of boundaries that used to separate different markets.

Unfortunately, theoretical and empirical economic work has shed little light on the benefits and costs of alternative arrangements of financial system structure. The vast literature on economies of scale and scope in banking has been unable to explain the persistent increase in concentration. Universal banking and integrated financial systems raise far more complex issues, and it is not surprising that there is a greater difference of opinion among economists on the merits and demerits of universal banks than there is perhaps on the existence of economies of scale and scope.

Universal Banking in Canada

Universal banking has been extensively debated in many countries in recent years, but perhaps nowhere as thoroughly and openly as in Canada. **Charles Freedman** reviews the arguments for and against universal banking and discusses the rationale for the solutions adopted in Canada. Freedman notes that there are two principal uses of the term universal banking: one definition refers to the ability of banks to engage in the securities business; the other to their ability to own and control nonfinancial entities. Banks in Canada are primarily interested in underwriting corporate bonds and equities, and not in owning and controlling industrial and commercial companies. The narrow definition is, therefore, more appropriate in the Canadian context.

Freedman also draws a clear distinction between upstream and downstream linkages between banks and nonfinancial corporations. Upstream linkages exist when nonfinancial companies own and control banks, and downstream linkages exist when banks own and control nonfinancial corporations. Upstream linkages generally give rise to greater concern among policymakers and regulators.

The Canadian financial system has traditionally been compartmentalized by function between chartered banks, trust and mortgage loan companies, cooperative credit institutions, insurance companies, and securities dealers. Most of the largest institutions have been widely held, either because it has been required by law as in the case of the big chartered banks (known as schedule I banks) or because they have been constituted as mutual entities (as in the case of credit cooperatives and some of the largest life insurance companies). However, some large trust companies have recently come under close ownership as parts of industrial and commercial conglomerates. Regulatory responsibility has been divided between the federal and provincial governments, with sole federal government responsibility for banks, sole provincial responsibility for credit cooperatives and securities dealers, and dual (federal and provincial) responsibility for trust and insurance companies.

The traditional separation of functions has been blurring over the past twenty-five years or so: banks have expanded into consumer credit and mortgage finance; trust companies, credit cooperatives, and securities dealers into payment services; trust companies into consumer credit and even commercial lending; insurance companies into savings instruments, such as single premium deferred annuities that closely resemble fixed term deposits; commercial banks into various forms of insurance; and so on. The blurring of demarcation lines, the need to create a level playing field for all financial institutions and to establish a sound and robust regulatory framework, and the competitive impact from developments in overseas markets have prompted the Canadian authorities to consider legislative changes with far-reaching implications for the structure and functioning of the Canadian financial system.

Freedman addresses the issues of ownership, self-dealing, conflicts of interest, and corporate governance that are at the heart of the debate about integrated financial systems. He notes that although the ownership issue has been the most contentious one, the authorities have concluded that large banks and insurance companies should continue to be widely held, but smaller financial institutions could be closely held and commercially linked. On self-dealing there is widespread agreement on the need to impose strict limits on transactions with related parties. Conflicts of interest could be handled through better information disclosure, establishment of effective monitoring machinery, and a reliance on reputational considerations that would prevent banks and other financial institutions from abusing privileged information. Strengthening of the functioning of boards of directors and of the role of external auditors would be two essential elements of tackling corporate governance issues.

Freedman then discusses the impact of the 1987 change in legislation that allowed commercial banks and other financial institutions to acquire securities firms. He considers three rationales for the legal separation of banking and securities business: the assumption of excessive risks by banks and its impact on deposit insurance; the potential conflicts of interest between bank lending and underwriting; and the concentration of financial power. He notes that banks in Canada are not permitted to engage in the trust business, but otherwise the traditional separation between banks and the securities business was based on custom rather than legislation. In contrast, in the United States, there is a legal separation between commercial and investment banking, but commercial banks are allowed to engage in trust business. These contradictions reflect historical accidents but clearly weaken the rationale for enforced separation. In Canada, factors motivating change included the growth of syndicated lending, the advent of securitization of corporate financing business, and the need for increased capital by securities dealers. Following the change in securities legislation in 1987, Canadian banks, both domestic and foreign (but not insurance or trust companies), entered the securities industry, mostly by acquiring existing securities firms. There was also an influx of several foreign dealers.

As noted in chapter 13, Freedman's paper was completed before the latest legislative developments. In fact, following a long process of debate and consultation, the Canadian government adopted on December 13, 1991 (date of Royal Assent), a new regulatory framework for all financial institutions, consisting of four new acts governing banks, trust and loan companies, financial cooperative associations, and insurance companies. The new financial services legislation will come into force sometime in 1992.

Recognizing the unavoidable integration of financial services, the new regime enables every institution to offer a complete range of financial services, in many instances through subsidiaries. The expression "financial services" is not defined, thus providing flexibility to expand and adjust to a fast-changing environment both in Canada and abroad. An important feature of the new legislation is its high degree of standardization of rules applicable to different types of institutions. Thus, new banks, insurance companies, and trust companies will be incorporated in the same way. The rules governing related party transactions, directors' liability, board composition, shareholdings, insider trading, and the role of external auditors are common to all and are, for the most part, identical. With respect to permitted in-house activities, financial institutions are confined to the provision of financial services. Banks will be barred from insuring risks, issuing life annuities, and acting as insurance agents. Insurance companies will be able to do everything banks do except take deposits.

Insurance companies and banks will be unable to engage in the trust business or in underwriting corporate bonds and equities. The former activity remains the exclusive function of trust companies, while the latter belongs to securities firms. However, banks and insurance companies will be able to own subsidiaries specializing in these and other areas, including each other's area of expertise. The list of permitted subsidiaries is quite long and effectively open ended. For instance, banks are allowed to own insurance, reinsurance, trust, loan, securities, investment (mutual) fund, venture capital, factoring, equipment leasing, and financial holding companies, as well as any entities that primarily provide financial services. There is no requirement for specialized subsidiaries to be organized through a holding company structure.

Thus, the Canadian system has not only adopted the concept of universal banking but has also authorized the emergence of "allfinanz" or "bancassurance," which refers to the marriage of banking and insurance, and it is spreading rapidly in Europe. One limitation that applies to banks and represents a political concession to insurance agents is that banks will not be allowed to sell insurance products through their branches, nor to use their large customer databases for insurance marketing purposes. However, use of credit card distribution networks is permitted so that this restriction may turn out to be less binding in practice.

The Debate on Financial Conglomerates in Italy

An intense debate has been going on in Italy for several years on the merits and demerits of universal banking and linkages between banks and industrial companies. As noted by **Mario Draghi,** after a long period of regulation and sheltered existence, Italian banks have been faced with a pressing need for restructuring and recapitalization. Unlike Canada, where the benefits and costs of upstream linkages were at the periphery of the debate, the Italian debate has focused on whether the necessary structural changes can be achieved by the banking sector alone or whether they need the participation of the industrial sector, which has restructured itself with astonishing success.

Draghi reviews the arguments for and against such linkages in the context of past and recent developments in Italian banking and the changes in the European Economic Community (EEC) legislation that are prompted by the creation of the single European market. He provides a brief historical review of the experience of universal banking in Italy before the 1930s. The failures of that era led to the establishment of a rigidly controlled system that imposed a clear separation between short- and long-term business, between commercial and investment banking, and between banking and industry. It also led to the public ownership of large commercial banks that coexisted with a number of public law banks and savings banks and dominated the Italian financial system.

Draghi discusses the merits and demerits of both universal banking and upstream linkages. He cautions that universal banking, which appears to have been quite successful in Germany, would not necessarily be equally successful if it was transplanted into other countries. He places particular emphasis on the conflicts of interest inherent in a universal banking system and on the difficulty of monitoring and controlling the behavior of universal banks.

Draghi also notes that leaders of large industrial conglomerates have exerted considerable pressure for the right to acquire controlling stakes in banking institutions. The main arguments in favor of upstream linkages are the provision of private capital and the potential transfer of strong management skills. The main arguments against are the potential excessive concentration of power, the large conflicts of interest, and the burden on monitoring and surveillance for preventing abuse of privileged information.

Draghi then discusses the legislative changes prompted by the creation of the single European market and the passing of the Second Banking Directive of the EEC. He notes that the banking directive provides for the authorization of universal banks with extensive powers, subject to various risk concentration limits, but does not preclude nonbanks from having controlling interests in banks. The EEC directive does not prevent national authorities from imposing stricter rules on national banks but, as Draghi emphasizes, more restrictive rules would undermine the competitive position of national institutions.

Draghi reviews the recent legislative changes, especially the provisions of the so-called Amato Law, and their impact on the Italian banking structure. The new law covers the merger, transformation, and recapitalization of Italian banks and improvements in bank supervision. The law authorizes public law banks to convert themselves into corporations. Although it does not promote bank privatization as such, it states that privatization may be authorized if it is instrumental in strengthening the Italian banking system, increasing its capital, and meeting public interest goals. However, it imposes strict conditions, such as requiring the approval of both the Bank of Italy and the Council of Ministers and provisions that preclude control of privatized banks by nonbanks or by individuals.

The Amato Law in combination with new antitrust legislation impose clear limits on upstream linkages and require the creation of holding company structures for undertaking the various financial activities authorized by the second directive. Following the enactment of these laws and other changes in regulations, Italian banking has undergone considerable restructuring. There have been several important bank mergers, public law banks have changed their status into corporations and have floated new equity on the markets, and freed from branching restrictions banks have proceeded to more than double their branch networks. Banks have also established specialized securities firms. However, Italian banking legislation is likely to undergo further radical change in the near future in order to bring it into line with EEC developments.

The Role of Holding Company Structures

Despite reservations about excessive risks and concentration of power, universal banking has been adopted by most OECD countries as well as a growing number of developing countries, especially in Latin America and Eastern Europe. The two major countries where universal banking is not yet fully authorized are Japan and the United States. In Japan, the existence of *keiretsu* conglomerates with strong links between banks, insurance companies, and other financial institutions (as well as industrial companies) has effectively created universal financial institutions. In the United States, the current administration proposed a radical reform of banking legislation that would have removed the legal separation between commercial and investment banking, banking and insurance, and banking and commerce. However, the proposed reform did not win congressional support.

While approving universal banking, most countries have imposed limits on upstream linkages that would prevent industrial and commercial companies from controlling financial institutions, especially large banks and insurance companies. The one question that remains unresolved regards the structure of universal banking operations. In the United States, the holding company structure has been proposed and actively considered as a better structure for conducting universal banking. In a holding company structure, nonbanking activities are undertaken by subsidiaries of a parent holding company rather than by subsidiaries of the bank.

The arguments for and against the holding company structure are reviewed by **Samuel Talley**. Talley notes that proponents of the holding company structure argue that it would allow the public to derive the benefits of universal banking without placing the stability of the system in jeopardy. This is because clear limitations would be placed on transactions between the bank, its parent company, and its other subsidiaries. For instance, any transactions would have to be effected on market terms. In addition, the holding company structure would create a level playing field for both banking and nonbanking competitors, while the bank would be protected from risky activities that would be undertaken by nonbanking subsidiaries.

Talley notes, however, that in practice it may be difficult to insulate banks from holding company problems. The "corporate veil" may be pierced if the group is perceived as one entity by the courts, if problems at the holding company level affect confidence in the soundness of the bank, and if holding company problems lead to adverse transactions with the bank in violation of existing "firewall" rules. Talley also notes that there is limited evidence in the United States against the insulation view.

Two ways in which a holding company structure can avoid problems is by creating a fail-proof bank (also known as a "narrow" bank) and by creating a fail-proof parent. The fail-proof bank proposal would force banks to separate their traditional deposit and lending functions. Banks accepting deposits from the public would be confined to investing in risk-free assets, such as treasury bills or perhaps high quality commercial paper. Talley notes that this proposal has considerable theoretical merit, but would require a wrenching change in the structure and operation of the banking and financial system. A basic problem would likely be that the amount of liquid bank deposits would greatly exceed the supply of risk-free assets.

The fail-proof parent proposal would require all risky activities to be conducted in nonbank subsidiaries, thus insulating both the bank and the parent company from problems at the subsidiary level. Under this proposal, the parent company would not be allowed to issue debt, while the bank would not be allowed to engage in most types of transactions with either the parent company or its nonbank subsidiaries. Talley argues that the fail-proof parent proposal has many advantages over the other proposals in that it would provide greater protection to the bank and would create a level playing field for different types of activities.

Conclusion

What conclusions could be drawn from this overview of issues in financial regulation? The first point, which cannot be overemphasized, is that the 1980s was not a decade of deregulation, but rather a period of extensive regulatory reform. There was decreased reliance on economic regulations that inhibit competition, innovation, and efficiency but an increasing importance of prudential and other regulations that promote stability and fairness.

Second, there is now widespread consensus that macroeconomic and allocative regulations may be justified under special circumstances, but that over time there should be greater reliance on market mechanisms for monetary and credit control and for allocating scarce financial resources.

Third, a question that is still open concerns the speed and sequence of financial reforms. The contrasting experiences of Japan and Chile support a cautious and gradual approach. Abrupt liberalization after a long period of repressive control may be quite dangerous—Chile had negative interest rates at least from 1945 to 1973. The experience of Indonesia also confirms that caution is important but suggests that there may not exist a unique and optimal sequence of reforms.

Fourth, there is very strong consensus on the importance of prudential, organizational, and protective controls. Although particular types of control, such as the Basle risk-weighted capital ratios, are sometimes questioned, there is little disagreement on the need for capital adequacy and strong banking supervision. However, because they face greater uncertainty and risks, banks in developing countries should perhaps be subject to higher capital ratios than those recommended under the Basle agreement.

Fifth, there is ample recognition of the importance of speedy and decisive intervention to prevent insolvent institutions from magnifying losses. This is underscored by the experience of the banking crises and restructuring in Malaysia, Norway, and the United States.

Sixth, the role of deposit insurance is still unclear. It is instrumental in protecting small savers, but otherwise its role in preventing bank runs, promoting competition, or stimulating better regulatory mechanisms is open to serious objections. Deposit insurance suffers from a high risk of moral hazard.

Seventh, the regulatory issues of nonbank financial intermediaries are very similar to those of banks. For life insurance companies, price and product controls, which inhibit competition, are being replaced by solvency controls. In addition, the use of insurance (and pension) funds for financing large public sector debts at below market yields is being replaced by investment rules that emphasize safety and profitability.

Eighth, the most controversial type of controls are still structural controls that impose geographic or functional limitations on the activities of financial institutions. There is general agreement against geographic restrictions, especially for institutions operating in areas with a common currency. There is also a worldwide trend in favor of universal banking and even in favor of close links between banks and insurance, but there is generally less support for close links between banks and industrial companies. This is particularly so for upstream linkages that involve industrial companies owning or controlling large banks and insurance companies.

Ninth, it is widely accepted that universal institutions pose a serious challenge on regulators and supervisors. Countries with weak supervisory agencies would be well advised to promote simpler and more transparent structures, at least until they are able to strengthen their regulatory and supervisory mechanisms.

Tenth, despite the worldwide trend toward universal banking, there is considerable controversy regarding the desirability and benefits of this trend. Many analysts emphasize the difficulties of regulation by function and reliance on conduct rules for overcoming excessive risk-taking, conflicts of interest, and abuse of privileged information. These analysts favor structural controls that limit the scope for fraud and mismanagement. But other analysts argue that the threat of regulation, reputational considerations, and provisions for legal redress against offending institutions would be effective in policing universal institutions.

Is There a Role for Portfolio and Growth Limits?

Despite the acknowledged importance of prudential regulations, no country appears to have developed a robust regulatory framework. Banks and other financial institutions in a large and growing number of countries have suffered from excessive risk-taking, mismanagement, and fraud. Capital adequacy controls and greater supervision have not succeeded in preventing large losses and failures, although it is fair to say that few countries, if any, have fully and consistently implemented such controls. At the time of writing this chapter, most Anglo-American and Scandinavian countries that have implemented extensive financial deregulation in the 1980s suffer from the consequences of excessive and uncritical expansion of credit as well as from widespread mismanagement and a significant amount of fraud.

One school of thought attributes the phenomenon of large and widespread financial failures in part to a lack of experience and expertise. Mistakes have been made because, after a long period of tight regulation, banks and other financial institutions have failed to develop adequate internal systems of controls. According to this view, financial failures will decline in frequency as well as intensity once institutions learn how to operate and compete in the new deregulated environment.[9] To some extent, excesses occurred because prudential regulation and supervision were ineffective. Not only were incentive structures distorted in favor of risk-taking, but they failed to reward monitoring and risk assessment. Strengthening supervision and correcting the structure of incentives would minimize the likelihood of a repetition of these mistakes in the future.

An alternative view is that there is a systemic tendency of financial institutions to engage in destructive competition, to assume excessive risks, and to engage in imprudent and/or fraudulent activities. According to this view, the performance and behavior of financial institutions in the 1980s bears close resemblance to the 1920s. Without the stabilizing influence of deposit insurance and governmental readiness to provide financial support to avert financial panics, the world economy might have experienced the financial collapse and destruction of the Great Depression. Although macrofinancial controls for

---

9. See Caprio and Atiyas (forthcoming).

development purposes have clearly lost their traditional appeal, there may be some argument for imposing stricter portfolio limits and especially growth limits for purely prudential purposes.

The rationale for such types of controls would rest on two arguments: first, the need to ensure adequate risk diversification; and second, the need to ensure a smooth and reasonably sustainable expansion of business. In the United States, existing prudential controls, such as risk-based capital ratios and limits on individual risk concentrations, failed to address problems caused by high concentrations of portfolio risks. In fact, many deposit institutions suffered from excessive concentration of risks. In Texas, Colorado, and other states, this was caused by restrictions on interstate expansion, but in New England, where geographic restrictions were less binding, the banking sector had 48 percent of its total loan portfolio in real estate related loans in 1990. Portfolio limits would prevent this problem, or at least they could require a higher capital backing for higher levels of portfolio risks. Portfolio limits would, of course, need to take care of any covariance of risks between different types of loans.[10] Moreover, their introduction and subsequent revision would have to be implemented gradually to avoid big distortions in the flow of credit to particular sectors.

The rationale for placing limits on bank growth stems from the argument that fast-growing institutions tend to suffer from managerial problems. Rapid expansion stretches management information and control systems.[11] Growth limits that would apply on an annual as well as a longer time framework could provide sufficient flexibility to individual institutions, while ensuring that a spurt of rapid growth was followed by a period of consolidation before resuming a fast pace of growth.[12]

---

10. For instance, in Texas, where energy lending accounted for a big part of bank lending, banks diversified their loan portfolios by engaging in real estate lending, despite the fact that the two sectors were highly interdependent. When the oil price collapsed, loan losses were high on both types of loans.

11. Research at the Federal Reserve Board identifies rapid growth as the most consistent predictor of future bank trouble.

12. Growth regulations could, for instance, impose a 15 percent annual limit (presumably, in real terms) and a 50 percent cumulative rate over five years. As reported by White (see chapter 9), some savings and loan associations grew in the United States by 200 and 400 percent in three years or less.

How portfolio and growth limits could be applied without inhibiting competition and undermining efficiency remains unclear. However, it is an issue that is still open and could be revisited if more traditional controls fail to promote efficient, fair, and, above all, stable systems.

Bibliography

Berger, A. N., and D. Humphrey (1990). *The Dominance of Inefficiencies over Scale and Product Mix Economies in Banking.* Federal Reserve Board. Processed.

Berlin, Mitchell, Anthony Saunders, and Gregory Udell (1991). "Deposit Insurance Reforms—What Are the Issues and What Needs to be Fixed?" *Journal of Banking and Finance,* September.

Caprio, Gerard Jr., and Izak Atiyas (forthcoming). *Policy Issues in Financial Reform.* World Bank, CECFP. Processed.

Kay, John, and John Vickers (1988). "Regulatory Reform in Britain." *Economic Policy,* October.

Key, Sydney J., and Hal S. Scott (1991). *International Trade in Banking Services—A Conceptual Framework,* The Group of Thirty, Occasional Paper 35, Washington, D.C.

Shaffer, S (1989). "Challenges to Small Banks' Survival." *Business Review,* Federal Reserve Bank of Philadelphia, September/October.

Udell ,Gregory (1990). "Will Small Banks Survive? Small Banks and the Theory of Financial Intermediation." In A. Saunders, ed., *Recent Developments in Finance—Conference in Honor of Arnold W. Smarts,* New York: Business One Irwin, forthcoming.

Vittas, Dimitri, and Bo Wang (1991). *Credit Policies in Japan and Korea.* World Bank, PRE Working Papers, WPS 747. August.

Vittas, Dimitri (1992). *Contractual Savings and Emerging Securities Markets,* World Bank, DEC Working Papers, WPS 858. February.

2

CHANGING THE RULES OF THE GAME

Millard Long and Dimitri Vittas

Introduction

The financial systems of most countries experienced dramatic changes over the past decade or so in both financial regulation and structure. At one level, there was extensive deregulation as country after country eliminated or relaxed credit and interest rate controls and removed or softened restrictions on market entry and diversification. But at a different level, the past decade was characterized by a growing emphasis on prudential and other regulations that were increasingly deemed essential for the smooth and efficient functioning of financial systems. Thus, the decade of the 1980s was one of regulatory reform rather than simply one of deregulation. The most notable feature of financial regulation was the extensive and far-reaching change in the rules of the game rather than the adoption of a laissez-faire approach in finance.

Much of the change in regulatory approach was an endogenous response to forces in financial markets. Advances in electronic technology and telecommunications increased the international links of financial systems and weakened the effectiveness of many of the preexisting controls. Moreover, three decades of extensive regulation of credit flows and interest rates gave rise to many instances of misuse of selective credit flows. These prompted a reconsideration of the underlying philosophy that placed central emphasis on government direction of funds.

The changes in regulation and technology were accompanied by changes in financial structure. In most countries nonbank financial intermediaries and financial markets emerged as significant competitors to the commercial banks that had long dominated the financial system. In addition, changes in philosophical approach were fueled by the impact of an increasing volume of nonperforming loans on the financial position of commercial banks.

This paper tracks the evolution of regulatory thinking in the postwar period. It discusses the main criteria that could be used in evaluating financial regulation and structure and highlights the questions that policymakers need to address in reforming their regulatory frameworks and reshaping their financial systems.

Historical Perspective

In the 1950s and 1960s, the financial systems of most developing countries, especially the newly independent countries of Africa and Asia, were dominated by foreign-owned banks, with limited branch networks located in the capital and port cities, providing primarily short-term trade finance, much of which went to firms that were themselves foreign owned. In Latin America and Southern Europe, the role of foreign banks was less dominant, but the financial systems were similarly oriented toward short-term trade and working-capital finance. The governments of most countries decided the existing institutions did not provide the type of financing needed to develop their countries. Among other objectives, governments wished to promote industry and small-scale agriculture. They wanted financial systems that would mobilize deposits and make loans in the rural areas, provide long-term finance for investment, and fund local rather than foreign-owned firms.

To accomplish their objectives, governments introduced rather sweeping changes in financial practices. In Africa most governments tended to nationalize the largest commercial banks. In South Asia they nationalized practically all the commercial banks. In almost all developing countries governments took control of a substantial segment of the financial system. In addition, they started specialized industrial and agricultural banks under public control. With regard to policies in the financial area, governments directed financial institutions to lend to selected industries on subsidized terms. Interest rates were kept quite low, usually below the rate of inflation. In other words, governments used finance as a tool to reach their development objectives. Given the financial systems then in place, and the models of development prevailing in the 1960s, the approach taken was quite understandable.

By some measures, the policies followed were successful: banks did open many rural branches, government deficits were funded, and credit was channeled to priority sectors and local businesses. But the policies did not create robust financial systems. With rates of interest on deposits below the rate of inflation, much of the domestic saving did not go into financial assets. Some of the funds went abroad in capital flight, others into physical assets. Financial systems remained small in terms of assets and undiversified in terms of institutions and financial instruments. Because of the shortage of domestic credit, borrowers relied heavily on funding from abroad. For a sample of countries in 1987, twenty-two out of twenty-nine had foreign loans greater than the total of loans from the domestic financial system. Governments and public enterprise were the main recipients of domestic credit, receiving more than half the loans. Many private firms were crowded out of the market.

The problems created by the approach taken to finance were not so apparent in the 1970s when there was easy access to foreign funding. But after the onset of the debt crisis in 1982, it became much harder to borrow abroad. Governments and state enterprises turned to borrowing from the domestic markets, further crowding out the private sector and in many countries exacerbating inflationary pressures. While many developing countries were able to maintain price stability, the average rate of inflation in developing countries rose from 10 percent per year in the 1965-73 period, to 26 percent per year in 1974-82, and to 51 percent per year in 1983-87. The number of developing countries with inflation rates above 20 percent rose from four to fifteen to twenty-seven over the same periods (World Bank 1990).

The economic problems experienced by the developing countries in the 1980s are well known. In Africa and Latin America, but not in Asia, lack of access to foreign funds, higher interest rates, lower commodity prices, etc., have led to much slower growth. Recessions have reduced the incomes of business firms in both the public and private sectors; devaluations have increased the domestic burden of the firms' foreign debts; and much higher real interest rates in some countries have made domestic loans harder to service. As a result, many firms have been unable (or unwilling) to service their debts, and the level of arrears has built up dramatically in financial institutions.

The external debt crisis has had an internal counterpart of equal severity. The level of arrears is such that financial institutions in many developing countries have been decapitalized—in fact, losses are several times book capital. There have always been occasional bankruptcies in financial institutions, but never before, not even in the 1930s, has the problem affected as many institutions in so many countries. A growing number of countries are dealing with the problems in their financial sectors. But other countries have not dealt with the problem, or dealt with it only in the most pressing cases.

Reforming Financial Systems

To develop financial systems that can in the future finance their private sectors efficiently, countries need to undertake a variety of reforms. First, the financial institutions need to be restored to vitality. Second, countries must restore macroeconomic balance and adjust relative prices where distorted. Third, they must build their financial infrastructure by developing modern and effective information, legal, and regulatory systems.

Financial institutions and markets should make choices among investments to be funded on the basis of expected return and risk. Good information is needed in order to make those choices, to monitor firms' behavior after funding, and to take appropriate corrective action if things are not going as planned. For all three reasons, financial institutions require reliable company data, which in turn depends upon better accounting, auditing, and information disclosure rules.

Also, there must be adequate legal protection for both debtors and creditors. In some countries the company law, the banking and securities laws, and the bankruptcy law are all outmoded or weakly enforced. Financial agreements are legal contracts, and for finance to flourish there must be an adequate basis for drafting and enforcing contracts.

In most developing countries bank supervision has focused on the implementation of economic directives, such as credit allocation, to be certain bank lending was in compliance with government directives. Very little attention has been paid to the quality of the loan portfolios, the adequacy of capital, and the soundness of bank management. The huge losses now found in the banks' portfolios in many developing countries are testimony to the poor quality of this oversight function.

Both the financial needs of the countries and financial technology have changed substantially over the last twenty-five years. In many of the developing countries the laws and regulations, and, correspondingly, financial practices, have not kept pace. Governments need to pay more attention to prudential and less to economic regulation, leaving the decisions of who is to get credit and at what price to the bankers. The regulators need to focus on the safety and efficiency of the financial systems.

The line between economic and prudential regulation is thin. Any specific aspect of regulation may—and most do—have components of both. But the focus is different between using regulation to control credit allocation and pricing and using regulation to maintain a healthy and efficient financial system. It is not a matter of a complete reorientation of focus, but rather a reweighting of the importance of economic and prudential regulation. The rules of the game need to change. This does not suggest a laissez-faire approach—for all save a few academics believe that the financial process must be regulated— but a different orientation to regulation.

With regard to prudential regulation there is an emerging consensus in some areas, not in others. The area of consensus includes the points made above about limiting allocative controls and strengthening prudential controls and supervision. There is also agreement that there should not, in general, be discrimination, say, in terms of tax policy, among financial instruments and institutions. There is agreement on capital requirements, on criteria for entry and exit, on asset diversification, on limits on loans to insiders, on provisioning for nonperforming loans, etc.

With regard to the structural issues, there is far less consensus. There is little agreement on how to define institutions for regulatory purposes (e.g., what is a bank?) or what amounts to more or less the same thing, on how to delimit the financial services different classes of institutions should be allowed to provide. Indeed there is dispute whether regulators or market factors should set such limits. The dominant school of thought in Europe, though not in the United States, believes that financial intermediaries should be allowed to offer any combination of financial services they find most profitable. The concept of the universal bank flows from this approach; a universal license does not mean that a bank will provide all financial services, simply that it is allowed to choose what services it will provide. But even the exponents of universal banking have some differences about how such banks should be structured and regulated, namely whether the riskier services should be provided in the banks, by subsidiaries of the banks, or through subsidiaries of a holding company. The latter two models permit universal financial institutions but limit the activities that can be done by each subunit.

Today in Eastern Europe the systems' change has forced the restructuring of the entire financial system. The systems that are emerging in some of the countries in the first stage of reform do not seem to be appropriate.[1] But even in the remainder of the developing countries, the need to modernize their financial systems—and to deal explicitly with the pressing problem of widespread bankruptcy of financial institutions—is leading to significant changes in financial structure. Though not the only factor at work, the future structure of financial systems will be affected by regulation; to that degree at least, governments can influence the financial structures of their countries.

Alternative Models of Financial Structure

In using regulatory reform for shaping the structure of the financial system, policymakers can choose between several alternative models of financial structure. Historically, the main distinction was between bank-based and securities-based systems. Bank-based systems are those systems where banks operating as universal institutions

---

1. Long and Sagari (1991) discuss some of the issues involved.

dominate the provision of corporate finance, other than retained earnings. These banks typically offer both short- and long-term loans and both commercial and investment banking services. In securities-based systems, deposit banks confine themselves to short-term lending and other commercial banking services. Much of corporate funding is from the securities markets, which are more active than in bank-based systems in issuing and trading corporate securities.[2]

Increasingly the distinction between bank- and securities-based systems has lost its relevance, at least in developed countries. In terms of both the sources of finance and the services provided by various components of the system, differences have narrowed. Furthermore, in most OECD countries, internally generated funds have become the primary source of corporate finance, with banks and securities markets playing a secondary role in the financing of industrial corporations. Under these circumstances, the basic distinction between alternative models of financial systems has gradually shifted from one based on differences in sources of funding for industrial corporations to one based on differences in the handling of information problems.

The principal differentiation is between relationship-based and transaction-based systems. In relationship-based systems, banks and industrial companies cultivate close links and long-term relationships that govern not only the provision of finance but also the provision of other financial services, such as assistance with mergers and acquisitions. In transaction-based systems, the relations are less close; industrial corporations tend to assign their business on a case-by-case basis to the lowest bidder.

Different types of systems have different implications for financial regulation. Universal institutions are more difficult both to manage and to supervise. They also raise more problems of conflicts of inter-

---

2. Not all bank-based systems involve banks operating as universal institutions. In most developing countries, banks have traditionally specialized in trade and short-term finance while specialized institutions have provided long-term industrial and investment finance. Moreover, in many, perhaps in the majority of developing countries, governments have played a significant role in the financial system both through owning intermediaries and through directing the allocation of financial resources. However, whether financial systems can be more aptly described as credit-based or government-based, a feature they share in common with bank-based systems is the predominance of bank loans as opposed to corporate securities.

est and moral hazard. But as managerial and supervisory capabilities improve, universal institutions providing a range of services appear to have significant advantages in overcoming the problems of informational asymmetries and investment uncertainty.

Policymakers are not required to make irreversible decisions. Regulation can be adapted in the light of changing circumstances. However, regulatory caution suggests that policymakers should proceed slowly and at least initially encourage the creation of simple structures that are more transparent and easier to manage and supervise.

Evaluating Financial Regulation and Structure

Three criteria can be suggested for evaluating financial regulation and structure: stability, efficiency, and fairness.

STABILITY.   Financial systems the world over have been shocked by loan losses in the 1980s. For forty years the stability of financial systems had not been a significant concern; it is today. Much has been written about the new capitalization rules as specified by the Basle Committee. Clearly financial institutions with more capital and less leverage are less subject to shocks. But the stability of the financial system is also affected by its structure.

To protect the payment mechanism, regulators could limit access to the payment clearing and settlement system to so-called "narrow" banks that would be allowed to engage in only the safest activities. Only those institutions would be allowed to issue liabilities insured by government. Milton Friedman proposed in the early 1950s to require intermediaries with access to the payment system to hold 100 percent reserves. Recent suggestions on narrow banks are more liberal but would require banks issuing demand deposits to hold only safe assets.[3]

---

3.   The concept of the "narrow" bank is a recent innovation by academic economists. However, narrow banks have long existed in several European countries in the form of postal giros that offered transaction accounts and invested in government securities. It is interesting to note that postal giros have gradually been merged with postal savings banks and later on have been converted into, or merged with, fully fledged commercial banks with universal functions. Thus, historically and absent regulatory impediments, the model of narrow banks has yielded to that of

This approach would increase the stability of the payment system but not necessarily that of the credit system, for other intermediaries would hold the riskier assets. If a country were threatened by wide scale bankruptcies and debt deflation, the government might still be compelled to intervene.

Another financial structure that would be more stable with regard to credit would be Islamic or "non-par" banking in which payments on all liabilities would be contingent on asset performance. Non-par banks would resemble mutual funds. Their successful operation would require well-developed financial markets and adequate supervision and disclosure of information.

These are only two examples, but they illustrate that the stability of the financial system will be affected by its structure as well as its capital. A practical issue affecting stability concerns the effectiveness of supervision. Structures involving universal banks appear to be harder to supervise than more specialized institutions. This suggests that countries in which supervision is poorly developed might consider limiting the scope of activities of their intermediaries until supervision can be improved.

EFFICIENCY. The relationship between structure and efficiency is clearly complex. As a practical matter we observe in many countries growing concentration in financial markets and expansion in the range of financial services offered by individual institutions, suggesting economies of both scale and scope.[4] In the research literature the issues of economies of scale and scope in finance still seem unresolved. Evidence from developed countries suggests that banking systems with high levels of concentration tend to have lower margins and operating costs as well as higher profits. Banks in Canada, the Netherlands, and Sweden, all of which are characterized by highly concentrated banking systems, have outperformed banks in the United

---

banks with wider powers. This raises doubts about the feasibility and economic efficiency of narrow banks.

4.   One suggested economy of scale is the realization that institutions can be too large for the government to allow them to fail; hence the liabilities of large intermediaries may be considered more secure. From the social perspective, this may be a diseconomy of having large intermediaries.

States, Norway, and Italy, where banking systems tend to be fragmented and concentration is low (Vittas 1991).

In many of the developing countries the financial markets are dominated by a few large, often inefficient banks that may control as much as 80 percent of financial assets. Their size may be based less on economies of scale and more on restrictions on new bank licenses, on interest rate and credit controls that discourage competition, on forced branching, etc. In many of these countries the efficiency of the financial markets would probably be increased by greater competition, which could come from licensing new banks and by allowing international trade in financial services.

With issues of structure we are as concerned with economies of scope as scale. Portugal, in reforming its system in anticipation of the single European market after 1992, opted for universal banks on the grounds that to restrict function would put its banks at a competitive disadvantage with banks from other European countries that allow universal banking. Of course, that presumes there are economies of scope; there are no disadvantages in terms of efficiency to specialized intermediaries if scope economies do not exist. Canada recently allowed the banks to enter the securities business and over a short period of time the banks came to dominate the business, suggesting the existence of economies of scope. The Canadians are now considering whether to allow the banks to offer insurance as well.

For developing countries, the question of the desirability of universal banking is hard to resolve. First, as already noted, universal institutions are more difficult to supervise effectively. Second, allowing universal banking might exacerbate the dominant position of large banks. The experience of developed countries shows that securities markets develop faster in countries where banks' activities are limited to short-term commercial finance and less rapidly in countries with universal banking. In countries allowing universal banking a broad array of financial products appears less likely to develop. Whether this indicates that universal banks can efficiently provide the financial services needed by corporations or whether large banks have been able to block the development of competing institutions is unclear. Product and market development needs to be considered in assessing efficiency and structure.

There is also a question of competitive equality. In the early 1980s the World Bank was asked by the Philippine government to prepare a report on the advantages of universal versus specialized banking. Two departments in the World Bank gave the government contrary advice: one for, the other against, universal banking. Those in favor argued that universal banking would increase the availability of term finance; those against maintained that because of implicit and explicit government insurance, universal banks would be able to provide cheap term finance, but only by passing some of the risk to taxpayers through understated deposit insurance premiums. Thus, universal banking would forestall the development of the securities markets and might even over the longer run reduce the availability of term finance.

FAIRNESS. Fairness covers many issues such as protecting users of financial services from abusive behavior by financial institutions, creating a level playing field for competing institutions, and tackling the problems caused by potential conflicts of interest. The interests of small savers, investors, borrowers, and policyholders, who are deemed to be nonprofessional users of financial services, are safeguarded by appropriate protective regulations. The interests of professional users, including participating financial institutions, are best protected by appropriate regulations regarding disclosure of information and market practice.

Serious conflicts of interest can arise when the ownership and management of financial and nonfinancial firms are not kept separate. It has been argued in the case of both Germany and Japan that the close ties between financial and nonfinancial firms have contributed significantly to the development of the productive sectors. After providing funds, lenders must supervise and enforce their contracts with borrowers. It has been recognized in the German and Japanese cases that interlocking ownership and control allows lenders to monitor borrowers' activities more effectively, thus allowing banks to take financing risks that would be unacceptable if post-lending control were not well developed.

Because of the poor quality of information and the difficulty in enforcing contracts, the problems of asymmetric information, moral hazard, and adverse selection are more serious in developing countries. Because contracting with related firms is far less risky than contracting with outsiders, there has been a tendency in developing countries for conglomerates to evolve. But there are well-known cases in developing countries where interlocking control—in both the public and private sector—of productive and financial enterprises has led to less than arm's length decisionmaking on loans, leading, in some cases, to rather disastrous misallocation of resources. Such arrangements, when in the private sector, are likely to lead to excessive concentration of wealth and power. Interlocking control has also been used to prevent competition within the industrial sector by excluding potential competitors through control of finance.

Those concerned about conflicts of interest argue for strict separation of control and management of banking and industrial firms. But in fact historically ownership and management of financial and nonfinancial firms has been linked in most countries, possibly because it improves information flows and economizes on managerial skills. Strict separation of function may limit abuse, but it may also slow the process of development. Hence this is an important and contentious issue.

Of course in the United States concern over conflicts of interest goes beyond the interlocking of industrial and financial firms. Conflicts can also arise from interlocking financial services. For instance, the proceeds from an underwriting by a bank can be used to repay outstanding loans to the bank. To limit such frauds, the United States has attempted to impose "Chinese walls" among different types of financial services. Of course finance and fraud are inseparable, but interconnected financial activities have been said to make fraud that much easier. There seems to be some reconsideration of that view going on at the present time, with the regulators allowing banks to provide some underwriting services even in the United States. The regulators today seem to feel that while they cannot eliminate such conflicts, through supervision they are now better able to control them. But considerations of the potential conflicts of interest and the ability of a country's supervisors to control them must enter into decisions on structure and regulation.

Questions of Regulation and Structure

The analysis presented indicates the complexities of these structural issues and the difficulty of reaching a consensus. There are clearly tradeoffs between the three criteria suggested above to evaluate regulation and structure. These will lead to different decisions among countries about preferred structures and therefore about the proper regulatory environment. In making decisions about regulation and structure, the following questions need to be addressed by policymakers. These questions do not have general answers but must be answered in the context of particular countries:

1. In terms of ownership and management, what should be the "allowed" relationship between financial and nonfinancial corporations? Related to this is the question of the scope and extent of public ownership.

2. Within the financial sector, are there principles for deciding what products can safely and efficiently be offered by a single financial institution? In other words, should the regulatory system encourage or discourage the formation of universal, as distinct from more specialized, financial intermediaries?

3. In countries electing to have broad-based intermediaries, what are the advantages and disadvantages of different forms of arrangements: universal banks, narrow banks that are part of financial holding companies, or banks that own but are legally separated from subsidiaries that offer other financial products?

4. Is regulation by function to be preferred to regulation by institution? Regulation by function appears to be a way of avoiding the problems of overregulation and unequal treatment of institutions engaging in similar functions, but is it feasible? Closely related to the last issue, is it feasible to define intermediaries for regulatory purposes? That is, can the regulators reasonably define in terms of assets and liabilities as well as in terms of other financial services a narrow bank, a finance company, a leasing company, a broker-dealer, and so on? A number of suggestions that have been made about regulation depend on the regulators being able to impose reasonably clear rules.

5. How is financial structure affected by limiting deposit insurance to some institutions, imposing reserve requirements on some institutions but not others, double taxation of dividend income, and so on?

6. Nonbank intermediaries and markets raise other regulatory issues. Insurance companies, like banks, must be subjected to solvency regulation and supervision. Also like banks, entry and exit constraints, pricing control, and excessive intervention on investment decisions affect their development. The question of consumer protection is also important in the insurance business as in banking.

7. For their part, securities markets require trading and disclosure rules to ensure both efficiency and fairness. How detailed should these rules be? Is there a danger of overregulation impeding the development of markets?

8. An issue that is shared by payment clearing systems and settlement and clearing systems for securities transactions is who should have access to such systems and under what criteria and conditions.

9. Finally, one problem posed by diversified financial systems for countries at an early stage of development is the heavy burden of regulation and supervision. Perhaps such countries may be better off with simpler financial systems based on competitive and sound commercial banks.

In conclusion, in the last fifteen years, there have been very marked changes in financial regulation and structure in both developing and developed countries. These reflect in part a change in philosophy and in part changes in technology and the internationalization of markets. The regulations that are being changed were in many cases the outgrowth of the excesses of the 1920s, followed by the financial collapse in the 1930s. As was said in the *1989 World Development Report* (World Bank 1990):

> "The lessons to be learned from the experience of the high-income countries is that the financial decisions of private agents are also imperfect.... Market-based financial systems, like public ones, are subject to fraud and instability. The goal is not perfection but a system which mobilizes resources efficiently, minimizes allocative mistakes, curbs fraud, and stops

instability from turning into crises....A main concern of financial regulation has been the achievement of stability without undermining efficiency. But finance remains a dynamic field, changing far too rapidly to achieve a perfect balance between the freedom needed to stimulate competition and growth and the control needed to prevent fraud and instability."

Bibliography

Long, Millard, and Silvia Sagari (1991). *Financial Reform in Socialist Economies in Transition*. The World Bank, PRE Working Papers No. 711. June.

Vittas, Dimitri (1991). *Measuring Commercial Bank Efficiency*. The World Bank, WPS 806, November.

World Bank (1990). *Financial Systems and Development*, (The 1989 World Development Report), World Bank, PRE, Policy and Research Series 15.

3

THE IMPACT OF REGULATION ON FINANCIAL INTERMEDIATION

Dimitri Vittas

Introduction

Financial regulation has a pervasive impact on the structure and efficiency of financial intermediation. It is perhaps the most important determinant of differences in financial structure that are exhibited by countries at a similar level of economic development and with access to common technologies. Regulation also affects the efficiency of financial institutions through its impact on competitive practices, financial and technological innovation, and transaction costs.

Historical accidents and differences in financial culture also influence the shape and behavior of a country's financial system. The importance of regulation lies in the fact that it is shaped by policymakers and is, therefore, amenable to radical change. In contrast, historical accidents are by definition outside the control of policymakers, while financial cultures reflect habits that change slowly over time.

Although financial regulation is amenable to radical change, it is not an exogenous process imposed from without on a country's financial institutions and markets. Rather, both regulation and deregulation are part of an endogenous response to changes in financial systems, and especially to financial crises and to real or perceived problems in the functioning of financial systems.

Regulation is also influenced by political and social pressures. Some of these reflect the interests of special groups, which often include the firms that are subject to regulation. Others reflect basic beliefs and perceptions of different societies about the role of the financial system and its interaction with the "real" sectors of the economy. Like regulation itself, social and political beliefs are not exogenous, but are shaped by the historical performance of the financial system. Historical accidents, in particular, have as large an impact on values and perceptions as they have on regulatory practices.

Thus, the aversion to inflation that characterizes current attitudes in Germany is rooted in the disastrous experience with hyperinflation in the 1920s and again in the 1940s. Similarly, the reliance on direct credit controls in many countries, both developed and developing, in the first two decades after World War II can be attributed to the massive failures of financial institutions and the devastating impact of the Great Depression. In a similar vein, the hostility toward foreign banks in many developing countries was bred during colonial times when foreign banks were little more than colonial institutions.

But although historical accidents have a strong impact on the formation of social and political values and beliefs, their influence fades with the passage of time. New historical experiences cause a gradual change in attitudes and lead in due course to a reconsideration of prevailing policies.

The endogeneity of the whole process may suggest a fatalistic approach, but this need not be so. There is a positive and most important role to be played by political leadership when the values and beliefs of society about the structure and role of financial systems are contrary to the fundamental regulatory requirements of efficient and stable financial systems. Political leadership is very important in the area of prudential regulation and supervision where supervisory agencies need to be awarded decisive powers of intervention and crisis resolution (Polizatto 1992). It is also crucial for the success of financial restructuring operations when political considerations must be set aside in order to ensure the viability of restructured institutions. But political leadership is perhaps even more important in creating a sound and robust framework of regulation that contributes to higher efficiency and stability in the first place and thus avoids the need and cost of later interventions.

Assessing the impact of regulation on structure and efficiency is a complex exercise because a variety of regulations are required to meet a variety of objectives. There is no simple correspondence between objectives and effects. Moreover, there is a constant interaction between regulation and market practice. Financial innovation and technological progress undermine the effectiveness of regulation and often cause radical changes in regulatory philosophies. A constant process of evaluation and adjustment may be required to maximize the benefits (and minimize the costs) of financial regulation.

To be effective, political leadership requires a thorough understanding of the merits and demerits of different types of regulations and different regulatory approaches. There is an interesting contrast between the widespread perception of financial deregulation in the 1980s with the growing realization of the need for prudential and other regulations that ensure the soundness and stability of financial systems. Understanding the rationale for removing some regulations and introducing others is essential for the design and implementation of effective regulatory reform.[1]

This paper discusses the rationale and objectives of financial regulation and reviews its impact in both developing and developed countries over the past forty years or so. The paper highlights the interaction between different types of regulation and emphasizes the importance of a sound and robust financial constitution.

Objectives of Financial Regulation

The Rationale of Financial Regulation

Financial intermediaries and markets are subject to extensive regulation in both developed and developing countries. To be sure, finance is not unique in this regard. Other industries, such as utilities, pharmaceuticals, airlines, and nuclear energy, are also subject to extensive regulation for both good and bad reasons. The main rationale for fi-

---

1. The contrast between deregulation in some areas and more extensive regulation in others is similar in many respects to that between trade and investment liberalization, on the one hand, and strengthening of competition or antitrust policy, on the other. (For a discussion of competition policy and its interaction with trade liberalization, see Boner and Krueger 1991.)

nancial regulation is the existence of market failure in financial systems arising from externalities, market power, and information problems.

Externalities include the risk of systemic failure (i.e., the risk of failure of one or more institutions as a result of the actual or threatened failure of another), the infection effect (i.e., the general lowering of standards and prices caused by excessive competition), and network effects (i.e., the costs and benefits of linking together competing institutions to a common network). Other externalities are the achievement of macrostability (to avoid the distortions in relative prices, incentives, and expectations caused by high and volatile inflation) and the enhancement of the allocative efficiency of the financial system (to ensure the financing of projects and sectors, including small firms, that have dynamic efficiency benefits).

Concern about market power stems from the fear that dominant firms may undermine both allocative and dynamic efficiency (the former by charging high prices and earning excessive profits and the latter by avoiding competitive pressures). Finally, information problems arise from poor price and product information, from the free rider problem, and from informational asymmetries between the suppliers and users of financial services.[2]

Market failure is a necessary but not sufficient condition for regulation. The other condition is that regulation can correct market failure in an effective and efficient way. Much of the debate among alternative theories of regulation is about the cost and effectiveness of regulation rather than about its rationale.

Types of Financial Regulation

Whatever its rationale, the ultimate goals of financial regulation are the achievement of efficiency, stability, and fairness, not only in the financial sector but also in the economy at large. To achieve these ultimate goals, governments adopt various direct controls and interventions that can be classified in six categories depending on their particular objectives:

---

2. For an interesting discussion of the rationale for financial regulation, see Kay and Vickers (1988).

- Macroeconomic controls—to maintain overall control over the level of aggregate economic activity and contain major internal and external imbalances (reserve requirements, direct credit and deposit ceilings, interest rate controls, and restrictions on foreign investments);
- Allocative controls—to influence the allocation of financial resources in favor of priority activities (selective credit programs, compulsory investment requirements, and preferential interest rates);
- Structural controls—to control the structure of the financial system (entry and merger controls, geographic restrictions, and limits on the range of activities of different types of financial institutions);
- Prudential controls—to preserve the safety and soundness of individual financial institutions and sustain public confidence in the stability of the financial system as a whole (authorization criteria, minimum capital requirements, limits on the concentration of risks, and reporting requirements);
- Organizational controls—to ensure the smooth functioning and integrity of financial markets and information exchanges (rules of market-making and participation, disclosure of market information, and minimum technical standards);
- Protective controls—to provide adequate protection to users of financial services, especially consumers and nonprofessional investors (information disclosure to consumers, compensation funds, and ombudsmen offices to investigate and resolve disputes).

Differences in financial structure may also arise from differences in company law that affect the formation of different types of companies (joint stock companies, limited partnerships, etc.) and in the organization of a country's social security system. The effect of these regulations is similar to that of structural controls on financial institutions.

MACROECONOMIC CONTROLS. Macroeconomic controls, and especially the use of direct credit ceilings, have often been motivated by the paramount importance of controlling the expansion of credit and maintaining price stability. The case for the use of macroeconomic controls is strengthened in many countries by the absence of adequate market mechanisms for the operation of indirect methods of monetary and credit control. However, both economic theory and historical experience suggest that the macroeconomic objectives of financial regulation can be achieved more efficiently by market-based mechanisms that do not distort competition between individual institutions and among different types of financial institutions. Rather than relying on the use of direct credit ceilings and interest rate controls that stifle competition and inhibit innovation, governments should stimulate the development of efficient money and government bond markets.

ALLOCATIVE CONTROLS. Allocative controls have been motivated by the desire to compensate for the tendency of financial institutions, and especially of commercial banks, to finance either low risk activities, such as short-term trade finance, or high risk speculative projects with short payback periods, such as real estate development. Commercial banks are generally less willing to finance investment projects with high risks and long payback periods, even though they may have beneficial effects on total factor productivity. They are also generally reluctant to finance small firms without adequate collateral, even though such firms may be innovative and promise high returns. The rationale for intervention is then the need to direct financial resources to uses with dynamic efficiency benefits. Allocative controls are often combined with macroeconomic controls that aim to limit the total supply of credit without raising the level of interest rates.

However, the existence of this externality provides a good example of the argument that market failure is a necessary but not a sufficient condition for regulation. There are many reasons why commercial banks may be unwilling to lend for projects with long payback periods or to small firms without adequate collateral: investment projects may be subject to high uncertainty, which may be compounded by high inflation and macroeconomic instability; commercial banks may be relying on short-term deposits and may thus be unwilling to assume the higher interest rate and credit risk exposure of long-term lending; accounting and auditing standards may be very weak, limiting the quantity and quality of information available to lenders, especially on the performance and prospects of small firms; and legal procedures for collateral, foreclosure, and debt recovery may be very ineffective.

The absence of capital markets and other sources of long-term finance (including venture capital and equity finance) may compound the shortage of investment and small firm finance, but the imposition of allocative controls involving directed credit programs and preferential interest rates is unlikely to be effective if no action is taken to improve the legal and accounting systems or to develop more appropriate sources of funding. Moreover, without a better monitoring of both banks and their borrowers, allocative controls suffer from the problem of moral hazard, as subsidized resources tend to be diverted to unauthorized uses.

Very few countries have been able to design and implement effective allocative controls. Where they have worked, these have been based on the achievement of overall macroeconomic stability and the development of quite effective monitoring systems. In fact, the general case for allocative controls has been undermined by the failure of most countries to design and implement effective and efficient controls. In general, the experience of most countries implies that the scope of allocative controls should be limited and that any subsidization of the cost of credit should also be small.

STRUCTURAL CONTROLS. Structural controls are mainly motivated by economic and political considerations. For instance, the legal separation of commercial and investment banking and other restrictions on the permitted types of activities of banks mainly aim at preventing undue concentration of economic and financial power. Structural controls often discourage, or even prohibit, the maintenance of close links between the suppliers and users of financial services because of the potential conflicts of interest that may arise and the potential abuse of information and financial flows. Restrictions on new entry by foreign banks (including restrictions on interstate banking in the United States) aim to protect the position of indigenous institutions. In addition, controls on the expansion of operations in foreign countries are often motivated by the desire to channel financial resources in the domestic (or local) market.

Structural controls aim to deal mainly with problems caused by market power. But by putting limits on the size and diversification of individual firms they may cause a fragmentation and segmentation of the financial system and may also prevent large firms from achieving economies of scale and scope. They may also weaken the incentives of individual institutions to invest in the acquisition, processing, and dissemination of information and may thus aggravate the free rider problem.

PRUDENTIAL CONTROLS. Prudential controls aim to reduce the risk of systemic failure and avoid the disruptions caused by financial crises. They require financial institutions to be adequately capitalized, professionally managed, diversify their risks, adopt proper accounting policies, report their true financial position and be subject to effective supervision. They impose "fit and proper" tests on the managers and owners of financial institutions to minimize adverse selection and detailed conduct rules to guard against moral hazard.

Prudential controls are necessary because financial institutions are susceptible to both imprudent and fraudulent behavior. Experience has shown that private financial institutions make mistakes and their decisions are imperfect and prone to excesses. Market-based financial systems, like public ones, are subject to fraud and instability. A main concern of prudential regulation is the achievement of stability without undermining efficiency, though it is not clear to what extent prudential controls can be devised that are based on market mechanisms and do not distort competition and financial behavior.

ORGANIZATIONAL CONTROLS. Organizational controls aim to cope with the externalities caused by the existence of networks such as stock and other trading exchanges, payment clearing systems, and information networks. By setting out the rights and obligations of market participants on objective criteria, such as technical competence and financial standing, they promote the efficiency and integrity of networks without discriminating against new institutions.

PROTECTIVE CONTROLS. Protective controls deal with the information problems that affect the relations of financial institutions with their customers, especially small ones. These arise from the existence of informational asymmetries between the suppliers and users of financial services and from poor price information. In most markets, the main informational asymmetry is the inability of consumers to judge the quality of the service being purchased. But in banking and insurance, asymmetric information also affects the suppliers of financial services. Financial institutions often lack adequate information on the behavior of their customers that may affect their creditworthiness and insurability.

One way to deal with asymmetric information is by specifying contracts that impose restrictions on behavior and discriminate between high and low risk customers. However, these may be open to abuse by individual institutions, and regulation about contract terms and conduct rules is required to protect the interests of consumers. Protective controls may also be required to ensure the quality of price information that is provided to consumers. This need is greater where products are not standardized and markets are fragmented and where there is price dispersion and uncertainty about the quality of products.

Interaction and Overlap of Financial Regulations

Although financial regulations are usually introduced with a particular objective in mind, they tend to have effects that cut across different objectives. For example, credit ceilings are mainly applied for macroeconomic purposes, but they also restrain banks from engaging in an uncontrolled and imprudent expansion of credit and thus serve to fulfill a prudential objective. Moreover, because they tend to stifle competition among banks, credit ceilings also have a structural effect.

Similarly, global interest rate controls can have both macroeconomic and prudential objectives, while branching restrictions tend to have both structural and prudential effects. In many countries, interest rate and branching controls were introduced after the Great Depression in order to curtail excessive and destructive competition among banks. In the insurance industry, price and product controls are extensively applied for prudential rather than allocative purposes, but such controls also have pervasive effects on the structure of insurance markets.

Even the modern approach to prudential regulation, which emphasizes risk-based capital requirements, subject to a minimum capital for new entrants, has structural effects since it may discourage new entry and may differentiate in favor of some activities as a result of the risk weights that are applied to different types of assets.

Organizational controls are clearly essential for the development of financial networks, but such controls may discriminate against particular groups of institutions, such as foreign banks, and may thus have direct effects on the structure of financial markets.

Regulations for consumer and investor protection may also have both prudential and structural effects. To protect the interests of investors, financial institutions may be induced to adopt more prudent practices, while increased requirements for information disclosure and the cost of compliance with an array of complex regulations may increase operating costs and thus discourage new entry.

Structural controls are motivated by political considerations to prevent excessive concentration of market power, but by limiting the risks that different institutions can assume they may also have prudential effects. On the other hand, some structural controls may undermine the effectiveness of prudential regulation. This is because they may cause a fragmentation of the financial system into a large number of small institutions with limited capital resources. Both the risk of systemic failure and the risk of infection are likely to be greater in fragmented systems. In contrast, consolidated financial systems with a high degree of concentration are likely to be more stable and much less exposed to systemic risk. Structural controls on foreign investments by domestic institutions may have adverse prudential effects in that they may impede risk diversification and increase the fragility of individual institutions.

There is clearly a tradeoff between the various objectives of financial regulation and especially between controls that stimulate competition, efficiency, and innovation on the one hand and those that promote stability, safety, and fairness on the other.

In this regard, it is worth emphasizing that the most important and fundamental regulatory action is the enactment of what may be called the basic financial constitution of a country. This should cover the structural, prudential, organizational, and protective regulations discussed above and should govern what financial institutions are permitted to do, where they can operate, who is allowed to own or manage them, and what basic conditions they have to meet.

A sound and robust financial constitution would not place arbitrary entry, branching, and merger restrictions on individual financial institutions and would encourage them both to diversify their risks and to accumulate substantial capital reserves that would then be available to absorb losses. In many ways, it would define the ability of financial institutions to exploit economies of scale and scope and generally operate on a sound and managerially efficient basis. Individual financial institutions would have a strong incentive to develop effective internal audit and control systems, thus reducing the amount of external policing that financial supervisors have to undertake and placing a smaller burden on the resources of compensation funds.

A sound and robust financial constitution should be complemented with a system of effective supervision. Financial supervision is important in order to ensure that the various rules and regulations are complied with. Traditionally, supervision was mostly concerned with ensuring compliance with the various credit and exchange controls, but increasingly greater attention is focused on ensuring the adoption of prudent and sound practices. It also has a crucial part to play in preventing attempts to cover up losses and thus stopping them from being magnified out of control.

Other forms of regulatory action include financial accommodation through the lender of last resort facility to deal with short-term liquidity problems and financial restructuring, and through intervention by the appropriate authorities to deal with more permanent solvency crises. Compensation funds in general, and deposit insurance in particular, also have a role to play, especially in protecting the interests of small investors. But if compensation funds and deposit insurance attempt to safeguard financial stability by preventing runs on fragmented and fragile individual institutions, they are likely to create major distortions in incentives and suffer from the problems of moral hazard and adverse selection.

In the United States proposals for reforming deposit insurance have received extensive publicity following the debacle of thrift institutions. But discussing deposit insurance in isolation from other regulatory issues is not very meaningful. Indeed, a financial constitution that avoids the fragmentation and segmentation of the financial system and discourages the continuing existence of fragile institutions can lead to greater stability and efficiency than any reform of deposit insurance.[3]

The Impact of Financial Regulation and Deregulation

Financial Regulation in Developing Countries

Financial regulation in developing countries was very extensive in the immediate post-war or post-independence period. Most regulations had macroeconomic, allocative, and structural objectives, while prudential regulation and supervision were conspicuous by their absence, as were controls to protect consumers and nonprofessional investors. To a large extent this reflected the emphasis placed on two of the sources of market failure identified above: externalities and market power. Information problems generally received little attention in most developing countries. Moreover, the ability of the regulatory system to correct market failures was taken for granted.

Although prudential regulations were mostly absent, direct controls had a prudential effect by inhibiting banks from expanding too fast and engaging in imprudent and excessive competition. On the other hand, failure to provide for prudent policies on suspending interest accrual on nonperforming loans and for loan provisioning against doubtful debts resulted in many cases in a buildup of nonperforming loans and unrecognized losses that undermined the financial standing of both commercial and development banks (World Bank 1990).

Moreover, failure to monitor the performance of borrowers, especially large state-owned firms in strategic sectors, resulted in both overleveraging of individual companies and abuse of subsidized credit facilities. In many countries, industrial and financial conglomerates used their control over finance to capture economic rents by passing cheap credits to related firms, engage in speculative ventures, and deny credit to potential competitors.

---

3.   The recent proposal of the U.S. Treasury for a major overhaul of banking regulation implicitly recognizes the importance of these points. The proposal aims to abolish the legal separation between commercial and investment banking, between banking and insurance, and between banking and industry or commerce. It also aims to reform the structure of financial regulation and the operation of deposit insurance (U.S. Treasury 1991).

Extensive exchange controls limited the scope for risk diversification and isolated domestic financial systems from developments in international financial markets. Foreign financial institutions, especially deposit banks and insurance companies, were prevented from entering domestic markets and from engaging in a beneficial transfer of financial technology and financial innovation.

To be sure, most developed countries, ranging from Scandinavia to Central Europe and the Mediterranean Region and farther away to Australia and New Zealand, also applied similar types of controls. The main difference between developing and developed countries was in the extent and severity of controls. In general, these were far more extensive and comprehensive in developing than in developed countries, and this had a discernible impact on the functioning and efficiency of national financial systems.

Apart from stifling competition and inhibiting innovation, financial regulation also had an impact on the overall structure of financial intermediation. In several countries, nonbank financial intermediaries, such as finance and leasing companies, were left out of the tight regulatory regime, either by design or by accident (Cho 1989). As a result, such companies were able to grow by paying high interest rates, although in many countries (e.g., Malaysia, Thailand, Sri Lanka, and Pakistan) finance companies engaged in imprudent or fraudulent operations and caused financial crises and losses for depositors.

In the 1980s several developing countries, following the precedent set by some developed countries, such as France and Japan, used financial regulation as a means of stimulating the development of capital markets. These involved both allowing higher interest rates on company debentures than on bank deposits and providing strong fiscal incentives for issuing and investing in company securities.

Another way in which regulation affected the structure of financial intermediation was through the establishment of national provident funds or more generally through the promotion of contractual savings institutions. Two countries, Singapore and Malaysia, established employee provident funds with high contribution rates and substantial long-term savings. In Korea, Zimbabwe, Chile, and a few other countries, various types of contractual savings institutions, covering life insurance and pension plans, were encouraged to grow and play a significant part in the mobilization of domestic long-term financial savings and the development of capital markets.

Financial Regulation in Developed Countries

Macroeconomic and allocative controls, including credit ceilings, interest rate controls, reserve requirements, and directed credit programs, were extensively used in most developed countries, especially during the period of reconstruction and high growth following the end of World War II. This was particularly the case in Japan (Patrick 1984, Teranishi 1986), but was also true of most continental European countries.[4] However, Germany and the United States made little use of credit ceilings, while Germany, the Netherlands, Switzerland, and the United Kingdom either had no recourse to interest rate controls and branching restrictions or removed them at quite an early stage.

Many countries imposed extensive structural controls, separating commercial and investment banking; limiting the scope of activities of specialized housing, rural, and savings banks; and restricting the expansion of regional institutions, although Germany and some other European countries refrained from imposing structural controls and generally allowed both their commercial and savings banks to operate as universal banks. Among OECD countries, the use of structural controls was most extensive in the United States, Italy, Norway, and Japan.

In the United States structural controls, especially branching restrictions dating from the 19th century, caused a fragmentation of the banking and thrift industries that increased their fragility and susceptibility to financial crises. Following the massive failures of banks and thrifts in the 1930s, two deposit insurance funds were created to prevent runs on individual institutions and, thus, protect the stability of the system. The thrift industry was also subjected to a series of controls and restrictions that maximized its exposure to interest rate, sectoral, and geographic risks.[5]

---

4. For a review of financial regulation in the 1960s and 1970s in several developed countries, see Vittas et al. (1978).

5. The recent experience of U.S. savings and loan associations contrasts sharply with the continuing prosperity and success of U.K. building societies. The impact of regulation on the thrift industries in the United Kingdom and the United States is discussed in Vittas (1991).

The fragmentation of the banking industry and the absence of nationwide banks stimulated the development of corporate securities markets and the growth of investment banking. In the post-war period, the structural controls imposed on banks have been instrumental in contributing to the growth of the commercial paper market and to the emergence and growth of money market mutual funds.[6]

In the United Kingdom the institutional segmentation between commercial (clearing) banks and merchant banks was not imposed by regulation, but reflected the traditional concerns and prevailing practices of major banks. The absence of branching controls and other rigid regulatory restrictions permitted the emergence of large commercial banks with nationwide operations that were able to diversify progressively into other areas, such as hire purchase finance, merchant and investment banking, mutual funds, insurance broking, and, more recently, stockbroking and real estate broking. In contrast to commercial banks, savings banks and building societies were compelled to specialize in collecting retail deposits from households and investing them in government securities in the case of savings banks, and housing loans in the case of building societies. However, neither type of institution was prevented from expanding operations on a national scale.

Most countries paid little attention to prudential, organizational, and protective regulations, although Germany and Switzerland imposed rather strict prudential controls on both banks and insurance companies.[7] In the United Kingdom, prudential regulation was mostly based on informal arrangements. This was facilitated by the small number of banks and the greater consolidation of the U.K. banking system. In contrast, in the United States the use of deposit insurance

---

6. In this respect, it is worth noting that the commercial paper market has expanded at a rapid pace in Spain, Portugal, and France, countries where banks have been subjected to extensive credit ceilings; but not in other European countries such as the United Kingdom, the Netherlands, or Germany. Moreover, money market mutual funds have generally thrived in countries with strict controls on interest rates on retail deposits, such as the United States, Japan, France, and Australia; but not in the United Kingdom, Sweden, and other European countries where deposit institutions have been free from interest rate restrictions and high interest has been offered on various types of bank accounts.

7. For a discussion of insurance regulation in Germany, see Finsinger et al. (1985), Finsinger and Pauly (1986), and Rabe (1992).

and the large number of deposit institutions necessitated the imposition of detailed prudential controls and the development of an extensive machinery of examination and supervision. Because of the fragmented structure of the U.S. banking system, the supervisory process was forced to rely on large numbers of skilled examiners for probing the integrity of bank managers and second guessing their business decisions. Policing costs were externalized and bank losses were covered to a large extent by deposit insurance funds and ultimately by taxpayers if the reserves of the funds were not adequate. In more consolidated banking systems, policing costs were internalized and losses at the branch level were absorbed to a greater extent by bank shareholders.

The limited use of macroeconomic and allocative controls but extensive reliance on structural controls in the United States contrasts rather sharply with the experience of most European countries. As documented by banking historians, the fragmentation of the banking and thrift industries reflects a strong tradition of localism in American banking that was based on populist policies motivated by fear of the concentration of power that large banks from out-of-state centers might acquire.[8] Neither politicians nor economists have done much to dispel this fear.

The restrictions on the geographic expansion of banks have prevented the emergence of large banks with nationwide operations. In some states, branching restrictions have confined banks to very small geographic areas. Geographic restrictions have been eroded in recent years, although the fragmentation of the industry still persists. One could argue that economists have undermined potential support for consolidation of the banking and thrift systems by downplaying the potential economies of scale and scope of large banks. By focusing on the production side of banking services and neglecting potential economies in risk and marketing, they have largely failed to establish a strong case for greater consolidation. Politicians responded to the financial crisis of the 1930s by introducing deposit insurance, despite some early concerns about the distortion of incentives, but failed to allow a consolidation of both industries.

---

8.   See Hammond (1957) and Krooss and Blyn (1971).

The fear of out-of-state banks may have made sense when communications were poor and the ability to regulate and supervise large institutions with nationwide operations may have been limited. But improvements in communications and regulatory practices should have removed any concern about the ability to control large institutions and prevent them from abusing their market power. Lack of political leadership, which may partly be explained by the belief that deposit insurance imparted a sufficient degree of financial stability, has allowed this irrational structure of regulation to persist. However, as already noted above, the recent thrift crisis and the poor financial condition of a large number of banks suggest that a major overhaul of bank and thrift regulation is now likely.

Financial Deregulation in Developed Countries

Most developed countries have undertaken extensive deregulation of their financial systems since the late 1970s, although the focus and pace of deregulation have varied considerably across countries. In many countries, deregulation has primarily affected the provision of corporate financial services.

A good example of this approach is Japan, where financial deregulation has involved the progressive relaxation of restrictions on domestic and foreign bond issues and the liberalization of interest rates on bank loans and large deposits (Hoshi et al. 1989). In retail banking many regulations are still imposed, limiting opportunities for branch network expansion and controlling interest rates on retail deposits.

Financial deregulation has been accompanied by an explosive growth of activity on the securities markets, which now play a central part in the Japanese financial system. The creation of markets for financial futures and options has further increased the flexibility of the financial system. Although the role of banks in corporate finance has declined, close links between banks and industrial companies, and extensive cross-shareholdings among firms belonging to conglomerate groups continue to predominate.

In France, deregulation has been more extensive and has involved the abolition of the legal separation of commercial and investment banks, the lifting of branching restrictions, and the relaxation of interest rate controls on loans and large deposits. But controls on retail deposits have continued to apply, and use has been made of fiscal incentives to encourage households to invest in marketable securities and contractual savings. As in the case of Japan, there has been a large expansion of activity in the money, capital, and derivative markets.

In Germany, financial deregulation has been less extensive, mainly because the system was already quite free from structural controls.[9] Because of the traditional emphasis on prudential and anti-inflationary concerns, authorization of new financial instruments (such as negotiable certificates of deposit, floating rate and zero coupon bonds, and indexed instruments) was considerably delayed, and this held back the development of active money markets. Moreover, securities markets for corporate equities and bonds have continued to be underdeveloped.

The underdevelopment of German securities markets may be explained by five factors: first, the close links between corporations and the universal banks, which provide financial and managerial support for expansion plans and restructuring operations and may thus mitigate the need for strong financial independence by the corporate sector; second, the preference of most medium-sized companies to operate as limited partnerships;[10] third, the imposition of turnover taxes that affected, in particular, the development of markets for short-term securities, such as commercial paper; fourth, the limited role played by pension funds in the German financial system as many company pension schemes are based on internal reserves that are reinvested in the sponsoring companies and are not available for investment in marketable securities; and fifth, the recurrent crises in the German financial system, which have undermined the confidence of the saving public in marketable securities and have interrupted the evolution of the

---

9.   See Deutsche Bundesbank (1986) and Broeker (1989).

10.   It is not clear why unlisted German firms are reluctant to go public. For firms with less than 2,000 employees, an important reason may be the desire to avoid the burden imposed by company law on listed companies through the provisions for codetermination (i.e., the requirement that half the seats on supervisory boards of listed companies must be reserved for representatives of workers). For larger firms, which are subject to codetermination irrespective of legal form, the reluctance to go public may be related to fears about losing company control and perhaps also to the lack of any clearly perceived benefits from listing.

German financial system toward a more varied and balanced structure.[11]

Financial deregulation in the United Kingdom has involved the abolition of credit ceilings and exchange controls and the reform of the stock exchange to allow membership by banks and other financial institutions. On the other hand, prudential controls have been progressively enshrined in legislation, in line with international developments. There has also been a major overhaul of organizational and protective regulations. The new regulatory framework covers all firms engaging in financial services and is based on a combination of statutory agencies and self-regulatory organizations. It is supported by a network of ombudsman offices for the independent examination of consumer complaints and by a series of compensation funds for the protection of small investors in all kinds of financial assets.

In the United States deregulation has involved the removal of interest rate controls and a gradual but slow relaxation of branching restrictions. In addition, the wide-ranging restrictions on the activities of thrift institutions were removed in response to the losses suffered in the late 1970s, although their new powers led to the thrift debacle that resulted from the provision of deposit insurance with deficient supervision (White 1992).

There is now considerable and growing pressure for an overhaul of the whole system of bank and thrift regulation. Interest rate deregulation has already been completed and interstate barriers have been substantially reduced and are likely to be completely eliminated in the near future. The three remaining issues are the reform of deposit insurance, the legal separation of commercial and investment banking (or more generally the issue of universal banking), and the permissible level of market concentration. There is also some concern about the growing volatility of financial markets and the need to coordinate the regulation of different types of markets.

---

11. Historical crises occurred as a result of the boom and bust of company promotions in the 1870s, World War I and the hyperinflation of the 1920s, the suspension of market mechanisms in the 1930s, and the devastation of World War II. Universal banks played a crucial part in promoting industrialization before World War I; and they were called upon again to play an equally crucial part in financing and supporting the economic reconstruction effort of the post-war period.

Financial Deregulation in Developing Countries

In developing countries, the experience of financial deregulation has been more varied. Many countries have taken measures to develop money and capital markets, promote nonbank financial intermediaries, and strengthen prudential regulation and supervision. There has also been a general reduction in the scope and intensity of macroeconomic and allocative controls. However, developing countries continue to place greater reliance than developed countries on direct credit controls, while prudential, organizational, and protective controls have yet to be fully developed.

Structural controls have been reformed in favor of market-based mechanisms, although many countries continue to restrict entry of foreign banks to the domestic market or to place strict limits on their range and level of activities. In countries where commercial and development banks were under public ownership, privatization programs have been implemented slowly and with caution, to some extent because of the limited size of the domestic capital markets. Universal banking has been permitted in a growing number of countries, even though prudential regulation and supervision are not as well developed as in most high income countries.

Financial deregulation has generally been more successful in countries that have maintained moderate price stability and have adopted a gradualist approach in implementing their reforms. In countries where inflation has been too high and the exchange rate has tended to be overvalued, deregulation has been accompanied by considerable distortions in incentives and has resulted in extensive instability, in terms of both high real interest rates and massive defaults (Cho and Khatkhate 1989).

Conclusion

The experience of both developed and developing countries suggests that regulatory change tends to happen when there are large economic disruptions. Thus, extensive financial regulation was introduced in the aftermath of the Great Depression. More recently, financial deregulation in the 1970s was motivated by the large increase in the level and volatility of inflation, exchange, and interest rates.

Regulatory change also takes place more easily if it can be accomplished without requiring cumbersome legislative changes. A corollary of this idea is that the threat of regulation in a society where regulatory action is not subject to long delays may be as effective as actual regulation. In fact, the threat of regulation may be as important a concept in explaining the behavior of incumbent firms in highly concentrated industries as the threat of potential competition. It may, for instance, be an important factor in Germany where the large universal banks have been reticent in exercising their influence on corporate affairs, although another factor may have been the need to build and sustain a reputation of good and responsible behavior.

In both developed and developing countries financial regulation is now moving toward the elimination or substantial reduction of macroeconomic, allocative, and structural controls and toward the adoption or substantial strengthening of prudential, organizational, and protective controls. One issue that continues, however, to remain unresolved is the question of the role and scope of universal banks.

In developed countries, a consensus is emerging in favor of universal banks as one type of institution among a wide range of specialized financial intermediaries and a wide network of financial markets. The most important remaining issue concerns the organizational form of universal groups and, in particular, the usefulness of a holding company structure as opposed to direct involvement in universal banking activities through departments or subsidiaries of the parent company.

In developing countries, the question of universal banking is closely linked with the development of more effective prudential and supervisory mechanisms. Universal banking relies to a large extent on functional and conduct regulation and implies a greater need for collecting and analyzing detailed information and for taking prompt corrective action.

In the past, universal banking has produced negative results in several developing countries, though in large part these may have been encouraged by the laxity of supervision and/or the availability of heavily subsidized credits that provided strong incentives for excessive borrowing and for abusing the system. In a less distorted regulatory framework and with more effective supervision, universal banking may be able to make a more positive contribution to economic and financial development even in developing countries.

Political leadership has a substantial part to play in reforming the regulatory system. Experience shows that structural controls that are mainly motivated by political considerations, such as preserving the monopoly position of domestic banks or protecting the turfs of different types of financial institutions, can be very damaging. Many of the problems facing the U.S. financial system, such as the fragmentation and fragility of the banking system, the financial crisis of the thrift industry, and the segmentation of the banking and nonbanking parts of the financial system, can be attributed to the adverse effects of structural regulations.

Among developed countries, political leadership would be required to remove any remaining restraints on geographic and sectoral diversification of financial institutions. The most important task is the creation of a sound and robust financial constitution that governs what financial institutions are permitted to do and what basic conditions they have to meet. As far as possible, the regulatory framework should be neutral between different types of financial intermediaries and markets.

In developing countries, political leadership would be required in undertaking and implementing a major reform of the regulatory framework that would emphasize the prudential, organizational, and protective objectives of financial regulation and downplay the importance of macroeconomic, allocative, and structural objectives.

A major challenge facing political leadership in developing countries lies in reforming structural regulations to allow foreign financial institutions to play a more active part in the domestic financial system. In earlier periods, foreign banks behaved like colonial institutions, exploiting local resources and contributing relatively little to local economic and financial development. But in the modern world foreign institutions (banks, insurance companies, securities firms, etc.) are more likely to be beneficial by transferring financial technology, training local staff, providing effective competition to the large domestic institutions that often dominate the financial systems of developing countries, and instilling greater stability in local financial markets.

Political leadership would also be required in implementing an ambitious privatization program. These would permit competitive market forces and decentralized decisionmaking to play their full part in mobilizing and allocating financial resources and in monitoring the performance and controlling the behavior of the ultimate users of financial resources.

Postscript

One question that has not been explicitly addressed in this paper concerns the relevance of differences in financial arrangements. The financial systems of different countries exhibit considerable differences in both structure and practice, and regulation is clearly a major determinant of such differences. But how important are they for economic performance and development?

Unfortunately, economic theory is not very helpful in answering this question. As Gertler (1988) pointed out, the working hypothesis of most economists has long been that the structure of financial intermediation is irrelevant.[12] This approach contrasts sharply with the widespread belief among policymakers, bankers, and other financial practitioners that financial intermediaries and markets play important roles in economic development and stability.

A comparison of data on long-run economic growth, as reported by de Long (1988), and financial structure suggest that countries characterized by a greater reliance on bank finance and close links between banks and industrial companies have achieved higher rates of economic growth, especially in relation to their economic potential, than countries with market-based systems. The first group of countries includes Japan, Germany, other continental European countries, and

---

12. "Irrelevance" propositions represent a long tradition in economics. They cover the "money is a veil" argument, which implies the associated concept of the long-run neutrality of money, even though it is incompatible with the view that inflation distorts relative prices, fuels speculative behavior, and misallocates resources. They also cover the "finance is a veil" argument, which argues that the financial structure of corporations is irrelevant for their market value and that investment and financing decisions can be completely separated. This proposition is at variance with observed practice in financial markets, which emphasizes the importance of matching the maturities of assets and liabilities, maintaining stable dividend payouts, minimizing the cost of capital, and avoiding excessive reliance on debt finance.

(at least regarding close links between industry and finance) the United States in the pre-Depression era. The second group covers mostly Anglo-American countries (the United Kingdom—with Scotland as a special case of an economic region suffering relative decline—Australia, New Zealand, and, to a lesser extent, Canada and the United States in the post-Depression era).

Differences in financial arrangements are only one of the factors that may explain differences in economic performance. Other factors, such as the stance of macroeconomic policies, the functioning of the labor markets, the availability of natural resources, and historical accidents, are also important. However, the growing emphasis that is being placed in theoretical work on information asymmetries, long-term relationships and commitments, and the building of reputations suggests that differences in financial arrangements may be important and that views about the irrelevance of the structure of financial intermediation may change.

The new approach is likely to pay less attention on the distinction between bank-based and market-based systems and to focus more on the distinction between financial systems that emphasize long-term relationships and those that emphasize a more transactional approach. The former encourage closer monitoring of the operations of industrial companies and overcome the problems of asymmetric information. They also create mechanisms for more effective support of long-term expansion or restructuring operations.

There is some evidence that bank-based systems are better able to cultivate close links between banks and industrial companies (Vittas 1986). But strong evidence that such links have beneficial effects on investment and aggregate activity is still limited, although a recent study of corporate investment in Japan shows that companies that have severed their links with banks have been more constrained by their internally generated funds in their investment operations than companies with continuing close links (Hoshi et al. 1989).

Bibliography

Boner, Roger A., and Reinald Krueger (1991). *The Basics of Antitrust Policy— A Review of Ten Nations and the EEC.* World Bank, Industry and Energy Department, Industry Series Working Paper 43. February.

Broeker, Guenther (1989). *Competition in Banking*. Paris: OECD.

Cho, Yoon Je (1989). "Finance and Development: The Korean Approach." *Oxford Review of Economic Policy*, Winter.

Cho, Yoon Je, and Deena Khatkhate (1989). *Lessons of Financial Liberalization in Asia—A Comparative Study*. World Bank Discussion Papers 50, World Bank, Washington D.C.

De Long, Bradford (1988). "Productivity Growth, Convergence, and Welfare: Comment." *American Economic Review*, December.

Deutsche Bundesbank (1986). "Innovation in International Banking." *Monthly Report*, April.

Finsinger, Jorg et al. (1985). *Insurance—Competition or Regulation, A Comparative Study of the Insurance Markets in the United Kingdom and the Federal Republic of Germany*. Institute of Fiscal Studies, Report Series No. 19. London.

Finsinger, Jorg, and Mark Pauly (eds.) (1986). *The Economics of Insurance Regulation*. Hong Kong: Macmillan.

Gertler, Mark (1988). "Financial Structure and Aggregate Economic Activity." *Journal of Money, Credit and Banking*, August.

Hammond, Bray (1957). *Banks and Politics in America from the Revolution to the Civil War*. Princeton, N.J.: Princeton University Press.

Hoshi Takeo, Anil Kashyap, and David Scharfstein (1989). "Bank Monitoring and Investment: Evidence from the Changing Structure of Japanese Corporate Banking Relationships." NBER Working Paper No. 3079. August.

Kay, John, and John Vickers (1988). "Regulatory Reform in Britain." *Economic Policy*, October.

Krooss, Herman, and Martin Blyn (1971). *A History of Financial Intermediaries*. New York: Random House.

Patrick, Hugh (1984). "Japanese Financial Development in Historical Perspective." In Gustav Ranis et al.: *Comparative Development Perspectives*. Boulder, Colorado: Westview Press.

Polizatto, Vincent (1992). "Prudential Regulation and Banking Supervision" (this volume, chapter 10).

Rabe, Thomas (1992). "Life Insurance Regulation in the United Kingdom and Germany" (this volume, chapter 12).

Teranishi, Juro (1986). "Economic Growth and Regulation of Financial Markets: Japanese Experience During Postwar High Growth Period." *Hitotsubashi Journal of Economics*, December.

U.S. Treasury (1991). *Modernizing the Financial System, Recommendations for Safer, More Competitive Banks*. Washington, D.C.: U.S. Department of the Treasury. February.

Vittas, Dimitri (1986). "Banks' Relations with Industry—An International Survey." *National Westminster Quarterly Review*, February.

_____ (1991). "The Regulation of the Thrift Industries in the U.K. and the U.S." World Bank, CECFP. Processed. July.

Vittas, Dimitri et al. (1978). "Banking Systems Abroad." Inter-Bank Research Organization, London.

White, J. Lawrence (1992). "The U.S. Savings and Loan Debacle: Lessons for the Regulation of Financial Institutions" (this volume, chapter 9).

World Bank (1990). *Financial Systems and Development (The 1989 World Development Report)* World Bank, PRE, Policy and Research Series 15.

4

FINANCIAL LIBERALIZATION: THE CASE OF JAPAN

Akiyoshi Horiuchi

An observed characteristic of the process of economic development over time, in a market-oriented economy using the price mechanism to allocate resources, is an increase in the number and variety of financial institutions and substantial rise in the proportion not only of money but also of the total of all financial assets relative to GNP and to tangible wealth. However, the causal nature of this relationship between financial development and economic growth has not been fully explored, either theoretically or empirically. (Patrick 1966, p. 174)

This paper investigates the process of Japan's financial liberalization since the end of World War II. The first part examines the relationship between financial regulation and economic development in the high growth era, specifically in the period from 1960 to the early 1970s. During this time, the Japanese financial system was comprehensively regulated and lacked flexible market mechanisms. It is not an exaggeration to say that rapid economic growth was achieved under the predominance of nonmarket mechanisms, such as long-term relationships between banks and borrowing companies.

By defining the degree of financial deepening according to the ratio of total debt issued by the nonfinancial sectors to gross national product (GNP), financial deepening did not occur much during most of the high growth era, although it rose substantially at the very early stage (see table 4.1). Since the mid-1970s and the end of the high growth era, however, the degree of financial deepening has increased remarkably. This seems to suggest that though the comprehensive regulation hindered Japan's financial deepening to some extent, well-functioning market mechanisms in the financial system were not indispensable to the rapid economic growth.

The second part of this paper looks at the financial liberalization that started in the mid-1970s. The emphasis is on structural changes in the financial system that occurred after the high growth era and forced the authorities to liberalize financial regulations. Thus, the financial liberalization was not a cause but a consequence of economic development in Japan.

The growth of international and securities markets since the late 1970s has been pressing the Japanese government to reorganize the financial regulatory regime. As the relative importance of the open capital markets increases in the financial system, an informational infrastructure must be built up to preserve the stability of financial transactions in open markets. Currently, the infrastructure, which consists of disclosure rules, regulations on insider trading, and a system of credit ratings, remains to be fully developed in Japan.

Financial Regulation in the High Growth Era

The Japanese economy suffered serious turmoil immediately after World War II. Warfare had destroyed most of the nation's productive facilities. When the Pacific war ended in August 1945, the level of industrial production was less than 10 percent of the average level during 1935–37 and agricultural production had fallen to around 60 percent of the 1933–35 average. Goldsmith (1983) describes the contrast between the immediate postwar years and the early 1950s:

> In absolute terms, the basket of commodities and services at the disposal of the average Japanese in 1953—¥81,000, or $225 at the exchange rate—although worth considerably more in purchasing power, cannot be regarded as paradisiacal. But it must have seemed so to the average Japanese. The return to a reasonably satisfactory standard of living, only slightly below the previous high point of the mid-1930s, after the terrors of the later phases of the Pacific War and the physical and moral deprivations of the first postwar years, must have appeared to him, indeed, like paradise regained. (page 131)

Generally speaking, post-war economies tend to exhibit high inflation; while the population holds a large amount of money and financial assets, physical production is greatly reduced. By decreasing the real value of financial assets, postwar inflation restores the

Table 4.1: The Proportion of the Nonfinancial Sector's Total Debt to GNP
(in percent)

Year	Total	Borrowing (From private financial insts.)	Securities	Trade credit	Total
1953	61.7	49.4	20.8	29.9	112.5
1954	64.1	50.0	23.7	29.5	117.1
1955	66.4	51.3	25.0	29.7	121.2
1956	72.7	57.1	26.9	33.3	133.0
1957	77.9	62.0	26.4	34.2	138.5
1958	88.3	70.3	30.5	37.9	156.9
1959	93.7	75.0	32.6	47.4	173.8
1960	94.7	76.8	32.8	47.2	174.7
1961	93.1	76.3	32.8	53.7	179.6
1962	101.7	83.8	35.5	58.4	195.7
1963	109.9	92.0	35.7	64.5	210.2
1964	109.3	91.0	35.7	65.5	210.6
1965	114.0	94.8	36.6	65.0	216.0
1966	113.6	94.3	38.1	65.2	217.1
1967	113.3	94.1	38.2	69.9	221.5
1968	111.1	92.0	37.1	68.0	216.3
1969	112.5	93.4	36.0	70.8	219.6
1970	113.4	94.8	34.4	70.0	218.0
1971	126.1	106.0	35.7	67.9	229.9
1972	135.3	114.6	37.2	69.4	242.1
1973	134.6	113.1	34.6	77.7	247.2
1974	130.1	107.5	33.9	70.4	235.0
1975	136.4	110.1	38.3	71.0	246.2
1976	139.3	110.3	42.4	69.2	251.3
1977	138.5	108.4	47.1	63.7	249.5
1978	139.1	106.9	54.3	64.2	257.8
1979	142.1	106.7	58.4	67.3	268.0
1980	143.2	105.9	61.7	68.3	273.3
1981	152.2	111.6	68.2	69.5	290.2
1982	161.8	117.4	73.0	68.0	302.9
1983	173.9	126.5	82.1	69.8	325.9
1984	179.2	130.9	85.2	70.7	335.2
1985	183.9	135.4	88.3	68.8	341.9
1986	194.2	144.7	94.0	63.9	352.8

Note: The nonfinancial sector consists of the central government, public and private corporations, local authorities, and the personal sector. Borrowing includes borrowing from both private and public financial institutions. Securities consists of fundraising by issuing stocks and bonds.

Source: Bank of Japan, *Flow of Funds Accounts*.

equilibrium between the financial and real sectors of the economy. Japan was no exception in this respect. During 1945–51, the indexes of the wholesale and retail price levels rose 98-fold and 100-fold, respectively.

From the mid-1950s onward, however, Japan's economic development was remarkably rapid. The annual rate of increase in real GNP was 7.2 percent from 1953 to 1959, and 11.0 percent from 1960 to 1969. We define the period from 1960 to the early 1970s as the era of high growth in Japan. During this time, the inflation rate in terms of the GNP deflator was less than 5 percent. Clearly, the macroeconomic performance of the Japanese economy was excellent (see chart 4.1).

The Financial System in the High Growth Era

The Japanese financial system was under comprehensive regulation during the high growth era that principally consisted of regulations of the interest rates on bank deposits, bank loans, and other financial instruments; restrictions on the development and introduction of new financial products and services; market segmentation regulations; and foreign exchange controls. These regulations were anticompetitive in the sense that they suppressed competition, particularly price competition, in financial markets.

Some of the regulations were not as effective as they appeared to be. For example, banks circumvented controls on loan rates by requiring borrowers to deposit compensating balances. The "effective" loan rates were, to some extent, adjusted through changes in the amount of compensating balances, although the process of adjustment was rather sluggish.[1] On the whole, however, the Japanese financial system lacked both flexible market mechanisms and effective competition, primarily because of financial regulation.

REGULATION OF INTEREST RATES. The Temporary Interest Rate Adjustment Law, introduced in 1947, imposed ceilings on interest rates, thereby hindering price competition among financial institutions. Japanese banks have been able to determine deposit and loan rates through a cartel permitted by this law. It was only in 1979 when

---

1. The compensating balance mechanism was sometimes criticized during the high growth era as making ineffective the low interest rate policy.

Chart 4.1: Annual Rates of Increase: Real GNE and Deflator, 1953-85
(percent)

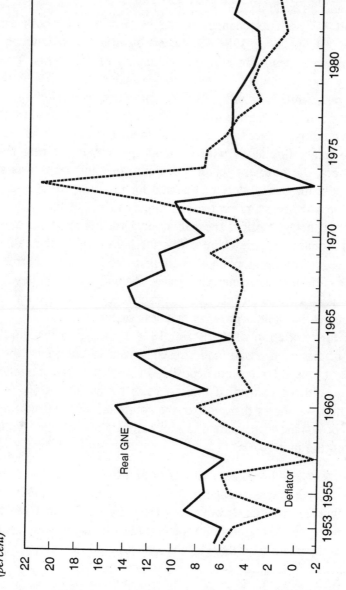

Source: Bank of Japan.

the negotiable certificate of deposit was introduced that a bank deposit with an uncontrolled interest rate was available to nonfinancial companies and households.

Chart 4.2 presents changes in the interest rates on both time deposits and loans since 1954. This chart clearly shows how controlled these interest rates were until the beginning of the 1970s. Their immobility was particularly conspicuous when compared with the call money rate, which was uniquely free from direct control.[2]

Banks and other financial institutions adjusted the amounts of their reserve holdings by trading in the call money market where the interest rate freely fluctuated with demand and supply. During the high growth era, the business sector's demand for bank loans was strong. As a result, the banks' derived demand for reserves was strong, which exerted upward pressure on the call money rate. Especially in periods of tight monetary policy, the call money rate jumped far above 10 percent. Some observers claimed that the high level of the call money rate was an abnormal phenomenon that needed to be corrected to normalize the Japanese financial system. Actually, the high level of the call money rate was an inevitable consequence of the strong demand for loans by the rapidly growing business sector in Japan.

The high inflation of 1973 and 1974 depreciated the purchasing power of financial assets and caused savers to complain about the control of interest rates on deposits. In response, the monetary authorities adjusted controlled interest rates far more flexibly than before. Chart 4.2 shows that most of the controlled interest rates on both bank deposits and loans started to move in parallel with the call money rate from the mid-1970s.

REAL RATE OF INTEREST. It is sometimes carelessly stated that the Japanese government pursued a policy of low interest rates to stimulate economic growth. However, as Horiuchi (1984) and McKinnon (1988) point out, the controlled interest rates in Japan were relatively high in comparison with those of the United States and other advanced

---

2.   Although the Bank of Japan (BOJ) did intervene in the process of determining the call money rate until the mid-1950s and after 1957, private banks colluded to establish the "appropriate" level of the call money rate with the BOJ's implicit approval.

Chart 4.2: Nominal Interest Rates in Japan, 1954-87
(annual rate, percent)

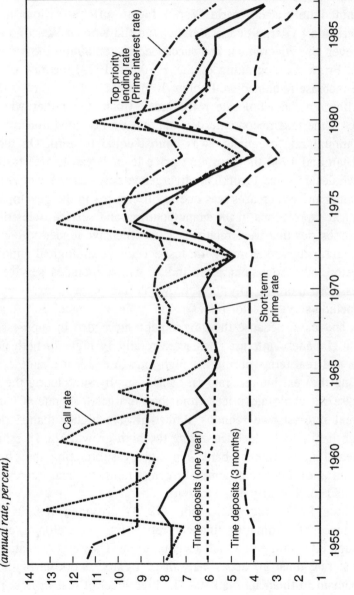

Source: Bank of Japan.

economies at that time. Of course, a high level of nominal interest rates does not necessarily mean a high cost of capital. Thus, it is important that we pay attention to inflation and the real rate of interest.

Immediately after World War II Japan suffered serious inflation, exacerbated by large budget deficits and the Korean War of 1950–51. However, the government had succeeded in containing the inflation by 1951. From the beginning of the 1950s to 1972, the rate of annual price increase remained well below 10 percent.

Although the wholesale price index fluctuated rather widely because of the macroeconomic demand and supply conditions, the average annual rate of change was almost equal to zero. On the other hand, around 1960 the consumer price level began to rise faster than the wholesale price level. The divergence between the wholesale and consumer price increases was due to differences in the development of technical innovations in the manufacturing and service industries: service industries that were relatively labor intensive tended to lag behind manufacturing industries with respect to technological innovation. Therefore, the consumer price index, which includes service sector prices, rose more rapidly than the wholesale price index, which does not include service sector prices.

In any case, because the government succeeded in suppressing inflation, Japanese interest rates were relatively high, in both nominal terms and real terms during the high-growth era. For example, in calculating the real interest rate on bank loans by subtracting the rate of increase in wholesale prices from the nominal loan rate (Chart 4.3), the real interest rate remains almost always higher than 5 percent, though it gradually declines during the high growth era. In estimating the real interest rate of bank deposits by subtracting the consumer price inflation rate from nominal interest rates, the real interest rate is estimated to be nearly equal to zero.

Shaw (1973) and McKinnon (1973) provided insight on the importance of eliminating financial repression in developing countries in order to stimulate capital accumulation. They argue that the real interest rate must go up as a result of flexible working of the price mechanism in financial markets. The high level of real interest rates in Japan in the high growth era could be seen as a successful case

Chart 4.3: Real Rate of Interest, 1954-87
(percent)

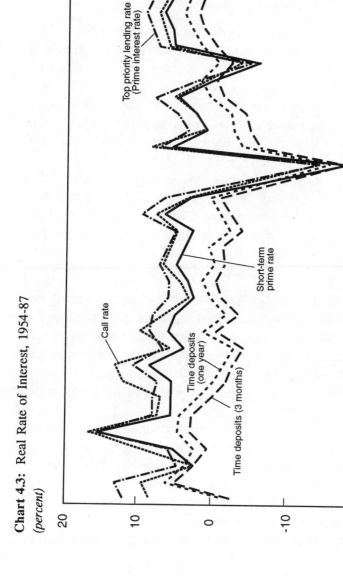

Source: Bank of Japan

corresponding to their thesis. It should be noted, however, that this high level of real interest rates was not produced by a pure market, because comprehensive controls on interest rates hindered the full-fledged working of financial markets during the high growth era.

Successful Containment of Inflation

Today, many developing economies are suffering from high inflation. Thus, Japan's success in holding down inflation during its period of high growth is noteworthy. The success can be attributed to the Bank of Japan's effective control of the money supply and bank credit. Stimulated by active investment from the business sector, the Japanese economy tended at times to excessively expand, or overheat. At such times, however, the Bank of Japan quickly adopted tight money policies, that effectively cooled down the overheating and prevented the general level of prices from rising too rapidly. The wage rate in Japan was also very flexible, so any slowdown of real economic growth was accompanied by relative declines in wage rates (Chart 4.4). The flexibility of the price-wage system indicates that the Bank of Japan's monetary policy during the high growth era had credibility with the public. Where did this public trust come from?

THE CONSTRAINT OF THE BALANCE OF PAYMENTS. During the high growth era, Japanese authorities had to consider the constraint of the nation's balance of payments situation when managing macroeconomic policy. The high level of capital investment by the business sector, which was the linchpin when Japanese economic growth exceeded domestic savings, caused the balance of payments to deteriorate.

However, at that time, the government would not consider devaluing the yen. Moreover, there were rather strong restraints on capital imports imposed by the government. As a result, any deterioration in the current account led to a rapid depletion of official foreign exchange reserves, which were extremely scarce. Therefore, any decrease in foreign exchange reserves served as a reliable signal of a current or upcoming shift in monetary policy toward a more restrictive stance.

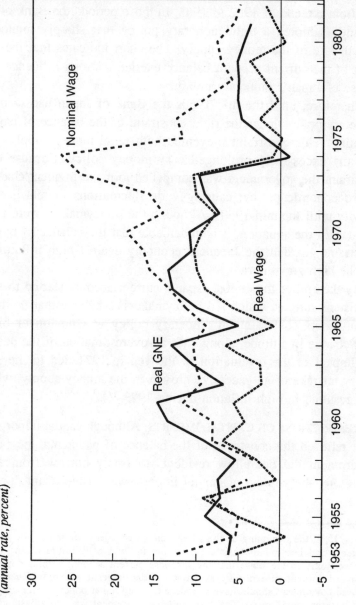

Chart 4.4: Changes in Real and Nominal Wage Rates, 1953-82 *(annual rate, percent)*

Source: Bank of Japan

Chart 4.5 illustrates this situation. The Japanese current account deteriorated in the latter half of 1956, from late 1960 to early 1961, and from the end of 1962 to 1963. In those periods the Bank of Japan instantly adopted a tight monetary policy that sharply reduced the growth rate of the money supply. The chart indicates that the movement of the current account balance exerted a strong influence on the course of Japan's monetary policy.

Therefore, until the mid-1960s the Bank of Japan had to manage monetary policy under the rigid constraint of the balance of payments situation. This constraint prevented both rapid money supply growth and any excessively prolonged easy money policy. Because of this constraint the government was compelled to make frequent changes in macroeconomic policy, causing wide fluctuations in real economic activity until the mid-1960s. Although the policymakers were not satisfied with the situation, it is undeniable that the balance of payments constraint guarded the Japanese economy against high inflation during the high growth era.

By the end of the 1960s, Japan's current account started to show a consistent surplus, which led policymakers to believe that the balance of payments constraint on monetary policy was no longer binding. This change in attitude, along with an overestimation of the deflationary impact of the revaluation of the yen in 1971, led to the serious policy mistake of an excessive growth in the money supply, which in turn resulted in high inflation during 1973–74.[3]

RESTRICTIONS ON CAPITAL IMPORTS. Although capital imports could have relieved the constraint of the balance of payments, the Japanese government did not allow residents to freely borrow from abroad. Therefore, the volume of capital imports was insignificant during the

---

3. Until the beginning of the 1970s, the external equilibrium of the balance of payments had become inconsistent with the internal equilibrium of the domestic macroeconomy in the sense that the Japanese current account surplus could not be eliminated without an excessive expansion of the domestic economy. Therefore, the Japanese government should have introduced an additional policy instrument oriented to the external equilibrium. The most suitable instrument was the adjustment in the yen exchange rate. But the government was so eager to retain the fixed exchange rate regime that the excessively expansionary policy was adopted in 1972–73 with a view to avoiding the revaluation of the yen, eventually leading to high inflation.

Chart 4.5: Current Account (million US$) and Changes in Money Supply
(percent)

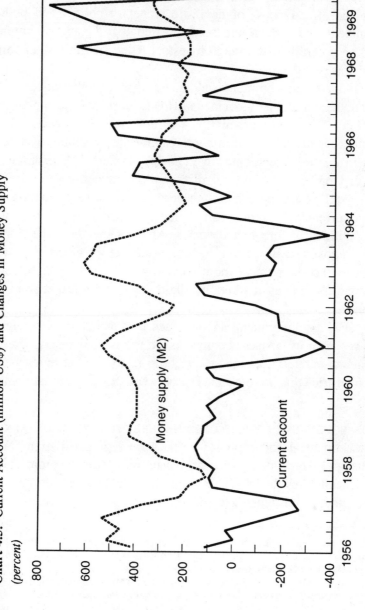

Source: Bank of Japan

period.[4] The restrictions on capital imports were adopted for two reasons: the government was concerned that free capital flows would decrease the effectiveness of domestic monetary policy, and both the government and the private sector feared that Japanese companies would be controlled by foreign investors if the free inflow of foreign capital was permitted.[5]

In 1960, the government announced a plan to liberalize international trade and capital movements. However, in reality, capital flows were liberalized only gradually. The monetary authorities did not hesitate to introduce controls on capital movements in order to maintain control over domestic financial markets. For example, the Bank of Japan started the foreign reserve requirement system in 1962, which required Japanese banks to hold liquid assets denominated in foreign currencies at more than a predetermined ratio of their short-term liabilities in foreign currencies. At the same time, the Bank of Japan imposed ceilings on banks' total net position in foreign currencies. The purpose of these regulations was to keep tight control over domestic money markets by limiting the mobility of short-term capital.

In 1967, the government adopted measures to liberalize foreign direct investment in Japanese companies. At the same time, however, the government carefully retained the right to restrict direct investment in those industries that were deemed to be weak in international competition.[6]

CONSEQUENCES OF THE CLOSED NATURE OF FINANCIAL MARKETS. Japanese financial and capital markets were segregated from foreign markets, and the economy did not depend on borrowing from abroad. It is difficult to evaluate whether this financial segregation had a favorable impact on Japan's economic development. As has already

---

4. Of course, we cannot say that actual borrowing from abroad was insignificant. For instance, loans from the World Bank were utilized to build the main part of the Japanese highway network.

5. Major companies started to strengthen their mutual shareholdings to guard themselves against foreign takeovers after the liberalization plan of 1960.

6. For example, the following industries were among those "protected" against direct foreign investment: electric appliances, radio sets, TV sets, plate glass, cameras, synthetic fibers, Western-style restaurants, laundries, and shipbuilding.

been seen, interest rates were relatively high in Japan, so had it not been for restrictive controls, a substantial amount of capital would have flowed into Japan, loosening the constraint of the balance of payments. As a result, the Japanese monetary authorities could have pursued a bolder and more expansionary monetary policy and, in this sense, freer capital inflow might have promoted further development.

The relaxation of capital controls, however, would have forced the government to face the tradeoff between economic growth and inflation instead of the tradeoff between economic growth and external balance. The government probably would have accepted more inflation to achieve quicker development. This, however, would have eventually disturbed the stability of the financial system, which would have eventually damaged the potential for economic growth.[7]

At the same time, with the relaxation of constraints on capital movements, Japan's financial markets would have been vulnerable to financial disturbances in foreign markets. Therefore, under the regime of fixed exchange rates, the strict regulation of capital movements helped the government maintain the stability of financial conditions in domestic markets.

The rigid controls on capital movements, especially those on capital imports, narrowed the opportunities of Japanese companies for raising funds. In the domestic financial system, the banking sector played a primary role as intermediator. Thus, the financial segregation from the overseas markets strengthened the dominance of the banking sector in the Japanese financial system, thus hindering the development of a well-organized, open securities market.[8] If Japanese companies could have more freely relied on funds from foreign markets, the dominance of the banking sector in Japan might have been challenged to some extent.

---

7. For example, the Ikeda Cabinet of the early 1960s, famous for its income-doubling plan, was eager to stimulate Japan's economic growth by easy monetary policy.

8. A topic to be addressed later in this paper.

The Underdeveloped Nature of the Money Markets and Capital Markets

Japan's economic growth seems to suggest that rapid development of real economy is quite possible without well-developed money markets and capital markets. The working of the price mechanism in these markets was insignificant, due in part to regulation. The volume of transactions through the markets was very small. However, the underdeveloped nature of the financial markets does not necessarily mean that the Japanese financial system was inefficient during the high growth era. Rather, it can be posited that the financial system worked in a different fashion than that of the United States and other advanced economies.

MECHANISMS IN THE MONEY MARKET. The call money market, that is, the interbank money market, was already well developed shortly after World War II. The call money rate was flexible in adjusting the supply and demand in the market.[9] However, nonfinancial companies and households were not permitted to participate in the call money market. The financial system lacked open money markets in which participation was not limited to financial institutions. Nonfinancial agents with surplus funds could not choose financial assets other than those whose rate of interest was controlled (for example, bank deposits, bank debentures, and loan trusts).

Markets in short-term government bonds and government bills, which in Japan are customarily called the TB and FB markets, could have been the core open money markets, because they are free from credit risk and are highly homogeneous. If they had been part of an open money market, agents could have adjusted their liquidity position by transacting in the markets, and the Bank of Japan could have conducted its monetary policy through these markets.[10]

Because the government was to maintain a balanced budget principle until the mid-1960s, such public debt was scarce. Although government bills were issued to cover temporary shortages of funds of the treasury, and the average amount of the bills was not small, almost all

---

9. See chart 4.2.

10. In reality, due to the lack of open money markets, the Bank of Japan carried out monetary policy primarily through the control of its lending to private banks.

bills were held by the Bank of Japan and governmental institutions. This was because their issue rates were fixed at such low levels by the government that private investors did not regard them as good instruments. Obviously, the artificially low level of issue rates is what has prevented the development of a secondary market in government bills. Even today, the Japanese financial system lacks well-developed TB and FB markets, which could be the core of the money market. In this sense, the Japanese money market is still underdeveloped, a fact that some economists regard as a serious hindrance to the internationalization of the yen.

Gensaki transactions, in which there is a prior promise either to repurchase or to resell the same security after a fixed time has elapsed and at a fixed price, have been an important method for Japanese nonfinancial institutions to adjust their liquidity positions. But they became important only after the mid-1970s when a large number of government bonds were issued, because government bonds were convenient instruments to be used as a basis for *gensaki* transactions.

The lack of open money markets worked to stabilize the Japanese financial system in the sense that large scale financial disintermediation, or the substantial shift of funds from bank deposits with controlled interest rates to money market instruments with market-determined interest rates, did not occur. The lack of open money markets also maintained the banking sector's dominance in Japan's financial system.

INACTIVE SECURITIES MARKETS. According to economic theory, a well-organized securities market is indispensable for the efficient distribution of risk-bearing. In particular, the equity capital market will, by expanding the possibility of distributing risk, promote investment in risky but high return projects. Cho (1986) emphasizes the importance of the equity capital markets in the context of economic development.

The thrust of this theory, however, does not seem to hold in the case of Japanese economic development. During the high growth era, securities markets were generally inactive compared with the bank loan market. Although Japanese companies raised a substantial amount of funds by issuing common stock during the early 1960s, the briskness of the stock market did not last long.[11] The stock market suffered from a sharp decline in the mid-1960s, which caused a mini-crisis in the securities markets. Some big securities companies fell into financial distress, and in 1965 the Bank of Japan had to take emergency measures as the lender of last resort to rescue these securities companies.

The corporate bond market also played a minor role in the Japanese financial system. The *Kisaikai,* an association composed of trust banks and underwriting securities companies, determined both the issue terms (that is, yield to subscribers) and the quantities of issue of corporate bonds. The issue terms were fixed at artificially low levels of interest. Not all companies could enjoy this favorable issue condition. The most important role of the *Kisaikai* was to severely limit the amount of funds companies could raise in the bond market so as to prevent the bond market from becoming an effective competitor with the bank loan market.[12]

Even today, the *Kisaikai's* role continues to be important, although its importance has gradually decreased. Most Japanese companies bitterly criticize the *Kisaikai's* specific procedures of corporate bond determination. This problem is discussed in greater detail in a later section.

Thus, both disorder in the securities markets in the mid-1960s and the *Kisaikai's* restrictions on bond market development lowered the relative importance of corporate fundraising in securities markets and ensured the predominance of the bank loan market in the landscape of Japan's corporate finance in the latter half of the high growth era. However, the reason for the predominance of the bank loan market during the high growth era cannot totally be explained by these conditions. Rather, on the basis of economic theory, it was quite natural that the bank loan market played a predominantly important role in the process of Japan's economic development after World War II.

---

11. In those days, almost all new issues took the form of allotment of stocks to incumbent shareholders at par value substantially lower than market value. Therefore, new issues were not a method of fundraising from general investors outside the corporation. New issues at market value have become gradually important since around the early 1970s.

12. The banking sector has been important not only as a constituent of the *Kisaikai* but also as the largest investor in the bond market.

THE ROLE OF BANKS IN THE PROCESS OF ECONOMIC DEVELOPMENT. Theoretically, it is often posited that the bank loan and other credit markets suffer from asymmetric information among lenders and borrowers, which leads to agency cost inefficiencies.[13] However, long-term relationships among banks and borrowing companies can effectively reduce these agency cost inefficiencies by encouraging more efficient monitoring and a better exchange of information among lenders and borrowers.[14]

The stock market is not always immune from the inefficiencies arising from imperfect information. A number of scholars in the field of business finance have made this point clear. For example, Myers and Majluf (1984) argue that with imperfect information, managers can exploit outside investors by issuing new stocks to finance investment projects whose profitability is mistakenly overvalued by outsiders. Rational investors foresee this possibility of insider exploitation, take the active issue of stocks by a company to be a signal of their overvaluation of the company concerned, and accordingly lower their valuation of the company. Therefore, it will not always be advisable for companies that have good investment projects to finance these projects by issuing stock. They may refuse to issue stock, and therefore may pass up valuable investment opportunities. Companies will tend to rely on internal sources of funds and prefer debt to equity if external financing is required. This is just one feature of the potential inefficiency of the stock market that is based on the agency cost approach, which was pioneered by Jensen and Meckling (1976) and others.

It is therefore clear that the efficient working of the stock market needs informational infrastructure, which includes a well-ordered set of rules of disclosure and penalties on insider trading. This minimizes the asymmetry of information among investors and corporate fundraisers, and eliminates fundraisers' incentives to exploit outside investors. It may be costly, however, to build such an infrastructure in

---

13. See Stiglitz and Weiss (1981) and Cho (1986).

14. In Japan, banks are allowed to hold up to 5 percent of the issued common stock of individual companies. Thus, they can simultaneously be both lenders and shareholders. According to some scholars, this financial integration at the level of banks has been useful in overcoming the conflict of interest between lenders and shareholders and in reducing agency costs.

developing economies where diversified investors are not accustomed to the sophisticated methods of modern capital markets.

In such a situation, financial intermediation through the banking sector may be more effective in mobilizing domestic savings than direct fundraising through the stock markets and other securities markets. In Japan's case, the banking sector seems to have provided financial services to the corporate sector that were equivalent to those supplied by an open capital market in the high growth era.

Financial Regulation and Economic Growth

As previously mentioned, comprehensive regulation does not appear to have hindered Japan's economic growth. The working of the price mechanism in the financial system was weak, and certain money and capital markets did not exist at all. The controls on interest rates, the market segmentation, the actual prohibition of entry into the financial industry, and other regulations were anticompetitive in the sense that they suppressed free competition in the financial industries, and thereby stabilized the profits of individual financial institutions. In spite of both the thoroughness of financial regulation and the lack of market mechanisms, the Japanese economy grew much faster than anyone expected at the beginning of the high growth era.

The experience of Japan shows that when pursuing financial allocation suitable to rapid economic growth, the relationship between banks and borrowing companies can be an effective substitute for an open capital market, which crucially depends on flexible prices and interest rates.

What about the costs that were associated with financial regulation? Some observers did not think such costs were that significant. For example, Suzuki (1987) made the following argument:

"The tempo of financial innovation was slow until the end of the 1960s. Moreover, the types of financial innovation centered on those which eased the technological limitations of financial transactions or which attempted to lower the cost burden to customers. But the regulations and customs which ruled during the high growth period—that is, interest rate controls, separation of areas of business of financial institutions, exchange rate controls, and collateral requirements—were appropriate to the economic and financial structure of the time, and thus these controls were not particularly costly to corporations and households." (pages 44, 45)

However, in contrast to this argument there is evidence indicating that the anticompetitive regulation of Japanese financial markets provided large rents to financial institutions, especially banks. Certainly to some degree this was at the expense of nonfinancial corporations and households.

Chart 4.6 presents the ratio of profits to total assets for both the banking and manufacturing sectors. Of course, because of different accounting rules between banking and manufacturing, the profit rates of these industries cannot be directly compared. Chart 4.6 suggests interesting changes in the relative profitability of these industries. The profit rate of all banks was relatively high during the high growth era, but has showed a declining trend since the early 1970s when the process of gradual liberalization of the financial system began. On the other hand, the profit rate of manufacturing fluctuated widely since the beginning of the 1960s and dropped sharply immediately after the first oil crisis. The profit rate of manufacturing, however, has not declined for long periods since the mid-1970s.

These different movements in the profit rates indicate that structural changes in the financial system and accompanying liberalization since the 1970s have erased the profits that the banking industry enjoyed during the high growth era because of the anticompetitive regulations.

THE ROLE OF PUBLIC FINANCIAL INSTITUTIONS. This paper does not explicitly investigate the role of government in the financial system. Sakakibara and Feldman (1983) provide an excellent summary of the financial activity of the Japanese government during the high growth era. According to them, government activities through public financial institutions were important. This was in sharp contrast with the very modest scale of public fiscal expenditure during the period.

There has been controversy regarding the effectiveness of the government financial activities in stimulating Japan's economic growth. The loan amounts supplied by public financial institutions tended to concentrate in declining and stagnant industries (for example, coal mining and shipping) during the high growth era. At the same time, rapidly growing industries did not rely much on borrowing from public financial institutions. In this sense, public intermediation of

Chart 4.6: Profit Rates per Total Assets, 1960-88

(percent)

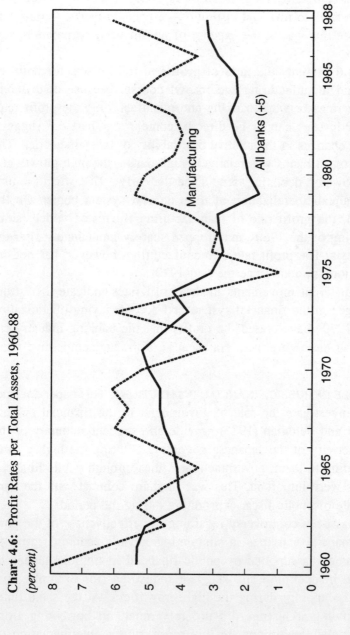

Source: Bank of Japan

credit does not seem to have had a close relationship with Japan's rapid industrial growth.[15]

Some people argue that public financial institutions, in particular the Japan Development Bank, were important because they conveyed valuable information about the government's industrial policy to the private sector through the public financial institutions' lending behavior. If this thesis is correct, then the quantity of publicly intermediated credit does not necessarily matter. In any case, it still remains to be definitively investigated what specific roles these institutions played in the process of economic development.

As financial liberalization proceeds, the public financial institutions have begun to compete more and more with private banks and other financial institutions. In a sense, they constitute a group of vested interests developed in the high growth era. Japan will have to solve the thorny problem of how public financial institutions are to be treated in the process of financial liberalization.

DIRECT INTERVENTION OF THE GOVERNMENT INTO FINANCIAL ALLOCATION. Did the Japanese government directly intervene in the private decisionmaking about fund allocation under the controlled interest rate regime? In the early 1960s the Ministry of International Trade and Industry planned a statute that would have forced private banks and other financial institutions to obey government orders concerning fund allocation. This would have been the revival of the direct public control on financial allocation that the government adopted during and immediately after World War II and had abolished in the mid-1950s.

However, because the Ministry of Finance and the private banks opposed the statute, the plan was not realized. Thus, the government did not control the fund allocation of private financial institutions; rather, it left fund allocation to the financial intermediation of private financial institutions. At most, the government coordinated and influenced private sector fund allocation in indirect ways.[16]

---

15. See Hamada and Horiuchi (1987).
16. See Horiuchi (1984).

Structural Changes and Financial Liberalization

After the first oil crisis in 1973, the growth rate of the Japanese economy substantially decreased. The decline in the real growth rate was accompanied by structural changes in the financial system, which compelled the government to liberalize some of its financial regulations.

The Japanese monetary authorities were reluctant to liberalize or reorganize the system of financial regulation that prevailed in the high growth era. Their reluctance was mainly because of the difficulty of compromising diverse vested interests that were protected by the segregation of financial business and other anticompetitive regulations. In particular, the anticompetitive regulations benefited small-scale banks and other financial institutions that could not attain economies of scale. Such financial institutions were opposed to the full scale liberalization of Japan's financial system.

The structural changes occurring in financial markets, however, made the traditional financial regulations obsolete. Anticompetitive regulations tended to hinder the response of big banks to changes in the demand for financial services, and to make the financial system as a whole more vulnerable to external shocks. Therefore, it was inevitable that the authorities would amend the current regulatory system, the main part of which consisted of anticompetitive controls.

The government started a gradual process of financial liberalization in the late 1970s. The most important of the liberalization measures was the revision in 1980 of the Foreign Exchange and Foreign Trade Control Law. This section examines the interactions between structural changes and the reorganization of financial regulation since the mid-1970s.

Structural Changes in Financial Markets

A large amount of literature surveys the structural changes in Japan's financial markets since the mid-1970s, such as those written by Cargill (1985), Suzuki (1987), Hamada and Horiuchi (1987), and Shinkai (1988). The above-mentioned works emphasize the following structural changes in Japanese financial markets: the large scale flotation of government bonds, the internationalization of financial markets, and the rapid accumulation of financial assets.

RAPIDLY INCREASING GOVERNMENT DEBT. The end of the high growth era implied a change in Japanese money flows. Specifically, the corporate sector's demand for funds decreased dramatically, and the government, in turn, increased its demand: the volume of government bonds increased from ¥5.8 trillion in 1972 to ¥154.5 trillion in 1988.

The government had already abandoned the balanced budget principle when it issued government bonds in 1965 to finance the budget deficit. Until the mid-1970s, however, the Bank of Japan had assisted the government bond issues by buying most of the bonds one year after they were issued.[17] This operation may be called the "monetization of government debt," which is often associated with excessive money supply growth. Fortunately, the amount of government debt issue remained small until the mid-1970s. Therefore, the monetization in itself did not lead to inflation.[18]

The government broke away from the monetization of government debt in the latter half of the 1970s when the amount of government bond issues began to increase sharply. The increased volume of non-monetized government bonds stimulated the development of the secondary bond market. The trading volume of various bonds in the Tokyo market was ¥17.7 trillion in 1972; by 1988, the trading volume reached ¥4,279 trillion, a more than 240-fold increase. More than 90 percent of the trading in the bond market in 1988 was related to government bonds, including TB and FB.

The development of the bond market extended the opportunity for households and nonfinancial companies to choose liquid assets other than bank deposits. *Gensaki* (repurchase) transactions based on long-term government bonds expanded greatly, and became strong competitors for banks' time deposits. But because the certificate of deposit

---

17. It was reported that the Bank of Japan eventually bought about 85 percent of the government bonds issued during the period of 1966–74.

18. The Bank of Japan did allow an excessive growth in the money supply from 1971 to 1973, which caused the high inflation of 1973–74. But this mistake was due to the bank's overestimation of the deflationary impact of the revaluation of the yen in 1971.

(CD) was introduced in 1979, *gensaki* transactions have decreased in relation to CDs. One reason for their relative decline is that the securities transaction tax is imposed on them, while the CD and the large scale time deposits with free interest rates are exempt. In 1980 medium-term government bond funds were introduced by securities companies. These are open-ended investment trusts that invest 50 percent or more of principal in medium-term government bonds with two- to four-year maturities. These have also been a serious threat to the banking sector.

The banks, therefore, introduced some instruments with interest rates that were free from regulation to compete with the expanding tradable bond markets. In 1979 banks were permitted to issue negotiable CDs, and in 1985 interest rates on large scale time deposits (¥1.0 billion or more) were liberalized.[19] The authorities introduced this liberalization because they correctly regarded the current controls on interest rates as destabilizing the business performance of banks.

SECURITIES MARKETS AND FINANCIAL LIBERALIZATION. The increase in government fundraising in the securities markets has influenced the basic structure of the Japanese financial system. As fundraising by the government has become more important, the securities business has become more profitable in the financial system. Related parties have hotly debated whether the separation between banking and the securities business is appropriate in Japan. In 1984 the Ministry of Finance allowed dealing in public bonds by banks as well as securities companies. Thus, the separation of the securities and banking business narrowed, and the competition between banks and securities companies intensified.

IMPACT OF INTERNATIONALIZATION. The internationalization of the Japanese economy exerted pressure for financial liberalization in the following ways. As financial activities became global, the relatively rigid controls on domestic financial transactions induced financial institutions and other agents to move from domestic to foreign financial markets in order to obtain various financial services at lower

---

19. The minimum denomination of time deposits with freely determined rates has since been reduced to ¥10 million.

prices. This exodus can often lead to a decline in domestic financial markets unless they themselves are liberalized.

This process has been particularly conspicuous in the bond markets. Table 4.2 presents the amount of funds Japanese companies raised both in domestic and foreign capital markets from 1977 to 1988. According to this table Japanese companies have actively issued corporate bonds, especially convertible and warrant bonds, since 1980; nearly half of these bonds have been issued in foreign markets. Moreover, most of the ultimate buyers of these bonds have reportedly been Japanese investors. The *Kisaikai's* restrictive rules on issuing domestic bonds and the unduly expensive trusteeship fees that bond issuers are required to pay have pushed bond transactions out to foreign markets. In 1984 the rules were somewhat loosened with respect to convertible bonds. This relaxation was apparently meaningful, because the amount of convertible bonds issued in the domestic market has substantially increased since that time.

Because the Japanese economy became more global, Japanese financial institutions have greatly expanded their activities in foreign markets. While foreign financial institutions and governments begin to regard the rapid expansion of Japan's financial institutions as excessive, foreign financial institutions call for Japan's financial liberalization and equal access. Many claim that the expansion of Japanese financial institutions in overseas markets has been promoted by financial regulation in their own domestic markets, and that financial liberalization in Japan would make it much easier for foreign financial institutions to penetrate Japanese markets.

In this respect, the U.S. government played an important role. When the U.S./Japan yen/dollar committee was established in 1983, the U.S. government strongly requested that the Japanese government liberalize its domestic financial regulations. The committee was organized to bring about an appreciation of the yen in order to reduce Japan's huge trade surplus with the United States. Many observers were doubtful that effective financial liberalization would aid in the

Table 4.2: Composition of Fundraising by Japanese Companies in Domestic and Foreign Capital Markets
(billion yen)

Fiscal year	Convertible Total	Convertible Foreign	Straight Total	Straight Foreign	Warrant Total	Warrant Foreign	Stock Total	Stock Foreign	Total Total	Total Foreign
1977	383.4	220.9	1,397.4	156.6	0.0	0.0	768.1	58.7	2,548.9	436.2
1978	709.1	432.1	1,443.8	130.5	0.0	0.0	1,046.3	13.4	3,199.2	576.0
1979	917.5	564.0	1,485.1	187.0	0.0	0.0	675.3	14.8	3,077.9	765.8
1980	613.6	517.1	1,177.1	183.6	0.0	0.0	1,267.8	107.7	3,058.5	808.4
1981	1,558.5	1,032.2	1,321.8	52.8	64.3	44.3	2,080.6	287.4	5,025.2	1,417.0
1982	1,049.8	632.3	1,728.5	681.0	113.2	66.2	1,078.0	62.6	3,969.5	1,442.1
1983	2,060.8	1,199.8	1,095.0	412.0	342.3	325.3	927.2	77.8	4,425.3	2,014.9
1984	2,846.1	1,234.6	1,847.2	1,127.2	440.2	437.2	864.1	49.5	5,997.6	2,848.5
1985	2,538.5	953.0	2,380.1	1,436.6	937.0	882.0	662.0	10.7	6,517.6	3,282.3
1986	3,957.4	489.4	2,856.5	1,876.3	2,106.3	2,002.8	632.1	0.6	9,552.8	4,369.3
1987	6,139.6	1,084.6	1,905.4	990.4	3,471.5	3,471.5	2,122.9	39.0	13,639.4	5,585.4
1988	8,073.1	1,078.6	1,877.4	1,128.4	5,022.7	5,022.7	4,579.0	16.5	19,552.2	7,246.2

Source: Nomura Research Institute.

appreciation of the yen.[20] However, this committee succeeded in persuading the Japanese government to present a precise time schedule of financial liberalization. By the end of 1988, the Tokyo Offshore Market was established. In this market financial transactions denominated in yen are carried out free of regulation among nonresidents. The Tokyo Offshore Market can be regarded as one of the Japanese government's responses to the request from abroad to internationalize the Japanese yen.

The growing inconsistency between financial regulations in domestic markets and liberalized transactions in international markets is also noteworthy. If Japanese financial institutions were allowed to freely extend their activities in both international and foreign markets, the effectiveness of domestic financial regulations would substantially decrease. Therefore, the monetary authorities have had to constrain financial institutions' activities in foreign markets in order to preserve the effectiveness of domestic regulations.

The most notorious case is the so-called "three-bureau agreement" of the Ministry of Finance concerning the securities business of the Japanese banks' subsidiaries in international markets. Specifically, by this measure of administrative guidance, the securities subsidiaries of Japanese banks are not permitted to be the lead managers of Japanese corporate bond issues. In other words, a subsidiary of a securities company must be the lead manager when a Japanese company issues bonds in a foreign market. Needless to say, this administrative guidance is designed to maintain the effectiveness of the domestic regulation separating the securities business from the banking business.

SOME CONSEQUENCES OF ECONOMIC GROWTH. Japan's successful economic growth in itself destabilized the status quo of financial regulation. The volume of household financial assets increased rapidly during the era of rapid economic growth. Thus, households gradually became more interest-rate sensitive, in the sense that they were ready to take advantage of better terms when managing their portfolios. At the end of the 1970s, households were not satisfied with the controlled deposit interest rates. This was also true of corporations. The accumu-

---

20. For example, see Frankel (1984) and Shinkai (1988).

lation of financial assets was essential preparation for full-fledged financial liberalization in Japan.

Generally speaking, nonfinancial corporations achieved excellent performance during the high growth era. They established a reputation of being reliable borrowers in both domestic and foreign financial markets. Thus, their demand for the assistance of banks has substantially decreased. At the beginning of the 1980s, major companies began issuing bonds and stocks and reducing their reliance on bank loans. This process, called securitization, implies a drastic change in the structure of demand for financial services, and it has forced financial authorities and related parties to reconsider the regulations concerning the segmentation of business areas that characterized the financial system during the high growth era.

Reorganization of Financial Regulation in Japan

The Japanese monetary authorities are confronting three areas of policy concern as the financial structure changes: rearranging the safety net in the financial system, building up the infrastructure that stabilizes the expanding securities markets, and making more effective use of the antitrust law in the financial industries. This section discusses both the monetary authorities' actual responses to these issues, and other possible responses that could be considered.

REARRANGEMENT OF THE SAFETY NET. Financial liberalization will foster competition in banking and other financial industries, and will increase the risk of failure of individual financial institutions. For example, the proportion of banks' liabilities with uncontrolled interest rates relative to the total of their liabilities has dramatically increased since 1980. This means the banks' market risk significantly increased. Bank failure will become much more probable than it has been during the last three or four decades.

Bankruptcy can be regarded as a form of restructuring managerial resources, and as a necessary result of risk-taking. Thus, bank failures in themselves will have to be permitted to occur. The authorities, however, must treat them carefully to prevent them from causing widespread financial panics. To this end, an actual safety net, mainly consisting of deposit insurance and the central bank's role of lender of last resort, needs to be carefully used.

Strengthening the safety net, however, will incur the problem of moral hazard on the part of banks and depositors.[21] Thus, strengthening of the safety net must be supplemented by more careful prudential regulations, which limit the extent of risk-taking by financial institutions. The Japanese monetary authorities agreed to the 1988 BIS regulatory standards of capital adequacy, showing their intent to make prudential regulation more substantial. This policy stance is quite timely.

INFRASTRUCTURE OF OPEN CAPITAL MARKETS. The volume of securities transactions has rapidly increased in Japan. It is reported that the total market value of outstanding stocks in the Tokyo Stock Exchange far surpassed that of the New York Stock Exchange in 1988. Therefore, many people may be surprised to hear that Japan's securities markets lack a sound infrastructure. But it is the author's opinion that an informational infrastructure, consisting of rules of disclosure, regulations on insider trading, and efficient systems of credit rating, has not been well established in Japan.

For example, stock prices of particular companies often show abnormal changes just before the companies announce important matters related to their future profitability. Such abnormal changes in stock prices suggest the existence of insider trading, which is likely to lessen public confidence in the fairness of the stock exchange. The authorities must strengthen the infrastructure for securities transactions in order to stabilize the financial system with rapidly expanding securities markets. The current organization of the Ministry of Finance has been well suited to operating anticompetitive regulations. But it is not structured to be efficient in establishing the proper infrastructure for the securities markets.

THE IMPORTANCE OF THE ANTITRUST LAW. In the high growth era, long-term relationship among banks and borrowing companies played an essential role in efficiently intermediating between savers and capital investors under imperfect information. Banks, especially big

---

21. See, for example, Kane (1985).

Chart 4.7: Composition of Major Companies' Fundraising, 1967-88
(percent)

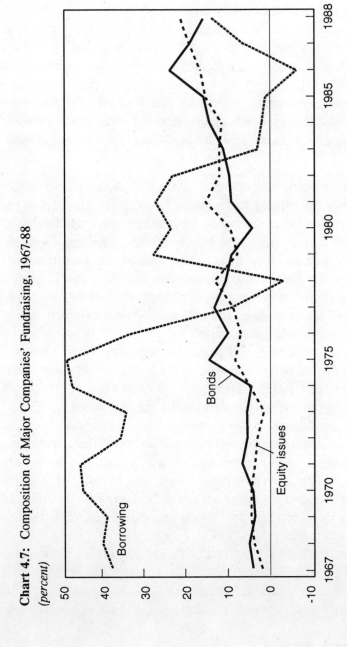

Source: Bank of Japan

ones, accumulated relevant information concerning major companies through long-term relationships.[22] The underdeveloped nature of Japan's credit rating system is related to the fact that much of the information on companies was concentrated in the banking sector, especially big banks. This has caused some observers to be concerned about the danger of banks' dominance over the Japanese financial system after market segmentation regulations are liberalized. This concern seems inconsistent with the fact that major companies have greatly reduced their dependence on borrowing from banks (chart 4.7). It should be noted, however, that big banks have preserved a close relationship with major companies through transactions in various financial services other than lending.

Banks appear to have some advantage over other financial institutions, in particular securities companies, because of their accumulated information. It may be difficult for other domestic and foreign rivals to compete with Japan's big banks in the business of financial transactions with Japan's major companies. Therefore, while deregulation is expected to increase the efficiency of financial industries, there is some danger of existing financial monopoly power. In principle, the antitrust law should cope with this danger. But the Japanese antitrust law has been notorious for its ineffectiveness. The Japanese authorities must make this law more effective as they pursue full scale liberalization of the financial system.

Conclusion

The rapid economic growth in post-war Japan was achieved under rigid financial regulation; almost all interest rates on bank deposits and loans were controlled, and the securities markets remained underdeveloped. Therefore, high growth was achieved without a flexible market-oriented financial system. The Japanese government preserved the stability of the financial system by adopting anticompetitive regulations. These regulations, however, restricted effective competition in the financial industries, thereby benefiting banks and other financial institutions, probably at the expense of households and nonfinancial businesses. The government preserved the stability of the financial

---

22. See Horiuchi, Packer, and Fakuda (1988).

system under this rigid control by containing inflation. The constraint of the balance of payments under the fixed exchange rate regime helped the Bank of Japan avoid excessive monetary expansion.

The Japanese financial system crucially depended not on flexible market mechanisms, but rather on nonmarket mechanisms such as long-term relationships between banks and businesses. The nonmarket mechanisms worked relatively well under imperfect information.

The financial accumulation resulting from the rapid economic growth and the dramatic changes in money flows after the high growth era led to the structural change of the Japanese financial system. This was important for stimulating Japan's financial liberalization. Thus, the financial liberalization was not a cause of rapid economic growth but a consequence of economic development. The Japanese monetary authorities are reorganizing both the safety net and prudential regulations. Their attitude is a rational response to the structural changes in the financial system. The open capital markets have increased in their importance in Japan's financial system, but the necessary informational infrastructure has not yet been fully developed. The government will have to pay close attention to the development of the necessary infrastructure for the efficient working of Japan's securities markets.

Bibliography

Cargill, F. T., (1985). "A U.S. Perspective on Japanese Financial Liberalization." BOJ Institute for Monetary and Economic Studies, *Monetary and Economic Studies* 3, May.

Cho, Y., (1986). "Inefficiencies from Financial Liberalization in the Absence of Well-Functioning Equity Markets." *Journal of Money, Credit, and Banking*, Vol.18 , No.2, May 1986.

Frankel. J. A., (1984). *The Yen/Dollar Agreement: Liberalizing Japanese Capital Markets*, Institute for International Economics.

Goldsmith, R. W., (1983). *The Financial Development of Japan, 1868–1977*, Yale University Press.

Hamada, K., and A. Horiuchi, (1987). "The Political Economy of the Financial Market." in K. Yamamura and Y. Yasuba, eds., *The Political Economy of Japan, Vol.l, The Domestic Transformation*, Stanford University Press.

Horiuchi, A., (1984). "The 'Low Interest Rate Policy' and Economic Growth in Postwar Japan." *The Developing Economies,* Vol. 22, No. 4.

_____, F. A. Packer and S. Fukuda, (1988). "What Role Has the 'Main Bank' Played in Japan?", *Journal of the Japanese and International Economics* 2 (2).

_____, (1989). "Informational Properties of the Japanese Financial System." *Japan and the World Economy* 1 (3).

Jensen, M. C., and W. H. Meckling, (1976). "Theory of the Firm: Managerial Behavior. Agency Costs and Ownership Structure." *Journal of Financial Economics*, Oct. 1976.

Kane, E. J., (1985). *The Gathering Crisis in Deposit Insurance.* MIT Press.

McKinnon, R. I., 1973. *Money and Capital in Economic Development*, The Brookings Institution.

_____, (1988). *Financial Liberalization and Economic Development: A Reassessment of Interest-Rate Policies in Asia and Latin America,* Occasional Paper No. 6. International Center for Economic Growth.

Myers, S. C., and N. S. Majluf, (1984). "Corporate Financing and Investment Decisions When Firms Have Information that Investors Do Not Have." *Journal of Financial Economics*, 13.

Patrick, H., (1966). "Financial Development and Economic Growth in Underdeveloped Countries." In *Economic Development and Cultural Change*, Vol. 14, No. 2

Sakakibara, E., and R. A. Feldman, (1983). "The Japanese Financial System in Comparative Perspectives." *Journal of Comparative Economics* 7 (March).

Shaw, E. S., (1973). *Financial Deepening in Economic Development.* Oxford University Press.

Shinkai, Y., (1988). "The Internationalization of Finance in Japan." In T. Inoguchi and D. L. Okimoto, eds., *The Political Economy of Japan, Vol. 2, The Changing International Context*, Stanford University Press.

Stiglitz, J. E., and A. Weiss, (1981). "Credit Rationing in Market with Imperfect Information." *American Economic Review* 71.

Suzuki, Y., ed., (1987). *The Japanese Financial System*, Oxford University Press.

5

INDONESIAN FINANCIAL DEVELOPMENT: A DIFFERENT SEQUENCING?

David C. Cole and Betty F. Slade[1]

Introduction

Indonesia in the 1980s provides a highly successful example of both substantial deregulation and rapid development of the domestic financial system in the context of a very open foreign exchange system. Most developing countries and many developed countries have clung to some forms of foreign exchange controls long after freeing up many aspects of their domestic financial system. Several Latin American countries in the late 1970s and early 1980s suddenly removed most domestic and foreign financial controls and, after an initial period of favorable response, subsequently experienced severe instability and inflation. This led to a new dogma among financial development specialists to the effect that liberalization or deregulation of a financial system should follow a sequential path, starting with relaxation of internal trade controls and maintenance of a "realistic" exchange rate to get relative prices in line with world market prices. Then it would be appropriate to free up domestic financial controls over interest rates and credit allocation; and finally, when everything else was in order, to remove controls over foreign capital flows. Only

---

1. Harvard Institute for International Development, Harvard University.

in this way, it was claimed, could excessive foreign capital inflow and, more critically, capital outflow be avoided.[2]

Indonesia, however, essentially removed all foreign capital controls in 1971, when its foreign exchange position was still relatively precarious. The main reason for taking this action at that time was that the government could not exert effective control over foreign capital movements anyway. Singapore was a major financial and trading center in the midst of Indonesia, and commodities and finance flowed freely between the two countries in spite of controls. Attempts to enforce foreign exchange controls wasted scarce administrative resources and were seen as doing more harm than good to the domestic economy.

Removal of foreign capital controls was preceded by major macroeconomic stabilization adjustments to counteract the hyperinflation and negative growth of the early to mid-1960s. These measures included elimination of fiscal deficits, restrictions on domestic credit, positive real interest rates on bank deposits and loans, encouragement of both foreign direct investment and foreign aid inflows, and implementation of dual exchange rates, one fixed and one floating, that were unified and pegged at the time of freeing up exchange controls.[3]

Since 1971, avoidance of controls over foreign capital movements has been a cornerstone of Indonesian economic policy. Another not unrelated tenet of policy has been a balanced domestic government

---

2.   There is a considerable literature on the sequencing of liberalizing reforms. The most prominent recent statement was in the World Bank's *World Development Report 1989*, pp. 127-8, where it is suggested that "Until (domestic financial market) reforms are well under way, it will probably be necessary to maintain controls on the movement of (foreign) capital." The report continues, "If, however, a country already has an open capital account, the government should give priority to maintaining macroeconomic stability to avoid destabilizing capital flows. After substantial progress has been made toward reform, the government can move to the final stage: full liberalization of interest rates, the elimination of the remaining directed credit programs, the relaxation of capital controls, and the removal of restrictions on foreign institutions."

Shaw (1973) proposed that all reforms should be implemented at the same time. After this was tried in the Southern Cone of Latin America, with disastrous results, Harberger, Dornbusch, McKinnon, Frenkel, and Edwards, among others, have sought to explain the reasons for the failure and the lessons for other countries. Much of this literature is discussed in Edwards (1984).

3.   These measures are consistent with the sequencing policy prescriptions of McKinnon and Edwards, discussed in the previous footnote.

budget. Maintenance of these policy stances was made easier by the large inflow of oil earnings after 1973, but it has been continued through the 1980s despite the decline in oil revenues and other disturbances in the international financial markets.

The inflow of oil earnings from 1973 to 1982 also removed many incentives for domestic financial development within Indonesia. Finance was abundant, either from domestic sources or from foreign institutions that were willing to lend to Indonesian enterprises on the basis of expected future earnings derived either directly or indirectly from oil. Trade-distorting restrictions were imposed and the state-owned oil company, Pertamina, became almost like an autonomous development agency, investing in capital intensive industrial and infrastructure projects with little concern for their economic viability. After several years Pertamina's excesses were curbed, but restrictive trade policies and emphasis on import-substituting industries continued throughout the oil boom period.

The main concerns of the monetary authorities during this period were to control domestic credit expansion and foreign borrowing. The domestic objective was addressed through imposition of credit ceilings on each bank, which had the effect of limiting the growth of the domestic banking system. But with the open foreign capital system, excess funds of banks, businesses, or individuals were readily invested abroad. The limit on foreign borrowing was enforced most effectively over the state-owned oil company, Pertamina, after its excessive appetite for foreign loans was curbed in 1976. Other enterprises were able to borrow abroad either on their own name or against compensating deposit balances at banks in Singapore or Hong Kong. Thus, the monetary policies of the oil-boom era, combined with the open foreign capital system, shifted the locus of much financial activity, both lending and borrowing, offshore. Domestic activity of financial institutions hardly grew at all relative to GDP and became increasingly focused on state-owned banks serving state-owned enterprises, or carrying out government-sponsored credit programs as so-called "agents of development."

Since 1983, following the sharp reduction in oil earnings, the Indonesian government has been pursuing a policy of financial reform to stimulate the growth and improve the effectiveness of the domestic financial system, still within the context of an open foreign exchange system. The first phase of this reform, initiated in 1983 along with a major devaluation and fiscal retrenchment, was focused on the banking system. It involved the removal of credit ceilings and interest rate controls on commercial banks and, as a consequence, eliminated the central bank's main instruments of monetary policy. This reform resulted in rapid growth of the whole commercial banking system, and a significant gain in the share of the private domestic commercial banks, at the expense of both the government-owned banks and foreign banks. It also led to a period of experimentation with various techniques and instruments for influencing the supply of money, interest rates, and foreign exchange movements. The reform moved the financial system part way toward a market-price basis of operation but, with many restrictions remaining on entry and initiation of new activity, the markets were only partially effective.

Subsequent to the 1983 reforms, there were several financial crises, usually manifested as sudden, large losses of foreign exchange reserves by the central bank and sharp increases in the interbank interest rate. These crises could have, and in many other countries probably would have, led to imposition of some form of foreign exchange controls. But in Indonesia this solution, though sometimes speculated about in the press, was never seriously considered by the government. Instead, the officials used other measures to stem the outflow of foreign exchange and bring down the interbank interest rate. Initially these measures were somewhat harsh, such as the 45 percent devaluation of the exchange rate in September 1986 and the withdrawal of practically all available legal reserves of the banking system in June 1987, but since that time the measures have become more finely tuned and subtle in their application. This contributed to greater stability and confidence in the management of financial policy.

It also laid the foundation for a further series of financial reform measures from 1988 through early 1990 that were directed at promoting more fundamental structural and operational changes of the financial system. The recent reforms, which are still evolving, have consisted of a mixture of changes in regulations that (1) opened up entry of new domestic and foreign joint-venture banks, their geographical dispersion, and range of activities; (2) stimulated the development of domestic money and capital markets; and (3) promoted a broad range of new types of financial institutions and services. These reforms have been supported by efforts to strengthen government's supervisory capabilities to ensure that financial services will be provided within the framework of a fair and competitive market environment.

So far, the most recent reforms have led to rapid growth and diversification of financial activity. There have been no significant financial crises, and the volatility of interest rates and expectations has been diminishing. The monetary authorities have learned to use their monetary policy instruments quickly to respond to potential dangers, while continuing fiscal balance and healthy growth of non-oil exports have helped to build confidence in the prospects for financial stability.

The question arises as to whether Indonesia is a special case of a country that had to follow a "less than optimal" sequence of policy reform by force of circumstances, and managed to succeed largely due to good luck; or whether it represents a reasonable, or even a better, sequence of financial reform. It is our view that the open capital account policy has imposed a healthy degree of restraint on both fiscal and monetary policy in Indonesia over the past two decades. This has been reinforced by capable economic policymakers who have been quick to respond to emerging difficulties. In fact, economic policy has been most effective during times of balance of payments stringency, and has tended to become more lax when oil earnings were most abundant, and when the economic policymakers were less influential. An open capital account both incites and requires good macroeconomic management. A country that is incapable of achieving such management probably needs foreign capital controls to limit the danger to its foreign exchange reserves and permit some control over the allocation of foreign exchange to priority uses. But such a sequencing may actually be a "second best" approach. For countries that are capable of reasonably sound macro policies, the Indonesian approach may be worthy of consideration.

Financial Growth and Structural Change in Indonesia

The Indonesian financial system has experienced two growth spurts since recuperating from the destructive effects of hyperinflation in the mid-1960s. These longer-term trends are best indicated by the ratio of broad money (M2) to gross domestic product (GDP), as shown in table 5.1. During the mid-1960s, the Indonesian financial system had experienced a classic implosion as a consequence of the government relying mainly on the central bank to meet its operating expenses. The inflation rate reached a high of some 600 percent in 1966, and the ratio of M1 (or M2) to GDP was less than 4 percent. The first growth spurt was from 1968 to 1972, when the M2 to GDP ratio rose from 6 percent to 13 percent. During this period the monetary authorities set relatively high nominal interest rates on bank time deposits of the government-owned banks, and the central bank (Bank Indonesia) provided a partial subsidy for those interest rates. Over the next decade, from 1973 to 1982, the M2 to GDP ratio showed a mild upward trend reflecting a rise of about 2 percentage points in both the M1 and the quasi-money ratios.

The second important growth spurt started in 1983 and has continued into 1990. This latter period of rapid growth was manifested initially by a drop in the M1 to GDP ratio and a large increase in the quasi-money ratio, resulting in only a moderate increase in the M2 to GDP ratio. Subsequently, the M1 ratio has stabilized and the quasi-money ratio has continued to rise rapidly. This second growth spurt resulted mainly from the removal of credit and interest rate ceilings in June 1983, and the growing competition among banks to attract deposits, especially time deposits, since that time.

Over the more than two decades from 1968 to 1989, the ratio of narrow money (M1) to GDP approximately doubled. Since narrow money is primarily a means of payment, this suggests that the monetization of the economy has roughly doubled over this period. On the other hand, the ratio of quasi-money, or time and savings deposits, to GDP has increased from practically 0 to 24 percent in the two decades. It was the rise in this ratio that accounted for most of the growth in the two spurts. Since quasi-money is mainly longer-term deposits, it is more indicative of increases in financial savings that are held in the form of claims on the domestic banking system.

Both of these measures are limited in that they do not include certain other means of payment and forms of financial saving that from time to time have been important in Indonesia, namely, foreign cur

Table 5.1: Monetary Ratios

Year	Currency (CU/GDP) (1)	Demand deposits (DD/GDP) (2)	Quasi-money (QM/GDP) (3)	"Narrow" money (M1/GDP) (4)	"Broad" money (M2/GDP) (5)
1968	3.58	1.86	0.57	5.44	6.01
1969	4.27	2.50	1.84	6.77	8.61
1970	4.79	2.96	2.47	7.75	10.22
1971	4.56	2.77	3.39	7.33	10.72
1972	5.09	3.80	4.12	8.90	13.02
1973	4.99	3.91	4.23	8.90	13.12
1974	4.13	3.71	4.31	7.84	12.15
1975	4.48	4.48	5.22	8.97	14.19
1976	4.62	4.86	6.08	9.48	15.16
1977	4.78	5.02	5.50	9.80	15.30
1978	5.11	5.15	5.45	10.26	15.71
1979	4.45	5.26	5.27	9.72	14.99
1980	4.40	5.81	5.51	10.21	15.72
1981	4.40	6.76	5.56	11.16	16.71
1982	4.70	6.70	6.33	11.40	17.73
1983	4.29	5.45	9.13	9.74	18.88
1984	4.14	5.43	10.42	9.56	19.99
1985	4.58	5.85	13.47	10.43	23.91
1986	5.21	6.18	15.59	11.39	26.97
1987	4.64	5.54	17.02	10.19	27.21
1988	4.48	5.84	19.80	10.32	30.12
1989	4.63	7.22	23.52	11.85	35.37

The table is headed "Percent of GDP" spanning columns (1)–(5).

Sources: Bank Indonesia, *Monthly Report*, various issues; Bank Indonesia, *Weekly Report*, various issues; Central Bureau of Statistics, *Indonesian Statistics*, various issues.

rency, foreign exchange deposits, and other claims held abroad. Undoubtedly part of the spurts in domestic time and savings deposits in the high growth periods reflect the repatriation of claims held abroad, but we have no reliable way of estimating the magnitudes involved.

It is noteworthy that the periods of high domestic financial growth are not necessarily correlated with the periods of high real growth of the Indonesian economy. The initial period of financial growth occurred at a time when the economy was growing quite rapidly, but was mainly due to recovery from a long period of mismanagement and deterioration. During the decade of high economic growth and high investment deriving from the oil boom, the domestic financial system languished. Finally, after the decline in oil prices when real growth became more erratic, domestic financial growth accelerated. This is a first, crude indication that domestic financial growth was influenced more by financial policy measures than by the overall growth of the economy. It also suggests that during the years of high economic growth and increases in real income, a substantial portion of the increases in savings that would be expected to be associated with those higher incomes was placed abroad.

A broader measure of financial development can be obtained by looking at the total assets of various types of financial institutions. These inevitably include some double counting because, for example, the assets of insurance companies include deposits at banks, which in turn are matched by bank assets. Of greater significance, a sizable portion of the assets of Bank Indonesia consists of loans to deposit money banks (DMBs), which are then on-lent to their customers.

Another distortion arises from the likely overstatement of the real, or market, value of many financial assets, such as bad loans of the banks and, on the other hand, the understatement of the market value of real assets. Despite all these limitations and the gaps in the data for earlier years, the data shown in annex table 5.1 in annex 1 and in graphs 5.1 and 5.2 in annex 3 give an indication of the relative size and growth of various types of financial institutions in Indonesia over the past two decades.

The best overall measure of financial size and growth is the ratio of financial assets to GDP (ratio B), because this ratio omits the double counting of Bank Indonesia loans to deposit money banks. This ratio has risen from about 23 percent of GDP in 1969 to 75 percent of GDP in 1988.

During the initial growth spurt (1968–72), the DMBs raised their share of total financial assets relative to Bank Indonesia (BI). This is seen most readily by comparing the line item "total assets of DMBs less loans from BI" with the line item "total assets of BI" in graph 5.2. In 1969 the DMBs' net assets were equal to roughly half of the total assets of BI, but by 1972 they were about 25 percent greater than the total assets of BI. This change was largely due to the effective mobilization of deposits by the DMBs, especially the government-owned banks, during this period.

By 1982, however, total assets of DMBs less loans from BI were once again less than the total assets of BI. After the second growth spurt (1983-present), this figure had again risen to 184 percent of the total assets of BI. But it must be noted that there had also been substantial growth in the total assets of other financial institutions namely, insurance companies, leasing companies, pension funds, nonbank financial institutions (NBFIs), and the State Savings Bank (BTN). Although data for these other financial institutions are not available for the earlier period, they were probably of negligible importance. Their recorded growth in recent years has been very rapid and has accounted for an important part of the rise in the ratio of financial assets to GDP, as shown in graph 5.2 and table 5.1 in the annex.

The Sequence of Financial Reforms

High Bank Time Deposit Rates, 1968–72

In September 1968, when inflation was decelerating but still running at a rate of about 50 percent per annum, and the economy was just beginning to recover from the profligate Sukarno years, the first major move was made to revive and reform the financial system. This consisted of a large increase in bank time deposit interest rates from 30 percent to 72 percent per annum on one year time deposits and a rise in maximum bank lending rates to 60 percent.[4] The difference

---

4. This was one of the early cases of adoption of a "high interest rate" policy. It built upon the experience of Korea, which adopted such a policy in 1965 following recommendations of J. Gurley, H. Patrick, and E. Shaw, as described in Cole and Park (1983).

Table 5.2: Annual Inflation Rates, Nominal and Real Interest Rates

| Year | Annual inflation rates | | Interest rates[1] | |
	CPI (1983=100)	CPI % change	Nominal	Real
1968	10.99	125.20	72.0	-24.0
1969	12.95	17.88	60.0	35.7
1970	14.56	12.36	24.0	10.4
1971	15.14	4.00	24.0	19.2
1972	16.16	6.73	18.0	10.6
1973	21.11	30.63	15.0	-12.0
1974	29.77	41.03	15.0	-18.4
1975	35.37	18.83	15.0	-3.2
1976	42.43	19.96	15.0	-4.2
1977	47.09	10.98	12.0	0.9
1978	50.95	8.19	9.0	0.7
1979	61.43	20.57	9.0	-9.6
1980	72.78	18.48	9.0	-8.0
1981	81.66	12.20	9.0	-2.9
1982	89.45	9.54	9.0	-0.5
1983	100.00	11.80	18.0	5.5
1984	106.42	6.42	18.3	11.1
1985	108.51	1.97	15.0	12.8
1986	124.09	14.36	15.0	0.6
1987	139.23	12.20	17.5	4.7
1988	150.48	8.08	18.5	9.6
1989	159.67	6.11	16.5	9.8

1. Rate on one-year time deposits of state banks. Real rate is deflated by CPI of current year.
Sources: Central Bureau of Statistics, *Indonesian Statistics*, various Issues.

between the deposit and lending rates was covered in part by centralbank subsidy payments. This measure led not only to the rapid increase in bank time deposits shown in table 5.1, but also to a large inflow of foreign exchange and a 25 percent appreciation of the floating exchange rate in a 6-month period.[5] It also permitted more rapid expansion of central bank credit that, together with the growing deposit resources of the commercial banks, led to a substantial real increase in the availability of bank financing. As both domestic credit and foreign exchange became more available and less expensive in real terms, businesses were able to rehabilitate and, in some cases, expand their productive capabilities.

Over the next few years, economic conditions improved steadily, so that by 1971 the government was able to move to a decontrolled foreign exchange system with a unified rate pegged to the U.S. dollar. The nominal deposit interest rate was reduced to 24 percent in 1971 and 18 percent in 1972, but real rates remained positive because of the practical disappearance of inflation (see table 5.2). The direct subsidy on time deposit interest was reduced, but not totally eliminated. Financial institutions continued to grow and provide a mixture of commercial and term financing, which was augmented by a large inflow of foreign financing for major development projects as well as for business investment.

At that point in time, it was reasonable to conclude that the partial financial reform process of 1968, in the context of a broad macroeconomic policy reorientation and, after 1971, an open capital account, had been very successful. The supply of domestically provided financial services had more than doubled relative to GDP. Price level and exchange rate stability had been achieved, and real interest rates had been brought down to levels consistent with continued growth of savings and investment. There was still much room for improvement in the management and operation of financial institutions and a deepening of financial markets, but progress on all these fronts was readily apparent.

Financial Restriction and Displacement (1973–83)

The rise in oil prices in 1973 immediately affected Indonesia, generating balance of payments surpluses and budgetary revenues that

---

5. At this time Indonesia had a dual exchange rate system, with one rate for most imports pegged to the U.S. dollar, and a second floating rate that was traded through the banks between exporters and importers of nonessential goods. It was the floating rate that appreciated following the interest rate increases.

soon boosted domestic spending and inflation. The central bank was unable to control the growth of reserve money and therefore shifted to credit ceilings on the commercial banks in an attempt to control growth of the money supply. Interest rate ceilings, which had been carried over from earlier years, were kept well below the inflation rate so that real deposit rates became negative (see table 5.2). As a consequence, bank deposits increased only moderately as a share of GNP.

Much of the investment and working capital of business for the next decade was financed not through bank deposit mobilization, but by the government budget or by funds from abroad. The large government budget was funded through a combination of oil export revenues and continuing inflows of foreign assistance. The foreign financing of the business sectors consisted of direct foreign loans and equity investments, and also sizable borrowings from banks in nearby financial centers such as Singapore and Hong Kong. Because of the ceilings on domestic bank lending, and also the low interest rates on bank deposits, many Indonesian businesses found it expedient to hold substantial deposit balances abroad and to use those balances as collateral for loans from abroad. At the same time, any domestic banks that had surplus funds beyond their domestic loan ceilings tended to place those funds abroad in foreign exchange deposits or securities in order to obtain better rates of return. The open capital account system and the stability of the foreign exchange rate made these relatively risk-free operations. Thus, the ceilings on domestic credit did not become a significant constraint on the availability of financial services for most Indonesian businesses of medium to large scale. They simply shifted their financial activities offshore.

Smaller businesses and households, especially in the rural areas, were not well served by the formal financial institutions, but there was ample liquidity within the country as a whole, and a large network of semiformal and informal institutions in both urban and rural areas saw to it that financial services were available wherever they were profitable.[6] The abundance of financing and domestic spending raised the inflation rate to an annual average of 25 percent from 1973 through

---

6. See Patten and Rosengard (1989) and also Jennifer and Paul Alexander (1986).

1977 as measured by either the GDP deflator or the consumer price index. The ratio of deposit money bank total assets to GDP declined from 20.4 percent to 19.7 percent during the same period.

The tranquility of this combination of domestic and foreign financing was shaken in 1978 when the government carried out a surprise 50 percent devaluation of the rupiah relative to the U.S. dollar (see table 5.3). The primary purpose of the devaluation was to correct for the disparity in inflation rates between Indonesia and the rest of the world in order to reduce disincentives to domestic producers of tradable goods—the so-called "Dutch disease." But the financial effect was to give those domestic banks and businesses that had large credit balances abroad a sudden windfall profit on their net foreign exchange assets, and to impose a corresponding cost on all those with net foreign indebtedness. Once the devaluation was done, expectations of further devaluation were reduced, so borrowers were again encouraged to make use of foreign financing. The expansionary effects of this were then reinforced by the second increase in oil prices in 1979. Indonesia continued to have ample sources of financing despite negative real interest rates and repression of the domestic banking institutions.

In the late 1970s, the Indonesian government attempted to stimulate development of the capital markets in Jakarta.[7] It set up a new agency (BAPEPAM) to manage and regulate the stock exchange, and a government-owned corporation (DANAREKSA) to underwrite new issues and offer investment fund units to the public. The main objectives of these early efforts were to increase Indonesian ownership of foreign joint ventures operating in Indonesia, and also to broaden public participation in the capital markets. After an initial spurt of activity, the markets reverted to a relatively dormant state, and never did succeed in raising much capital.

The 1983 Reforms

The decline in oil prices beginning in 1982 signaled a sharp reversal in Indonesia's circumstances and brought on a second round of

---

7. See Dickie (1981) for a lengthy discussion of the early stages of development of the Jakarta capital markets.

Table 5.3: Rupiah/U.S. Dollar Exchange Rates and Annual Depreciation Rates *(end of year)*

Date	Rupiah rate	Annual percent depreciation
December 1968	326.00	38.72
December 1969	326.00	0.00
December 1970	378.00	15.95
December 1971	415.00	9.79
December 1972	415.00	0.70
December 1973	415.00	0.00
December 1974	415.00	0.00
December 1975	415.00	0.00
December 1976	415.00	0.00
December 1977	415.00	0.00
December 1978	625.00	50.60
December 1979	627.00	0.32
December 1980	626.75	-0.04
December 1981	644.00	2.75
December 1982	692.50	7.53
December 1983	994.00	43.54
December 1984	1,074.00	8.05
December 1985	1,125.00	4.75
December 1986	1,641.00	45.87
December 1987	1,650.00	0.55
December 1988	1,731.00	4.91
December 1989	1,800.00	4.01

Note: The annual percent depreciation is calculated using the Bank Indonesia selling rate for the US$ by the formula:

$$\% \text{ DEP}(t) = [FE(t) - FE(t-1)]FE(t-1)] \times 100$$

where FE(t) is the end-of-month rupiah per dollar rate, and FE(t-1) is the rate at the end of the previous month.
Source: Kompas Newspaper, Indonesia.

retrenchment and reorientation of macroeconomic measures in 1983, coinciding with the installation of a new cabinet following reelection of President Suharto. The first move was made in the fiscal area as government scaled back sharply on budgetary commitments for large investment projects to keep within available revenues and maintain the balanced budget principle. This was followed by another large devaluation of the rupiah by 38 percent at the end of March 1983. This devaluation was intended not only to encourage exports and restrain imports, but also to help make up for the loss in budgetary revenues from oil exports.

The third major move was in the area of financial policy. The central bank announced removal of all bank credit ceilings, and also of interest rate ceilings on the government-owned banks. (Previously, private banks had not been subject to interest rate ceilings, but they were subject to credit ceilings, and this had limited their interest in mobilizing deposits.)

The fourth move, announced in September 1983, was a broad tax reform, introducing a value added tax and shifting from a schedular to a global income tax. Implementation of the tax reform was a gradual process over the next several years and proved crucial in sustaining government revenues in the face of further declines in the oil prices. The financial reform, on the other hand, was quicker to take effect and produced a substantial increase in bank deposits and loans within the first seven months of its enactment.

One of the great unknowns in Indonesia, with its totally open capital account system, is, as we have noted previously, just how much of any change in domestic financial asset holdings is simply a shifting of activity from offshore to onshore or vice versa. The rise in the ratio of total bank assets to GDP between the end of 1982 and 1989 was from 25.5 percent to 45.4 percent. Such a high growth of bank assets, occurring during a period when GNP per capita was growing at only about 3 percent per annum in real terms and the terms of trade were moving strongly against Indonesia, did not reflect a comparable real increase in national saving. It also did not reflect accurately the increase in financial saving. Instead, it was some combination of increased real saving, increased saving in the form of financial assets, and repatriation of past financial savings from overseas.

At the time of the financial reform in June 1983, one of the major concerns was that there might be a rapid inflow of past foreign asset accumulations that could cause a sudden increase in domestic reserve

money, credit, and money supply, with possible inflationary consequences that could undermine the positive effects of the devaluation.
Similar inflows of foreign capital in 1973-74 had led to imposition of
credit ceilings in the first place, and removal of those ceilings in 1983
left the monetary authorities with no real instruments for controlling
the growth of the money supply, except possibly through increases in
reserve requirements. There was, in fact, some return flow of foreign
exchange in response to both the devaluation and the rise in domestic
interest rates during the latter half of 1983, but there was no large increase in bank credit, domestic spending, or inflation.

A major reason for this was the sluggish response of the government-owned commercial banks (state banks) to the removal of loan
ceilings. The state banks, still operating in the bureaucratic control
mode, were accustomed to making prospective borrowers wait for
months for loan approvals, and they did not change their style quickly
despite the rapid buildup of their deposits in response to higher interest rates. Instead the state banks found it expedient to increase their
foreign exchange holdings abroad or to lend excess funds through the
newly active Jakarta interbank market to the private banks, which were
much more aggressive in expanding lending. Over the next several
years, from March 1983 to September 1989 the private national banks
increased their share of total bank assets from 11 to 24 percent, reflecting their strong response to the removal of credit ceilings.

This pattern of deposit mobilization by the state banks, which was
then intermediated through the private banks to the ultimate borrowers, worked quite well without causing any serious pressures on interest
or exchange rates, until September 1984, when the Indonesian financial system experienced not an excess of liquidity from foreign capital
inflow, but instead a liquidity squeeze. This was due to the absence of
any effective instrument for supplying liquidity or adjusting the available liquidity to changes in other factors affecting the supply of reserve money in the financial system. A sudden transfer of government
deposits to the central bank reduced the supply of reserve money and,
without any offsetting adjustment from the central bank, caused the
liquidity squeeze.

Normally such a squeeze would have been met by a short-term inflow of funds from abroad under Indonesia's open foreign exchange

system, but this liquidity squeeze was exacerbated by a concurrent accelerated depreciation in the central bank-set exchange rate that made the commercial banks very reluctant to sell foreign exchange, even for a few days, to cover their reserve requirements. As a consequence, the domestic interbank interest rate on overnight funds shot up to 90 percent per annum, which was the annualized rate of daily depreciation of the exchange rate (see table 5.3). Bank Indonesia belatedly responded to the liquidity crisis by supplying large amounts of three- to six-month credits through the discount facility into the banking system, bringing the overnight interbank interest rate down below 15 percent in a few days.

Another way in which the liquidity squeeze might have been alleviated was through bank borrowing from the central bank's discount window. While such a facility existed, the banks were so reluctant to present themselves to Bank Indonesia with a reserve problem that they opted for overnight money from the interbank market at the 90 percent interest rate.

Bank Indonesia had assumed that the discount window was a workable mechanism for supplying emergency reserves to banks, and had concentrated instead on developing an instrument with which to mop up reserves when it felt there was need for such action. Since there were no government debt instruments in existence because the government did not engage in deficit financing, Bank Indonesia initiated the issuance of its own securities (Sertifikat Bank Indonesia, or SBI) in February 1984. These SBIs were sold in limited quantities, mostly to the state banks, in the first half of 1984, but they were not of sufficient magnitude, even if they had all been redeemed before maturity, to meet the liquidity squeeze of August and September 1984.

This experience demonstrated the many problems of implementing indirect monetary controls and the necessity of building up the institutional base for their use. Specifically, it highlighted the need for the central bank to keep better track of the available supply of reserve money in the financial system, to develop further its instruments for controlling the supply of reserve money, and to avoid too predictable depreciation of the currency.[8] When the new monetary policy instruments, such as SBIs and bankers' acceptances (SBPUs or Surat Berharga Pasat Uang), were first introduced, the plan was that their issue prices would fluctuate according to changing market conditions, and that active secondary markets would develop. But because BI in effect stood ready to supply to banks or buy from banks whatever amounts they desired, but at "cut-off" interest rates determined by Bank Indonesia, the secondary markets did not emerge. This practice did succeed in stabilizing the interest rates on these instruments and accustomed the banks to buying and selling them, but it precluded the development of a real secondary market, which could have facilitated BI's control over reserve money.[9]

In addition to setting the short-term interest rate, the central bank also set the foreign exchange rate and the premium on the foreign exchange swap facility that it offered to those qualified financial institutions and businesses with future foreign exchange commitments.[10] (Initially, the swap facility was offered in limited quantities, but the quantitative limits were removed in October 1986, following the devaluation.) Thus the central bank controlled the following key prices: the SBI and SBPU money market interest rates, the foreign exchange rate, and the rate on foreign exchange swaps. It also stood ready to be the residual supplier of any excess demand or buyer of excess supply, within broad limits, in all these markets.

This pattern of price setting, coupled with its willingness to meet excess demand, made the central bank particularly vulnerable to speculation about changes in the foreign exchange rate. Such speculation had been fostered by the three sudden and large devaluations in 1978, 1983, and 1986. Whenever rumors spread in the financial markets that there might be another devaluation, most financial institutions

---

8. Binhadi and Meek (1988) present a detailed discussion of the process by which Bank Indonesia sought to develop an appropriate set of money market instruments. We will not duplicate that discussion here, but merely highlight some of the problems that have arisen while these instruments were being developed, and trace their effects on the overall growth of the financial system.

9. See Cole and Slade (1990).

10. The swap facility was offered by Bank Indonesia to permit reswapping of swaps that the banks had offered to their customers as a way of hedging future foreign exchange obligations connected with borrowing from abroad. The reswap rate posted by Bank Indonesia was fractionally lower than the rate charged by the banks.

and businesses took advantage of the open capital markets and bought foreign exchange or sold it to the central bank with a swap agreement. Very large movements in short-term interest rates would have been required to counteract such speculation, and the central bank was reluctant to permit such moves in the short-term rates that it controlled. As a consequence, the interbank borrowing rate, which the central bank did not control, became very volatile, as shown in annex table 5.2.

In the second quarter of 1987, there was a speculative run on the rupiah; the overnight interbank rate rose to 37 percent. The authorities, having concluded that there was no underlying justification for another devaluation, took drastic measures to reduce the supply of reserve money and force a return flow of foreign exchange to cover bank reserve requirements.[11]

The effect of these strong measures has turned out to be positive in one very important sense: it made clear that the government was prepared to defend the exchange rate and perhaps avoid any further large devaluations. This change in market expectations helped to reduce the upward pressure on domestic interest rates. The cost was at least a temporary loss to the central bank of one of its market-based instruments for short-term liquidity management, the SBPU, although the banks continued to use the SBPUs as a discountable bill for lending to their customers or borrowing on the interbank market.

The 1983 financial reforms and the followup measures to develop the tools of indirect monetary policy succeeded in greatly expanding

---

11. The forced reduction in reserve money was accomplished through two means. First, commercial banks were required to repurchase their commercial bills (SBPUs) from the central bank—that is, the ceilings on such rediscounts for each bank were suddenly reduced to zero. The second means was through a government instruction to four state enterprises (which had large time deposit balances at the commercial banks) to use those deposits to buy SBIs. Both measures shifted large amounts of reserves from the commercial banks to the central bank. However, the forced redemption of the SBPUs dramatically reduced their use by banks for liquidity and thus restricted that instrument of monetary policy until May 1989; the forced purchase by the state enterprises of SBIs with six-month maturity at a set interest rate created a two-tier system of SBIs: longer maturities with fixed rates sold on a command basis; and short (seven-day) maturities auctioned at more variable rates and amounts as a flexible tool of monetary policy. These measures were adopted when both the governor of the central bank and the minister of finance were out of the country, and the minister of planning, Prof. J. B. Sumarlin, was both acting governor and finance minister. They were thus labeled by the press as "the Sumarlin shock."

domestic banking activity, supporting reasonably good rates of economic growth and restructuring of the economy despite the drastic decline in oil revenues. There were occasional bouts of financial instability manifested by capital flight and sharp increases in short-term interest rates, but the authorities were able to stem these outflows fairly quickly without imposing restrictions on capital movements or experiencing excessive losses of foreign reserves or serious inflation.[12]

The 1988–90 Reforms

In late 1988 the Indonesian authorities announced a broad new package of financial reform measures. This time the focus was primarily on the structure of the financial system, and the main themes were (1) to promote competition, particularly within the banking sector, by allowing for new entry, expanding of activities, reducing compartmentalization, and giving more bank autonomy in decisionmaking; (2) to promote confidence by stronger supervision of banks by Bank Indonesia and tighter prudential controls on foreign exchange positions, capital positions, and lending limits; (3) to promote rationality, internationalization, and confidence in the insurance sector; (4) to broaden the range of financial services by promoting the development of private sector activity in capital markets, venture capital, and other services; (5) to develop money markets, both primary and secondary, and to improve the use of monetary policy instruments; and (6) to shift from relatively fixed to more flexible interest and exchange rates.

---

12. Cho and Khatkhate (1989) give a much less positive assessment of the Indonesian financial reforms in their comparative study of financial liberalization programs in five Asian and three Latin American countries. They state that the Indonesian reforms led to high and unstable interest rates, and a drying up of longer-term financing. It is true that real interest rates did move from negative to positive levels, but, as shown in table 5.2, real deposit rates reached a maximum of 12.8 percent in 1985 and were lower in other years. Loan rates were 3 to 4 percentage points higher, which was probably not out of line with returns on investment. The limitations on longer-term funds reflect a misperception of financial practice in Indonesia. Most banks extend loans for multi-year periods, but they renew and reprice them annually. Foreign financing is also very significant and is of a multi-year nature, often backed by deposit balances held in the foreign banks by the Indonesian borrower. Given the continuing high levels of private investment during this period, there is no indication of a serious lack of term financing.

Specific measures set forth in the four main regulatory packages known as PAKTO 27, PAKDES II, PAKMAR and PAKJAN 1990 are shown in annex II.

Concurrent with these regulatory changes was a shift to more flexible management of both the exchange rate and money market interest rates. Gradual, steady depreciation of the rupiah against the U.S. dollar, through a kind of crawling peg, was designed to give more certainty, thus discouraging unfounded speculation about a major devaluation. At the same time the movements in the premium on the foreign exchange swap facility were to be linked to the prevailing spread between rupiah and dollar time deposit interest rates. Regular weekly auctions by the central bank of one-week, four-week, and thirteen-week SBIs became more consistent with the prevailing interest rates in the secondary market, at least through 1989.

The most significant aspects of the deregulation packages were those that provided new opportunities for engaging in practically all aspects of financial activity. The Indonesian government opened the doors to new licensing of domestic banks. It also permitted the opening of branches in major cities for the foreign banks already operating in Indonesia, and the licensing of new joint ventures between foreign and Indonesian banks. The way was also opened for joint ventures in the areas of insurance, securities companies, and other types of financial institutions.

The PAKTO reforms, in particular, gave a stimulus to the development of the domestic short-term money markets. Restrictions on interbank borrowing were removed. Along with a reduction in the required reserve ratio to 2 percent of all bank third-party liabilities, all commercial banks were initially required to buy specified amounts of three- and six-month SBIs to offset 80 percent of the reduction in required bank reserves. After this initial forced sale at fixed interest rates, the banks were encouraged to begin using and trading these SBIs as instruments for managing their liquidity needs. Bank Indonesia appointed a group of fifteen banks and NBFIs as market makers and two as brokers in these money market instruments as a further encouragement to development of a secondary market. Also, over time, Bank Indonesia improved the management of its daily and weekly auctions of seven- to ninety-one-day SBIs so as to support the growth of the secondary market and let interest rates respond to changing liquidity conditions.

Another measure that helped to shift money market activity from overseas foreign exchange markets to domestic rupiah money market instruments was the imposition on May 1, 1989, of net foreign exchange open position limits on all banks equal to 25 percent of their total capital. This measure, along with a shift from same-day settlement to two-day settlement of foreign exchange transactions with Bank Indonesia and the more gradual adjustment of the exchange rate, seemed to have diminished short-term movements in and out of foreign exchange as the main means of liquidity management by the banks throughout 1989. Instead the banks shifted over to the domestic money markets where transactions averaged Rp 300 billion, or approximately US$150 million per day as of November 1989. The outstanding volume of money market instruments was probably in the range of Rp 5 to 6 trillion, with SBIs averaging Rp 3 trillion. For purposes of comparison, narrow money supply (M1) was about Rp 15 trillion, the total reserves of the deposit money banks were about RP 1.7 trillion, and required reserves about Rp 0.7 trillion.

In the first half of 1990 there was some retrogression in these generally favorable money market developments. The monetary authorities decided to try to push down domestic rupiah interest rates, possibly in part to offset the adverse public response to reduction in credit subsidies announced in January. Whatever the reason, Bank Indonesia pushed down the SBI auction rates and encouraged all banks to lower their deposit rates. This quickly led to an outflow of foreign exchange reserves from Bank Indonesia and reduced demand for SBIs. The banks switched from SBIs to foreign exchange and other financial assets for managing their excess liquidity. After several months of substantial foreign exchange outflow, Bank Indonesia retreated from its low interest rate policy, and as both SBI and other money market interest rates firmed, the foreign exchange outflow was reversed.

Capital markets in Indonesia had been very quiet following their initial activity in the late 1970s. However, in December 1987 (PAKDES I) the government took the first steps to activate the moribund capital market. Foreign investors were, for the first time, allowed to buy and sell on the exchange, up to 49 percent of issued capital.

(However, only eight of the twenty-four stocks listed on the exchange were not already majority-owned by foreign interests, thus the opportunities proved limited.) The limits on price movements on the exchange were also lifted; in addition, licensing requirements for brokers and dealers and other capital market supporting professions were set forth, as were clearer procedures for new issues, in regulations known as PAKDES I. The "Bursa Parallel," or over-the-counter market, was authorized.

PAKTO 27 (October 1988) included several more measures that encouraged capital market development: a withholding tax of 15 percent was imposed on interest income from time deposits, previously tax free, thus improving the competitiveness of debt and equity shares as assets, while financial institutions were allowed to issue shares to the public, enhancing the potential supply of shares.

In December 1988 (in the set of reforms known as PAKDES II), important capital market provisions were included: private securities exchanges could be set up, the priority of Danareksa, the state-owned securities and investment fund company, to underwrite 50 percent of all new issues was removed, and joint venture firms in newly authorized financial services (of major relevance are securities companies) were authorized with up to 85 percent foreign participation.[13] In November 1989 securities companies were given the right to seek licenses for underwriting.

These measures set the stage for rapid development in the Indonesian capital markets. A privately owned and managed Securities Exchange was set up in Surabaya in June 1989.[14] New broker and dealer firms were permitted. As of March 1990 there were 143 brokers and dealers. New securities companies sprang up (twenty-seven as

---

13. Danareksa is a state-owned financial enterprise set up by Presidential Decree in 1977. It operates the only authorized "open-end" investment funds in Indonesia; it has brokerage and dealing operations, and has been a dominant underwriter. Until December 1988 it had priority to buy (underwrite) 50 percent of all new issues. Before early 1990, the only other underwriters in Indonesia were the Indonesian Development Bank, BAPINDO, and the 12 NBFIs (joint banking ventures with both foreign and private ownership), which also have brokerage and dealing operations.

14. The Surabaya Stock Exchange enjoys cross-listing with the Jakarta Exchange and receives one-half the income of the Jakarta Exchange, even though its volume is relatively very small.

Table 5.4: Funds Raised Through New Issues of Bonds and Equity Shares on the Jakarta Exchange

	Issues (Rp millions)[b]		
Year	*Shares*	*Bonds*	*Total*
1977-1983	117,205	94,718	211,923
1984	13,951	60,000	73,951
1985	490	100,000	100,490
1986	769	150,000	150,769
1987	411	131,000	131,411
1988	57,481	320,000	377,481
1989	4,243,551	671,500	4,915,051
1990a	1,762,455	10,000	1,772,455

a. As of March 1990.
b. Includes stock splits, bonuses, and dividends.
Source: BAPEPAM, Laporan Bulanan, Maret 1990.

Table 5.5 Indonesian Capital Markets

Category	*As of end December 1987*	*As of end March 1990*
Market index	82.5	609.017
Number of broker/dealer	39	143
Number of Security Comp.	0	12
Number of firms listed:		
JSE	24	79
Bursa parallel	0	6
Number of bonds listed:		
JSE	16	47
Bursa parallel	0	3

Source: BAPEPAM, Laporan Bulanan, Maret 1990.

of March 1990), and competition in the underwriting business was opened up. The over-the-counter market, the Bursa Parallel, had its first listing in February 1989 (with six listings as of March 1990).

During 1989 the government under the dynamic leadership of the chairman of the state agency—the Capital Markets Executive Board—made a concentrated effort to encourage new issues after years of total inactivity. The response was outstanding. Table 5.5 compares the capital market activity at the end of 1987 with that as of March 1990. The number of companies listing shares and bonds increased from 24 (listing shares only) to 101 in total. The Jakarta Stock Index (JSE Composite Index) moved from 82.5 to 609.0 (see table 5.5).

The supply response has been significantly encouraged by the fact that a number of foreign-based investment funds designed for portfolio investment in Indonesia have been set up since late 1987.[15] The first "foreign-based country fund" (actually for Indonesia and Malaysia) bought shares at the Jakarta Stock Exchange in November 1988, initiating a surge of foreign interest, with domestic investors riding on the heels. In fact, acknowledging a benefit from the growing demand of foreign investors, the government issued a decree in September 1989 whereby foreign investors were allowed to buy 49 percent of the shares in any new primary issues and of the already listed shares in all sectors of the economy except private banking. This was a major policy change because formerly either or both the Foreign Investment Board (known as 3KPM) and the Ministry of Trade regulations restricted certain categories of firms from selling their shares to foreigners. This decree has ruled that so-called "joint ventures" (known as PMA firms) are domestic investors, and that they too may sell up to 49 percent of listed shares to other foreign investors.

There have been concerns expressed about the overly rapid growth of the stock exchange, the large number and value of new issues, the

---

15. These funds are foreign based and theoretically do not sell units to Indonesian investors. The government welcomes these funds and has made no effort to restrict them other than considering them as "foreign investors." At any rate the lack of any foreign exchange controls generally puts the operations of these funds beyond Indonesian supervisory authority. As of early 1990, there were over 16 such funds with substantial interest in Indonesian securities, besides the so-called regional funds.

high price to earnings ratios and expectations of capital gains on new issues, and the problems of clearance and settlement following trades. Official pronouncements have indicated that the Jakarta stock exchange will soon be turned over to private management, that Bapepam will thereafter concentrate its activities into that of a securities regulation agency. Bapepam and other Ministry of Finance officials are currently developing far-reaching regulations concerning security market activities, but it is all being done in the context of providing a framework for fair, competitive development.

Summary

Financial development in Indonesia has been characterized by two periods of rapid growth in bank deposits and assets, from 1968 to 1972 and from 1983 to the present day, and more recently by a broad opening up of opportunities for new entry and new activities that began in 1988 and is in the process of fundamentally changing the structure of the financial system. Financial development has been driven mainly by changes in government policies rather than changes in the rates of economic growth. The domestic financial system was also affected by the Dutch disease, along with other parts of the domestic economy from 1973–82, but it has largely recovered as a result of various policy changes since 1983.

The recorded growth of the domestic financial system has reflected partly real growth of holdings of financial assets and liabilities by Indonesian entities, and partly the repatriation of such holdings from abroad, as well as new inflows of investments by foreigners. We have no good way of estimating the relative magnitudes of these several parts. The offshore financial markets in Singapore and Hong Kong play much the same role for Indonesia that the urban, informal money markets play in other countries with repressed domestic financial systems, such as Korea and Taiwan, and have the same problem of lack of reliable information.[16] There is an important difference, however, in that the offshore markets are modern, sophisticated, relatively safe, and largely beyond the reach of the Indonesian monetary authorities. The

---

16. Neither the Singapore nor the Hong Kong governments will provide the Indonesian government with any information on the flows or stocks of financial assets transacted or held by Indonesian entities within their territories.

only policy instrument the authorities might have would be a change in the exchange rate, and the most likely change, a devaluation, rewards those who hold savings offshore.

Since 1971 the open capital account has permitted both Indonesians and foreigners to engage in easy substitution of foreign and domestic assets.[17] At times this has been destabilizing, but overall it has been a healthy influence. It has forced the Government to avoid fiscal deficits, and it has necessitated that monetary and other financial policies be formulated in ways that would not precipitate capital flight. Once the political decision was made to open up share portfolio investment to foreigners, there were no further constraints.

Three large devaluations, in 1978, 1983 and 1986, on the one hand, helped to keep domestic prices in line with world prices, but also contributed to continuing expectations of further large devaluations. While the latter two devaluations helped to reverse capital flight for a time, these beneficial effects were soon overtaken by fears of further devaluations, which were readily manifested in the volatile, uncontrolled interbank interest rates since 1983. The strong contractionary medicine, known as the "Sumarlin Shock," was administered in mid-1987, and the subsequent, more stable management of crawling-peg exchange rate adjustments, seem to have dampened fears of further big devaluations for the time being and permitted further actions to promote financial development.

On the question of the sequencing of liberalizing reforms, Indonesia followed the McKinnon-Edwards advocated sequence from 1966 to 1971, first correcting macro distortions and freeing up trade controls, then raising domestic interest rates, and finally removing foreign exchange controls. Beginning in 1973, the Indonesian authorities reimposed credit and interest rate controls and also introduced many protective, trade-distorting measures. The authorities maintained the open capital account, however, because the sizable inflow of oil earnings provided ample foreign exchange resources. The authorities did find it necessary to impose external borrowing limits

---

17. Foreigners were forbidden to invest in the portfolios of firms before the end of 1988, and were also restricted in many areas of direct investment in the early years of the 1980s.

on selected state-owned enterprises, especially Pertamina, the state-owned oil company.

In 1983, when oil revenues declined, Indonesian authorities chose not to reimpose foreign exchange controls, but decided instead to devalue, to tighten up on fiscal policy, and to free up domestic financial controls. In 1986, the authorities began to reduce trade distortions by reducing tariffs and import quotas, carrying out a second large devaluation and providing new incentives for non-oil exports. Since Indonesia already had an open capital account, the authorities chose to bring other domestic policies into conformity with the open economy model rather than closing down the foreign capital controls until the rest of the domestic policies were in order. As we have suggested, this resulted in some financial instability and periodic foreign exchange outflows, but strong corrective macro policies have kept these pressures from getting out of hand.

Since early 1989, the newly emerging money and capital markets have added substantially to the liquidity and attractiveness of domestic financial asset holdings. Greater confidence in exchange rate policies, along with attractive rupiah interest rates and restrictions on banks' net foreign exchange positions, have all led to increased demand for rupiah-denominated financial assets. As these markets broaden and deepen, they are likely to become more stable and able to absorb occasional shocks.

Bank Indonesia is actively trying to impart stability to the domestic money markets and the foreign exchange markets, and has enjoyed considerable success in recent years. There is still some tendency to try to hold money market interest rates and depreciation of the exchange rate below market clearing levels, resulting in the need to make abrupt adjustments when foreign exchange pressures become apparent. There is also still a need to improve the regulatory structure of the banking system and capital markets and assist the development of new institutions, such as private investment funds, pension funds, and insurance companies, all of which should provide greater continuity, stability, and growth to the financial system.

Annex I

Annex Table 5.1: Total Consolidated Bank Assets by Type of Bank
(at end of fiscal year; March 31) (Rp billions)

Group of banks	1980	1981	1982	1983	1984	1985	1986	1987	1988	Sept. 1989
State banks*	6,073	8,305	10,857	14,298	16,544	21,184	25,129	29,544	34,657	61,076
Private national banks	688	983	1,356	2,079	3,076	4,402	6,149	8,060	11,225	21,522
Regional development banks	266	402	488	589	769	1,004	1,174	1,252	1,558	2,516
Foreign banks	661	720	936	1,603	1,729	2,258	2,418	2,585	2,894	4,419
Total	7,688	10,410	13,637	18,569	22,118	28,848	34,870	41,441	50,334	89,533

(as percentage of total)

Group of banks	1980	1981	1982	1983	1984	1985	1986	1987	1988	Sept. 1989
State banks*	78.99	79.78	79.61	77.00	74.80	73.93	72.06	71.29	68.85	68.22
Private national banks	8.95	9.41	9.94	11.20	13.91	15.26	17.63	19.45	22.30	24.04
Regional development banks	3.46	3.86	3.58	3.17	3.48	3.48	3.37	3.02	3.10	2.81
Foreign banks	8.60	6.92	6.86	8.63	7.82	7.83	6.93	6.21	5.75	1.93
Total	100.00	100.00	100.00	100.00	100.00	100.00	100.00	100.00	100.00	100.00

* Includes BAPINDO and excludes BTN.
Source: Bank Indonesia, Annual Report, 1980/81–1988/89.

Annex Table 5.2: Interest Rates on Jakarta Interbank Call Money
(*interest rates: percent per annum*)

Year/month	1983			1984			1985			1986			1987			1988			1989		
	Lowest	Highest	Weighted average	Lowest	Highest	Weighted average	Lowest	Highest	Weighted average	Lowest	Highest	Weighted average	Lowest	Highest	Weighted average	Lowest	Highest	Weighted average	Lowest	Highest	Weighted average
January	3.50	28.80	12.90	6.00	90.00	18.98	1.50	25.00	9.95	10.50	23.00	13.79	9.00	16.50	14.50	11.00	14.50	12.28	11.00	21.75	14.07
February	15.00	22.00	16.95	14.50	31.00	19.33	7.00	25.00	9.58	10.50	18.00	12.12	12.00	23.00	16.66	11.00	19.00	13.55	12.00	25.00	13.74
March	16.00	25.00	17.19	17.20	19.16	18.21	8.50	21.00	12.16	10.80	16.50	12.65	12.50	16.87	14.20	11.00	21.00	14.47	10.00	21.00	13.66
April	15.00	36.00	18.55	12.00	22.00	16.47	8.00	24.50	13.23	13.25	20.00	15.22	12.50	17.00	13.65	13.00	20.00	14.34	9.50	20.50	13.30
May	9.00	28.80	15.51	11.75	20.00	14.05	9.50	17.00	12.16	11.00	19.00	14.62	12.00	17.00	13.58	11.25	26.00	15.59	7.00	18.50	11.08
June	7.00	16.00	9.03	14.50	21.00	17.37	7.50	17.00	10.68	11.50	17.00	13.55	12.75	20.00	15.14	12.50	18.75	14.05	10.00	16.50	12.25
July	7.00	18.00	8.03	14.00	25.00	16.48	1.50	16.75	9.24	11.50	16.00	12.75	16.00	37.00	23.50	12.00	18.50	14.83	8.50	19.00	12.85
August	3.50	18.00	10.02	13.00	21.00	16.77	5.50	12.50	6.86	11.00	14.00	12.39	10.75	46.50	16.25	12.00	21.50	15.03	8.00	18.00	12.01
September	7.00	19.00	13.03	16.75	37.00	22.58	7.50	12.50	8.34	11.00	16.00	12.22	10.00	21.00	13.25	12.50	19.00	15.08	8.50	17.00	12.02
October	9.00	16.50	13.16	20.00	90.00	46.80	8.00	15.75	10.24	11.00	19.00	12.87	9.00	15.50	11.77	13.50	28.00	17.94	8.00	18.00	12.02
November	10.00	16.50	13.03	8.00	45.00	14.71	9.00	13.00	9.85	11.00	17.00	12.55	9.50	13.00	11.75	10.00	40.00	18.11	8.25	21.00	12.01
December	12.50	20.50	14.52	7.00	23.00	9.62	10.00	14.50	11.45	11.50	23.00	14.75	10.00	15.00	12.18	10.00	22.00	14.70	7.50	12.50	12.23

Source: Bank Indonesia, *Weekly Report*, various issues.

Annex Table 5.3: Indonesia Financial Assets
(rupiah billions: end-of-year data)

	1969	1972	1977	1982	1987	1988	Sept. 1989
Total assets of financial institutions							
1. Bank Indonesia[1]	417	675	13,703	113,706	35,554	42,445	38,880
2. Deposit money banks (DMBs) A[a,1]	291	983	4,030	15,922	48,202	63,284	85,929
a. National foreign exchange banks	217	735	3,199	12,724	37,499	50,051	67,409
b. Foreign banks	37	126	370	1,172	2,779	3,215	4,626
c. Development banks	7	66	288	1,336	3,699	5,046	6,384
d. Nat. non-foreign exchange banks	30	57	172	690	4,225	4,972	7,510
3. Deposit money banks B[b,1]	211	834	3,349	12,180	37,941	49,812	71,656
4. State Savings Bank (BTN)[1]	n.a.	n.a.	30	451	1,883	2,272	2,704
5. Nonbank financial institutions[2]	n.a.	n.a.	125	805	2,497	3,063	2,949
6. Insurance companies[2]	n.a.	n.a.	n.a.	587	3,457	3,906	n.a.
a. Life insurance	n.a.	n.a.	n.a.	173	677	799	n.a.
b. Loss insurance	n.a.	n.a.	n.a.	355	1,013	844	n.a.
c. Social insurance	n.a.	n.a.	n.a.	59	1,768	1,930	n.a.
7. Leasing companies[2]	n.a.	n.a.	31	73	1,626	1,751	n.a.
8. Pension funds[2]							
a. TASPEN	n.a.	n.a.	n.a.	27	7,920	1,105	n.a.
b. Other[c]	n.a.	n.a.	n.a.	n.a.	n.a.	224	n.a.
9. Securities[3]							
a. Listed bonds[d]	n.a.	n.a.	n.a.	n.a.	536	856	1,417
b. Listed equity shares[d]	n.a.	n.a.	3	96	133	190	794
10. Total financial assets (A)/GDP[e]	26.04%	31.07%	35.29%	51.09%	76.13%	85.44%	n.a.
11. Total financial assets (B)/GDP[f]	23.10%	28.27%	31.96%	45.10%	67.89%	75.78%	n.a.
12. Total financial assets (C)/GDP[g]	10.69%	18.41%	20.61%	29.15%	47.58%	55.00%	n.a.

Annex Table 5.3: Indonesia Financial Assets *(continued)*
(rupiah billions: end-of-year data)

	1969	1972	1977	1982	1987	1988	Sept. 1989
Other data							
13. Bank Indonesia[1]							
a. Gold and foreign assets	65	239	1,057	3,730	13,442	11,724	9,862
b. Claims on DMBs	80	149	681	3,742	10,261	13,472	14,272
14. DMBs[1]							
a. Foreign assets	24	203	578	4,013	7,806	8,397	8,156
b. Foreign liabilities[h]	57	222	457	2,403	5,415	7,683	7,200
15. GDP current prices[4]	2,718	5,339	20,469	62,476	124,539	139,452	159,977

n.a. = not available

Notes: a. Based on consolidated balance sheets.

      b. Equivalent of line (2) minus line (13.b).

      c. Only partial data available.

      d. Values at initial offerings.

      e. Total financial assets = Sum of lines 1, 2, 4, 5, 6, 7, 8, 9, and GDP is from line 15.

      f. Total financial assets = Same as footnote (e) minus line (13.b) and GDP is from line 15.

      g. Total financial assets = Same as footnote (e) minus line 1. GDP is from line 15.

      h. Since 1983, total foreign exchange liabilities are the sum of foreign currency deposits and foreign liabilities from BI Monthly Report, table 1.g.

Sources: 1. Bank Indonesia, *Indonesian Financial Statistics*, various issues.

      2. Ministry of Finance—Directorate of Financial Institutions and Accountancy.

      3. Capital Market Executive Agency, *Fact Book of the Indonesian Capital Market—Statistical Supplement*, various issues.

      4. Central Bureau of Statistics, *Indonesian Statistics*, various issues.

Annex II

DEREGULATION PACKAGES: OCTOBER 1988–MARCH 1989

PAKTO 27 (October 1988)
PAKDES II (December 1988)
PAKMAR (March 1989)
PAKJAN (January 1990)
PAKTO 27 (October 1988)

A. Banks

1. New Entry Permitted

Capital Requirements:

- Wholly owned by Indonesian nationals: General banks: Rp 10 billion Rural banks: Rp 50 million.
- Up to 85 percent owned by foreign banks (Joint Ventures) General banks: Rp 50 billion.
- Branches of Foreign Banks in Indonesia: No new entry
- NBFIs: No new entry.

Other Requirements:

- New Joint Ventures: Joint ownership by domestic banks and foreign banks (maximum of 85 percent of shares by foreign partner).
- Domestic bank must be classified "sound" 20 of last 24 months.
- Location restricted to 7 major cities.
- Within 12 months, outstanding export credits must equal 50 percent of total credits outstanding.

Foreign bank partner must:

- Have representative office in Indonesia;

- Be reputable in country of origin;
- Be from country with reciprocity agreement with Indonesia.

2. *New Branches*

- Banks wholly owned by Indonesian nationals:
  Must have 20-months "sound" classification of last 24 months.
  Can open branches anywhere in Indonesia.
- NBFIs:
  Must have 20-months "sound" classification of last 24 months.
  Can open one branch only in each of 7 major cities.
- Existing Foreign Bank Branches in Indonesia:
  Must be classified as sound.
  Can open one sub-branch only in each of 7 major cities.
  Within 12 months, outstanding export credits must equal 50 percent of total credits outstanding.
- Rural banks:
  No restriction on branch office in same district as head office.
  Must be located outside Jakarta, provincial capitals and municipalities; otherwise must move or become a General Bank (capital at RP 10 billion).

3. *Foreign Exchange Banks*

- Branches of existing Foreign Exchange Banks automatically have right to deal in foreign exchange.
- Domestic non-foreign exchange banks may deal in foreign exchange if:
  Classified "sound" 20 of last 24 months.
  Total assets greater than Rp 100 billion.

4. *Certificates of Deposit*

- All banks, except rural banks, and NBFIs can issue certificates of deposit.
  (RP1 million & 30-day minimum.)

B. Money Changers

Licenses issued for unlimited period; no specific restrictions on entry.

C. Other Measures

1. State enterprises may put 50 percent of deposits with private national banks, development banks and NBFIs, up to 20 in one single bank.
2. Maximum legal lending limits were imposed on banks and NBFIs (as percentage of lender's capital):
   20 percent to a single borrower.
   50 percent to a group of borrowers.
   Various restrictions on borrowing by Board of Commissioners, shareholders, other affiliates, and staff.
3. Reserve requirements on banks lowered from a nominal 15 percent to 2 percent of liabilities to third parties. Lagged reserve accounting adopted. 3-month and 6-month PAKTO SBIs issued.
4. Maximum limit on interbank borrowing eliminated.
5. SBI maturities extended from only 7 days up to 6 months. Auction process strengthened.
6. Final withholding tax of 15 percent imposed on the interest of time deposits. Exemption allowed for certain "savings" schemes. Anonymity preserved.
7. Banks and NBFIs can issue new shares on capital market.
8. Swap premium of BI made to reflect market conditions. swap maturity lengthened.
9. Two day settlement for foreign exchange transactions by BI.

PAKDES II (December 1988)

1. Allows for establishment of private securities exchanges. Securities can be traded on more than one securities exchange.
2. Priority of Danareksa to purchase 50 percent of new issues is eliminated. Simple "priority" is retained.
3. Permits licensing of wholly-owned Indonesian firms and joint ventures in the financial service activities shown in (4) with up

to 85 percent foreign capital participation. Existing firms must adjust within 2 years.

4. Licensing of single and multi-activity firms in:
   a. Leasing Companies
   b. Venture Capital
   c. Securities Trading
   d. Factoring
   e. Consumer Finance
   f. Credit Card
5. Banks permitted to set up subsidiaries for 4(a) and (b), and to engage in (d) through (f) without separate license. Must obtain license for (c).
6. Capital Requirements for Single Activity:
   - Wholly owned by Indonesians:
     Factoring, Securities Trading, Credit Card and Consumer Finance: Rp 2 billion
     Leasing, Venture capital: Rp 3 billion
   - Joint Ventures:
     Factoring, Securities Trading, Credit Card and Consumer Finance: Rp 8 billion
     Leasing, Venture Capital: Rp 10 billion
7. Capital Requirements for Multi-Activity:
   - Wholly owned by Indonesians: Rp 5 billion
   - Joint Ventures: Rp 15 billion
8. Regulations for Insurance:
   a. Joint Ventures allowed; up to 80 percent foreign share.
   b. Regulations set forth for solvency, admitted assets, retention ratios.
   c. Supervision strengthened.

PAKMAR (March 1989)

1. Clarifies and interprets PAKTO 27 concerning:
   a. Licensing mergers of banks.
   b. Definition of "Capital" and "Groups" used to calculate lending limits. "Exempted credits" defined.
   c. Definition of "Export Credits" used in requirements for foreign and joint venture bank operations.

    d. Shares of foreign banks in joint ventures.

2. Eliminates ceiling on offshore loans by banks and NBFIs.
3. Banks and NBFIs are restricted to maximum net open position equal to 25 percent of capital.
4. Announcement of schedule for removal of subsidy on interest rates on export credits within the year.
5. Exempts "existing" rural banks from PAKTO provisions.
6. Eliminates existing requirement that medium- and long-term bank loans must be approved by Bank Indonesia.
7. Allows BAPINDO and NBFIs to hold all types of equity.
8. Allows general banks to hold equity in financial activities with certain limits; can hold equity in other firms only with approval of the Minister of Finance.
9. Reaffirms underwriting authority to NBFIs and BAPINDO. Prohibits general banks from underwriting.

PAKJAN 1990

1. Abolition of Bank Indonesia subsidized refinancing facilities, which gave credit at (below market) interest rates from 3 percent to 14.5 percent to banks, which then lent to "priority" sectors at below market interest rates. Insurance was also provided by ASKRINDO, a government-owned agency, for much of this credit at low cost, partially with BI support.
2. PAKJAN 1990 abolished these facilities except for the following: to BULOG for certain food stocks, investment credit for development banks, NBFIs and Estates, working credits for farmers, and certain credits for cooperatives. However, interest rates on these were increased at least to near-market levels and the insurance scheme was made voluntary and at market rates.
3. National banks were required within one year to allocate a minimum of 20 percent of loan portfolio to small business, defined as having assets of less than Rp 600 million, excluding land, and each loan cannot exceed Rp 200 million. Failure to do this allocation would affect "soundness of the bank."

Annex III

GRAPHS

Graph 5.1: Ratio of Financial Assets to GDP

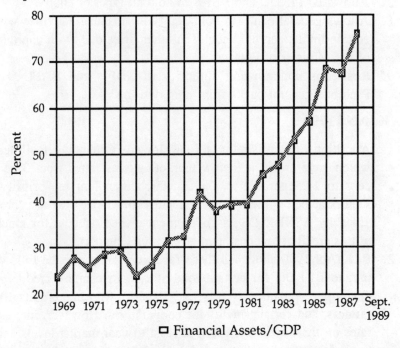

□ Financial Assets/GDP

Source: Appendix table 5.1, line 11.

Graph 5.2: Ratio of Financial Assets to GDP by Selected Categories

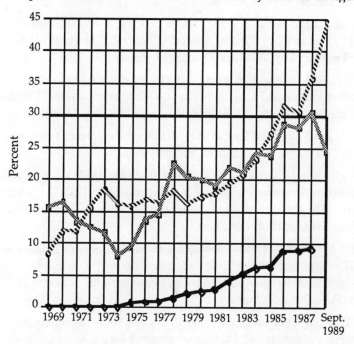

□ BI Asset/GDP   ○ DMBs Asset/GDP   ◆ Other Financial Asset/GDP

Source: Appendix table 5.1, line 11.

Bibliography

Alexander, Jennifer, and Paul Alexander (1986). "Finance and Credit in a Rural Javanese Market: An Anthropological Perspective." Paper presented at a Conference on Indonesian Financial Development, August.

Bank Indonesia, *Annual Reports*, various.

Binhadi, B. and Paul Meek (1988). "Implementing Monetary Policy in Indonesia." Chapter IV of *Visiting Specialist Papers*, 17th Seanza Central Banking Course, Sydney, Australia. October/November.

Cho, Yoon Je, and Deena Khatkhate (1989). "Lessons from Financial Liberalization in Asia and Latin America—A Comparative Study." World Bank *Discussion Paper*, No. 50, Washington, D.C.: The World Bank.

Cole, David C., and Yung Chul Park (1983). *Financial Development in Korea, 1945-1978*. Cambridge, MA: Harvard University Press.

Cole, David C., Yung Chul Park, and Betty F. Slade (1989). "Adapting Monetary Policy Instruments: Indonesian Experience." HIID Discussion Paper, No. 310, Cambridge, MA: Harvard Institute for International Development, Harvard University, June.

Cole, David C., Yung Chul Park, and Betty F. Slade (1990). "Indonesian Financial Development." Paper presented at the Conference on Indonesia in the 1980s, at Australian National University, December 1989, issued as HIID Discussion Paper No. 336. April.

Cole, David C., Yung Chul Park, and Betty F. Slade (1990). "Development of Money Markets in Indonesia." Draft paper prepared for the Research Project on Money Markets in Asia, organized by the Program on International Financial Systems of the Harvard Law School and the Harvard Institute for International Development, at Harvard University, Cambridge, MA. July.

Dickie, Robert B. (1981). "Development of Third World Securities Markets: An Analysis of General Principles and a Case Study of the Indonesian Market." In *Law and Policy in International Business*, Vol. 13, 1981.

Edwards, Sebastian (1984a). "The Order of Liberalization of the External Sector in Developing Countries." In *Princeton Essays in International Finance* No. 156, Princeton, N.J.: Princeton University Press. December.

_____ (1984). "The Order of Liberalization of the Balance of Payments: Should the Current Account Be Opened Up First?" Staff Working Papers No. 710, Washington, D.C.: World Bank.

Frenkel, Jacob A. (1982). "The Order of Economic Liberalization: A Comment." In K. Brunner and A.H. Meltzer, eds., *Economic Policy in a World of Change*. Amsterdam: North Holland.

McKinnon, Ronald I. (1988). "Financial Liberalization and Economic Development: A Reassessment of Interest-Rate Policies in Asia and Latin America." San Francisco, CA: International Center for Economic Growth.

_____ (1988). "Financial Liberalization in Retrospect: Interest Rate Policies in LDCs." In *The State of Development Economics*. New York: Basil Blackwell.

Organization for Economic Cooperation and Development (1989). *On the Sequencing of Structural Reforms*. In OECD Dept. of Economics and Statistics Working Papers No. 70. OECD, Paris.

Patten, Richard and Jay Rosengard (1989). "Progress with Profits: The Development of Rural Banking in Indonesia." Cambridge, MA: Harvard Institute for International Development. Unpublished.

Shaw, Edward S. (1973). *Financial Deepening in Economic Development*. New York City: Oxford University Press.

Sundararjan, V. and Lazaros, Molho (1987). "Financial Reform and Monetary Control in Indonesia." Presented at a conference sponsored by the Federal Reserve Bank of San Francisco, September 23-25.

Suwidjana, Njoman (1984). "Jakarta Dollar Market: A Case of Financial Development in ASEAN." Institute of Southeast Asian Studies, Occasional Paper No. 76.

World Bank (1989). *World Development Report 1989*. New York City: Oxford University Press.

6

FINANCIAL REFORM IN CHILE: LESSONS IN REGULATION AND DEREGULATION

Hernan Cortés-Douglas

Introduction

Financial sector reform in Chile was implemented in a context of far-reaching structural reforms. As such, the Chilean experience is a most interesting and complex laboratory case study. Not only because of the problems, mistakes, omissions, and dangers in the implementation of the reforms involved in the transition from a severely repressed economy and financial sector to a largely free market economy, but also because of the pioneering bank and enterprise restructuring used to deal with the crisis of 1982 and the important long-run transformation of the structure of the economy and the financial system.

Most accounts of the Chilean financial reform have stressed the errors and omissions in the process of economic reform. Less emphasis has been placed on the fact that in spite of serious errors and omissions during the implementation of reforms, the structure of the economy and of the financial sector changed dramatically, including a sophisticated banking legislation and a potentially important source of long-term financing.

The most important errors were the absence of prudential regulation and the inconsistencies of financial policies on the one hand and, on the other, the implicit subsidy to foreign exchange risk generated by the repeated pronouncements of the authorities about the nominal fixation of the exchange rate in spite of the evident symptoms of cumulative financial and macroeconomic disequilibrium.

These errors were compounded by the rise in 1980 and 1981 of a generalized perception of a permanent boom, with statements of government authorities helping to feed it. Corporations and individuals became highly overleveraged, and banks' portfolios turned extremely risky. Within this financial context, external shocks in the form of a sevenfold increase in real international interest rates in 1981 and the subsequent drop in terms of trade triggered the worst crisis since the 1930s.

On the macroeconomic side, generalized indexing, particularly of wages, became incompatible with the level of inflation and the fixed exchange rate, aggravating the crisis via reduced profits and decreased competitiveness. Although some authors have put the bulk of the blame on this particular macroeconomic disequilibrium, a growing consensus has emerged to give the key role in the crisis to the errors in the financial sector.

The trigger to the financial collapse of 1982 was the sequence of external shocks in the form of the steep rise in interest rates in 1981 and the drastic withdrawal of foreign credit in 1982, in the context of important overborrowing by private corporations and individuals. The larger conglomerates—*grupos*—tried to evade new and stringent regulations that limited the relationship between *grupo*-owned banks and the same *grupo*-owned corporations. Their deceiving of investors in the securities markets led to intervention of their banks, cascading to their corporations in January 1983. Chaos is the best word to describe the economic scenario at that date, after real GDP had fallen 14 percent the previous year and the government, committed to private enterprise development, had taken over 60 percent of the banking system!

Four years later, stability had been restored, in a consistent legal and regulatory framework. Spreads in the banking sector fell from 11.2 percent in 1983—as they were used to compensating portfolio losses associated with nonperforming loans—to 5.9 percent in 1987. Interest rates in real terms went from 40 percent per year in 1981–82 to 7.7 percent in 1987 and return on equity, negative in 1982, recovered to 13.7 percent per year in 1987. Real GDP grew steadily at an average rate of over 5 percent per year in 1984–87, and at a higher rate since.

The mechanisms used to restructure the banking system were debt reschedulings and foreign exchange subsidies to increase the repayment capacity of borrowers, sale of banks' nonperforming assets to the central bank, and direct recapitalization of banks and their subsequent sale to small shareholders (popular capitalism) in order to restore the banks' capital base. Increased transparency, the refocusing of supervision on the scrutiny of the banks' loan portfolio, and a sophisticated banking legislation completed the sector's rehabilitation.

The new financial structure includes an important segment of private pension funds, a dynamic financial sector where financial liabilities grew from 4.6 percent of GDP in 1970 to 94.5 percent in 1988 (Perez 1988), and an important growth of the equity market, from 30 billion in 1970 to 1,700 billion in 1988 (in pesos of constant purchasing power). Most importantly perhaps was a redefinition and clarification of the role of government in the financial sector, incorporated in the Banking Law of 1986, where prudential regulation is emphasized. These results were not obtained costlessly. The rehabilitation of the banking system required enormous resources from the central bank, nearing 25 percent of GDP, according to some estimates.

Initial Conditions

The effects of the reforms implemented after the coup of September 1973, and particularly the financial reform, can only be understood after a discussion of the extent of the distortions, disequilibria, and degree of excessive regulation of the economy and the financial sector as of 1973. Some of these disequilibria generated results that are key elements to explain the coup itself.

For the purposes of this paper three areas of important initial disequilibria will be distinguished. These areas are discussed in the following paragraphs.

The Oversized Public Sector

The public sector deficit reached 30 percent of GDP in 1973. In addition, through nationalization, expropriation, and seizures by unions, the number of industrial enterprises controlled by the government increased from 46 in 1970 to 507 in 1973, and all domestic banks became government controlled. Sixty percent of irrigated land had been expropriated by 1973, the government compensating only 10 percent of its commercial value. Furthermore, Chile's main export, copper, which at the time represented 80 percent of total exports, was nationalized without indemnification.[1]

The political consequences were foreseeable. The economic consequences were uncertainty, unrest, and strife in all sectors; the virtual paralysis of agriculture; unprecedented levels of inflation—as all this was financed by printing money; acute shortages; black markets; and rationing of all goods. The sweeping crowding out of the private sector led to the undercapitalization of virtually all sectors. This undercapitalization continued in the first years of the Pinochet regime, and became a key ingredient in the developments of the financial sector.

Inflation and Price and Exchange Controls

The combination of very high rates of monetary expansion with comprehensive and discriminatory price controls resulted in widespread and unprecedented shortages and very high and also unprecedented rates of inflation (over 500 percent in 1973). The government reacted via rationing, which in turn led to more unrest and strife, this time approaching class struggle. An important consequence was the abysmal distortion of relative prices, compounded by exchange rate distortions—a maze of multiple exchange rates—and the staggeringly high level of the black market exchange rate.[2]

Protectionism and Regulation of Markets

The high level of protectionism and excessive regulation of industry, commerce, transportation, and finance started before the Allende

---

1. The Frei administration bought 51 percent of the large copper mines owned by American companies. President Allende obtained Congress' approval to nationalize the mines, but deducted the "excess" profits obtained by foreign companies. This meant expropriation. The military government provided compensation later.

2. An example may clarify the extent of the latter distortions. In 1980 a private research institute I headed rented a large house as headquarters. The rent was US$60,000 per year. In 1973, the house had been bought by their present owners—members of a Catholic congregation—for US$7,000.

administration—essentially beginning in the 1930s, increasing through time, and being exacerbated between 1971 and 1973. Beyond the efficiency aspects, its most important consequences—from the standpoint of this paper—were the accumulation of excess demand for durable goods and for credit.

Decades of import prohibition created increasingly cumulative excess demands for good quality durable goods—the existing domestic ones being of very low quality and very expensive because of the monopolies created by protectionist policies. Decades of financial repression had similar effects: cumulative excess demands for credit at the individual and business levels, made worse by the severe undercapitalization of private businesses in the years immediately prior to 1973. Trade liberalization and financial liberalization unleashed these excess demands, the former feeding back into the latter and resulting in an explosion of credit.

An important part of the generalized overborrowing by corporations and individuals can be attributed to these excess demands for credit and durable goods and to the severe decapitalization of the private sector when the threat of expropriation was real. The high level of interest rates in 1975–78 is also, in part, a result of these latent disequilibria.

External Shocks, Reforms, and Stabilization

Thirty days after the coup, most price controls were eliminated (from over 3,000 items to 33), and the exchange rate was dramatically increased and essentially unified. As a consequence prices had a once-and-for-all jump in October 1973, with the result of wiping out the prevailing excess supply of money. Unfortunately, this effect was short lived, as the government increased the supply of money further.[3] The military government did return all enterprises that were illegally seized by the previous administration.

Reforms were scarce before 1975. In the first eighteen months of the military regime, no major structural reform beyond price liberalization was implemented. High terms of trade seem to have been opium to decisionmakers and prevented the reformers within the gov-

---

3. Refer to Solimano and Corbo, 1991.

ernment to have their advice heeded. The key economic posts were occupied by the military until April 1975, when the so-called "Chicago Boys" were promoted to these positions, fundamentally as a consequence of the crisis triggered by the precipitous drop in the price of copper in late 1974. After that date reforms were applied as in a blitzkrieg.

The crisis of 1975 started with the precipitous fall of the price of copper by nearly two-thirds late in 1974. To cope with this external imbalance—copper comprised 90 percent of total exports at the time—steep depreciations of the exchange rate were implemented. In the five-month period between December 1974 and April 1975, the exchange rate rose by 163 percent, as opposed to only 84 percent in the previous five months. The sharp increase in the rate of inflation in early 1975 appears to have resulted from this increase. The doubling of the rate of devaluation led to a 70 percent increase in the rate of inflation, with a very short lag.

On the fiscal side, an across-the-board reduction in public sector spending of 15 percent in domestic currency and 25 percent in foreign currency, as well as a 10 percent real increase in the income tax, full indexation of the tax system, and other tax reforms, reduced the fiscal deficit from 10.3 percent of GDP in 1974 to 3.1 percent in 1975 (in spite of a fall in real GDP of 12.9 percent in 1975). The local currency deficit of 5.5 percent of GDP in 1974 turned into a 1.2 percent surplus in 1975.

The effect on the balance of payments was also dramatic: the deficit for 1975, which was estimated by the monetary authorities at US$1,200 million at the beginning of the year, was reduced to $200 million-plus at the end of the year.

Although the impact of the policy measures was concentrated in a few quarters in 1975 and 1976, the combination of accelerated devaluation and credit and fiscal tightening led to a real reduction in expenditures of significant size, creating a massive reduction in output and an unprecedented increase in unemployment. The disequilibrium initiated in early 1975 did not disappear until the end of 1977.[4] The current account bore the burden as the only means of reestablishing

---

4. See Sjaastad and Cortés-Douglas, 1978.

equilibrium, which was accomplished in three years. The sharp fall in real GDP in 1975 was followed by a recouping of 3.5 percent in 1976 and 9.9 percent in 1977. By 1978 the real level of GDP was higher than the 1974 level.

Despite the critical situation of the economy, structural reforms, rather than being postponed, were accelerated. A brief description of the trade reform and the reform of public enterprises follows. Real sector deregulation, tax reforms, and other reforms will not be discussed because, although important, they have less direct effect on the results of financial reform.[5] This section ends with a discussion of the priority of reforms versus stabilization, and the postponement of anti-inflationary actions until 1977. This is crucial to understanding the results of financial reform.

Table 6.1: Trade Reform
(number of items subject to each tariff level)

Tariff Rates (percent)	January 1974	January 1975	February 1976	August 1977	July 1979
220-750	416	0	0	0	0
125-215	911	0	0	0	0
60-120	2,493	1,923	394	0	0
35-55	959	2,394	2,968	78	0
25-30	223	585	696	1,469	0
15-20	142	167	366	1,817	0
10	42	20	24	600	4,273
0-5	39	36	42	12	0
Average Nominal Tariff	105	57	44	15	10
Modal Tariff	90	55	50	13	10

Source: Cauas and de la Caudra, in Sjaastad and Cortés-Douglas, eds., (1981 pp. 230–31).

5.   See Edwards and Edwards (1986) for a fuller treatment.

Trade Reform

At the end of 1973, tariff and nontariff restrictions had reached record levels. The average nominal tariff at the end of 1973 was 105 percent, the modal tariff, 90 percent. Half the items had duties in excess of 80 percent. Only 4 percent of the items had tariffs lower than 25 percent.

In addition to tariffs, 187 items were prohibited and 2,872 items required previous deposits of 10,000 percent at the central bank during 90 days, which made importation prohibitive. Discretionary approval was a prerequisite for 2,278 items (a study concluded that this was used to prohibit the importation of 159 items). In summary, through these mechanisms more than 60 percent of imports were directly or indirectly prohibited. An estimate of the uniform tariff equivalent was calculated by Sjaastad to be 90 percent—similar to the modal tariff.[6]

Trade reform started in January 1975, eliminating tariffs above 120 percent and reducing the modal tariff from 90 to 55 percent (see table 6.1). By July 1979, a uniform tariff of 10 percent had been achieved.

The above description, and particularly the fact that 60 percent of the import items were effectively prohibited, strongly indicates the extent of the excess demand for these prohibited foreign goods, particularly cars, TV sets, and other durable goods. This situation had its origin in the Great Depression and continued until 1975, with the exception of a brief liberalization (1959–62) during the Alessandri administration. In synthesis, the Chilean economy had practically four decades of excess demand accumulation.

Public Enterprises: Privatization and Self-Financing

Public sector enterprises were not only drastically reduced in number but, as importantly, the remaining ones—essentially large enterprises in the mining, communication, and energy sectors—had to self-finance their projects under strict guidelines and without government guarantee.

---

6. In Sjaastad and Cortés-Douglas, 1981.

PRIVATIZATION. As of 1973, the government controlled 504 firms and all domestic banks. Its control over the nonagricultural sectors corresponded to the following shares (in percent):

Financial sector	85
Mining	85
Transport	70
Communication	70
Industry	40

Out of the 504 firms controlled by the government, 259 had been confiscated. In 1974 the military government returned 202 of them to their owners and by 1979 all of them had been returned.

In addition, between 1974 and 1976, ninety-nine firms were privatized, reaching a total of 135 by 1982, including many firms that had traditionally been government owned since the late 1940s. Thus in 1981 the government's share in industry had dropped to 12 percent; in transport, to 21 percent; and in the financial sector, to 28 percent (as this was the size of the only government bank—Banco del Estado—which had been government owned since its inception).[7]

The way firms were privatized was important for the outcome of financial reform. They were sold on credit with 10 to 40 percent down and the rest with ten year indexed loans at 10 percent real interest rate (except for banks, where two-year loans were used). Arellano (1983) criticizes the differential access to credit and nonenforced legislation against ownership concentration, which led to an impressive growth of new aggressive conglomerates—*grupos economicos*. The *grupos* bought banks on credit, and used loans from their banks to buy privatized firms, especially in the export and financial sectors. These new *grupos* borrowed heavily to finance down payments on privatized enterprises and banks. As firms were extremely undercapitalized, they also borrowed to finance important investments and restructuring expenditures—the latter made necessary by trade reform. By 1979 the *grupos* controlled 135 of the 250 largest private corporations.[8] A siz-

---

7. See Hachette and Lüders, 1988. As of 1981, both Mining and Communication remained largely in the hands of the state.

8. See Dahse, 1979.

able privatization process resulted in the creation of large and highly indebted enterprises.

SELF-FINANCING BY PUBLIC ENTERPRISES. As part of the drive to reduce the size of the government and give the private sector a key role in development, public enterprises were required to follow strict self-financing guidelines. These measures also achieved the short-run objective of first reducing the public sector deficit and then generating a surplus.

In addition, public sector projects were required to show a 17 percent rate of social return (á la Harberger), using sophisticated project evaluation methodologies, implemented by the Planning Office (ODEPLAN).

In synthesis, the conditions of privatization, the acute degree to which most firms were undercapitalized, and the drive for self-financing by public enterprises raised significantly the demand for credit during this period.

The Battle Against Inflation

An important feature of the macroeconomic scenario during the reform years was that priority was given to structural reforms over stabilization and control of inflation. It appears that authorities thought that by eliminating the public sector deficit, which they did, inflation would disappear. Inflation in both 1974 and 1975, however, neared 400 percent per year despite the forceful reduction of public sector deficit. Only late in 1976, a clear anti-inflationary program emerged.

The key issue is that financial reform started in a context of very high levels of inflation, which added dangerous obstacles to the reform process. As shown below, the combination of very high inflation and high reserve requirements significantly raised the cost of credit. The nominal fixing of the exchange rate—the instrument used for anti-inflationary purposes—in the context of the external and internal overborrowing in 1981 and in the absence of prudential regulation, had important effects in the transition period and in the depth of the crisis.

Had a clear anti-inflationary program—including a monetary reform and expectations policy—been implemented in 1975, it is conceivable that the severe macroeconomic hardship and financial distress of the early 1980s could have been avoided.[9]

The Anatomy of the Chilean Financial Reform

The central guidelines for financial reform were essentially the same as the reforms in other markets:

- Rely mainly on the private sector
- Foster competitive markets
- Eliminate discrimination among economic agents
- Eliminate controls and distortions.

Accordingly, selective credit controls, credit ceilings, and interest rate controls were eliminated; and reserve requirements and controls on capital movements were reduced. Universal banking was also fostered, allowing free entry into most financial operations to all intermediaries and imposing similar regulation procedures on all financial institutions.

Contrary to the uniform policy view in other markets, contradictory approaches were present with respect to the liberalization of the financial sector, though the free banking approach predominated in the crucial years of the reform.[10]

Privatization and Entry into the Financial System

In 1974, all domestic banks, excepting the Banco del Estado, were privatized, reverting the ownership situation to the pre-Allende years.

Until 1975, the only foreign bank was Citibank. This changed when foreign banks were allowed entry starting in 1976. However, the superintendent was reluctant to allow the number of domestic banks to increase. In 1981—the pre-crisis year—the financial system included one government bank, twenty-two private banks owned by Chileans, eighteen foreign banks, and thirteen finance companies. In contrast, in 1973 there were eighteen government banks and one foreign bank.

---

9. See Cortés-Douglas, 1975.
10. See de la Cuadra and Valdés, 1989.

Interest Rates and Indexing

In May 1975, indexing was allowed in all financial operations of one year or longer. In July 1976 it was extended to operations of 90 days or longer. In May 1975, free interest rates were established for institutions other than commercial banks and savings and loan institutions, for which a different schedule would apply. As a consequence, new finance companies mushroomed—operating without supervision—to take advantage of free interest rates and the competitive advantage over banks where interest rates were freed more than a year later. The lack of supervision was instrumental in the crisis of finance companies in December 1976 and their subsequent supervision by the Superintendency of Banks.

In June 1974 deposit rates were freed for commercial banks and savings and loans (S&Ls), but loan rates were kept controlled. In May 1975, the lending rate was also freed, jumping to 1,300 percent per year immediately (from a fixed 115 percent), with inflation close to 400 percent.[11] Savings and loan institutions were the hardest hit by interest rate liberalization, as they had the monopoly on short-term indexed deposits to finance long-term housing loans. There were no long-term indexed deposits. The explosion of high interest rates made S&Ls' indexed deposits unattractive, leading to their bankruptcy in 1976.

Credit Ceilings and Reserve Requirements

In April 1976, credit ceilings were eliminated after an unsuccessful attempt in the last quarter of 1974. Credit ceilings increase the inflation tax base, therefore a precondition for their successful elimination was fiscal equilibrium.[12]

At the same time that credit ceilings were eliminated, a program to drastically reduce reserve requirements was initiated. Reductions were phased in five steps, with a duration between eighteen months, the initial ones, to eight and twelve months, the last ones.[13] Finally, in

---

11. This led to a policy reversal in October 1975, where lending and deposit rates were fixed, but in January 1976 they were freed again.

12. de la Cuadra and Valdés (1989) have an extensive analysis of this.

13. As with credit ceilings, early reductions of reserve requirements, which started in October 1974, had been reversed by August 1975.

December 1980, reserve requirements ended up being 10 percent of demand deposits and 4 percent of time deposits, essentially similar to voluntary reserves. In April 1976 they were 85 percent on demand deposits, and 55 percent on time deposits.

To ease the burden on financial intermediaries interest was paid on required reserves between May 1976 and September 1979. The rate paid on reserves varied during that period, increasing from 70 percent to 100 percent of the rate paid on time deposits until April 1979, then decreasing to 50 percent of such rate and then being discontinued in September 1979.

Capital Requirements and Credit Limits

Capital requirements for banks were indexed in November 1974. The maximum debt was maintained at twenty times the banks' capital.

In 1974, limits on ownership of bank shares were set at 1.5 percent for individuals and 3 percent for firms. By creating "paper" companies, the *grupos* evaded this ruling. The authorities did not pursue this matter and instead these limits were eliminated in 1978.

Universal Banking

In addition to eliminating prohibitions on indexing and ceilings on interest rates and credits, all intermediaries were allowed to attract passbook savings accounts—which were the monopoly of the government bank—and mortgage operations—a monopoly of S&Ls.

The general approach was to regulate specific operations and not institutions. The only exception was that finance companies could not accept demand deposits and be involved in the financing of foreign trade. Development banks, on the other hand, became indistinguishable from commercial banks.

Access to International Markets

The opening of the economy to foreign inflows has been one of the most controversial reforms.[14] A myriad of restrictions on foreign borrowing were present at the beginning of the period, and some of

---

14. Analysis of one or more of its aspects can be found in Sjaastad and Cortés-Douglas (1977), Mathieson (1982), McKinnon (1982), Arellano and Ffrench-Davis (1983), Edwards (1988), Morandé (1988), and Valdés (1989).

them were introduced or increased afterward to tax or control capital inflows. But these became exceptions in a process that fundamentally eliminated most restrictions. In April 1980, only two of them were in place:
- Loans with an average maturity of less than two years remained prohibited.
- Permitted loans with a maturity of less than sixty-five months remained subject to a required reserve of 10 percent.

The most important restrictions and their evolution were:
- Limits on foreign borrowing—Until December 1977 only foreign trade loans could be financed with foreign borrowing. After that date, banks could use foreign borrowing to lend for any purpose, but only in foreign currency, the exchange risk being transferred to the domestic borrower. The ratio of foreign borrowing to capital and reserves of banks was reduced from 2 to 1 in January 1975, then it was increased steadily until it was set free in June 1979.
- The stock limits for loans in foreign currency were increased from 25 percent of banks' capital and reserves in January 1978 to 70 percent in April 1979, and set free in June 1979.
- Maximum monthly flow that banks could lend in foreign currency—This limit was established in January 1978 at 5 percent of banks' capital and reserves. It went up and down but most of the time was the largest of 5 percent of capital and reserves or US$2 million per bank, until it was freed in April 1980. The combination of these two liberalizations led to an explosive increase in foreign borrowing and lending in foreign currency.
- Average maturity on foreign borrowing and reserve requirement—In April 1978, foreign loans with an average maturity of two years or less were prohibited, and noninterest-bearing reserve requirements were imposed on the rest, ranging from 25 percent for twenty-four- to thirty-six-month loans to 10 percent for forty-eight- to sixty-five-month loans, and zero for sixty-six or more months. This restriction forced banks to contract longer-term debt, which was the objective of the central bank.

The predominant view at the Central Bank was that total liberalization was dangerous as it would lead to massive capital inflows, destabilizing the anti-inflationary effort.[15] This view was openly criticized by businessmen and economists, blaming it for the persistence of very high interest rates, for discriminating among borrowers given their differential access to foreign borrowing, and for being based on an assumption of instability in the supply of foreign capital. This lack of support led to the final liberalization that took place in April 1980.[16]

Dynamics of the Financial Reform

It is important to distinguish several subperiods in the process of the Chilean financial reform. From 1975 to 1978, real interest rates were very high—as high as 80 percent per year—and credit had an explosive growth. From 1978 to early 1981, corporations and banks enjoyed very high profits, real interest rates declined in 1979 and 1980, and a perception of a permanent boom became dominant in 1981, leading to extreme levels of external and internal overborrowing. Finally, the crisis started in 1982, the takeover of banks was in January 1983, and, after a brief populist period, conservative policies were initiated in 1985.

The High Levels of Real Interest Rates, 1975-78

Interest rates in Chile were substantially higher than international rates during the period following liberalization of interest rates in 1975. In fact, their real levels since the decontrol of interest rates in 1975 were staggering. In the first few years after this freeing, insulation of the domestic capital market from the international capital market and uncertainty about the exchange rates made the interest rate a domestic phenomenon in Chile.[17]

Bank credit to the private sector experienced explosive growth, increasing 600 percent in real terms between the end of 1975—a record low level of real credit—and 1979. Deposits in the same period increased 300 percent in real terms and banks' foreign liabilities increased 200 percent in the same period.

---

15. See de la Cuadra, 1982.
16. Refer to de la Cuadra and Valdés, 1989.
17. See Sjaastad and Cortés-Douglas, 1977.

In spite of this phenomenal increase in domestic credit from the time it was freed, in the second semester of 1975, real interest rates in Chile were extremely high in comparison with those of the rest of the world and those of traditional Chilean levels. During certain months of 1976, lending rates of banks and other financial institutions in Chile *were as high as 80 percent per annum in real terms* (i.e., corrected for the internal rate of inflation).

From the viewpoint of an external investor, real interest rates were even higher because the rate of devaluation of the peso during 1976 and 1977, on average, lagged behind the rate of internal inflation. A substantial amount of foreign capital entered the country, partly in response to these very high real rates of return, but exchange rate and other controls apparently prevented international capital movements of a magnitude sufficient to completely disconnect the stock of internal credit from money. Thus, the fact that real cash balances were abnormally low during much of the post-fiscal reform period (i.e., since mid-1975) implied that the stock of real bank credit was also abnormally low.

The post-fiscal reform period was again characterized by a rather high rate of inflation, albeit much lower than before. Inflationary expectations, together with the devaluation policy, were apparently sufficient during 1975 and most of 1976 to maintain inflation high despite a sharp decline in the fiscal deficit.

As a matter of fact, the decline in domestic lending rates and the domestic spread was fundamentally caused by important and steady reductions in reserve requirements and also, but later in time and therefore to a lesser extent, by gradual lifting of barriers to capital movements.

The link between high interest rates and the dearth of capital formation, which started at the end of the Frei Administration, for private investment and continued in later years needs to be further investigated. For public investment, the decline began with the Allende administration policies—which emphasized redistribution and therefore consumption—and were continued by the Pinochet regime through the structural reform of the public sector.

Business firms' financial position was quite strong by the end of 1979 due to the decline in interest rates, particularly in 1979; a significant increase in the value of their assets; and the completion of the recovery from the recession initiated in 1975.

The same was true with banks. Starting in 1978, banks enjoyed very high profits. As a percentage of net worth, profits went from 18.5 percent in 1978 to 23.5 percent in 1980. Profits were the result of financial liberalization, the high rates of growth of the economy (over 8 percent between 1978 and 1980), and the reduction of interest rates in 1979 and 1980.

Therefore, and in spite of the mistakes in policy implementation, banks and business firms were on solid ground in 1979. In 1980 and 1981, the general perception was that the financial and economic boom the country was enjoying was going to be permanent. But in 1981, international interest rates shot up. The story continues.

The Political Economy of Financial Reform

The many inconsistencies that plagued financial reform are difficult to understand if a monolithic team of policymakers is assumed. Most analyses of the financial liberalization implicitly assume that the dictatorial character of the Chilean polity and the homogeneity demonstrated by the policymaking team (the "Chicago Boys") in other sectoral reforms were sufficient to guarantee a monolithic view on financial reform. de la Cuadra and Valdés (1989) are the exception. From the vantage point of an insider—de la Cuadra was a senior member of the policy team—they argue that three opposing views were present during the financial reform.

The predominant view at the beginning of the reform was a Free Banking Approach held by the minister of finance, the president of the central bank, and others. They were against any involvement by the government, including government guarantees, and believed that bank failures were no different from any other failure.

The Prudential Regulation Approach included the vice-president of the central bank, de la Cuadra, and other senior managers at the central bank. In their view, the government should guarantee bank liabilities and therefore regulate to control the risk of bank failures.

The Superintendent of Banks—not a Chicago Boy—and others at the superintendency (SIB) favored the view that the financial market should continue to be repressed. They believed that depositors should be bailed out in case of failures; and since risk-taking by banks could not be controlled, repression was needed to ensure that banks would not grow—and negative interest rates would keep the risks low.

Eventually the facts defeated the Free Banking Approach and favored the predominance of the Prudential Regulation Approach. Several years, however, were lost in this process, years in which adequate prudential regulation was absent and in which an extremely fragile financial sector developed.

In the following sections we shall discuss how these opposing views, compounded by other problems, were important in increasing the costs of financial reform.

The Bankruptcy of S&Ls

Savings and Loan Institutions were private, but regulated by the government. In 1974, they still followed the original American S&L model; in the Chilean variant, which needed to take inflation into account, S&Ls had the monopoly on short-term indexed instruments. They were required to use these funds for long-term mortgage lending and loans to construction companies; their deposit rates were fixed by the board of regulators and were exempted from reserve requirements. They could not invest in money market instruments or banks' liabilities.

In 1974, the central bank returned to S&Ls their excess reserves. As described, the only use of these funds was long-term lending for housing or to construction companies. S&Ls could not even use them to lower deposit rates, as they were fixed by the board of regulators— which, incidentally, was biased toward the objective of increasing the supply of housing. Therefore, in mid-1974 S&Ls began using these excess reserves to increase their lending dramatically. Depositors continued increasing their indexed deposits in S&Ls, which, added to zero required reserves, led to a 100 percent rate of growth in real terms of S&Ls in 1974.

Starting in January 1975, people withdrew their deposits in S&Ls because of the high levels of interest rates in other intermediaries and the recession brought about by the fall in the price of copper. Government officials, before and after this date, declared that the government would subsidize S&Ls to prevent their bankruptcy.

However, in June 1975, after deposits had substantially fallen, the government froze the most important short-term instrument of S&Ls by limiting withdrawals to US$100 per month, and offering to substitute them by long-term bonds priced in the secondary market at 60 to 80 percent of their value.

This measure led to a complete loss of credibility in government guarantees as of June 1975. As a consequence, it was announced that "for the next 18 months, there [would] be no implicit guarantee of bank deposits" (de la Cuadra and Valdés). This is very important when contrasted with the next episode.

The lesson from the S&L episode is that financial liberalization measures need to be carefully harmonized and coordinated. A savings and loans system full of restrictions is consistent with a repressed financial system, but it is inconsistent and bankrupt when the rest is liberalized and shocks lead depositors away from it.

Banco Osorno's Failure and Moral Hazard

The absence of implicit or explicit guarantees on deposits after the S&L crisis, the absence of prudential regulation, and the free entry of finance companies were the principal elements of the financial system from 1974 to December 1976, which can be described as a period of essentially free banking.

In December 1976, one bank, Banco Osorno, and nine finance companies became insolvent. The citizens became aware of the total lack of supervision affecting both formal and informal financial intermediaries and realized that their distrust of financial intermediaries was well-founded.

The Banco Osorno *grupo* used the bank to buy several large firms privatized in 1976, then lent to these firms and issued guarantees to others without recording them. de la Cuadra and Valdés (1989) conclude that Banco Osorno abused the depositors' trust, this episode being a clear case of moral hazard against depositors.

In December 1976, while the failures proceeded, depositors shifted their deposits toward the larger banks. The reaction of the government was to guarantee Banco Osorno's deposits and small deposits of the formal finance companies, but to not guarantee deposits in informal ones. An explicit government guarantee on small deposits for all formal institutions was also instituted.

Advocates of the three views within the government had different readings of this crisis and accordingly fostered different policy measures.

In the free banking view, fraud and bad management explained the failures and thus these institutions should have gone bankrupt. To counter fraud, legislation defining these crimes more precisely was passed to enable depositors to defend themselves better in court. Only small depositors would be guaranteed as the costs of information or suing were deemed to be higher for them than the benefits.

Prudential regulation advocates obtained new powers and a larger budget for the superintendency—forty professionals of the central bank went to work as inspectors for SIB, which raised the number of inspectors from ten to fifty—and also obtained the government's guarantee for small depositors. In addition, limits on the volume of guarantees issued by banks were implemented for individuals and corporations, the capital requirements for finance companies were raised to three-fourths of that of banks, and they were banned from acting as brokers for commercial paper. Informal finance companies were prohibited.

Prudential advocates could not, however, enforce a fast implementation of prudential regulation. Not only were the free-banking advocates opposed, but in addition, implementation was delayed by the Superintendency of Banks—at the time the bastion of advocates of financial repression.

The differential treatment of Banco Osorno, the formal finance companies, and the small informal finance companies clearly indicated to the public that large institutions would not be allowed to fail. This impression gained further credibility in 1977 when eight small and four large credit cooperatives failed. The four large ones were taken over by the government and all depositors were bailed out, regardless of size. The eight smaller ones were treated as formal finance companies, with owners of large deposits losing their money.

By 1977 this evidence clearly indicated that an implicit guarantee for larger financial institutions was present, and that free banking was over. The advocates of free banking did not acknowledge this fact, and continued to believe that free banking was feasible. They entrusted information on the banking system to private external auditing firms and discouraged prudential regulation. That this view predominated still in 1979 was clear from the next episode: the case of Banco Espanol.

The Case of Banco Espanol

In March 1979, the superintendency banned the accrual of interest on delinquent loans. In February 1980, an important step was taken: the superintendency undertook the first attempt to classify loans. Banks were required to classify their thirty largest debtors in a four point risk scale. Four months later, SIB reported that "some institutions did not have the information necessary to identify their debtors," and in several, "the loans were disbursed...with absolute ignorance of the uses to which they would be put." This meant that some loans were undocumented, which was illegal since 1978.

In April 1980, two months after the announcement of the risk classification system, an external auditing firm that so far had approved Banco Espanol's balance sheets unquestioningly—characterizing them as average—reported that on 37 percent of the bank's portfolio no information was available in order to know the borrowers' ability to pay, and that debtors had renewed their loans repeatedly without interest paid at renewal.

The bank's owners foresaw takeover by the government in April 1980 and sold it to another business conglomerate. The authorities, advocates of free banking, failed to require the new owners to increase the capital of the bank, which is what a prudent regulator would have done.

These results of the initial risk classification system led the superintendency to further action. The number of largest debtors to be classified was extended to 80 in June 1980, to 300 in April 1981, and finally to 400 in February 1982. With this figure, 75 percent of the loan portfolio of the banking system was covered.

Most importantly, in November 1981, four banks—including Banco Espanol—and four finance companies were taken over by the superintendency, which together accounted for 7 percent of total loans. All depositors and creditors were guaranteed, with losses being paid by the government.

This episode clearly showed that the auditing firms behaved as in a textbook case of the "capture" theory of regulation. To most observers it became evident that external auditors were incapable of enforcing adequate supervision standards, particularly when in April 1981 the same auditing firm mentioned above declared that all of Banco Espanol's problems had been solved, and seven months later the bank was taken over by SIB.

Most importantly, the November 1981 takeover left no doubt that the implicit guarantee on all deposits was operating. In spite of this, proponents of free banking obtained the approval of a law a month later in which an optional deposit insurance up to $3,500 (dollars) and covering 75 percent of that sum could be purchased by each depositor. As expected very few depositors bought it, as it was clear from the recent takeover that the government had de facto guaranteed all deposits.

The superintendency continued its quest for regulation, requiring a general loss provision of 0.75 percent of loans and, at last but too late, in March 1982 requiring provisions according to the risk classification, allowing the banks a period of thirty-three months to comply. Too late because the depression of 1982 had already begun and the financial sector was extremely fragile.

Conglomerates and the Intervention of 1983

The superintendency had earlier—in August 1981—obtained changes to the Banking Law, changing the definition of individual debtors with the purpose of drastically limiting the lending by *grupo*-owned banks to firms owned by the same *grupo*. Thus, by the new definition, the debt of an individual debtor included that of all firms where the individual owned or controlled more than 50 percent, plus the prorated share of debts in firms where the individual owned or controlled between 10 and 50 percent.

Contrary to the generous timetable to comply with provisions according to the degree of risk, absolutely no time at all was allowed for firms of the same conglomerate to adjust to these important limitations to lending, in spite of the large amounts of these loans in the banks' portfolios. Conglomerates therefore evaded these new regulations. They continuously started and closed shell companies and increased their number so as to keep the participation of the conglomerate in each of them at 9.9 percent. They also colluded and swapped loans between conglomerates and used them to cancel loans within each of the conglomerates. Finally, they used triangular loans establishing shell companies abroad, giving them a loan and then lending it back to their companies in Chile. The two largest conglomerates established banks abroad—in the United States, Panama, and Uruguay—and lent to these "foreign" banks; they in turn lent back to firms of the conglomerate in Chile.

The lessons are twofold. It was a mistake for the superintendency to fail to provide an adequate time for the conglomerates to reduce their loans to their own firms, particularly given their sizable amounts and the fact that their investment programs could not be reversed instantaneously. Second, it was clear that the conglomerates could use to their advantage the informational asymmetry they enjoyed and they did use it when they had to.

The conglomerates were pressed in 1981 by the effect of the five-fold increase in real interest rates on their very large levels of indebtedness. They were the first symptoms of the financial crisis of 1982.

The *grupos'* exceptional growth until 1981 had largely been financed with debt. As such, they were highly exposed to interest rate risk. As international real interest rates increased from 1.5 to 10.7 percent, and inflation was dwindling, real interest rates in pesos went up from 12 to 35 percent. The reduction in asset values compounded the problem for *grupos* and other sectors as well.

The *grupos* were the principal beneficiaries of the implicit subsidy on foreign exchange risk. This distortion stemmed from the fact that SIB could not include in its loan classification scheme an independent assessment of banks debtors' exposure to foreign exchange risk and interest rate risk because it would have run counter to the Minister of Finance and the Chief Executive's statements on the permanent stability of the nominal exchange rate.

Rollover of *grupo* losses in the banking system was reduced by SIB's enforcement of modifications to bank regulations. But loopholes in the regulation of securities issues (under the control of the

Superintendency of Securities and Corporations [SVS]) allowed one of the largest *grupos* to roll losses over in the securities markets. The Cruzat conglomerate used mutual funds under its control to lend to its own firms. Depositors were attracted by the high rate of growth of mutual funds. As SVS never required *grupos* to publish consolidated balance sheets, investors discovered too late that the satisfactory growth of mutual funds was caused by manipulation of the price of securities issued by Cruzat's firms.

In spite of the central bank's scheme in July 1982 to allow deferral of losses, banks delayed the implementation of guarantee execution and case-by-case rescheduling, and continued to renew loans across the board, in spite of their being illegal. A generalized expectation of bailout—which never materialized—was the reason behind it.

To stop the generalized rollover of loans, the government intervened the banking system in January 1983, taking over the flagship banks of the two largest conglomerates and forcing the liquidation of three other banks. The government's diagnosis at the time was that the *grupos* were largely responsible for the overborrowing of the private sector and acted to force the *grupos'* larger corporations to go bankrupt (by simply refusing to renew their loans—most of which had a maturity of ninety days).

The Financial Crisis of 1982

Scenario for a Crisis

The dominant features of the domestic crisis scenario were the overextended and potentially insolvent condition of the banking sector and the heavy overindebtedness of business firms.

The private sector—encouraged by the perception of a permanent bonanza in the Chilean economy and in the context of inadequate financial regulation and enforcement as described earlier—engaged in a . frantic drive for credit, both externally and internally. The former increased the foreign debt of the private sector (the public sector had attained a surplus in its budget in the 1977–81 period). This increase in foreign borrowing acted as a shock absorber of the external disturbances of 1980, which started with the U.S. recession and were transmitted via the appreciation of the dollar, reducing the value of exports and increasing the price of importables. While the American economy was in recession, a boom occurred in Chile; it was a period with unprecedented expectations of prosperity. However, the financial boom left banks overextended and business firms heavily overindebted.

PERCEPTION OF A PERMANENT BOOM. Overborrowing was fostered by a general perception of a permanent boom in the economy. This belief led, among other things, to an overvaluation of capital goods such as land, stocks, and so on. In the banking sector, it also led to an overvaluation of investment projects and loan guarantees, and a strong increase in the demand for credit. The expectations of a permanent boom were coupled with:
- The extraordinary increase in capital inflow since 1979
- Evidence that when things go sour, the monetary authority pays the bill of the large financial intermediaries
- A legal system that allowed the overprotection of personal wealth through "shell" firms and property transfers to wives and others.

All this together generated a financial "bubble" that made the financial sector extremely fragile.

The massive expansion of both peso credit (at more than 50 percent a year in real terms) and dollar credit (at more than 25 percent a year in real terms) that took place in 1979, 1980, and 1981 are an indication that a phenomenal demand for credit arose since 1979.

MASSIVE INFLOW OF FOREIGN FUNDS. The private sector increased foreign borrowing to the limit, especially after the most important restrictions were lifted in 1979. The existence of excess demand for credit, particularly in the early stages of reform; the high level of interest rates; and the appreciation of the dollar vis-á-vis other OECD currencies were certainly important. But as the generalized debt crisis has eloquently shown, supply factors were also very important, particularly the recycling of petrodollars by American and other banks. This activity created a world excess of credit supply, which resulted in the lowering of risk evaluation by these financial institutions. Morandé's (1988) analysis provides evidence that foreign inflows systematically preceded the peso appreciation, and Valdés

(1989) points out that the imprudent period of foreign borrowing in Chile in 1981 was clearly related to the perception of a permanent boom.

FOREIGN EXCHANGE RISK. The enactment of the banking law of August 1981, which placed limits on lending by conglomerate banks to their own enterprises, coincided with critiques of national economic policy by the media, which were associated with the conglomerates. These particularly criticized the pegged exchange rate, which was identified with Finance Minister De Castro. Uncertainty about the permanence of the exchange rate at its fixed level began then and did not subside until the devaluation of June 1982.

The intervention of Banco Espanol and seven other banks and finance companies had the cost of increasing domestic credit by $700 million dollars, with an equivalent loss in international reserves. For knowledgeable observers, particularly in the private sector, this was an indication that the strength of the fixed exchange rate had been undermined.

As authorities continued proclaiming that the fixed exchange rate would be maintained at all costs, the accrual of an implicit subsidy on foreign exchange risk was readily visualized, and heightened the acceleration of foreign borrowing. It was equivalent to the government extending a guarantee for foreign exchange risk. As the next section shows the subsidy materialized starting in 1982.

HIGH INTEREST RATES. Interest rates in pesos were still more than twice the dollar interest rates throughout the three years of the fixed exchange rate regime. Curiously enough, the spread between the peso deposit rates and London Inter Bank Offer Rate (LIBOR) was quite stable on average but very high; indeed, the annual averages were between 1.0 and 1.6 per month in 1979–82 (although the monthly figures fluctuated between a low of 0.89 and a high of 2.67 a month), that is a spread in excess of 13 percent for the year.

The very high, persistent level of interest rates in pesos in Chile is one of the main characteristics of the period under analysis. Short-term bank deposit rates in real terms averaged 20 percent a year in 1977 and 26 percent in 1978, then dropped to 5 percent in 1979 and 1980. They resumed their previous high levels at 29 percent a year in

1981 and exceeded 30 percent a year in the first semester of 1982. In other words, real interest rates in peso deposits were almost always between 20 and 30 percent a year.[18]

In synthesis, among the most important lessons of the period is that the crisis of 1982 in Chile cannot be explained without a thorough consideration of the problems of financial regulation and real interest rates. With a feeble banking system, a high level of indebtedness, and a relative price disequilibrium deepened by the mandated wage increase of August 1981, the international recession was transmitted with untold severity to the Chilean economy. Due to these factors the transmission was lagged and multiplied. It produced a recession without parallel since the 1930s.

WAGE INDEXATION AND THE FIXED EXCHANGE RATE. The inconsistency between the fixed exchange rate and wages indexed to past inflation—where inflation is declining abruptly—clearly damaged the competitive position of Chilean tradables, particularly exports. This was particularly clear in August 1981, when wages were increased by law by 14 percent, while inflation was zero or negative in previous months, and export prices were falling because of external shocks. The relative impact of this disequilibrium was minor relative to the size of the interest rate shock and to its impact on a heavy overleveraged corporate sector, banking system, and individuals. An indication of this difference is given by the fact that real wages increased about 20 percent during the fixed exchange rate period, compared to a 500 percent increase in real interest rates.

External Shocks and the 1982-83 Recession

External shocks began with the appreciation of the dollar against other major currencies in late 1980. This revaluation caused the dollar prices of many Chilean imports to fall (reversing the previous situation in which Chilean tradables' prices were increasing faster than the U.S. price indices). It also brought domestic inflation down in 1981 to

---

18. The nominal level of peso deposit rates in 1979 and 1980 averaged 35 percent per year and was equivalent to international interest rates plus a relatively stable and high spread. Together with domestic inflation of 30 percent per year, the result was real rates of only 5 percent per year for the 1979-80 fiscal year.

negative 4 percent according to the WPI, and 9 percent according to the CPI. In addition, export prices fell due to the dollar appreciation, particularly for copper and agricultural and forestry products, which represented a large proportion of the total value of exports.

The trigger of the crisis was the rise in international interest rates in the last quarter of 1981; together with the reduction of inflation, they were responsible for the shooting up of the real interest rates in Chilean pesos from 5 percent per year in 1980, to 30 percent per year in 1982. The construction sector, which had boomed in 1979 and 1980 (23.9 percent and 25.7 percent real growth, respectively), was brought to a complete halt, initiating the economy's recession.

The feeble situation of the banking system, and the high levels of debt of business firms and people in general, multiplied the effect of this phenomenal increase in interest rates and translated themselves into a deep recession, exacerbated by the massive withdrawal of foreign credit at the end of 1981.

The automatic wage escalator clauses for past inflation added a wage increase of 14 percent in August 1981, with practically zero inflation. Business enterprises—heavily indebted—were thus caught by a 500 percent increase in real interest rates in 1981, an increase in real wages of about 20 percent (from July 1979, when the exchange rate was fixed, to December 1980) while their prices were mostly falling (the WPI index showed a drop of -4 percent in 1981), and export prices were plummeting due to the dollar appreciation.

All of this occurred before the abrupt reduction of capital inflow at the end of the third quarter of 1981. Just as the enormous capital inflow in 1980 and 1981 in excess of $500 million per quarter with a peak of $830 million and $1 billion dollars in the second and third quarters of 1981, respectively, triggered the price rise in Chilean tradables in 1980 and the increase in expenditure relative to income, so the reduction in the capital inflow at the end of 1981 required a corresponding reduction in relative nontraded goods prices and a reduction in expenditure. But the economy was already squeezed by the dollar appreciation that had started almost a year earlier.

Wage-escalation policy, coupled with the rise in real interest rates, made the adjustment of nontraded goods prices an extremely long and painful process (deflation was needed first to reverse the trend of wages).

No policy reactions took place previous to the onset of the crisis. Particularly, as discussed previously, no timely effective action was taken in the most vulnerable area of the economy: the financial sector. In mid-1982, the media carried the alternative "solutions" to the crisis: "devaluation or reduction in wages." The cancer of the financial system continued undiagnosed.

In June 1982, a 19 percent devaluation was effected to correct the distortion in relative prices, but the public expected a higher rate of devaluation, and consequently a run on the peso proceeded. Even more important, and as was to be expected, a devaluation in the context of an open capital account, when both the responsible ministers and the chief executive had, since August 1981, repeatedly declared that devaluation would not be a solution but an evil, produced a total loss of confidence in the authorities and their economic policies.

When comparing the 500 percent increase in real interest rates with the 20 percent increase in real wages in 1981, it is evident which was the critical factor in the depression, particularly given the extraordinarily high level of corporate indebtedness. It is also clear how mistaken it was to place as alternative solutions to the recession a reduction of wages versus a devaluation, as the media reported since mid-1981, and the authorities finally acquiesced in mid-1982. The crucial problem was financial, and that of relative prices was secondary.

The loss of confidence provoked by the devaluation ensured that the run on the peso was sizable, and its effects on high-powered money and international reserves were also important.

The outcome was economic depression. In 1983 the economy was depressed, with international reserves driven down, peso monetary aggregates falling in nominal terms, as they were not demanded but replaced by a demand for dollars, with huge debt payments forthcoming, a bankrupt financial system, and unemployment surpassing 25 percent of the labor force.

Bank Restructuring and Financial Reform

After the crisis erupted, the authorities took decisive action to prevent the total collapse of the financial system. They intervened in several banks, including some of the largest private ones, and ended up controlling over 60 percent of bank deposits (Larrain 1989). They provided emergency support to all banks and rescheduled their loans to industrial and commercial companies. The central bank assumed all the bad loans, which accounted for 28 percent of the total loan portfolio of the banking system.

Once the impending threat of a total financial collapse was averted, the authorities proceeded to build a robust and sound financial system. The banks were reprivatized, some by encouraging small savers to buy shares through subsidized credits (popular capitalism). However, they imposed tough restrictions on the payment of bank dividends to old shareholders. Any profits in excess of necessary retained earnings and dividends for new shareholders had to be used for repaying the debt to the central bank. The role of prudential regulation and supervision were much strengthened and strict limits were imposed on business with related parties.

At the same time, the authorities continued to strengthen the prudential regulation and supervision of insurance companies and pension funds. The insurance sector had been deregulated before the banking crisis. Its deregulation was continued with a strong emphasis on solvency monitoring instead of product and tariff controls. The reform of the social security system through the authorization of special pension fund companies (known as Administradoras de Fondos de Pensiones or AFPs) and compulsory individual capitalization accounts was based on the introduction of very tight regulations. The total assets of the pension fund system grew from 1 percent of GNP in 1981 to over 26 percent in 1990 (Vittas and Iglesias, 1992).

Considerable reform was also undertaken in the securities markets. The privatization of several public utilities and other state-owned companies boosted the development of the capital market. The pension funds played a crucial part in the privatization process, although measures to encourage dispersion of corporate ownership among other firms met with limited success.

The failure of financial reform in the late 1970s and early 1980s and the subsequent successful radical transformation of the Chilean financial system underscored a most valuable lesson from the Chilean experience. Prudential regulation and supervision are necessary ingredients, alongside macroeconomic stability and an undistorted structure of incentives, for a robust, efficient, and fair financial system.

Bibliography

Arellano, J. P. (1983). "De la liberalizacion a la intervención: el mercado de capitales en Chile 1974-1983." *Estudios Cieplan* 11. December.

Arellano, J. P. and R. Ffrench-Davis (1983). "La apertura externa en Chile." *Estudios Cieplan* 10.

Cortés-Douglas, H. (1975). "Stabilization and Currency Reform in Chile." OAS Capital Markets Program. Processed.

Dahse, F. (1979). *Mapa de la Extrema Riqueza.* Edit. Aconcagua.

de la Cuadra, S. (1982). "Sobre la apertura externa." in *Estudios Monetarios.* Banco Central de Chile.

de la Cuadra, S., and S. Valdes (1989). "Myths and Facts about Instability in Financial Liberalization in Chile: 1974-1983." Catholic University of Chile. Processed.

Edwards, S. (1984). "The Order of Liberalization of the External Sector in Developing Countries." *Princeton Essays in International Finance* 156, December.

Edwards, S., and A. Cox Edwards (1987). *Monetarism and Liberalization: The Chilean Experiment.* Cambridge, MA.: Ballinger Publishing Co.

Hachette, D., and R. Lüders (1988). *Privatization in Argentina and Chile..* Internal Discussion Paper No. 18, World Bank.

Larrain, Mauricio (1989). "How the 1981-83 Chilean Banking Crisis was Handled." World Bank, PRE Working Papers, WPS No. 300, November.

Morande, F. (1988):."Capital inflows in Chile." In F. Morande and K. Schmitt-Hebbel, eds., *Del Auge a la Crisis.* Instituto Inter-Americano de Mercados de Capital and Trades. Santiago, Chile: Georgetown University.

Mathieson, D. (1982). "Financial Reform and Capital Flows in a Developing Economy." *Staff Papers*, IMF, vol. 29.

McKinnon, R. (1982). "Liberalización financiera y tasas de interes." *Cuadernos de Economia.*

Solimano, A., and V. Corbo (1991). "Chile's experiences with stabilization revisited, "in M. Bruno, S. Fischer, E. Helpman and N. Liviatan, eds., *Lessons of Economic Stabilization and its Aftermath,.* Cambridge, Ma.: MIT Press.

Sjaastad, L., and H. Cortés-Douglas (1978). "The Monetary Approach to the Balance of Payments and Real Interest Rates in Chile." *Estudios de Economia*, I Semester.

Sjaastad, L., and H. Cortés-Douglas, eds. (1981). "La Politica Economica de la Reforma Comercial en Chile." In *Cuadernos de Economia* 54-55, special number.

Perez, F. (1988). "El mercado financiero en Chile." *Cuadernos de Economia* 76.

Valdés, S. (1989). "Origenes de la crisis de la deuda." *Estudios Publicos* 33.

Vittas, Dimitri, and Augusto Iglesias (1992). "The Rationale and Performance of Personal Pension Plans in Chile." World Bank, CECFP. January. Processed

7

BANK RESTRUCTURING IN MALAYSIA, 1985–88

Andrew Sheng

The Macroeconomic Background

Introduction

Malaysia is a small middle income oil-exporting developing economy with an area of 329,800 square kilometers, a population of 16.5 million, and well endowed with natural resources, being the world's largest exporter of rubber, palm oil, tin, tropical hardwoods, and an important producer of cocoa and pepper. The country is also a net exporter of crude oil and natural gas. Industrialization has reached the stage at which manufacturing now accounts for 22.5 percent of GDP, and manufactured products accounted for 45 percent of gross exports in 1987. In 1988, Malaysian GNP was US$31.6 billion, with a GNP per capita of US$1,869. The openness of the economy can be seen from the high ratio of external trade to GNP of 130 percent in 1987, and the historical sensitivity of the external payments position to changes in the terms of trade (figure 7.1).

Historically, Malaysia has been considered a model of cautious economic management. The government has a stated policy of maintaining a surplus in its current account budget, strong external reserves backing for its currency and low inflation. In the 1960s, the country enjoyed a steady expansion in average annual real GDP of 5.2 percent with inflation of less than 1 percent annually. In the turbulent 1970s,

Table 7.1: Malaysia: Principal Macro Indicators

Indicator	1980	1981	1982	1983	1984	1985	1986	1987	1988
GNP growth (% p.a.)[1]	8.8	7.5	4.6	3.9	6.7	-1.2	2.5	4.8	8.6
GDP growth (% p.a.)[1]	7.8	6.9	5.9	6.3	7.8	-1.0	1.2	5.2	8.1
GDI/GNP (percent)	31.6	36.3	39.1	40.4	36.0	29.7	27.1	25.8	27.1
GNS/GNP (percent)	30.4	26.1	25.0	28.0	30.7	27.3	27.3	32.9	32.8
Merchandise trade balance (M$ mln)	5,238	-243	-1,758	1,002	6,986	8,883	8,781	14,830	14,777
Current account balance (M$ mln)	-620	-5,633	-8,409	-8,117	-3,917	-1,522	133	6,480	4,934
As percent of GNP	-1.2	-10.1	-14.1	-12.4	-5.3	-2.1	0.2	8.6	5.8
Fed. govt. overall balance[2] (M$ million)	7,104	-11,015	-11,171	-9,183	-7,075	-5,707	-7,506	-6,153	-3,900
As percent of GNP	-13.8	-19.8	-18.7	-14.0	-9.5	-7.9	-11.3	-8.2	-4.6
Total debt/GNP (percent)[3]	19.5	27.6	40.7	48.5	50.2	58.7	76.1	67.4	55.5
Debt service ratio[4]	1.8[5]	7.1	9.3	9.8	11.8	15.8	18.7	16.0	13.3
Consumer price index (percent)	6.7	9.7	5.7	3.7	3.6	0.4	0.6	0.8	2.5
Exchange rate (MS/SDR) (percent)	1.7	8.6	1.9	4.6	3.0	-10.8	-16.3	-10.0	-3.2

1. At constant prices.
2. Covers only federal government.
3. Total debt: Public and publicly guaranteed, publicly nonguaranteed private, and private sector term debt.
4. Ratio of total debt service to exports of goods and services.
5. Refers to debt service ratio of federal government only.
Source: Bank Negara Malaysia.

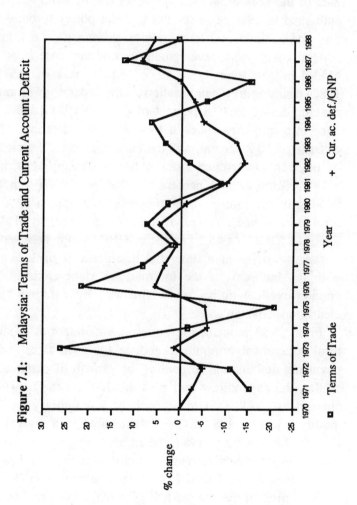

Figure 7.1: Malaysia: Terms of Trade and Current Account Deficit

Malaysia grew by an average of 8 percent in real terms, with a peak GDP growth of 9.3 percent in 1979, but inflation rose to an average of 6 percent, peaking at 11.1 percent in 1981 (table 7.1).

Decline in Growth

In the light of its strong financial position and to counteract the impact of the severe international recession of 1980-82, the government embarked in 1980 on a counter-cyclical policy to build up infrastructure and an industrial base, relying primarily on external borrowing. Federal government development expenditure rose from an average of M$3-4 billion annually in 1977-79 to a peak of M$11.5 billion in 1982, resulting in a deterioration in the federal government overall financing deficit to 19.8 percent of GNP in 1981 (figure 7.2). The decline in commodity prices in 1981-82 saw a deterioration in the terms of trade of 10.2 percent, and the current account deficit in the balance of payments worsened from a near-balanced position in 1980 to M$8.4 billion or 14.1 percent of GNP in 1982. The net result was a tripling in the foreign debt from M$10 billion in 1980 (matched by foreign exchange reserves of the same amount) to M$31.8 billion at the end of 1983, or 48.5 percent of GNP. As the debt service ratio also began to worsen at a time that international bank lending declined with the outbreak of the international debt crisis in 1982–83, the counter-cyclical policy to be financed by external borrowing was clearly unsustainable.

From 1983 onward, the government undertook a stringent structural adjustment program to reduce the twin fiscal and balance of payments deficits and to control the growth of external debt, in particular, the expenditure and debt incurred by the nonfinancial public enterprises (NFPEs). On the back of a temporary recovery in commodity prices in 1983–84, which resulted in a revival of growth in GDP to 7.8 percent in 1984, the adjustment program paid off with the balance of payments current account deficit cut to 5.3 percent of GNP and the overall fiscal deficit cut to 10.1 percent of GNP.

Beginning in the second half of 1985, however, commodity prices worldwide took a sharp unprecedented drop across the board, and proceeded to worsen in the course of 1986, with major falls in the prices of crude oil and palm oil. The terms of trade worsened by 4.5

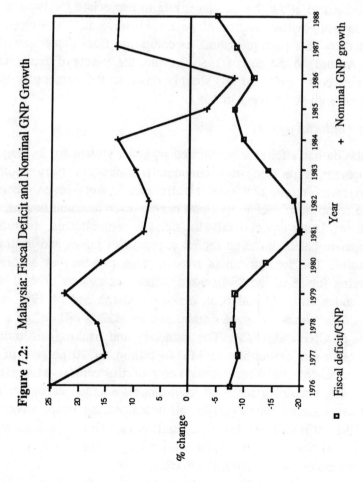

Figure 7.2: Malaysia: Fiscal Deficit and Nominal GNP Growth

□ Fiscal deficit/GNP   + Nominal GNP growth

percent in 1985 and a further 15.5 percent in the next year. Together with the cutback in public sector expenditure, GNP in current terms declined for the first time in a decade for two consecutive years, by 2.9 percent in 1985 and 7.9 percent in 1986. As revenue declined, the overall fiscal deficit again deteriorated to 11.3 percent of GNP, after the modest recovery in 1985, so that the government was forced to retrench further expenditure, bringing development expenditure down to M$3.2 billion in 1987, the lowest level since 1979. The government also decided to allow the exchange rate to depreciate freely as a key move to address the balance of payments problem. The ringgit depreciated by 16.7 percent against its composite from September 1985 (Plaza Accord) to the end of 1986. Despite the effects of depreciation on import costs, inflation fell sharply down to 0.6 percent in 1986, compared with 9.7 percent in 1981.

The Financial System

Malaysia has a fairly sophisticated financial system for its stage of development. It has thirty-nine commercial banks (twenty-two domestic, sixteen foreign, and one Islamic bank), forty-seven licensed finance companies, twelve merchant banks, seven discount houses, and a host of other specialized financial intermediaries, including development banks, building societies, provident funds, and insurance companies. The foreign banks have a large presence in Malaysia, accounting for 16 of the 38 licensed banks, one quarter of total bank loans, and a fifth of total bank deposits. At the end of 1987, total assets of the financial system amounted to M$203 billion, or 269.2 percent of GNP (table 7.2). The monetary and banking institutions, with total assets amounting to M$140 billion, or 70 percent of the total, are under the direct supervision of the central bank, Bank Negara. The remaining financial institutions are under the supervision of various agencies. For example, all deposit-taking cooperatives are under the Ministry of National and Rural Development, some development banks are under the Ministry of Public Enterprises, and others are under the Ministry of Finance.

The degree of monetization as measured by the ratio of broad money to GNP was 94 percent in 1986, compared with Korea (94 percent), the United States (82 percent), United Kingdom (77 percent), and Australia (73 percent). Malaysia also has an active foreign exchange and capital market, with a liberal exchange control regime and free convertibility of the ringgit for all major foreign currencies. The Kuala Lumpur foreign exchange market has an average monthly turnover of M$20 billion, while the Kuala Lumpur Stock Exchange is one of the more active stock exchanges in the developing world, with a market capitalization of M$97.2 billion (US$37.8 billion) in the first half of 1988. In 1986, equities as a percentage of total financial assets in Malaysia were 24 percent, about the same level as Canada, as compared with 4 percent for Korea and 9 percent for Taiwan.

Impact of the Recession on the Financial System

The Banking System

The impact of the recession on the financial system can be better appreciated against the background of events that led to the sharpest deflation in Malaysia since the post-Korean War recession of 1952–53. Since the early 1970s, the banking system had undergone a continuous and rapid expansion as the nation enjoyed an unprecedented period of real growth. As incomes rose with favorable commodity prices and the arrival of significant oil income, national savings increased sharply, with concomitant growth in savings with the banking system. In the first half of the 1970s, the growth of assets of the commercial banks had accelerated from an average annual rate of 19.1 percent to 24.4 percent in the second half. The double digit growth was maintained in the early 1980s until 1984, when it slowed down sharply to record a growth of 7 percent by 1987. Of particular significance was the rapid growth in loans, which averaged 22.8 percent in the decade 1975-84. As liquidity began to tighten due to the slower growth in national savings in the early 1980s with the decline in commodity prices, the loans to deposits ratio of the banking system rose from an average of 75 percent in the 1970s to over 90 percent by 1983. The expansion in banking was evident not only in terms of asset size, but also in its branch network and employment. Since 1970, the bank's branch network had expanded from 336 to 770 at the end of 1986, while employment had quadrupled from just

Table 7.2: Malaysia: Assets of the Financial System

Asset	Annual change 1986	1987	At end 1987 % Share	
	MS billion			
Banking system	<u>11.3</u>	<u>11.0</u>	<u>140.6</u>	<u>69.3</u>
Monetary institutions	9.0	9.6	110.0	54.2
central bank	3.8	3.8	24.2	11.9
Commercial banks[1]	5.2	5.8	85.8	42.3
Non-monetary institutions	2.3	1.4	30.6	15.1
Finance companies	1.8	1.6	21.3	10.5
Merchant banks	0.1	...	6.3	3.1
Discount houses	0.4	-0.2	3.0	1.5
Nonbank financial intermediaries	<u>5.4</u>	<u>6.4</u>	<u>62.4</u>	<u>30.7</u>
Provident, pension and insurance funds	4.6	4.8	42.0	20.6
Employees provident fund	3.8	3.8	32.3	15.9
Other provident funds	0.4	0.3	3.5	1.7
Life insurance funds	0.4	0.6	4.7	2.3
General insurance funds	...	0.1	1.5	0.7
Development finance institutions[2]	0.3	0.2	4.6	2.3
Savings institutions[3]	-1.2	0.4	7.2	3.6
Other financial intermediaries [4]	1.7	1.0	8.6	4.2
TOTAL	16.7	17.4	203.0	100.0

. . . = negligible
1. Include the Islamic bank.
2. Include all development banks.
3. Include the National Savings Bank, and deposit-taking cooperatives.
4. Include building societies and capital market funds.
Source: Bank Negara Malaysia.

under 10,000 to over 40,000 at the end of 1985. In addition, the larger domestic banks also began to expand abroad, with 45 foreign branches at the end of 1986 and foreign assets of M$11.2 billion, or 15 percent of total assets.

On the real side of the economy, the halcyon years of the second half of the 1970s and early 1980s, with real GDP growing at an average annual rate of 8.6 percent between 1976-80, a strong exchange rate, and an influx of foreign investment, saw a major shift in domestic investments toward real estate and speculation in equities. In the decade from 1976-85, the country showed signs of contracting the "Dutch disease," where an appreciation in the exchange rate caused a shift toward nontradables, as represented by banks lending to property (figure 7.3). Fueled by strong corporate profits and speculation, the Kuala Lumpur Stock Exchange Composite Index saw a sustained bull run from 100 in 1977 to a peak of 427 in early 1984. The influx of expatriate workforce, particularly arising from oil and other foreign investments, pushed quality office and residential rentals to unprecedented peaks in the early 1980s. This resulted in a bout of speculation in property, fueled also by the ready availability of bank credit. Between 1975 and 1983, rental and prices of good quality residential and commercial property roughly tripled. A Bank Negara survey conducted in 1983 on property development in Kuala Lumpur indicated that prime commercial property projects completed in 1986 would be five times that completed in 1983. By the end of 1986, total new banking system loans to the broad property sector (construction, housing, and real estate) amounted to 54.8 percent of total new loans, compared with 32.2 percent in 1980. The proportion of total property loans to total bank loans outstanding rose from 26.4 percent at the end of 1980 to 35.9 percent at the end of 1986.

In the third quarter of 1985, however, the gradual slide in commodity prices (evident since mid-1984) began to tumble, reducing total export income by 2.6 percent and 5.9 percent in 1985 and 1986, respectively. The crude oil price fell 62 percent from its peak, while palm oil prices fell 57 percent to M$579 per ton in 1986, below the cost of production. The composite commodity index dropped by 9.8 percent in 1985 and a further 24 percent the following year. Real GDP growth became negative (-1 percent) in 1985 for the first time since 1975, while nominal gross national income declined by 2.9 percent in 1985 and 7.9 percent in 1986. The consequence of the recession was a sharp contraction in cash flow for many companies in Malaysia, since their income declined sharply in the face of weak ex

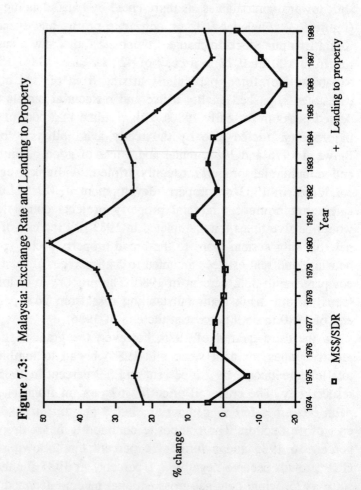

Figure 7.3:   Malaysia: Exchange Rate and Lending to Property

port sales and poor domestic demand, including delayed debt collection, while committed outflows, particularly in the property sector, continued to drain resources. Share prices slid by 59.8 percent from their peak in early 1984, and total market capitalization declined by 44 percent to M$46.7 billion at its lowest point in April 1986. As inflation fell to almost zero, the growth of narrow money, M1, became negative by the end of 1984, while growth of broad money, M3, also slowed down sharply to 3.6 percent by 1987, the slowest rate seen for 15 years (figure 7.4).

During this period, private sector expenditure was initially slow to adjust to the declining income, resulting in a drawdown of private sector savings. Growth of deposits with the banking system fell sharply from 20.3 percent in 1984 to 3.8 percent on an annual basis in October 1986. For the corporate sector, excluding deposits from the oil sector, growth in deposits was negative in 1986 by 7.1 percent and by 19.2 percent on an annual basis in October 1986. The banking system's loan growth moderated to 6 percent at the end of 1986, compared with 36.5 percent in 1980.

The combination of tight liquidity, low inflation, and a sharp decline in share and property prices brought sharply into focus the financial overcommitments of many entrepreneurs. Those who had built up their gross assets based mainly through speculation in shares and properties, and financed through excessive gearing, were caught in a triple squeeze, with a sharp decline in income flows, collapse in asset values, and a rise in debt servicing. In 1983, at the height of the property boom, prime commercial property in Kuala Lumpur was valued at M$450 per square foot, with a monthly rental of M$3.20 psf. By 1986, overbuilding and forced selling had driven values down to M$180 psf, while rentals fell to $0.90 psf.

As the slowdown in the economy gathered momentum in the course of 1985, tightening liquidity and bad economic news caused rising depositor nervousness. In July, the failure of Overseas Trust Bank (OTB) in Hong Kong led to a spate of rumors against a large domestic bank, which sparked off a series of runs against its branches. Although the run was quickly dispelled, it was the first time runs had appeared in Malaysia for nearly 20 years. In September, the first of

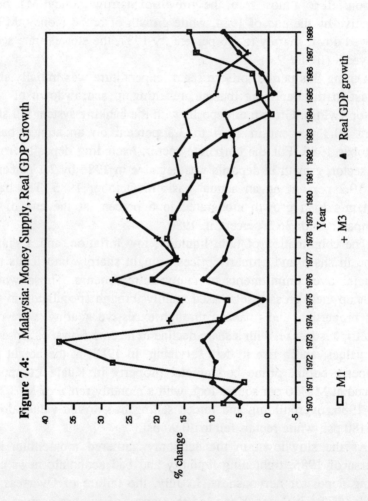

Figure 7.4:   Malaysia: Money Supply, Real GDP Growth

the failure of deposit-taking institutions (Setia Timor Credit and Leasing), a small credit leasing company engaged in illegal deposit-taking, emerged, causing further isolated runs against several licensed finance companies. These were also quickly dispelled. However, in December 1985, the collapse of a large public-listed company in Singapore, Pan-Electric, led to the unprecedented closure of the Kuala Lumpur and Singapore stock exchanges for three days. A run then occurred on a medium-size finance company associated with the (subsequently arrested) businessman with interests in Pan-Electric. This run subsided after liquidity was provided by Bank Negara and with the appointment of an experienced professional to manage the finance company. Thus began a spell of sporadic runs throughout 1986 against the weaker financial institutions, culminating in the failure of the deposit-taking cooperatives in July and August, which made the dangers of systemic failure a real possibility throughout the year.

The traumatic events of 1985–86 were as much a shock to bank management as to their borrowers. Throughout the last two decades, the Malaysian banking system had enjoyed a period of rising profits, with pre-tax profits peaking at nearly M$1 billion in 1984 (figure 7.5). In a period of uninterrupted growth and rising property (and hence security) values, bad loans were negligible, and as late as 1983, specific and bad debt provisions averaged only 1 to 1.5 percent of total loans. Foreclosed property could easily be sold at values higher than loans outstanding. However, with M$37.3 billion wiped off the stock market capitalization and property prices falling under selling pressure, the banks began to face the specter of rising nonperforming loans and bad and doubtful debts in 1985–86.

The dangers of rapid expansion into loans and new areas of growth during times of prosperity without fully understanding the implications became first evident to the Malaysian banking system from the experience of the BMF affair in 1982. Bumiputra Malaysia Finance (BMF), the Hong Kong finance company subsidiary of the largest domestic bank, Bank Bumiputra, nearly failed through the extension of M$2.4 billion loans to several Hong Kong corporations and individuals and subsequently became nonperforming. The parent bank absorbed the losses, and the national oil corporation, Petronas, was brought in to become the largest shareholder by injecting fresh capital

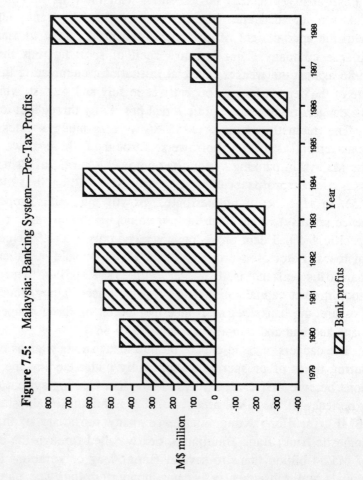

Figure 7.5:   Malaysia: Banking System—Pre-Tax Profits

into the bank. Petronas bought M$1,255 million in loans from the bank, and the balance of M$1 billion in nonperforming loans was written off in 1983, recording one of the largest losses in the history of Malaysian banking. The trial for the key persons involved is still continuing.

Malaysia has historically maintained a fairly high level of supervision over the banking system. The central bank has two departments supervising the banking system, with one in charge of off-site monitoring, and the other in bank examinations. Universal banking is not practiced in the country, and the banks are not allowed to acquire industrial and commercial shares without permission from the central bank, or to buy property in excess of their own operating needs. To identify the impact of the recession on the banking system, the central bank introduced uniform guidelines in 1985 for financial institutions on the treatment of non-accrued income or interest-in-suspense (IIS). At the beginning of the crisis in 1984, bad debt provisions and interest in suspense were only M$2 billion, or 3.5 percent of total loans of the banking system. Bad debt provisions at 2.3 percent were not out of line with international standards, such as that for the major British clearing banks of around 2 to 2.5 percent of total loans. However, by the end of 1988, total interest-in-suspense and bad debt provisions amounted to M$11.7 billion or 14.5 percent of gross loans of the banking system. These provisions covered approximately 47 percent of total nonperforming loans, a relatively high level compared with the average provisions of 25 to 40 percent for the international banks exposed to the highly indebted countries. The fastest rising component was IIS, indicating difficulties of the private sector in servicing debt during the recession. Between 1984 and 1988, IIS grew at an average annual rate of 72.9 percent from M$664 million to M$5.9 billion, while bad debt provisions rose at a slower rate of 42.3 percent from M$1.3 billion to M$5.7 billion (table 7.3).

The impact of these large provisions was to cut bank profits across the board. Even the best managed foreign banks showed substantially lower profits and several reported hefty losses, which were covered by fresh injection of capital. However, the most severely affected were four medium-sized domestic commercial banks that incurred heavy losses, particularly from their involvement in the property sector. All four banks had a relatively recent history: one being majority state owned, whose licence was issued in 1979; two were restructured banks from branches of foreign banks in the last 10 years; and the last was a joint-venture bank. The four banks collectively expanded their loan base aggressively between 1980-85, increasing their market share from 7.2 percent to 8.8 percent by the end of 1985. Overstretched managerial resources, poor internal procedures and controls, and instances of fraud and mismanagement led to lax control over costs and the burgeoning of nonperforming loans. The central bank had to step in to change the management and the board of directors, and to make arrangements to inject fresh capital into these banks, including direct central bank capital into three of these banks.

Table 7.3: Banking System: Outstanding Interest in Suspense and Bad Debt Provisions

Fiscal year	Interest in suspense M$ millions	Bad debt provisions M$ millions	Total as percentage of total loans
1984	664	1,346	3.5
1985	1,500	2,493	5.6
1986	2,844	4,056	9.7
1987	4,242	5,188	12.9
1988	5,932	5,722	14.5

Source: Bank Negara Malaysia.

Among the forty-seven licensed finance companies, which were traditionally providers of consumer and housing finance, problems also emerged among those that aggressively lent to finance real estate development and shares, especially the new entrants to the field. In 1980, only two finance companies reported small operating losses. By 1984, eleven out of forty-seven finance companies reported losses totaling M$17 million (out of industry profits of M$227 million), of which eight were new finance companies started between 1979-85. The finance companies also lagged behind the commercial banks in building professional expertise in commercial credit operations, and were slower in restricting loans to the property sector. Consequently, the industry was hit relatively severely, and by 1987 losses had risen to

M$252 million. The central bank had to assume control of four fi-
nance companies that were unable to inject new capital to cover their
losses. Fortunately, many of the other finance companies had strong
shareholders (one-third were subsidiaries of banks) and were able to
cover their capital deficiencies.

Nonbank Financial Intermediaries

As a group, the nonbank financial intermediaries account for 31
percent of the assets of the Malaysian financial system. However, the
bulk of the assets were accounted for by the provident and pension
funds, and the national savings bank, whose assets were primarily in
government bonds or deposits with the banking system. The seven development banks in Malaysia, with total assets of M$4.6 billion, also
incurred some losses during the recession, but since most of them were
state owned and funded, they had sufficient capital funds to cushion
them against the losses. The weakest link in the group of nonbank financial intermediaries was the group of deposit-taking cooperatives
(DTCs) and a handful of illegal deposit-taking institutions (DTIs) in
the informal market, whose total assets altogether did not exceed M$5
billion, or 2.5 percent, of the total assets of the financial system.

These financial intermediaries emerged in the 1970s ostensibly as
part of the cooperative movement, but were quasi-finance companies
that acted to collect deposits to finance business activities without the
constraints of supervision by the central bank. The DTIs in particular
were pawnbrokers or credit and leasing companies that took deposits
illegally from the public to fund their lending or investment activities,
in contravention of the law, which required a license from the central
bank for deposit taking. The cooperatives, however, operated under
the legal loophole that cooperatives could take deposits from their
members, and all depositors instantaneously became members by
payment of a nominal fee. The Department of Cooperative
Development, in charge of nearly 3,000 cooperatives, was not
equipped to supervise the rapidly expanding and complex operations
of the group of thirty-five DTCs, which expanded their operations
rapidly in the last decade.

The first major sign of emerging financial distress was in
September 1985 when a DTI named Setia Timor (Eastern Trust) failed

to honor its deposit withdrawals. Press reports of a few DTI directors and staff absconding with funds highlighted the existence of illegal DTIs in the informal sector that attracted deposits by paying interest rates of 2 to 3 percent per month (or 24 to 36 percent per annum), as against the 8 to 10 percent per annum offered in the banking system. Over the course of 1985–87, the central bank investigated thirty-three illegal DTIs that failed, involving 8,000 depositors and total deposits of M$49 million. Depositor nervousness began to spread to the DTCs, and in early July 1986, a large DTC named Kosatu, with M$156 million in deposits from 53,000 depositors spread over sixty-seven branches, suspended payments.

The DTC crisis that erupted bears an uncanny resemblance to the problems of the savings and loans institutions in the United States. Spawning from a relatively slow growing cooperative movement in the 1960s, the thirty-five DTCs had found deposit taking a golden way to diversify out of traditional consumer financing and to expand their activities with minimal supervision over their lending and investment activities. Spearheaded by the Cooperative central bank, the largest of the DTCs, these thirty-five DTCs as a group had a membership of over one million, over 600 branches (as against 860 for the commercial banks), and total deposits of over M$4 billion. Other than a simple requirement to keep 25 percent of deposits in liquid form (which was often ignored), there were no statutory reserve requirements nor lender of last facilities for these DTCs. Audited accounts were sometimes up to two years behind time. These DTCs rapidly expanded into share and property investment, often to companies connected with DTC board members or staff. The twenty-four DTCs investigated had 106 subsidiaries or related companies, ranging from a newspaper to a cosmetics distribution firm.

With no conventional legal powers and administrative machinery to cope with the crisis, the government promulgated the Essential (Protection of Depositors) Regulations 1986 under the Emergency Act on July 23, 1986 in order to empower the central bank to freeze the assets of Kosatu and its principal officers, to impound their passports, and conduct an investigation. However, contagion spread quickly from Kosatu to the other DTCs, which quickly ran out of funds to meet deposit withdrawals. As matters reached crisis point, the government had to direct the central bank on August 5 to suspend and investigate these twenty-three DTCs.

The investigation, which mobilized seventeen accounting firms to do the work in conjunction with central bank examination teams, found that the twenty-four DTCs in distress had 522,000 members, 630 branches, and total deposits of M$1.5 billion. Twenty-one of the DTCs were found to be insolvent, with losses totaling an estimated M$683 million, or 38.8 percent, of total assets. Although the position varied from DTC to DTC, on the average, a DTC depositor would have lost at least 42 sen out of every M$1 deposited (table 7.4). The DTCs were also illiquid, since many of them did not maintain the minimum liquidity ratio of 25 percent of deposits and were in no position to meet significant deposit withdrawals. The problems were compounded by gross mismanagement, including overinvestment in land and property, lack of control over loss-making subsidiaries, widespread speculation in shares, imprudent lending to directors and interested parties, fraudulent misappropriation of funds, criminal breach of trust, and many conflicts of interest situations. Based upon the investigation results, Bank Negara reported nine cases of fraud and twenty-one cases of conflicts of interest and technical offenses to the police. Many court cases are still pending.

The investigations also revealed numerous instances of blatant disregard for rules and regulations. By opening branches freely (often

Table 7.4: Losses of Twenty-Four Failed Deposit-Taking Cooperatives (DTCs)

	Book value M$ million	Estimated losses M$ million	Percent of book value
Fixed assets	150.5	4.4	2.9
Housing projects	185.5	30.6	16.5
Investment in shares	263.6	93.6	35.5
Loans	948.0	532.8	56.2
Other assets	214.3	21.7	10.1
Total	1,761.9	683.1	38.8

Source: Report on the Deposit-Taking Cooperatives, November 1986.

without permission) and offering higher deposit rates and attractive commission schemes for their branch staff to collect deposits, the DTCs were engaged in a vicious cycle of Ponzi financing, borrowing from new depositors to meet deposit withdrawals and interest payments and to cover the mounting losses. Their fundamental structure was flawed with gross undercapitalization, and overcommitment in long-term and speculative assets, funded by short-term deposits. The lack of trustworthy and prudent management, together with undercapitalization and weak supervision, was a formula for disaster.

Almost all the DTCs were affected by the recession. The apex cooperative to the DTCs, the Cooperative central bank (CCB) with 363,749 members and total deposits of M$1.5 billion, also began to face problems of nonperforming loans. The 1987 audited accounts of CCB showed accumulated losses of over M$726 million, and a capital deficiency of M$652 million. The CCB was put into receivership and the government made available a standby facility of M$323 million to help its liquidity needs. By the end of 1987, Bank Negara had thirty-two DTCs under its investigation or supervision, involving total deposits of M$3.1 billion, or an estimated 77 percent of the total deposits of the thirty-eight identified DTCs (thirty-five original DTCs and three in Sabah) in the country.

Among the nonbank financial intermediaries, the *insurance industry* was also not spared from the ravages of the recession. In the financial year that ended 1986, fourteen out of sixty-one insurance companies did not comply with the minimum solvency requirement of 20 percent of their net premium income. Inspection findings of the Office of the Director General of Insurance revealed that solvency problems had been compounded by the underprovisioning of outstanding claims reserves, bad debts from poor agency collection, and falls in value of investments in quoted securities and landed properties. To coordinate supervision of the financial system as a whole, the duties and responsibilities of the director-general of Insurance, previously a department of the treasury, were transferred to the central bank with effect from April 1, 1988.

Issues and Resolution

Approach Toward Ailing Financial Institutions

Financial stress arising from a sudden downward shift in relative prices fundamentally causes a shrinking of enterprise balance sheets. This contraction occurs primarily through a reduced cash flow and deterioration in the profit and loss account. Initially, enterprises that were not able to adjust their expenditure to the shortfall in income begin to suffer large operating losses. In addition, they may also suffer substantial capital losses, since forced disposal of assets in order to realize cash, arising from a *liquidity crisis,* often leads to a *solvency crisis*. Faced with survival problems, many cash-strapped enterprises engaged in "distress borrowing," paying exceptionally high rates for funds just to meet temporary liquidity shortfalls. In 1985, the real rate of borrowing had risen to an unprecedented 11.8 percent per annum, compared with only 2 to 3 percent per annum in 1981 (figure 7.6).
An interesting point to note is that while distressed borrowers were forced to pay high real interest rates in their demand for funds, the banking system was generally unwilling to reduce lending rates even when general liquidity improved and deposit rates began to fall. Between 1985 and 1988, the gross interest margin of the banks actually rose from 4.2 to 5.2 percentage points (table 7.5). The reason was simply that the banks tried to maintain high lending rates, since they were either not collecting interest from their nonperforming loans due to the interest-in-suspense, or they were forced to recover lost profits due to higher provisions for bad debts. They therefore maintained lower deposit rates and high nominal lending rates, so that the depositors and even good borrowers had to "subsidize" the banks' losses in the nonperforming loans. At the micro-level, this was good for the banking system, since the banks would be able to recover profitability sooner through higher spreads and loan margins. However, at the macro policy level, high real lending rates were felt to be deterring new investments in the economy to aid the recovery process, while the continued low deposit rates were encouraging disintermediation in the banking system, as depositors shifted out of bank deposits into other

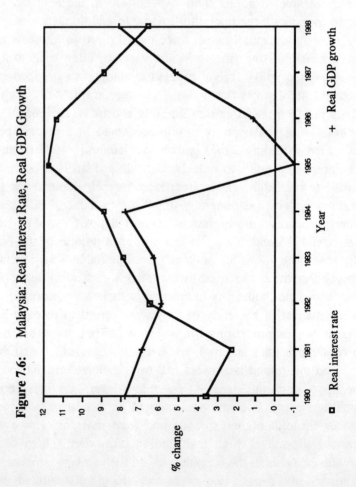

Figure 7.6: Malaysia: Real Interest Rate, Real GDP Growth

Table 7.5: Malaysia: Commercial Banks' Average Loan Margins
(in percent)

Item	1985		1986		1987		1988	
	% p.a.	*Share*	*% p.a.*	*Share*	*% p.a.*	*Share*	*% p.a.*	*Share*
Average lending rate	15.2	100.0	15.0	100.0	12.7	100.0	10.9	100.0
Minus cost of funds	11.0	72.4	10.1	67.3	7.6	59.8	5.7	52.3
Minus gross margin	4.2	27.6	4.9	32.7	5.1	40.2	5.2	47.7
Minus int. in suspense	1.4	9.2	2.1	14.0	2.3	18.1	2.5	22.9
Minus net margin	2.8	18.4	2.8	18.7	2.8	22.1	2.7	24.8
Minus overheads	3.5	23.0	3.2	21.4	3.2	25.2	3.2	29.4
Minus bad debt provisions	1.9	12.5	2.3	15.3	1.8	14.3	1.0	9.2
Minus net loan margin	-2.6	-17.1	-2.7	-18.0	-2.2	-17.4	-1.5	-13.8
Plus nonloan income	2.1	13.8	2.2	14.7	2.7	21.3	2.8	25.7
Minus net yield	-0.5	- 3.3	-0.5	- 3.3	0.5	3.9	1.3	11.9

p.a. = per annum
Source: Bank Negara Malaysia

assets. Accordingly, to ensure that the benefits of lower deposit rates could be "passed through" to the borrowers, the central bank had to use "moral suasion" to get the banks to reduce their interest rate margins. The banks were urged to achieve profitability and moderate loans margins through reductions in their operating costs. In other words, the banks had to significantly reduce their costs of intermediation.

A second factor to consider was the institutional premise that the central bank was established as a lender of last resort only to the banking system, to provide liquidity in times of stress. However, since Bank Negara was prevented by law from providing these facilities to institutions not under its charge, there was the danger that contagion from failing unsupervised financial institutions could spread to the monetary sector, that is, the licensed banks and finance companies. It was clear therefore that a financial safety net is only as strong as its weakest link. First, weaknesses in the less regulated or unregulated sectors in the financial system could pose a threat to the stability in the regulated sector through contagion. Second, the sharp fluctuation in the commodity, share, and property prices had subjected parts of the financial system to stresses and strains it was never designed to absorb. Third, the uneven quality of assets, management, capital base, and supervision within the financial system, including the informal sector, meant that an uncoordinated supervisory mechanism cannot cope with shocks emanating from the recession. A legal framework that clearly delineates supervisory powers and the administrative capacity to deal with future financial stresses had to be built.

Another key issue faced by Bank Negara in the wake of the significant number of sporadic runs against branches of financial institutions was whether a deposit insurance scheme was necessary. Bank Negara evaluated the feasibility of establishing a deposit insurance scheme to cover small deposits that would serve the purpose of keeping the small depositors at bay whenever news of instability befell any deposit-taking institution. However, a major disadvantage was that the burden of deposit insurance premiums would fall unevenly between the weaker and smaller institutions on the one hand and the larger and stronger banks and financial institutions on the other. Moreover, deposit insurance carries the inherent danger of "moral hazard," whereby bank management could be encouraged to take undue risks in the management of assets, since the fear of runs against deposit liabilities is removed. Consequently, on balance, it was considered not timely to launch the scheme.

The bank restructuring exercise was approached essentially from two fronts: monetary and regulatory. These objectives were, however, sometimes contradictory. Tighter monetary policy by raising interest rates had the effect of worsening the nonperforming loans of the banking system, as private sector borrowers could not service the high real interest rates from current cash flow. On the other hand, institutional adjustments at the micro level could not be achieved without macroeconomic changes, in terms of monetary policy as well as regulatory laws and guidelines. A top priority in monetary policy was to ease the contractionary effects of fiscal retrenchment and the deterioration in the balance of payments. However, the bank had considerable difficulty in reducing the abnormally high real rates of interest, even when deposit rates fell when liquidity recovered with improvements in the balance of payments in 1987. This was because of the reluctance of the banking system to reduce lending rates, due to their large overhang of nonperforming loans. The bank had to make major amendments to meet both objectives, including the removal of some prudential/monetary regulations in order to promote greater efficiency in the banking industry.

Monetary and Prudential Measures 1985–86

In 1985–86, Bank Negara introduced a series of monetary and policy measures designed to address the macroeconomic impact of the recession on the banking system. These included an extensive reform of the bank's export credit refinancing scheme to promote exports, the creation of a M$1 billion New Investments Fund to shift bank lending out of real estate to the productive (tradables) sectors of agriculture, manufacturing, and tourism, and a reduction in the liquidity and statutory reserve ratios of the commercial banks to lower their effective cost of funds. The bank also introduced a more flexible interest rate regime by freeing deposit rates, and encouraged the establishment of a secondary mortgage market to securitize long-term housing loans. Of key macroeconomic importance was the move to allow the currency to find its own level in the foreign exchange market, with only some intervention to stabilize sporadic speculative bouts.

At the same time that macroeconomic adjustments were taking place in fiscal, monetary, and exchange rate policies, and realizing that the adjustment process would begin to place considerable pressure on the banking system, the central bank also put into place in 1985–86 a number of regulatory changes designed to strengthen the structure of the banking system and its own regulatory powers to prevent and control damage arising from the recession. These included key changes to the banking laws and regulations to achieve the following:

- Introduction of the minimum capital adequacy requirements to be maintained by the commercial banks, which had the effect of raising the average capital ratio of Malaysian banks from 7.4 percent of total assets at the end of 1984 to 8.1 percent at the end of 1987;
- Dispersion in the ownership of financial institutions, by limiting the maximum holding of individuals, including family holding companies, in the equity of a financial institution to 10 percent, while any company or cooperative may not hold more than 20 percent;
- Introduction of penalties to prevent abuses of authority in the bank lending process;
- Powers to the central bank to lend against shares of, and purchase equity in, ailing financial institutions, to enable the bank, in the event of insolvency or illiquidity of a bank or finance company, to lend or to inject additional equity quickly into the problem institution;
- Restriction of bank credit to single customers to not more than 30 percent of shareholders' funds, to prevent the overconcentration of loans in any particular sector or customer;
- Prohibition of lending to directors and staff of banks and finance companies to prevent conflicts of interest and abuses;
- Introduction of guidelines on suspension of interest on nonperforming loans and provisions on bad and doubtful debts to ensure that the financial community followed sound, consistent, and prudent lending policies, and to standardize the accounting treatment of income from overdue loans and provisions;

- Establishment of board audit and examination committees, to reinforce the boards' supervision of bank management over the day-to-day affairs of the banks;
- Establishment of a central credit bureau to monitor and improve credit information on bank and finance company customers on a consolidated basis;
- Improvement of statistical reporting to the central bank, such as regular reporting on the size of nonperforming loans and exposures to share and property financing, loan margins, and bank productivity, through computerized data input;
- Improvement of on-site bank examination capability, by strengthening the bank examination staff force and conducting more frequent bank examinations.

A key legislative move to overcome the deficiencies of the existing bank legislation to combat illegal deposit-taking activities and to allow the central bank to act quickly in an emergency was the promulgation of the Essential Regulations in July 1986, which empowered the bank to:

- Investigate the affairs of any deposit-taker, including the power to enter and search any office or place of business; compel the production and retention of accounts, books, and documents; interrogate on oath or affirmation; and detain persons pending the completion of a search or interrogation;
- Order to freeze property and restrict departure from Malaysia, including the impounding of passports;
- Require the person to cease deposit-taking and refund the deposits taken;
- assume control of and carry on the business of the deposit taker or appoint someone to do so;
- Apply to the High Court to appoint a receiver to manage the affairs and property of the deposit taker;
- Petition the High Court to wind-up the illegal deposit taker.

To protect the public in the exercise of these wide powers, the central bank has to seek and abide by the advice of an advisory panel, comprising representatives of the private sector, the chairman of the association of banks, the treasury, and the attorney-general.

Modus Operandi of Rescue Packages

In assessing financial institutions, central banks the world over apply the famous CAMEL test, involving the assessment of *capital adequacy, asset quality, management quality, earnings capacity, and liquidity*. The experience of Bank Negara in the area of rescuing ailing financial institutions is that, except in the case of the DTCs, *liquidity* has never been a major problem with ailing financial institutions, since they could easily borrow funds from the interbank market or raise interest rates to attract funds to meet immediate liquidity needs. Two elements were, however, vital: *capital* and *management*. Adequate capital without good management is not sufficient to prevent losses. On the other hand, the best management cannot turn around an ailing institution if it does not have adequate capital. The first priority of any rescue plan is to restore operating profits, and this implies sufficient capital to cover all contingent and realized losses from assets revaluation, including nonperforming loans; and generate income to cover all costs.

A rule of thumb to test the viability of financial institutions is that *non-income earning assets must be supported by non-interest bearing liabilities*. The ailing financial institution should therefore be provided sufficient new funds to generate income to service its overheads and deposit liabilities. Inevitably, the rescue process involves four key processes—investigation and identification of the scope and depth of the losses; determination of the capital or new funds required to put the institution on a sound footing; the evaluation of various options, particularly in terms of who should foot the bill; and finally, the appointment of the right caliber persons to run the revamped institution.

Options for Rescue

The options available to rescue ailing financial institutions are generally as follows:

- Change management;
- Defer losses by staggering provisions, so as not to show large losses;
- Provide soft loans to subsidize operations;
- Buy out of nonperforming loans by another institution;

- Inject new capital by existing shareholders, by new shareholders, and by regulatory authorities;
- Merge with or absorb stronger institutions;
- Liquidate.

Changing management is a vital precondition in any rescue plan. Not only is the *competence* of management at stake, but the *credibility* of management with staff, creditors, depositors, and the regulatory authority is vital to the success of any rescue plan. Retaining old management of ailing institutions to manage affairs is like "leaving monkeys to look after bananas." The losses would inevitably escalate as existing management has every incentive to cover up its mistakes (and misdeeds) and to siphon off funds before they are detected. The choice of the other options depends on the prompt recognition of the extent of the losses and the apportionment of the losses to the shareholders, depositors, other creditors, or the government (directly through grants and subsidies) or indirectly through soft loans and aid through the central bank. The question of burden sharing lies at the heart of the bank restructuring exercise.

In the light of the prevailing circumstances, and given the budgetary constraint of the government during a period of high fiscal deficits, it was decided that the matter of ailing financial institutions should be addressed head on with the central bank shouldering the brunt of the burden of the investigation, diagnosis of problems, evaluation and execution of the rescue plans, as well as funding.

The Rescue of the Problem Banks

In general, the stance of the central bank in the rescue package was as follows:

- First, require the ailing institutions to recognize all losses and interest in suspense immediately, rather than attempting to stagger such losses by deferring the problem.
- Second, change management, by first revamping the board of directors and then appointing tested professionals to serve as chief executives, and thereafter to give more or less full discretion to the appointed board to do whatever is necessary to stem the losses and turn around the institutions.

- Third, require existing shareholders to inject as much capital as possible through a rights issue, and supplement such capital required to meet the minimum capital adequacy requirements through the central bank.
- Fourth, tighten reporting requirements of the ailing institution in "intensive care" to the central bank through regular reviews and discussion, including follow-up inspections.

The problems of the three ailing banks in which Bank Negara subsequently injected capital emerged from the inspections of these banks for the 1985 financial year. In all three cases, there was initially considerable bank management and shareholder resistance to recognizing immediately the enormity of the existing problems. Once it was clear that the problems were beyond the capability of existing management and shareholders to resolve, the central bank assumed control and appointed new directors and chief executives to undertake a thorough review of the depth and scope of the problems. In all three cases, rights issues were called and the central bank took up the shortfall in rights. Of the total losses of the three banks in 1985–86, amounting to M$1,203 million, the existing shareholders injected M$159 million in rights issues, Bank Negara injected M$672 million, and the balance was met through subordinated loans of M$401 million (table 7.6).

The shares subscribed by Bank Negara are held in trust for disposal later under a buy-back scheme, whereby those shareholders who participate in the scheme would be allowed to buy back their unsubscribed shares at par plus holding cost.

Table 7.6: Key Data of Three Ailing Commercial Banks

Category	1984	1985	1986	1987[2]
Total deposits	4,309	4,568	3,945	3,513
Total loans	3,898	4,326	4,466	3,367
Total pre-tax losses	39	591	612	2
Increase/(decrease) in capital [1]	38	(5)	162	1,130
Capital adequacy ratio (percent) (minimum: 4 percent)	4.3	3.0	2.8	5.2

1. Paid-up capital and subordinated loans.
2. Preliminary.
Source: Bank Negara Malaysia.

The Rescue of the Twenty-Four DTCs

Following the freeze and investigations of the twenty-four ailing DTCs in July and August 1986, pressures began to mount for a quick rescue plan. Emotions became highly charged as over 522,000 depositors (out of a population of 16.5 million) and approximately M$1.5 billion in deposits were involved. To assess public opinion on an appropriate rescue scheme, the government appointed a special Action Committee on Cooperatives (ACC), chaired by Bank Negara, with representatives from the government and the private sector. The depositors expressed very strong views that their deposits should be guaranteed in full by the government as a matter of legal and moral responsibility. The depositors also objected strongly to the conversion of their deposits into equity and also demanded prompt legal action against the DTC staff responsible for mismanagement, fraud, and criminal breach of trust.

The task of the ACC was to find an appropriate restructuring plan that would be acceptable to all. Among the options studied was a preliminary plan (loosely referred to as the 25:25:50 solution), which involved the payment of up to 25 percent of deposits in cash immediately, a further 25 percent in two-year deposits at a maximum of 6 percent per annum interest and the balance converted into equity. This scheme was designed as a general framework to restructure the cooperatives, but was rejected when it was prematurely leaked to the press.

The ACC also considered other options available including:

- *Place all twenty-four DTCs under liquidation.* This was rejected as forced selling would increase the losses of the DTCs.
- *Exchange deposits for unit trusts* (to help depositor liquidity). This was rejected as not all depositors would agree to a conversion, and most of the DTC assets could not qualify as trustee assets under the law.
- *Convert deposits into shares of a public company.* The transfer of DTC assets and liabilities into a public company would result in the transfer of the losses to the public company. Such a company could not be listed under existing equity flotation guidelines.

- *Merge several DTCs into one apex cooperative bank.* This would mean transferring the losses of the DTCs into a single institution. Merging different managements and staff of different DTCs would also compound the problems of rehabilitation.
- *Get full government guarantee of deposits.* This would imply that the government must be prepared to inject cash of M$1.5 billion ultimately, and bear losses of nearly M$700 million. Under the prevailing conditions of financial stringency and fiscal restraint, the government was not able to bear such large losses.

The ACC recognized the enormous complexity of the problems since the capital deficiency was at least M$680 million, thus any rescue vehicle would be faced with a mire of legal suits that could jeopardize any rescue scheme. After studying various options, the committee recommended a three-stage approach. For those DTCs whose net asset backing of each $1 of deposit was close to $1, the government should invite a number of strong banks or finance companies to assume their deposit liabilities and the attendant assets. To assist the rescue package, Bank Negara should provide soft loans to meet the liquidity needs of the banks and finance companies concerned. For those DTCs with large losses, the depositors should be offered a combination of cash and equity or convertible bonds.

The government white paper on the DTCs published in November 1986 adopted most of the recommendations of the ACC. As a matter of principle, the public should not be responsible for the large losses arising from the bad management of the cooperatives. The depositors would be able to receive the amount of their deposits in proportion to the net asset backing of their respective DTC. To help the reconstruction process, all rescue schemes that involved debt/equity conversion for the depositors would be based on the due process of law as approved by the courts.

The government also decided to change the cooperative laws to limit cooperatives to take only specific deposits from their members, such as for housing and education, and not savings and fixed deposits. The twenty-four DTCs would be placed under Bank Negara's supervision until all the soft loans had been repaid. To prevent law suits from creditors or depositors from jeopardizing the whole rescue package, receivers from accounting firms were appointed by the High Court to manage the assets of the twenty-four DTCs. The High Court also determined the ranking of payment to unsecured creditors, such as salaries and wages, legal fees, and essential services.

The white paper revealed that the twenty-four DTCs had invested nearly half of their total assets in connected lending or investments in subsidiaries and related companies and other shares. One-fifth of total assets was tied up in land, property, and housing. Another fifth was in loans to the cooperative members, while only 9 percent, as of the date of the freeze, was in cash and liquid assets, due mainly to large-scale deposit withdrawals during the run period.

The net assets available for distribution, after provisions suggested by the accountants of M$673 million, was M$890 million. This implied that the cooperatives had a total capital deficiency of M$601 million. After providing for secured loans and other creditors, *the net asset value per $1 deposit* for each DTC was estimated to range from 19 sen to as much as M$1.

The final rescue package was carried out in three stages. Stage one involved the "de-freezing" of the deposits of eleven cooperatives that had relatively small capital deficiencies. In January 1987, eleven DTCs (each of which had net asset backing per ringgit of deposits of close to M$1) received soft loans from the central bank, and reached agreement with their appointed banks or finance companies to take over their assets and liabilities, with full payment in cash to be made to all depositors over periods of up to five years *without interest*. These eleven DTCs had total deposits of M$191 million from 85,000 depositors.

Stage two of the rescue plan involved the group of twelve DTCs with moderate to heavy losses (which, on the whole, had an average asset backing of 39 sen per M$1 depositors). The scheme provided for a $1 for $1 return to all depositors through a combination of cash and equity, of which the cash component would be at least 50 percent of the deposits, while the balance would be converted into equity in a licensed financial institution that would absorb all the assets and liabilities of the twelve DTCs. In December 1987, an amendment to Section 31 of the central bank of Malaysia Ordinance, 1958, permitted the central bank to acquire equity in a finance company and to utilize it as a rescue vehicle under a government-approved scheme for the depositors.

Accordingly, the central bank acquired a small ailing licensed finance company, renamed it Kewangan Usahasama Makmur Berhad or KUMB, which in turn acquired the net assets and deposit liabilities of these 12 DTCs from their receivers. The 12 DTC depositors would be refunded in full through a combination of cash and equity depending on the net asset backing of each DTC, the minimum cash refund (over a period up to December 1989) being not less than 50 percent. The balance of the refund would comprise ordinary shares of M$1 each in KUMB. As soon as these shares become eligible for public listing, the intention is for KUMB to float its shares, so that the depositors stand to gain in capital appreciation if the share prices rise on flotation.

Stage three involved the largest of the DTCs, namely Koperatif Serbaguna Malaysia (KSM), which had deposits of $549 million and 166,000 depositors with an asset backing of about 50 sen per M$1 deposited. The government accepted the proposal by Magnum Corporation Berhad (MCB), a large public-listed company, and its licensed finance company subsidiary, Magnum Finance Berhad (MFB) to take over the net assets and deposit liabilities of KSM, which had indirect interests in MCB. Depositors of KSM would be repaid in full on a 50:50 basis, with 50 percent paid in cash in stages from 1987 to 1989, and the remaining 50 percent repaid initially in the form of irredeemable convertible unsecured loan stocks of MCB, at a price to be determined. The loan stock would be non-interest bearing for the first two years, and would be convertible into MCB ordinary shares at a predetermined rate over two years from 1989-91.

To enable the DTC rescue schemes to work, the central bank would provide, in the final analysis, M$720 million in soft loans at 1 percent per annum, plus M$280 million in commercial loans at 4 percent per annum for a term of ten years, to the rescuing financial institutions to implement the rescue schemes for the failed DTCs. Altogether, the rescue of the twenty-four DTCs involving deposits of M$1.5 billion, required M$1 billion in loans from the bank as well as M$23.4 million in professional fees incurred in the investigations and receivership (table 7.7).

Table 7.7: Summary of Rescue Plan for Twenty-four DTCs

Item	11 DTCs	KUMBI 12 DTCs	KSM Magnum	Total
Membership	84,632	270,740	166,388	521,760
Assets taken over (M$ millions)	181	257	407	845
Liabilities taken over (M$ millions)	191	709	592	1,492
Losses/shortfall (M$ millions)	10	452	185	647
Deposits converted into shares (M$ millions)	–	315	277	592

Source: Bank Negara Malaysia.

With respect to the persons responsible for the mismanagement of funds of the DTCs, twenty-two directors of eight DTCs were charged in court. Of these, four were found guilty and sentenced to jail, while the remaining are still awaiting trial.

Evaluation

Results and Lessons

The prompt action taken by Bank Negara to step in to intervene in the management and capital injection of the three ailing banks and the announcement of the rescue plans for the twenty-four DTCs during the course of 1987 and early 1988 had stabilized public confidence in the financial system and avoided the dangers of contagion spreading, at a time when the economy was in the trough of the recession. By the fourth quarter of 1986, commodity prices began an upturn, leading to an immediate injection of liquidity into the banking system from growing export income. As it turned out, 1987 proved to be a year of strong recovery, with GDP growing by 5.2 percent in real terms. The terms of trade improved by 12.4 percent, and the current account in the balance of payments recorded in 1987 a M$6.4 billion surplus, or 8.6 percent of GNP, with gross external reserves rising to M$19.4 billion, or 7.4 months, of retained imports. Although the budget of the Federal government remained in deficit, despite continued retrenchment of development expenditure, the financing deficit of the federal government was reduced sharply to 5.6 percent of GNP by 1988, allowing the government to prepay over M$4 billion of its external debts. By 1989, the national external debt had fallen sharply to M$42 billion or 43.9 percent of GNP, as against 76.1 percent in 1986. Clearly, the structural adjustment program was beginning to yield results.

In 1988, the economy continued to rebound with vigor, with real GDP growth of 8.1 percent. With the depreciation of the ringgit, the terms of trade improved by 12.4 percent in 1987, while export proceeds jumped by 24.6 percent in 1987 and 21.3 percent in 1988. As confidence revived, the KLSE market capitalization rose by 45 percent from the trough just after the October 19, 1987 crash to a recent peak of M$101.9 million on August 9, 1988. Similarly, property prices began to firm with strong sales in low-cost housing in urban centers and revival in commercial property prices from the trough of M$180 per square foot in 1986 to M$279 psf in early 1989. The reflation in asset prices and enterprise cash flow had their beneficial impact on bank profitability. Preliminary unaudited data on bank profits revealed a rebound in pre-tax profits to M$794 million in 1988, compared with M$125 million in 1987, as bad debt provisions fell by 28.1 percent. Most of the recovery was in the write-back of provisions for nonperforming loans, amounting to M$828 million in 1988, or nearly double the amount in the previous year.

Given the improvement in the banking environment, a radical switch in approach to the problem of nonperforming loans was made when the focus of loan rehabilitation was switched from the bank level to the enterprise level. The central bank established a M$500 million Enterprise Rehabilitation Fund in 1988, aimed at reducing the overhang of stalled projects and nonperforming loans. The fund, financed by Bank Negara and managed by a development bank, would provide seed capital to recession-hit Bumiputra (indigenous) enterprises that have been found to be fundamentally viable. The projects would be co-financed with the existing lenders, which would provide additional working capital for the turnaround enterprises. Specialist Turnaround Groups, comprising leading professionals in the fields of manufacturing, trading, agriculture, and property, would evaluate the viability of eligible enterprises for recommendation for assistance under the fund.

It may still be too premature to evaluate objectively the results of the bank restructuring exercise for the DTCs and ailing banks and finance companies. In the case of the twenty-four DTCs, eleven DTCs had already been resolved, with the refund of their deposits assured, while twelve others with weaker asset backing have been absorbed into a single licensed finance company, KUMB. The licensed finance company has been restructured with a strong board and new management and is busily engaged in the taking over of assets of the twelve DTCs. The three problem banks have since turned around from a combined audited pre-tax loss of M$679 million in 1986 to a preliminary combined unaudited profit of M$71 million in 1988. The capital restructuring program for the four finance companies is ongoing, but the losses have been stemmed. Some of them may be absorbed into larger and more efficient banks or finance companies. While there remain pockets of unresolved problem areas in the financial institutions, especially among the smaller finance companies, on the whole, the "Malaysian banking sector has regained health, and concern that the system would collapse has faded" (*Asian Wall Street Journal,* May 1989).

Losses and Costs

In summary, the sharp deflation in the Malaysian economy in 1985–86 manifested itself in large losses by various financial institutions. It was most evident among four of the thirty-eight commercial banks, four of the forty-seven finance companies and thirty-two deposit-taking cooperatives, as well as thirty-three illegal deposit-taking institutions. The DTIs in the informal sector were relatively small in number and size, accounting for less than 8,000 depositors and M$46 million in deposits. The impact on the four banks, four finance companies, and thirty-two DTCs that came directly under the control of Bank Negara was much larger. These institutions together had total deposits of M$9.4 billion, comprising M$6 billion for the four commercial banks and four finance companies and M$3.4 billion for the thirty-two DTCs, which would comprise in sum 10.4 percent of total deposits of M$90 billion of the financial system at the end of 1986. In aggregate, these forty institutions lost between 1985–87 about M$3.1 billion, comprising M$1.7 billion in the case of the banks and finance companies and M$1.4 billion in the case of the DTCs. These losses were equivalent to 4.7 percent of GNP in 1986. It is interesting to note that losses in the banking sector, which was tightly supervised by the central bank, amounted to 2.4 percent of total deposits in 1986, while losses in the lightly supervised DTC sector were as high as 40 percent of total deposits.

The rescue operations for these institutions have been costly, comprising M$1.3 billion in equity (M$672 million from Bank Negara for the three banks, and M$592 million conversion of DTC deposits into equity) and at least M$1.3 billion in assistance loans (comprising M$1 billion from Bank Negara for the twenty-four DTCs and M$323 million from the government for CCB). Not all these aid funds could be considered lost. Over time, with the sustained recovery of property prices, and a turnaround in operations, the equity component and a large part of the loans have a fair chance of being recovered.

The key lessons from the financial adjustment package in Malaysia may be broadly summarized as follows:

- Prompt action has to be taken decisively and immediately to address all problem areas in ailing financial institutions. The need to determine fairly accurately the extent of the damage and to address the problems of capital adequacy and competent management must be tackled with the greatest urgency. Failure to admit the size of the problems or delays in the resolution of these issues almost always compounds the problems and the costs involved.
- Problems in ailing financial institutions had generally been worse than they appeared at first sight. Only in very few examples had the reverse been shown to be true. This occurred mainly because of the problems of *transparency*. Many ailing financial institutions' managements were reluctant to recognize and report an accurate picture to the regulatory authorities once they began to face a deterioration in their performance. It takes a brave bank chairman to admit and pin down the true extent of the damage and recommend the necessary dosage of medicine required.
- The importance of additional equity capital has proved to be vital in any rescue package. Nonperforming loans can only be

supported by non-interest bearing capital. Lending high interest loans to tide over liquidity problems for an insolvent institution is pouring good money after bad. Without adequate capital and setting the gearing into the right levels, the strongest of management would have difficulty in turning around ailing institutions.

- For both the supervisory authorities and bank management, there is an urgent and important need to develop efficient and accurate reporting systems that can detect the true financial position of the financial institutions, including exposure to different types of risks. It is no longer sufficient to monitor institutions based purely on traditional balance sheet ratios. It is more important today to monitor frequently, sometimes on a month-to-month basis and in certain operations on a daily basis, the profit and loss account of the financial institutions in order to pinpoint the structural weaknesses in these institutions and their exposures to various risks.

- Prevention is better than the cure, as financial rescues are costly affairs. Devoting more resources to regular inspections and accurate monitoring would in the long run still be cheaper than rescue funding. As had been demonstrated in the case of the DTCs, light supervision without lender of last resort capabilities can result in large losses. However, as noted earlier, in an economywide deflation of asset prices, it is not possible to avoid losses completely.

- The process of financial institution supervision has to evolve with the times, as the lines of business demarcation in banking has become more blurred with competition, technological improvements, and internationalization. The supervisory authorities have to monitor not just the traditional monetary institutions, but also their interrelationships with the capital market, rural deposit institutions, development banks, and other financial institutions. In other words, the financial safety net, traditionally designed for the monetary sector only, may have to be widened and strengthened. The credit information in all sectors has to be pooled in order to have a good early warning system of problem areas. There are substantial economies of scale to be gained in coordination and pooling of resources in the supervision of financial institutions.

- Traditional banking laws and regulations must also change with the times. As technology evolves, the transmission of shocks within the system accelerates through the payments mechanism, while the scope for insider trading and white collar bank fraud and theft increases rapidly. The banking laws must therefore change to give scope for greater competition in financial products, while tightening prudential regulation against abuses of the system. At the same time, laws relating to bankruptcy (exit of enterprises) should be reformed to expedite and reduce the costs of bank restructuring. In June 1989, a new Banking and Financial Institutions Bill was tabled before Parliament to address these issues, including powers to the central bank to act quickly in future instances of financial distress in all sectors of the financial system.

- With greater internationalization, regulatory supervision over financial institutions not only have to be coordinated among sectors within an economy, but also internationally. The work of the Basle Committee is to be commended in this area.

- In the last analysis, after capital and proper control procedures have been put in place, the key to sound and healthy financial institutions still lies fundamentally in good quality management. Improved internal controls and procedures, and penalties against breaches of the law, code of ethics, and Chinese walls are still insufficient to deter insider trading, conflict of interests, and lending to interested parties, where large sums of money are involved. The temptations in financial institutions are great. Fraud in management must be detected promptly, and must be cut out early so that better procedures and professional, competent, and trustworthy management can be put into place as soon as possible.

- Finally, the bank restructuring exercise could only be achieved against the background of firm structural adjustment in the macroeconomic environment. The twin beneficial effects of fiscal retrenchment and depreciation of the currency brought a broad-based economic recovery, which assisted the bank restructuring process. Without the recovery of underlying enterprise profitability, a high level of national savings, and adequate foreign exchange reserves to cushion the system against shocks, the bank restructuring process would have been much more difficult and protracted. The political will and financial discipline to address the looming twin deficits in the balance of payments and the public sector were vital ingredients of the recovery program.

The success of Malaysia's financial adjustment program can only be evaluated objectively in the course of time. What has been an important ingredient in the structural adjustment program has been the determination and willingness of the Malaysian government to address the key issues at hand. In the long run it may well be that it was the twin factors of the fundamental resilience of the Malaysian economy and prudent economic management that had carried the day.

Bibliography

Bank Negara Malaysia (1983). "Management of the Banking System." In *Annual Report 1983*, pp. 19–25.

_____ (1984). "Management of the Banking System." pp. 26-35; "The Supply of High-rise Commercial Property and Condominiums," pp. 129-130. In *Annual Report 1984*.

_____ (1985). "Management of the Economy," p. 22; "Monetary Management," p. 29; "Management of the Banking System," pp. 32-43; "The Property Sector and Bank Financing," pp. 157-159. In *Annual Report 1985*.

_____ (1986). "Monetary Management," pp. 24-29, "Management of the Banking System," pp. 24-29; "Management of the Banking System," pp. 33-46; "The Deposit-Taking Cooperatives (DTCs)," pp. 119-124. In *Annual Report 1986*.

_____ (1987). "Monetary Management," p. 28; "Management of the Banking System," pp. 34-50. In *Annual Report 1987*.

_____ (1987). "Press Statement on Purchase of Shares in Problem Banks." PEN: 3/87/12 (BN).

_____ (1988). "Press Statement by the Governor on Details of the Rescue Package of the Remaining 13 Deposit-Taking Cooperatives." PEN: 1/88/44 (BN).

Malaysia, Government of (1986). "Report on the Deposit-Taking Cooperatives." Command Paper No. 50. November.

_____ (1986). "Investigation Report on Twenty-four Deposit-Taking Cooperatives." Attachment to Command Paper No. 50. November.

_____ (1987). "Solvency Provisions," pp. 16-17; "Inspections," p. 17. In *25th Annual Report of The Director General of Insurance, 1987*. Ministry of Finance.

Sheng, Andrew (1987a). *Capital Adequacy and Banking*. AFCM Luncheon Talk. October.

_____ (1987b). *Banking and Monetary Policies—A Framework for Economic Recovery*. MIM Ministerial Conference. November.

_____ (1988). *Regulation of the Banking System*. Lecture to BNM Staff. June.

Tan Sri Dato' Jaffar Hussein (1987). *The Management of the Banking System— Thoughts on Bank Regulation and Supervision*. Address in conjunction with the 10th Anniversary of IBBM, Malaysia. November.

World Bank (n.d.). *Malaysia: Industrializing a Primary Producer, Vol. 1* .

8

THE NORWEGIAN EXPERIENCE WITH FINANCIAL LIBERALIZATION AND BANKING PROBLEMS

Jon A. Solheim

Introduction

The following paper reviews the problems that have affected the Norwegian banking sector in recent years. First we will take a look at Norwegian economic policy, financial liberalization, cyclical movements, and structural developments of the credit market in the 1980s, followed by a presentation of banking developments and the particular nature of the problems faced by certain banks. Furthermore we will touch on the regulatory framework applying to banks and the role of the Guarantee Funds, the Banking, Insurance and Securities Commission, and Norges Bank in this context. Finally we will discuss the likely evolution of the regulatory framework for banks and the experience with financial liberalization.

Background

Economic Policy and Financial Liberalization

During the post-war period up to the mid-1980s, Norwegian economic policy was to a great extent characterized by direct regulations and selective use of policy instruments in monetary policy. The state banking system played an important role, the interest rate was set by the authorities at a level below the market rate, and there were extensive foreign exchange controls. There was a broad political consensus for the major elements of this policy. In the 1980s economic policy gradually became more market oriented. The change of political philosophy in a more liberal direction was influenced by developments in other industrial countries, but was also a result of increasing awareness of the costs, and the reduced effects, of existing regulations.

In 1984 direct regulation of bank lending was abolished, and there was a general shift in emphasis toward the use of indirect instruments to control the flow of credit. This coincided with a lack of political willingness to accept an increase in the Norwegian nominal rate of interest, despite rising domestic demand pressure. A commission that had reviewed the Norwegian tax system, a system marked by high taxes on capital (except housing) and on above-average incomes, presented its proposals in 1984. One proposal was to reduce interest deductibility. In Norway, all interest payments are deductible from gross income.

Since the highest marginal tax rate for households was about 70 percent, the incentive to borrow was substantial. The proposal was not, however, followed up by the political authorities at that time.

Fiscal policy was tightened somewhat in 1983-84, but was followed by an expansionary stance in 1985. Up to the end of 1985 oil prices were at a very high level. This generated strong growth in Norwegian export revenues, which in turn fueled expectations of continued strong income growth in Norway. Credit regulation was thus abolished at a time when strong real and expected income growth prevailed. The new lending situation led a rising share of income earners to take advantage of the easy access to credit at low real after-tax interest rates. As a result, overall domestic credit supply rose sharply, by 21 percent in 1985 and 20 percent in 1986.

The political authorities' priority of a stable nominal interest rate level, combined with a weakening of the external account position, led to the need for substantial central bank interventions in order to supply liquidity to the bank system to meet the strong demand for credit. At the end of 1986 central bank lending to banks stood at 14 percent of the banks' total assets compared with 1 percent at the end of 1984. In fact, because of the political objective of a stable nominal interest rate level, the central bank in the end had to finance a major part of the banks' credit expansion.

The Norwegian krone was devalued by 10 percent in May 1986, and economic policy was markedly tightened toward the end of 1986. Chart 8.1 shows that the strong growth in overall credit supply up to the end of 1986 was followed by a falling growth rate in subsequent years. The high level of recorded bank lending expansion in 1987 was affected by particular statistical factors and therefore does not reflect the underlying downward trend.

Cyclical Movements

Chart 8.2 shows that in the period 1981-84 economic growth in Norway was broadly on a par with the average of the OECD countries. In 1985-86 a strong cyclical upturn was a feature peculiar to the Norwegian economy, characterized by strong domestic demand, tight labor market, and growing inflation. Substantial investment and export growth in conjunction with a strong debt-financed increase in consumption under a deregulated credit market and the negative real after-tax interest rate fueled the cyclical upturn.

The growth in domestic demand and the fall in oil prices at the beginning of 1986 contributed to a dramatic deterioration of the current account in 1986 (chart 8.3). Since 1987 domestic demand has slowed considerably, partly due to the economic policy tightening but also as a result of the natural reaction following a period of high domestic demand and private debt accumulation. On the whole, economic developments in Norway from 1984 to 1989 were characterized by exceptionally large cyclical swings.

Chart 8.4 shows that the relatively stable, positive savings ratio of the household sector in the first half of the 1980s was replaced by a strong contraction in household savings in 1985 and 1986. This development was to some extent reversed in the period 1987-89. The reversal was partly due to the gradual restructuring of tax policy, making borrowing less advantageous. Despite the rising real after-tax interest rate, the savings ratio of the household sector was also markedly lower in 1989 than in the period 1980-84.

Credit Market Structure

The trend in market shares for various types of financial institutions is shown in table 8.1. The high market share of state banks in

Chart 8.1: Credit Supply and M2 (expanded)
(percent change from preceding year)

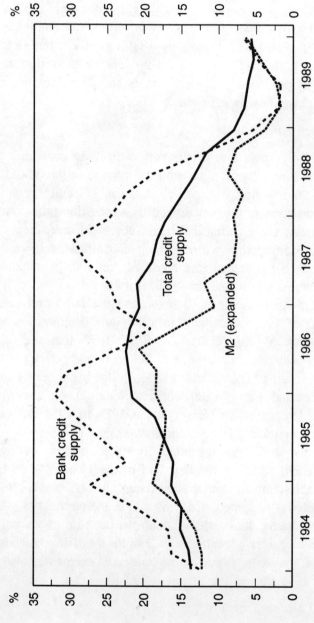

Chart 8.2: Growth of Real Domestic Demand

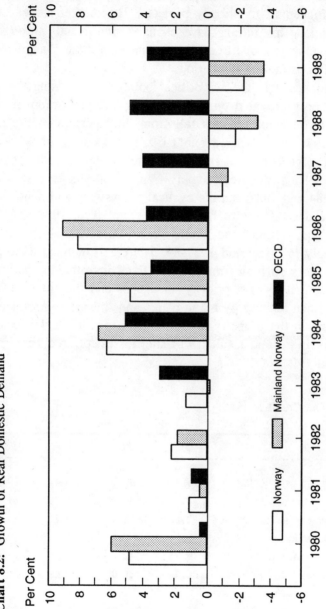

Per Cent

1980 reflects the fact that these banks were originally important means of channeling credit to priority projects. The market shares of the various financial institutions have changed significantly through the 1980s, a development that to a large extent reflects the changing regulatory conditions during this period.

In accordance with the authorities' policy of increasing the share of credit supply provided on market terms, the proportion of credit channeled through state banks fell from 38.8 percent of the credit market in 1980 to 21.6 percent in 1989. In the course of this period the role and organization of state banks have been markedly changed. On the other hand, the credit supply from private banks rose sharply between 1984 and 1987, but the cyclical downswing and major losses led to some deceleration of bank lending growth in 1988 and 1989. The credit supply from bond-issuing credit enterprises, however, also rose markedly in the period 1987-89. The credit of bond-issuing enterprises centers on basic financing of fixed investments, which are normally secured by first priority mortgages and thus carry a lower risk profile than lending by many banks and finance companies. The weaker trend in the property market and in the Norwegian business and industry in general resulted in rising losses for credit enterprises in 1989 and 1990.

Table 8.1: The Credit Market
(percent)

Category	1980	1984	1987	1989
Private banks	39.8	43.2	50.4	49.1
State banks	38.8	31.9	21.8	21.6
Private finance companies	2.2	3.4	3.2	3.1
Insurance companies	9.3	9.4	9.6	9.1
Private credit enterprises	9.9	12.1	15.0	17.1
Credit market total	100.0	100.0	100.0	100.0
Memo item: Total assets				
(NOK billion)	231.0	382.0	659.0	759.0

Note: Market shares based on total assets as of December 31 each year.
Source: Bank of Norway.

Developments in the Banking Sector—The Banking Problems

Main Developments

During the period of strong credit growth in 1984–86, competition for borrowers and market shares intensified. Important parameters of competition were rapid assessment of loan applications and greater willingness to run risks. The banks financed large investments in new firms and new areas of business, and the fledgling enterprises often had a low level of equity capital. However, the banks failed to match interest rates to the degree of risk involved. Moreover, lending decisions were decentralized, but this was not accompanied by new control routines.

As seen in chart 8.5, banks' loan losses showed some signs of increasing in the first half of the 1980s. The increase was most marked, however, after 1986. The heavy losses in 1987 were to a certain extent (about one-fourth) ascribable to the tightening of the definition of loan write-offs. The continued increase in losses in 1988–89 was not solely due to the banks' inadequate internal management systems, but also to the cyclical downturn in the years 1987-1989. Between 80 and 90 percent of the losses sustained were on loans to the corporate market, with a large share distributed on consumer-oriented sectors such as retail trade, the hotel and restaurant industry, and other services. Furthermore, a rising share of the losses referred to the aquaculture sector.

Chart 8.6 shows that banks' profits after losses were relatively stable up to 1986. As a result of banks' strong lending growth, starting in 1984, the proportion of short-term funds in banks' balance sheets obtained at money market rates rose. This led to increased funding costs and thereby to a weakening of banks' net interest ratio. This was in the first instance offset by an increase in income from securities and foreign currency trading. The increase in loan losses combined with losses on securities as a result of the stock market crash in the autumn of 1987 led to a negative result for commercial banks in 1987, the first time since World War II. Losses on securities trading were substantial in some of the commercial banks.

Chart 8.3: Current Account
(in billion NOK)

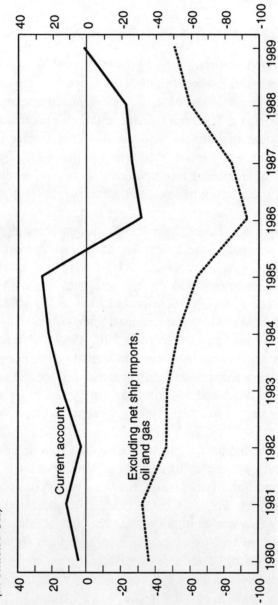

Chart 8.4: Household Sector Savings Ratio and Real After-Tax Interest Rates
(in percent)

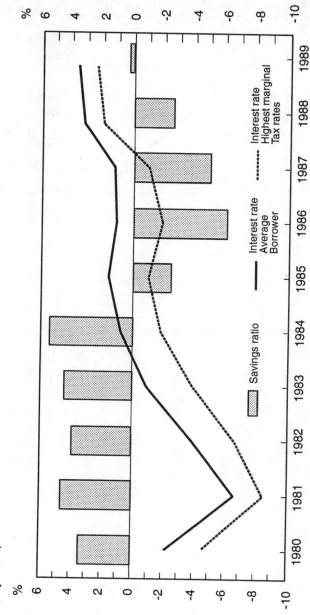

Chart 8.5: Losses of Commercial and Savings Banks

(million kroner)

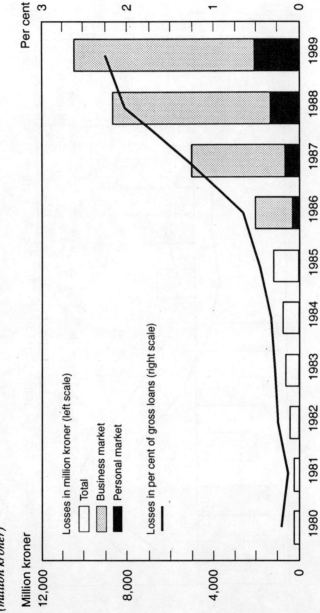

Chart 8.6: Profits and Losses of Commercial and Savings Banks
(in percent of average total assets)

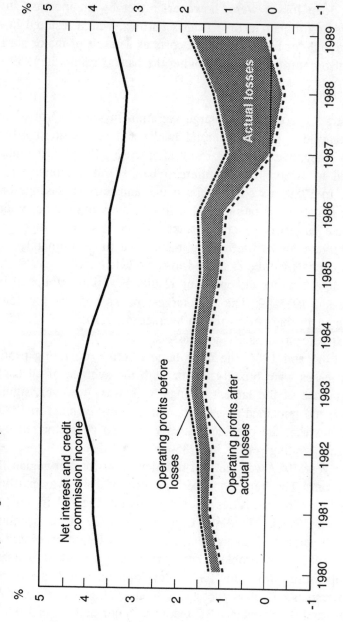

In 1988 and 1989 loan losses continued to increase. In 1989 the higher loan losses were, however, offset by an increase in banks' spreads and higher income from securities, which resulted in a profit (before tax) for banks. Reduced costs as a result of major staff reductions also contributed to improving the banks' results in 1989.

Banking Problems

Chart 8.6 conceals the large variation in banks' profits. In 1987, for example, eight commercial banks and seven savings banks reported a negative operating result after losses. In 1988, the number increased to twelve for commercial banks and eighteen for savings banks. In 1989, six commercial banks and thirteen savings banks reported negative operating results. In the following the development of the three largest commercial banks and the largest savings banks and the problem banks (defined as banks that have ultimately lost their equity capital) will be examined in some detail.

Table 8.2 shows the operating results of various groups of banks in the period 1985-89. The four largest banks and the problem banks accounted in this period for an average of, respectively, 52.5 percent and 5.0 percent of banks' total assets.

In 1985 and 1986, the three largest banks' operating profits after actual losses were broadly in line with the average of all banks. The performance of the largest savings bank was, however, significantly weaker, and remained so until its marked improvement in 1989. Table 8.2 shows that the problem banks were also characterized by below average operating profits in 1985-86.

The year 1987 was the first turbulent year for Norwegian financial institutions. The very poor performance of DnC was partly due to heavy losses on securities trading following the fall in stock market prices on "Black Monday," October 19, 1987. DnC accounted for about 80 percent of commercial banks' total losses on securities trading in 1987. The problem banks recorded a marked worsening of their operating profits in 1987, a development that was influenced by Sunnmørsbanken's heavy losses on loans and on securities trading.

DnC and Sparbanken ABC recorded major deficits in 1988 too, but the performance of the largest banks improved in 1989. In contrast, the situation of the problem banks deteriorated further, culminating in

Table 8.2: Operating Profits and Selected Balance Sheet Items, Expressed in Percent of Total Assets

Item	Problem banks[b]					All banks				
	1985	1986	1987	1988	1989	1985	1986	1987	1988	1989
Loans to the public	75.6	81.1	82.2	87.1	87.8	56.9	54.5	55.8	60.0	61.5
Deposits from public	69.1	57.0	56.5	54.1	58.3	61.9	49.8	47.4	51.2	53.2
Loans and deposits from Norges Bank	2.4	21.4	18.3	33.3	26.9	1.8	14.0	12.6	13.1	10.1
Equity capital[a]	5.4	4.3	3.5	−2.1	−5.0	6.8	5.1	4.8	4.9	5.1
Net interest and credit commission income	3.36	3.59	3.62	3.47	3.64	3.49	3.51	3.23	3.17	3.48
Operating profits before loss	1.01	1.22	0.90	0.76	0.49	1.42	1.49	0.88	1.18	1.79
Operating profits after actual losses	0.47	0.56	−1.29	−3.80	−8.25	1.10	1.01	0.01	−0.23	0.09

a. Equity, conditional tax-free reserves, and general loan loss provisions.
b. Sunnmørsbanken, Sparbanken Nord-Norge, Sparskillingsbanken Trøndelag, Sparbanken Romsdal, and Norion Bank.
Source: Bank of Norway.

1989 in a negative profit operating after actual losses of 8.25 percent of total assets.

A larger proportion of the problem banks' assets than that of the "average" bank was in the form of loans in the period 1985-89. Their lending growth, which was stronger and more concentrated on high risk projects than the lending growth of the average bank, was financed in larger measure by borrowing from Norges Bank. In 1988 as much as one-third of the problem banks' funding was provided by Norges Bank. In 1988 and 1989 a major share of the central bank loans to the problem banks were in the form of extraordinary liquidity loans where the central bank had set specific conditions.

Norwegian Credit Legislation and Structural Policy, Deposit Guarantees, and the Authorities' Role

Norwegian Credit Legislation

Norwegian credit legislation is provided for under various acts relating to banking, insurance, and other financial activities. The main features of the legislation are influenced by international trends and other elements of economic policy, with clear regulations regarding areas of activity, ownership rules, voting limits, equity capital requirements, and so on. Norwegian equity capital requirements have been reassessed, and they will by the end of 1992 be in line with the Cooke Committee's proposals and the European Community's (EC's) recommendations.

Structural Policy

In the course of the 1980s, structural policy for the Norwegian financial sector has undergone substantial changes. An important objective has been to ensure an adequate level of competition in the Norwegian market in order to achieve an efficient production of financial services. An important concern has also been to strengthen the financial soundness of financial institutions.

Another objective stated by the authorities in the early 1980s was to maintain and strengthen independent regional financial institutions. According to the guidelines for the banking structure policy an aim was on the one hand to build up strong autonomous regional commercial banks through mergers and establishment of branches, and on the other to build up a nationwide network of branches of a small number of large commercial banks. In the case of savings banks, the aim was to build up larger regional units.

Under the influence of the European development toward a single market, the guidelines of banking structure policy were markedly changed toward the end of the 1980s. A merger between the second and third largest banks, Bergen Bank and DNC, to form Den norske Bank (DnB), and between regional and nationwide banks have been approved in recent years. Moreover, the largest savings bank (Sparbanken ABC) has been permitted to merge with several savings banks outside its previous regional area. Moreover, Kreditkassen has merged with two regional commercial banks (Sunnmørsbanken and Sørlandsbanken). Less emphasis is now placed on the objective of independent regional banks. This is partly due to the weak results recorded by some of these banks. The regional banks' risk exposure has proved to be high because of their geographically limited area of activity.

To strengthen the international competitiveness of Norwegian financial institutions and to maintain a high level of competition in the domestic market, the authorities have taken various measures toward freer entry to the Norwegian financial market. The first foreign banks were established in Norway in the course of 1985, but by the end of 1989 they still accounted for only 3 percent of the total banking balance sheet. The policy initiatives are to open the way for establishment of branches of foreign banks (and not only establishment of subsidiaries) and for possible mergers between Norwegian and foreign institutions. Moreover, in effect from July 1, 1990 the foreign exchange regulations were abolished, leaving few restrictions on the freedom of residents to carry out capital transactions abroad.

Between 1980 and 1989 the number of savings banks was reduced from 322 to 150. Owing to the establishment of foreign banks and new banks, the number of commercial banks rose from twenty-four to twenty-eight in the same period. The two largest commercial banks, Den norske Bank and Kreditkassen, accounted for 77 percent of commercial banks' total assets at mid-1990.

The authorities' revised structural guidelines will imply that the market players are the ones who essentially determine the structure of the financial market. Even though the authorities will evaluate each individual case based on its effects on competition in the various markets, intervention will mainly occur if the structure generated entails indirect, negative effects that outstrip the business benefits. As a result, the new guidelines are likely to function primarily as a hindrance to undesired developments.

Deposit Guarantees

Under banking legislation, all banks must be members of a guarantee fund, either the Commercial Banks' or the Savings Banks'

Guarantee Fund. Both funds have the objective of supporting member banks' activities and of ensuring that they meet their commitments.

In contrast to most other countries, the Guarantee Funds play a central role in the Norwegian financial system's safety net. In this area the Norwegian structure shares some features with the U.S. system. In Norway, however, the Guarantee Funds are not public bodies, although both Norges Bank and the Banking, Insurance and Securities Commission are represented on their boards. Whereas the Banking, Insurance and Securities Commission is responsible for declaring an institution insolvent, the Guarantee Funds' role is to elaborate proposals for possible solutions, which ultimately must be approved by the authorities. The solution arrived upon is partly dependent on whether liquidation will be more costly for the Guarantee Fund than continued support. Moreover, the impact on confidence in the Norwegian financial system is also taken into consideration. If the Guarantee Fund does not provide the required support for continued operation, the Ministry of Finance is likely to put the bank under public administration.

The Savings Banks' Guarantee Fund guarantees all deposits except those made by banks, without any upper limit. The Commercial Banks' Guarantee Fund's Board may set a limit if so decided. However, it has been commonplace to assume that the Commercial Banks' Guarantee Fund will guarantee any ordinary deposits in the same way as the Savings Banks' Guarantee Fund. The handling in 1989 of Norion Bank, which was put under public administration, backs up this assumption.

The rules governing the accumulation of funds are somewhat different for the two funds. In both cases the funds are to consist of about 1.5 percent of the members' combined total assets. Furthermore, there are rules governing annual payments to the funds and members' responsibilities if the funds are utilized.

The Authorities' Role

Responsibility for supervision of financial institutions rests with the Banking, Insurance and Securities Commission. This body came into being when the Banking Inspection and the Insurance Council were amalgamated in 1986, providing a joint supervisory apparatus for the entire Norwegian financial sector, including securities markets. The Banking, Insurance and Securities Commission is subsumed under the Ministry of Finance. It monitors financial institutions based on a combination of analysis of accounts and of statements from financial institutions and by on-site inspections. In recent years, the commission's resources have been substantially strengthened, and its activities correspondingly stepped up.

Being the central bank, Norges Bank has prime responsibility for maintaining a stable financial system. Norges Bank's role in the event of a banking crisis must be seen in this light. In his annual address in 1988 Governor Skanland described Norges Bank's role as lender of last resort as follows:

"Should individual financial institutions find themselves in position which could affect general confidence in the credit market, Norges Bank—cognizant of its responsibility as the central bank—is prepared to take such measures as are necessary to bolster market confidence in our financial system."

In recent years Norges Bank has stepped up its monitoring of financial institutions. This is partly because the central bank, in the wake of deregulation, has become more engaged with the smooth working and efficiency of the financial system than previously. Another reason is the high level of the bank's liquidity loans to the banking system. These loans have required no collateral.

Treatment of Banks in Financial Straits

The sharp deterioration in banks' economic situation first became clearly apparent in 1987. Toward the end of 1987 the Banking, Insurance and Securities Commission made a thorough inspection of the activities of DnC. As a result of the critical report of the commission, the majority of the bank's top management was replaced in the beginning of 1988. Furthermore, the main strategy of DnC was changed from growth and market gains to improved solvency and traditional banking operations. To reduce costs, major cutbacks of staff were implemented. From the end of 1987 to the end of 1989 the staff of DnC was reduced by 27 percent in terms of manyears.

The commission also issued critical inspection reports on several other banks. This led, among other things, to major changes of

Sparbanken ABC's top management and business strategy. Particularly the largest banks acted swiftly to comply with the measures imposed by the commission. The subsequent performance of the large banks confirm that the measures have borne fruit.

At the beginning of 1988, the largest Norwegian finance company, which was 100 percent owned by the third largest insurance company, was hit by serious liquidity problems. The loans of the finance companies traditionally carry a high degree of risk, and they recorded dramatic loan loss increases in 1987 and 1988. Although the authorities did not provide direct financial support to the finance company, Norges Bank in the end extended a liquidity loan on overnight terms to the commercial bank that took over the company. The insurance company, which had suffered considerable losses on its finance company, was later taken over by a Swedish insurance company. Several other finance companies have subsequently incurred problems, and some have been wound up. There have been no interventions on the part of the authorities.

In contrast to the largest banks, the performance of the problem banks worsened further in 1988 and 1989. In the following we will take a look at the most important problem banks to which the Guarantee Funds and the authorities have provided direct support.

The Crisis of a Medium-Sized Commercial Bank in Western Norway

In 1988 the supervisory authorities became increasingly aware of the problematic situation of Sunnmørsbanken (total assets of NOK 7.4 billion at the end of 1988), which had its headquarters at Alesund. In the late summer of 1988, the Banking, Insurance and Securities Commission carried out a comprehensive inspection and established that the bank's equity capital would be exhausted by the end of the year. The plan to merge with a local savings bank consequently fell through, and it also became clear that none of the major commercial banks was interested in a takeover. After an extensive round of meetings where the authorities were involved, the Commercial Banks' Guarantee Fund declared on September 18, 1988 that it had issued a general guarantee for all Sunnmørsbanken's commitments. Concurrently, Norges Bank gave its assurance that the bank would be supplied with the necessary liquidity support. Norges Bank's loans were covered by the Guarantee Fund. The decision meant that deposits with Sunnmarsbanken were safe, and that domestic and foreign loans, including subordinated loan capital, would be covered.

The aim was that the bank should continue to operate under the Guarantee Fund's guarantee, and that efforts should be made to arrive at a lasting solution, which entailed as low as possible losses for the Guarantee Fund. Norges Bank provided substantial liquidity loans to Sumnersbanken at the rate applying for ordinary, short-term liquidity loans from the central bank. The Guarantee Fund appointed a new board for the bank, on which the central bank was represented.

Sunnmørsbanken was originally a strong regional commercial bank with substantial local equity participation. The local interests involved wished to maintain the bank's regional character, and gave the impression that they could raise the fresh capital required. It became increasingly clear that this was not feasible, partly due to the constant upward adjustment of the loss estimates. In January 1990, it was decided that Sunnmørsbanken should merge with Kreditkassen, at that time the largest Norwegian commercial bank. The Commercial Banks' Guarantee Fund has in all disbursed about NOK 900 million in support to this bank, corresponding to about 15 percent of the bank's total assets at the end of 1989. Even so, there is little doubt that an immediate liquidation would have been even more burdensome for the Guarantee Fund. Moreover, liquidation at that time could have had a considerable negative impact on confidence in the Norwegian financial system.

The Crisis of Two Medium-Sized Savings Banks in Northern Norway

Two relatively large savings banks had headquarters in Tromsø in North Norway, namely, Sparbanken Nord (total assets of NOK 7.6 billion at the end of 1988) and Tromsø Sparbank (total assets of NOK 7.1 billion at the end of 1988). In the 1980s, the two banks competed for market shares in the two northernmost counties. Both recorded sharp expansion in this period, based largely on funding via the money market and from Norges Bank. At the same time, North Norway's heavy dependence on the fisheries, which are traditionally subject to strong cyclical fluctuations, should be borne in mind.

As early as 1987, the authorities were aware of the growing problems facing the two savings banks in North Norway. In 1988, the Banking, Insurance and Securities Commission and Norges Bank kept in close touch on the issue. In the summer of 1988 a confidential report was prepared on possible solutions for the problems of Sparbanken Nord and Tromsø Sparbank. Its conclusion was that if market confidence was to wane, the banks risked finding themselves in a highly precarious liquidity position, which could necessitate supportive action on the part of Norges Bank.

In September and October 1988, Norges Bank granted extra liquidity loans to the banks as a result of extraordinary liquidity problems ensuing from weak earnings and heavy losses. As a condition for such loans, the central bank, in consultation with the Banking, Insurance and Securities Commission, imposed requirements in regard to the banks' further operations. In November 1988, an inspection revealed that the primary capital in both banks was to be regarded as exhausted. The condition set by the Banking, Insurance and Securities Commission for continued operation was a sufficient injection of new capital for both banks.

After an extensive round of meetings, the Savings Banks' Guarantee Fund decided to make available guarantee capital amounting to NOK 600 million. Concurrently, Norges Bank, after consultation with the Ministry of Finance, intervened with a large loan which would provide an overall subsidy effect of NOK 200 million over a five-year period. The total subsidy amount was approved as capital. A condition set for the measures was that the two banks should merge and that new boards be elected in accordance with the proposal of the Banking, Insurance and Securities Commission. Norges Bank was represented on this board. Another condition was that the boards should operate the banks with a view to limiting the Guarantee Fund's losses as far as possible,.

The merger between the two savings banks to form Sparbanken Nord-Norge was carried through on July 1, 1989. Developments in 1989 showed that the support measures adopted in November 1988 were inadequate. Accordingly, in October 1989 it was decided to inject substantial fresh capital into Sparbanken Nord-Norge. Three-quarters of this (or NOK 1,500 million) was provided by the

Guarantee Fund, and one-quarter by the authorities in the form of a write-down of NOK 500 million of the loan from Norges Bank.

The extensive direct official involvement in Sparbanken Nord-Norge should be viewed in light of the fact that the bank had two-thirds of the private bank market in North Norway. This part of Norway has traditionally received substantial economic support from the authorities, and since 1987 the region has been affected by a deep crisis in the fisheries sector. There were no potential merger partners, and Sparbanken Nord-Norge could not have been wound up without dramatic consequences for the entire northern region. Thus, the extensive direct support provided to this bank by the authorities is a reflection of the special circumstances of the case.

The Crisis of Other Smaller and Medium-Sized Regional Savings Banks

Since 1988 other smaller and medium-sized savings banks have also lost their capital. In these cases, the Savings Banks' Guarantee Fund has intervened with support in the form of guarantee capital, combined with various forms of liquidity support from Norges Bank subject to guarantee by the Guarantee Fund. Concurrently, the Guarantee Fund endeavored to bring about mergers with nearby savings banks. To achieve such mergers, the Guarantee Fund had to take over the bulk of the banks' losses.

The Administrative Solution for a Small Commercial Bank

Several new commercial banks were established in Norway in the period 1984-86. One of them recorded growing losses in 1988 and into 1989. In October 1989, the Banking, Insurance and Securities Commission informed the Commercial Banks' Guarantee Fund that Norion Bank's capital was probably exhausted. After scrutinizing the situation, the Guarantee Fund decided not to provide support for continued operation of the bank. Concurrently, the Guarantee Fund provided a guarantee for all deposits from nonbanks. The Ministry of Finance decided to put the bank under public administration. To facilitate the disbursement of deposits, Norges Bank provided a liquidity loan to Norion Bank against a guarantee from the Commercial Banks' Guarantee Fund. The bank is now in the process of being wound up.

Some Main Features of Solutions for Banks in Financial Straits

The above account shows that banking crises in Norway have not followed an absolutely uniform pattern in terms of receiving support from the Guarantee Funds and the authorities. Whereas, in the case of Sunnmørsbanken, the Commercial Banks' Guarantee Fund provided a general and unlimited guarantee, the Savings Banks' Guarantee Fund has in all instances confined itself to a guarantee carrying an upper limit. Moreover, in most cases the approach of the Savings Banks' Guarantee Fund has been to seek merger partners (i.e., savings banks) for the troubled savings banks. In the case of Norion Bank, the consequences of liquidation for confidence in the financial system were seen as so marginal that they were assigned no significance in the choice of a final solution.

In all cases where Norges Bank has intervened with liquidity support—with the exception of the subsidized loan to the savings banks in Northern Norway—the loans granted have carried the central bank's overnight lending rate. Norges Bank has at times injected substantial funds to the problem banks, mainly via the merger partners or subject to a guarantee from the Guarantee Funds. Furthermore, Norges Bank has supported the Guarantee Funds, partly by providing direct loans to the Savings Banks' Guarantee Fund and partly through loans to facilitate redeeming of deposit customers with Norion Bank when it was in the process of liquidation. In 1989 and 1990 special liquidity loans to banks in financial straits were in the range NOK 2 to 3 billion, or less than 5 percent of total central bank financing during the same period.

It should be emphasized that only in one instance—Sparbanken Nord-Norge—have the authorities, via Norges Bank, contributed to refinancing the bank. The authorities' involvement in the treatment of Sparbanken Nord-Norge is outlined in a report to Parliament (St.meld nr. 24, 1989-90). In the report it is stated that the support was provided largely on regional policy grounds. According to the report, "The Government will in future give crucial weight to the fundamental objections to central government involvement of a type and on the scale shown in the case of Sparbanken Nord-Norge. In the event of any future banking crisis in Norway, the Ministry of Finance assumes that the ordinary procedures provided for by law will be applied, and refers in this connection to the arrangements established through the guarantee funds."

In all other cases than Sparbanken Nord-Norge, the Guarantee Funds alone—that is, the banks themselves—have financed the restructuring of the bank in question. Apart from Sparbanken Nord-Norge, Norges Bank has only incurred losses on the winding-up of Norion Bank. However, the banking crisis has been a heavy burden on the Guarantee Funds. This is especially true of the Savings Banks' Guarantee Fund, whose capital currently consists largely of committed, unpaid guarantee capital.

Regulatory Response

The main impression is that the Norwegian guarantee system has worked well. The deposit guarantees, combined with the intervention of the Guarantee Funds and the authorities, have contributed to the absence of any dramatic flight of deposits from troubled banks, at the same time as the public's confidence in the banking system as a whole has been maintained. For most banks in financial straits, the solution has been to secure operations through mergers. Where the small commercial bank, Norion Bank, is concerned, placing the bank under public administration was, also in retrospect, the correct option. All in all, the authorities' involvement in the crises in question appears to have supported the confidence of international finance in the Norwegian financial system.

The crisis of recent years in the Norwegian financial arena has shown the need for changes in a number of areas. Although the Guarantee Funds have played a decisive and constructive role, consideration is currently being given to scaling back the scope of the deposit-guarantee arrangement. Whereas deposits from nonbanks currently are subject to a virtually unlimited guarantee, it is possible that ceilings will be proposed for guarantees for deposits by the nonfinancial sector at the same time as all financial institutions are excluded from the guarantee arrangements. A further aim may be to devise uniform rules for the Savings Banks and Commercial Banks' Guarantee Funds, and ultimately to institute a sole, joint fund. Whether the management of the funds should continue to be left to the banks or whether the authorities should play a greater role is also an issue that may be discussed.

As mentioned, a proposal has been put forward to bring equity capital requirements into line with the proposal of the Cooke Committee. The Norwegian Parliament has recently come out in support of the government's proposal for liberalization of structural policy in financial markets with regard to guidelines for mergers, rules governing foreign equity participation and so on. In many areas, the proposed changes are in line with the bulk of the rules now being elaborated by the EC.

The banking problems in the latter half of the 1980s has provided useful experience with the process of deregulating financial markets. The effects of liberalization have had a larger impact in Norway since the regulations were consistently more stringent than in other countries and the real after-tax rate of interest lower than in various countries with which it is natural to compare Norway. The excessively high level of loan losses and weak performance of the financial sector may, however, as stated by Governor Hermod Skanland in his annual address in February 1988, be regarded as due to a combination of bad banking, bad policies, and bad luck.

Inadequate credit risk assessment, poor management routines, and the desire to win market shares by higher risk-taking were elements of "bad banking." The authorities' responsibilities for "bad policies" refers partly to the too expansionary economic policy up to the end of 1986, and to the fact that the appropriate tax rules and interest rates were only brought into play after this. The supervisory functions should also have been more developed in readiness for the new market situation. However, it should also be acknowledged that the Norwegian financial institutions have suffered a stiff dose of "bad luck." The sharp drop in oil prices and consequent retrenchment that led to widespread surplus capacity rendered it more difficult for financial institutions to make correct credit assessments.

The problems faced by the Norwegian banking system have been compounded and prolonged by the lasting domestic recession. Bank losses have up to now remained at a very high level, impeding the required buildup of capital. As a result, the state of the Norwegian financial system is still looked upon with some misgivings by international finance. However, given the past two years' improvement in earnings before losses, and the signs that the Norwegian economy is in the process of a moderate domestic economic upturn, it is expected that the Norwegian banking system will show an improvement in operating profits after losses from 1991 onward.

In conclusion, the lesson is that the removal of credit and interest rate regulation should have been viewed in the light of, among other things, the current cyclical situation, the stance of tax policy, and the readiness of supervisory functions for the new market situation. Moreover, with the benefit of hindsight, the internal management systems in the financial institutions were poorly prepared for operating in a more competitive environment. Clearly, the Norwegian experience points to the need to see the deregulation process as a coherent whole in which several policy elements play a part.*

Editor's Note: This paper was completed before the deterioration of bank profitability in 1991. For a brief review of measures taken by the authorities to deal with the crisis, see the addresses by Governor Hermod Skanland to representatives of the international banking community in Frankfurt, Germany, on October 2 and in Bangkok, Thailand, on October 16 (Norges Bank, *Economic Bulletin*, 3/1991).

9

THE UNITED STATES SAVINGS AND LOAN DEBACLE: SOME LESSONS FOR THE REGULATION OF FINANCIAL INSTITUTIONS

Lawrence J. White

Introduction

The insolvencies of hundreds of savings and loan associations (S&Ls, or thrifts) in the United States in the late 1980s has been a searing event for regulators, politicians, and owners and managers of thrifts. The costs of these insolvencies will be huge and will largely be borne by the U.S. taxpayers.

The complete story of this debacle—what happened, why it happened, how it happened, and what must be done to ensure that it never happens again—is still not well understood. There are important (albeit costly) lessons that must be learned from this experience. These lessons have equal validity for the regulation of other financial institutions (e.g., banks, credit unions, insurance companies, pension funds) where governments accept explicit or implicit responsibility for protecting the liability holders or claimants from losses. Other countries can learn from the U.S. Government's sad experience.

This paper will attempt to provide a brief review of the story of the S&L debacle and extract the important lessons from it.[1] As a basis for what follows, we first describe the major forms of regulation that have applied to thrifts in the U.S., introduce a few key accounting concepts, and provide some important insights from these accounting examples.

---

1. A more complete review is found in White (1991a).

We then tell the story of the debacle. In the final two sections we derive the lessons from this experience and provide a brief conclusion.

S&L Regulation and the Insights from Accounting

S&Ls have generally been subjected to two major forms of government regulation: economic regulation and safety-and-soundness (or prudential) regulation.[2] Economic regulation, practiced at both the federal and state government levels, has been extensive, though it has changed over time in form and substance. Thrifts (at various times) have been limited in the types of activities in which they could engage, the types of investments they could make, the locations at which they could establish branches, the interest rates they could pay on deposits, and the interest rates they could charge on loans. This economic regulation has been generated by a range of motivations: American political concerns about the exercise of market power by financial institutions; a general fear of the economic and social power of these institutions; a political imperative to assure home buyers of a steady and low-cost stream of mortgage finance; and thrifts' own desires to shield themselves from competition.

The safety-and-soundness regulation of thrifts has also been extensive and has been practiced at both the federal and state levels; the availability of federal deposit insurance (through the Federal Saving and Loan Insurance Corporation, or FSLIC), though, has tended to increase the relative importance of the federal government's role in this form of regulation. Thrifts are limited in the types of investments that they can make (i.e., the types of assets they can hold) and the types of liabilities they can issue.[3] They are subject to minimum net worth (capital) requirements. Thrifts are expected to be operated in a safe and sound manner, with adequate plans and procedures to ensure such operation. The motivation for this form of regulation has been pri-

---

2.   Commercial banks are subject to similar forms of regulation; see White (1991a, chapter 3). Banks and thrifts are also subject to information and consumer protection regulation (e.g., requirements to provide customers with specified interest rate information on deposits and on loans and requirements that banks and thrifts adequately serve their local communities).

3.   These limitations on the types of investments that thrifts could make have been rooted partly in economic regulation motivations and partly in safety-and-soundness regulation motivations.

marily the desire to avoid imposing losses on depositors (or on the insurance fund backing up the depositors).

Because the focus of this paper is on safety-and-soundness regulation, it is useful to provide some simple accounting examples of a bank's or thrift's balance sheet; these examples will yield valuable insights for the process of safety-and-soundness regulation.[4]

Table 9.1 shows the balance sheet of a healthy bank or thrift. Its assets are the loans that it makes, since it expects to earn an interest re

Table 9.1: The Balance Sheet of a Healthy Bank or Thrift, as of December 31, 199X

Assets	Liabilities
$100 (loans)	$92 (deposits, insured)
	$8 (net worth)

Table 9.2: The Balance Sheet of a Marginal Bank or Thrift, as of December 31, 199Y

Assets	Liabilities
$92 (loans)	$92 (deposits, insured)
	$0 (net worth)

Table 9.3: The Balance Sheet of a Deeply Insolvent Bank or Thrift, as of December 31, 199Z

Assets	Liabilities
$60 (loans)	$92 (deposits, insured)
	-$32 (net worth)

---

4. These examples apply directly to credit unions as well; and with modest modifications they (and the lessons extracted from them) would apply to insurance companies and pension funds (i.e., other financial institutions where liability holders and claimants are likely to be in a poor position to be able adequately to protect themselves).

turn on the loan as well as to have the principal repaid. (We will assume that all values shown in the balance sheets are market values; this is an important assumption to which we will return below.) The institution's liabilities are the deposits it has taken in, since it owes these sums (is liable) to its depositors; we will assume that all deposits are covered by government deposit insurance (and that the safety-and-soundness regulator and the deposit insurer are the same). Net worth (or capital) is the arithmetic difference between assets and liabilities; it represents the owners' stake in the enterprise.

Table 9.2 shows a marginal bank or thrift, in which the value of its assets has declined to a level that is just equal to the value of its liabilities. Net worth is zero; the owners' stake has been wiped out.

Finally, Table 9.3 shows a deeply insolvent bank or thrift, in which the value of its assets has fallen far below the value of its liabilities.

There are a number of important insights that are yielded by these simple balance sheets.

First, even a healthy bank or thrift is relatively thinly capitalized, as compared with other enterprises in the U.S. economy. An enterprise's capital strength is usually indicated either by its ratio of net worth to assets (as is usually done for banks and thrifts) or by its ratio of debt to equity (net worth). Table 9.4 provides both of these ratios for major industry groupings in the United States. It is clear that banks and thrifts are much more thinly capitalized than is any other major sector.

Second, with their thin capitalization, banks and thrifts are the beneficiaries of high leverage: relatively small percentage changes in the value of the enterprise's assets will mean relatively large percentage changes in its net worth.

Third, corporations in the United States operate within a legal system of limited liability for the corporations' owners. The owners are normally not liable for more than their initial investment in the enterprise. They are thus buffered from the full consequences of large losses. In the context of limited liability and with thin capitalization, bank and thrift owners (and managers acting on behalf of owners) have incentives to take on greater risks than would otherwise be true, since they will enjoy the full benefits of the upside outcomes from risk-taking but are limited in their exposure to the downside (loss) consequences. Further, they would generally prefer to operate with as

Table 9.4: Measures of Corporate Net Worth for Major Industry Groups, 1985

Industry	Ratio of net worth to total assets	Debt-equity ratio
All industries	0.32	2.11 : 1
Agriculture, forestry, and fishing	0.32	2.12 : 1
Mining	0.45	1.21 : 1
Construction	0.28	2.52 : 1
Manufacturing	0.45	1.20 : 1
Transportation and public utilities	0.40	1.50 : 1
Wholesale and retail trade	0.29	2.49 : 1
Services	0.31	2.25 : 1
Finance, insurance, and real estate	0.26	2.90 : 1
Bank holding companies	0.08	11.07 : 1
Commercial banks[1]	0.08	11.00 : 1
Mutual savings banks	0.06	15.75 : 1
Savings and loan associations	0.03	31.12 : 1

1. Excluding bank holding companies.
Source: U.S. Internal Revenue Service data.

little net worth as possible, since lower net worth means a smaller ownership stake to be lost in the event that the downside consequences occur. And the owners would prefer to have as few regulatory inhibitions on their risk-taking as they can politically achieve.

Fourth, with limited liability applying to the owners, insolvency means that the liability holders must absorb the losses implied by the shortfall in assets. In the case of banks or thrifts, those liability holders would otherwise be the depositors; but with deposit insurance, it will be the deposit insurer who will bear the losses.

Fifth, if the protection of depositors (or the deposit insurance fund) is an important goal, bank regulators need to inhibit risk-taking by banks and thrifts through safety-and-soundness regulation.[5] Direct

---

5. This is the equivalent of the covenants that bond holders require in bond indentures and that banks insert in their lending agreements to corporate customers.

restrictions on activities is one means; minimum net worth requirements are another.

Sixth, net worth is an important protection for the deposit insurer.
It acts as a direct buffer for the insurer, since a larger level of net
worth means that there can be a greater fall in the value of the assets
before the insurer's obligation is triggered. Further, net worth means
that the owners have more to lose from the downside consequences of
risk-taking; higher net worth thus has important incentive effects in
discouraging risk-taking. In essence, from the deposit insurer's perspective, net worth has the same properties as a deductible clause in a
typical home or automobile insurance arrangement, since it offers the
same types of direct and indirect protections.

Seventh, since net worth and solvency are such important concepts
for the regulator, the accounting framework should be designed to
yield market values for assets, liabilities, and any off-balance-sheet
items; it is only market values that measure the available protection for
(or likely loss to) the deposit insurer. Unfortunately, the standard accounting framework ("generally accepted accounting principles," or
GAAP) is a backward-looking, historical cost-based system rather than
one that focuses on current values. This GAAP accounting framework,
accompanied by innovations in the securities markets, provides banks
and thrifts with ever-expanding opportunities to overstate their true
(market value) net worth, to the detriment of the deposit insurer.[6, 7]

Eighth, a useful component of the regulator's tool bag of devices
to discourage risk-taking would be insurance premiums that would
vary in relationship to the riskiness of the bank's or thrift's activities.
Unfortunately, the legislation establishing deposit insurance in the
United States in the 1930s mandated flat rate premiums that are in-

---

6. The major innovation of importance here is that of "securitization": the
process whereby either loans are standardized and thus made tradable like securities or
new tradable securities are created that have as their collateral the standardized loans;
see White (1991a, chapter 12) and Campbell (1988).

7. A major means of overstating net worth is through "gains trading," the
process whereby assets whose values rise above their accounting (historical cost)
value are sold to recognize the gains, while assets that are "under water" (below their
historical costs) remain in the portfolio at accounting values equal to their historical
costs.

sensitive to risk, and this aspect of the legislation has never been altered.

With this background, we can now turn to the story of the S&L debacle.

The Debacle

Until the late 1970s, the S&L industry was basically a sleepy, prosperous, and safe group of financial institutions. The major banking reforms of the 1930s had included the establishment of federal chartering and regulation of thrifts by a new agency, the Federal Home Loan Bank Board, and deposit insurance for thrifts through an arm of the Bank Board, the FSLIC.[8] Thrifts were seen as a vital part of the housing finance system of the United States and were confined largely to making home mortgage loans. During the post-war period of growing prosperity, expanding homeownership, and rising real estate values, thrifts grew and prospered.

There was, though, one serious flaw in this arrangement: Thrifts' mortgage loans were long term (typically, thirty years) with fixed rates of interest, while their deposits were short term (typically, passbook accounts). In the parlance of the financial markets, they were borrowing short and lending long. If the general level of interest rates were to rise sharply, they would be squeezed badly. Their incomes would be limited to their interest earnings on their portfolio of long-lived fixed-rate mortgages made in earlier years, while their costs would rise because of the higher interest payments that they would have to make to their depositors (to prevent the latter from withdrawing their funds in favor of higher yielding investments elsewhere).

This condition of sharply rising interest rates first arose in 1965-66, in the wake of the U.S. government's increasingly heavy involvement in the Vietnam War. The Congress' solution in 1966 for the thrifts' dilemma was to extend to them the system of interest ceilings on deposits (known as "Regulation Q") that had previously applied only to

---

8. State-chartered and -regulated thrifts were also able to obtain FSLIC insurance, which subjected them to an extra layer of federal regulation. This pattern of dual chartering with federal insurance was similar to the pattern that applied to commercial banks.

commercial banks. This solution worked for the next decade, because thrift depositors had few suitable alternatives and market interest rates did not rise too far above the interest rate ceilings.[9]

In the late 1970s, however, the thrifts faced another period of even more sharply rising interest rates, and this time Regulation Q could not solve their problems, because depositors now had a suitable alternative: money market mutual funds (MMMFs). Thrifts now could not avoid being squeezed, and many of them ran massive losses during the years 1980-82; these data are shown in table 9.5.[10]

Table 9.5: Profits or Losses by FSLIC-Insured Thrifts, 1978-83

Year		*Unprofitable thrifts as a % of all thrifts*	*Unprofitable thrifts' assets as a % of all thrift assets*	*Losses of unprofitable thrifts (US$ millions)*	*Profits or losses of all thrifts (US$ millions)*
1978:	H1	2.9	1.5	-25	1,869
	H2	2.7	1.3	-16	2,051
1979:	H1	4.7	2.6	-35	1,821
	H2	6.5	4.1	-50	1,792
1980:	H1	30.5	30.0	-335	478
	H2	35.5	33.0	-443	303
1981:	H1	69.1	74.8	-1,732	-1,506
	H2	84.8	91.3	-3,324	-3,125
1982:	H1	83.2	89.0	-3,390	-3,205
	H2	67.8	60.6	-2,085	-937
1983:	H1	38.4	33.0	-868	1,101
	H2	35.2	33.2	-1,021	843

Source: Federal Home Loan Bank Board data.

9. In 1970, to make sure that thrift depositors lacked good alternatives, the U.S. Treasury raised the minimum denomination treasury bill to $10,000, from the $1,000 that had previously prevailed; see Kane (1970). The average size deposit in a thrift in 1970 was $3,045.

10. These are the standard data that are usually presented for the thrift industry and show substantial losses. As is argued in White (1991a, chapter 5) these data surely understate the losses experienced by the industry, even if measured on a historical cost-based accounting system. And as Kane (1985, 1989) and Brumbaugh (1988) have

Table 9.6: Tangible Net Worth for All FSLIC-Insured Thrifts, 1978-83

Year		Number of thrifts	Assets (US$ billions)	Tangible net worth (US$ billions)	Tangible net worth as a % of assets
1978:	H1	4,051	465.0	26.1	5.6
	H2	4,048	497.3	28.0	5.6
1979:	H1	4,040	529.1	29.7	5.6
	H2	4,038	554.4	31.5	5.7
1980:	H1	4,021	572.6	31.9	5.6
	H2	3,993	603.8	32.2	5.3
1981:	H1	3,916	622.8	30.6	4.9
	H2	3,751	639.8	25.3	4.0
1982:	H1	3,533	658.0	14.7	2.2
	H2	3,287	686.2	3.7	0.5
1983:	H1	3,206	752.8	4.4	0.6
	H2	3,146	813.8	3.5	0.4

Source: Federal Home Loan Bank Board data.

Table 9.7: Annual Growth Rates[1] of FSLIC-Insured Thrifts, 1980-86

	1980	1981	1982	1983	1984	1985	1986
Total U.S.	7.2	7.8	7.3	18.6	19.9	9.5	8.7
Arkansas	6.0	4.2	-2.3	42.9	24.7	6.2	-2.0
Arizona	13.5	9.4	23.5	18.3	46.7	23.8	15.3
California	10.1	8.2	18.3	28.0	29.6	8.8	13.1
Colorado	13.0	8.6	-9.2	9.9	24.7	6.8	12.1
Florida	11.8	10.5	9.6	17.1	20.7	7.6	2.2
Kansas	6.6	5.3	5.9	21.2	28.8	20.9	11.9
Louisiana	10.5	8.0	11.5	20.3	18.1	3.7	5.2
Oklahoma	11.7	10.4	9.8	16.5	13.6	5.4	1.9
Texas	11.9	9.7	13.2	33.3	38.0	18.4	5.5

1. Percentage growth in assets, from previous year end.
Source: Barth, Bartholomew, and Bradley (1989).

argued, the losses of the industry, when measured on a market value basis, were considerably larger.

The Congress again addressed the thrifts' problem, as did many state governments for their state-chartered (but federally insured) thrifts, and this time developed a different solution: *economic deregulation*. In major legislation in 1980 and again in 1982 the Congress provided for the following: thrifts could offer adjustable rate mortgages (ARMs)[11]; federally chartered thrifts were allowed (in limited percentages) to make commercial real estate loans, commercial unsecured loans, and consumer loans (e.g., car loans, credit card loans), and even to take direct ownership positions in projects (some states, especially in the Sunbelt, were even more liberal in the investment authority that they granted to their state-chartered, but federally insured, thrifts); the Regulation Q ceilings on interest rates on deposits were to be phased out; and (in 1980) the maximum insured deposit amount was raised to $100,000 (from $40,000).

These economic deregulation actions were basically sensible. The authorization for ARMs was long overdue. The wider investment authorities, if used prudently, could allow thrifts to diversify their portfolios in ways that could increase their returns and decrease their risks. The elimination of Regulation Q also was long overdue, since it had disadvantaged depositors, introduced substantial inefficiencies into the banking system, and artificially stimulated the growth of the MMMFs. The increases in the insured amount is today considered a controversial action, but there was scarcely a murmur when it was passed in 1980; if a goal of deposit insurance is to stabilize depository institutions against depositor runs, then an increase in the insured amount was a step in the right direction.[12]

This endorsement requires an immediate caveat: These sensible actions of *economic deregulation* for thrifts needed to be accomplished by a substantial *strengthening* of the *safety-and-soundness regulatory system* and/or *an increased attention to economic incentives*. To see why this was so, it is useful to consider these deregulation actions in the context of the balance sheet examples of the previous section (tables 9.1 through 9.3).

---

11. Until 1979 ARMs had not been a permitted form of mortgage for federally chartered thrifts, and only a few states (notably Wisconsin and California) had authorized them for their state-chartered thrifts.

12. See White (1991a, chapter 10) for a more complete argument.

The wider investment authorities influenced the asset side of thrifts' balance sheets. Though these new powers could be used for sensible diversification, they also meant that thrifts now had greatly expanded opportunities for taking risks, since the new types of assets could carry high possible returns (but also yield large losses).

The phasing-out of Regulation Q and the increase in the insured amount operated on the thrifts' liabilities. Though, again, these expanded powers could be used sensibly, they could also provide the capabilities for getting the funds that would fuel the risk-taking opportunities. Small thrifts could advertise in the financial press that they paid market rates (or even above market rates) of interest on federally insured deposits; or they could engage deposit brokers to gather the funds for them. And, with the increase in the insured amount, the funds could be gathered in larger bundles, thereby reducing transaction costs.

Finally, the high interest rates and massive losses of the thrift industry in the late 1970s and early 1980s meant that their net worths had been greatly diminished or wiped out. Table 9.6 shows the relevant data. Also, the generally increasing competition between and among thrifts and banks and other financial institutions (e.g., money market mutual funds) meant that the implicit franchise value that had been associated with thrifts' previously protected economic position was also eroding.[13] With net worths that were either severely diminished or eliminated, thrifts thus faced incentives for risk-taking that were greatly enhanced.

Unfortunately, this combination of expanded opportunities, capabilities, and incentives for risk-taking was not understood in Washington, D.C. at the time. Instead, the policy community was mesmerized in the early 1980s by the hemorrhaging of the thrift industry and simply saw the need to provide relief measures that would staunch the bleeding.

Indeed, rather than strengthening the safety-and-soundness regulatory system, policy measures in the early 1980s actually weakened it! The Federal Home Loan Bank Board (at the behest of the Congress) lowered the net worth standards applicable to thrifts in 1980 and again

---

13. See Spellman (1982) and Keeley (1989).

in 1982. The accounting system—already inadequate because it focused on historical costs rather than on current market values—was weakened further through the Bank Board's regulatory modifications that allowed thrifts yet greater leeway to overstate their net worths. The numbers of the Bank Board's regulatory personnel—the field force of supervisors and examiners—were decreased between 1981 and 1984. The number of examinations relative to the size of the industry similarly fell.[14]

Hundreds of thrifts quickly took advantage of the new environment. Though a majority of the 3,287 thrifts insured by the FSLIC at the end of 1982 remained relatively cautious and conservative, a substantial minority expanded rapidly during the years 1983-85. Table 9.7 shows that the overall industry grew much more rapidly during these three years; for thrifts in individual states, especially in the Sunbelt, there were even sharper bursts of expansion. For a group of 637 thrifts that would eventually fail in the years 1986-89 (or, as of early 1989, were considered highly probable to do so), growth during 1983-85 led (on average) to a doubling of their sizes; and a subsample of seventy-four in this group grew by 400 percent or more during those three years.

Much of this growth was in the new, nontraditional assets that the deregulation actions of 1980-82 had authorized. In many instances, these rapidly growing thrifts were under the control of new entrepreneurs who had either entered de novo or taken over existing small thrifts. Unfortunately, all too often these new investments were ill-conceived, inadequately researched, overly optimistic, and/or excessively aggressive; in some instances, they were outright fraudulent.

What was clearly destined to be a bad situation was then made substantially worse by two exogenous events: the decline in the price of oil during the 1980s and especially the sharp decline in early 1986; and changes in the U.S. tax laws, which in 1981 had made real estate a

---

14. Also, in September 1983 the field office responsible for the states of Arkansas, Louisiana, Mississippi, New Mexico, and Texas was moved from Little Rock to Dallas. Though this move made a good deal of sense in the abstract, the timing was unfortunate. Few of the supervisors moved; the office had to re-staff itself. And, in the administrative confusion, the number of thrift examinations in those five states fell sharply in the twelve months following the move; see White (1991a, chapter 5).

tax-favored investment and then in 1986 reversed course and subjected real estate to less favorable treatment. Many of the new loans and investments of the rapidly growing thrifts were in real estate projects (e.g., shopping centers, office buildings, luxury resorts, apartment condominiums) in the Southwest and were based on assumptions of a high and rising price of oil and continued favorable tax treatment for real estate. When neither assumption held true, many of these projects collapsed, spelling losses for the thrifts that had lent to or invested in them.

After a delay in recognition, the Federal Home Loan Bank Board reversed its regulatory course and tightened its safety-and-soundness structure. During the years 1985-87 the Bank Board placed limits on growth by inadequately capitalized thrifts, raised the net worth standards, tightened the accounting rules, placed limits on the ability of state-chartered thrifts to take direct ownership positions in projects, and more than doubled the size of its field force of examiners and supervisors (and improved their training and their compensation). This regulatory tightening was desperately necessary and had the desired effects; by mid-1986 the growth binge was largely over. But, unfortunately, a large amount of damage had already been done. Far too many bad loans and investments had already been made and were embedded in the thrifts' balance sheets. From 1986 onward, especially as the real estate markets in the Southwest and elsewhere began to crumble, these assets would begin to be written down and losses would snowball, leading to hundreds of insolvencies.

In addition to tightening the regulations, the Bank Board also moved in early 1985 to strengthen the FSLIC insurance fund, since the prospect of substantial numbers of insolvencies threatened to swamp the fund. The insurance premiums that were levied on thrifts, which had been 8.33 cents per $100 of deposits, were raised to 20.83 cents. In early 1986, the Bank Board sent to the Congress a legislative proposal to "recapitalize" the fund (which primarily meant allowing the FSLIC to borrow against its expected future stream of premiums). The Congress finally passed this legislation in August 1987 (but with lower borrowing authority than the Bank Board had requested).

During the years 1985-88 the Bank Board disposed of 329 insolvent thrifts: 64 by liquidation and 265 by placing them with acquirers.

Table 9.8 provides the complete data on the Bank Board's disposals during the 1980s, including the aggregate assets of the insolvent thrifts and the estimated costs to the FSLIC. It is important to note that for both methods of disposal—liquidations and placements with acquirers—the FSLIC's costs of disposal were roughly equal to the negative (market value) net worth of the insolvent thrifts. Placements with acquirers tended to be less costly to the FSLIC because the "going concern" or "franchise" value of the thrift could thereby be preserved as an asset (and because acquirers could take advantage of tax advan

Table 9.8: The FSLIC's Liquidations and Placements with Acquirers of Insolvent Thrifts, 1980-88

	Liquidations			Placements with acquirers			Total		
Year	Number	Assets[1]	Estimated cost[2]	Number	Assets[1]	Estimated cost[2]	Number	Assets[1]	Estimated cost[2]
1980	0	$ 0.0	$0.0	11	$1.5	$0.2	11	$1.5	$0.2
1981	1	0.1	0.3	27	13.8	0.7	28	13.9	0.7
1982	1	0.04	0.003	62	17.6	0.8	63	17.7	0.8
1983	5	0.3	0.1	31	4.4	0.2	36	4.6	0.3
1984	9	1.5	0.6	13	3.6	0.2	22	5.1	0.7
1985	9	2.1	0.6	22	4.2	0.4	31	6.4	1.0
1986	10	0.6	0.3	36	11.9	2.8	46	12.5	3.1
1987	17	3.0	2.3	30	7.6	1.4	47	10.7	3.7
1988	22	3.0	2.8	179	97.7	27.1[3]	205	107.7	29.9[3]

1. In billions of dollars.
2. Costs to the FSLIC, in billions of dollars, on a present discounted value basis; neglects costs to the U.S. Treasury in the form of reduced tax collections.
3. Costs to the U.S. Treasury of reduced tax collections were estimated to be an additional $5.5 billion, on a present discounted value basis.
Source: Barth, Bartholomew, and Bradley (1989); Federal Home Loan Bank Board data.

tages that would be lost in a liquidation).[15] Also, acquirers were willing to accept notes and other promises of future payment, whereas liquidations required large amounts of up-front cash.

By the end of 1988, despite the hundreds of disposals of insolvent thrifts that had already occurred, there were still hundreds of insolvent thrifts waiting for disposal. It was clear that the FSLIC's resources had been far exceeded and that new Congressional legislation would be needed.

In February 1989 the Bush administration announced its plan for dealing with the insolvent thrifts. This proposal, with some modifications, was eventually enacted in August as the Financial Institutions Reform, Recovery, and Enforcement Act (FIRREA) of 1989. The major provisions of the act were as follows: It authorized $50 billion of new funding to continue the disposals of insolvent thrifts.[16] It raised the insurance premiums paid by the remaining (healthy) part of the thrift industry and taxed away some of their assets and future incomes. (The major part of the costs of the cleanup, however, would come from general treasury revenues.) It mandated higher net worth standards for thrifts (comparable to those applicable to commercial banks) and limited their operating flexibility (including a requirement that 70 percent of their assets must be devoted to housing-related investments). And it eliminated the Federal Home Loan Bank Board and the FSLIC and scattered their functions and responsibilities to three newly created agencies and to the Federal Deposit Insurance Corporation (which had previously provided deposit insurance for

---

15. By law the FSLIC could not proceed with a transaction with an acquirer unless the cost of the transaction was less than the cost of liquidation. For each transaction, analysts in the FSLIC computed the estimated present discounted value of liquidation; the FSLIC's cost of borrowing (approximately 10 percent) was used as the discount rate. The estimated cost to the treasury of the tax benefits to the acquirers were usually excluded from these calculations. For the eighty-six transactions concluded with acquirers in 1988, however, in only five would the inclusion of the estimated tax revenue losses to the treasury have raised the estimated cost of the transaction above the estimated cost of liquidation, and in all five the differences were small in absolute and/or percentage terms. Because rapid liquidation was not a realistic alternative, even these five transactions were defensible; see White (1991a, chapter 8).

16. Though the media almost always describes the disposals of individual thrifts as "bailouts" and refers to the FIRREA as the S&L "bailout" legislation, that term is not used in this paper because it is a misleading and inappropriate characterization of these disposal actions; see White (1991a, chapter 8).

commercial banks and now became the deposit insurer for thrifts as well).

In the ten months following the enactment of the FIRREA, the Resolution Trust Corporation (which had been created by the FIRREA and was structured as an arm of the FDIC) disposed of 207 thrifts (with $69 billion in assets) at an estimated present discounted cost of $25 billion. As of June 30, 1990, however, there were still 247 insolvent thrifts (with $139 billion in assets) in its caseload, and there were expectations that another 200 to 400 thinly solvent thrifts would likely slide into insolvency in the next year or two and require disposal.

As of the summer of 1990 it appeared that the costs of all of the thrifts' insolvencies would likely be in the range of $140 to $150 billion on a present discounted cost basis. (The figures of $350 to $500 billion that frequently appeared in the media were estimates of *undiscounted* cash flows that would extend over 40 years, including the annual interest costs on the borrowings of the FSLIC and the Resolution Trust Corporation.) It was also clear that the funding authorization of the FIRREA was inadequate and that the Congress would have to readdress the costs of the overall cleanup in 1991.

The Lessons

There are a number of vital lessons to be learned from this sorry tale. They have general application to the regulation of all depository institutions (and many other financial intermediaries) in the United States, as well as for other countries. They are especially important in circumstances where financial intermediaries have previously been subject to highly restrictive economic regulation (which is likely to have the side effects of restricting the opportunities for risk-taking and of creating implicit franchise value net worth) and are then exposed to economic deregulation and more extensive competition (which would erode that franchise value).

First, the overall regulatory framework must stress an ethos of prudence and fiduciary responsibility on the part of financial institutions' executives and directors.

Second, the safety-and-soundness regulatory agency must have adequate numbers of well-trained and well-paid examiners and supervisors.

Third, the accounting information provided to the regulators must be based on market value concepts. The existing accounting framework, which is backward-looking and cost-based, is not adequate for the needs of regulators.[17]

Fourth, minimum net worth (capital) standards must be based on a market value accounting framework, must be geared to the risks of the individual institution, and must be set high enough to keep the likelihood of insolvency at an acceptably low level. The so-called BIS or Basel agreement on international net worth standards for banks (which, because of the FIRREA, will also apply to U.S. thrifts) is a welcome step in the right direction, but it is nevertheless wholly inadequate. It is based on existing cost-based accounting frameworks rather than a market value accounting framework. Also, it focuses only on the credit (default) risk of broad classes of assets and wholly ignores portfolio effects and the covariance of returns among assets, as well as ignoring interest rate risk. And, finally, the relative risk categories and the absolute net worth levels specified in the BIS agreement have no empirical foundation.

Fifth, deposit insurance premiums should be based on the risks embodied in a financial institution's activities and portfolio, rather than structured as the flat rates that they are today.[18] Risk-based premiums and risk-based net worth standards are not complete substitutes, since the actual (market value) net worth level of the financial institution should be one of the elements of risk on which premiums should be based. Risk-based premiums can thereby provide an incentive for financial institutions to operate with *higher* levels of net worth than the bare-bones minimum requirements. (The deposit insurance premium structure would thus parallel that of most insurance companies, whereby the insured party can reduce its premiums by choosing a larger deductible.)

Sixth, the regulators need strong powers of early intervention and rapid disposal. They need to be able to intervene and take control of a

---

17. Further arguments along these lines are provided in White (1988a; 1988b; 1990a; 1990b; 1991b).

18. For countries where the guarantee to depositors is implicit rather than explicit, this logic suggests that the arrangement should be made explicit and risk-based premiums should be charged for the guarantee.

financial institution before it becomes insolvent; waiting until insolvency is reached (especially when insolvency is measured according to a cost-based accounting framework) almost always means waiting too long, with large consequent costs. And insolvent or near-insolvent financial institutions should be liquidated or placed with an acquirer rapidly. Delay is costly.

Seventh, the activities that should be permitted within the insured financial institution are those for which risks can be assessed (so that adequate net worth levels and insurance premiums can be specified) and that can be adequately examined and supervised by regulators. All other activities should be in the financial institution's holding company (or the holding company's other subsidiaries). Because financial institutions are so thinly capitalized, they are too easy to "loot" through improper transactions (e.g., excessive dividends to the parent, purchases from the parent at prices that are too high, sales to the parent at prices that are too low, loans to the parent at concessional rates or with inadequate collateral). Accordingly, all transactions between the financial institution and its parent (or its owners generally) must be tightly restricted and closely monitored.

Conclusion

The debacle of the S&Ls is a story that will surely be told and retold in financial histories for decades to come, much like the 1929 stock market crash and the South Sea Bubble and the Tulip Mania of earlier centuries. Many of the popular accounts have stressed anecdotes and personalities.[19] An implication of these accounts is that the primary remedy is to throw the villains in jail. Unfortunately, that approach diverts attention from the fundamental reforms in regulation that are vital.

Instead, as this paper has argued, we need to understand the basic economic forces that were at work in creating the S&L debacle. Only then can we understand how they might arise again in other contexts and how important the reforms advocated in Section IV are for forestalling another such debacle.

---

19. See, for example, Pizzo, Fricker, and Muolo (1988), Pilzer (1989), and Adams (1990).

Bibliography

Adams, James R. (1990). *The Big Fix: Inside the S&L Scandal.* New York: John Wiley & Sons.

Barth, James R., Philip F. Bartholomew, and Michael G. Bradley (1989). "The Determinants of Thrift Resolution Costs," Research Paper no. 89-03, Office of the Chief Economist, Office of Thrift Supervision. November.

Brumbaugh, R. Dan, Jr. (1988). *Thrifts Under Siege: Restoring Order to American Banking.* Cambridge, Mass.: Ballinger.

Campbell, Tim S. (1988). *Money and Capital Markets.* Glenview, IL.: Scott Foresman.

Kane, Edward J. (1985). "Short-Changing the Small Saver: Federal Discrimination Against the Small Saver during the Vietnam War," *Journal of Money, Credit and Banking*, 2 (November), pp. 513-522.

Kane, Edward J. (1985). *The Gathering Crisis in Federal Deposit Insurance.* Cambridge, Mass: MIT Press.

Kane, Edward J. (1989). *The S&L Insurance Mess: How Did It Happen?* Washington, D.C.: Urban Institute Press.

Keeley, Michael C. (1989). "Deposit Insurance, Risk, and Market Power in Banking," in Federal Reserve Bank of Chicago, *Banking System Risk: Chartering a New Course.* Chicago, pp. 101-116.

Pilzer, Paul Z. (1989). *Other People's Money: The Inside Story of the S&L Mess.* New York: Simon and Schuster.

Pizzo, Stephen, Mary Fricker, and Paul Muolo (1989). *Inside Job: The Looting of America's Savings and Loans.* New York: McGraw-Hill.

Spellman, Lewis J. (1982). *The Depository Firm and Industry: Theory, History, and Regulation.* New York: Academic Press.

White, Lawrence J. (1988a). "Mark to Market is Vital to FSLIC and Valuable to Thrifts," *Outlook of the Federal Home Loan Bank System*, 4 (January/February), pp. 20-24.

White, Lawrence J. (1988b). "Market Value Accounting: An Important Part of the Reform of the Deposit Insurance Systems," in Association of Reserve City Bankers, *Capital Issues in Banking.* Washington, D.C., pp. 226-242.

White, Lawrence J. (1990a). "Mark-to-Market: A (Not So) Modest Proposal," *Financial Managers' Statement*, 12 (January/February), pp. 27-37.

White, Lawrence J. (1990b). "The Case for Mark-to-Market Accounting," *Secondary Mortgage Markets*, 7 (Summer), pp. 2-4.

White, Lawrence J. (1991a). *The S&L Debacle: Public Policy Lessons for Bank and Thrift Regulation*. New York: Oxford University Press.

White, Lawrence J. (1991b). "The Value of Market Value Accounting for the Deposit Insurance System," *Journal of Accounting, Auditing, and Finance*, 6 (April).

10

PRUDENTIAL REGULATION AND BANKING SUPERVISION

Vincent P. Polizatto

Establishing a Sound Public Policy for Banks

Banks hold a unique position in most economies as creators of money, the principal depositories of the public's financial savings, the primary allocators of credit, and managers of the country's payment systems.[1] For this reason, governments establish public policy for banks in the public interest. In most market economics, the goals of these policies are to control the supply of money, prevent systemic financial instability, and ameliorate concerns about the efficiency and equity of financial intermediation. In socialized, or centrally planned economies, public policy for banks may differ—emphasizing instead the role of the banking system in channeling funds to priority sectors of the economy.

Because banks perform an intermediary function as gatherers of deposits and allocators of credit, they are necessarily highly leveraged, making them vulnerable to depositor withdrawals and losses of public confidence. Since most banking assets are usually held as loans and advances that cannot be easily valued, there is a lack of transparency as to the actual financial condition of any given bank. This lack of transparency further adds to the vulnerability of banks since deposi-

---

1. The term "bank" is used in this paper as a generic term covering all types of deposit and credit institutions (commercial and savings banks as well as building societies, savings and loan associations, and credit unions).

tors may be forced to act upon incomplete or inaccurate information and rumors concerning the health of such institutions.

From a public policy perspective, the government's goal to ensure the stability of the financial system should be of paramount importance.[2] The failure of a large bank or multiple bank failures may force a sudden contraction of the money supply, a failure of the payments system, a severe dislocation of the real economy, and real or implicit obligations on the part of the government. The failure of any bank, no matter how small, may lead to contagion and loss of confidence in the system, unless the government can demonstrate its ability to handle bank failures in an orderly and systematic fashion.

Public policy toward banks is captured or codified in the various laws, rules, and regulations promulgated by governments. These may generally be classified according to their intent as either economic or prudential regulation, although in some instances regulation has both economic and prudential aspects.[3,4] This chapter will primarily concern itself with the prudential aspects of regulation and supervision that are designed to remove or lessen the threat of systemic instability.

If prudential regulation is the codification of public policy toward banks, banking supervision is the government's means of ensuring compliance.[5] By providing timely and accurate information to policymakers, bank supervisors play a critical part in supporting the government's role as lender of last resort, deposit insurer, and/or investor of last resort when financial instability threatens an economy. Lacking such information, public policymakers may make faulty decisions in response to a problem, potentially worsening it. The more decision-

---

2. For more on prudential supervision as an aspect of public policy, see Bench, unpublished.

3. Economic regulation refers to regulation designed to achieve economic goals. Examples include reserve requirements (control of money creation), directed credit and credit allocation (lending to priority sectors in the interest of social and developmental objectives), financial transaction taxes (revenue generation for the fiscal budget), and so on.

4. Prudential regulation refers to the set of laws, rules, and regulations that is designed to minimize the risks banks assume and to ensure the safety and soundness of both individual institutions and the system as a whole. Examples include lending limits, minimum capital adequacy guidelines, liquidity ratios, and so on. These are discussed in greater detail later in the paper.

5. Banking supervision refers to the banking agency's ongoing monitoring of banks and enforcement of banking regulations and policies.

makers know about a problem, the more likely is the chance that confidence in the system will be maintained or restored through effective and timely action. Bank supervisors can provide this vital information and the means to prevent and correct unsafe and unsound banking practices.

Public Policy Goals for Banking Supervision

Public policy toward banks can differ from country to country. In many countries, banks are used as a means to achieve important developmental and social goals through programs such as rural branching and priority sector lending. However, these goals often conflict with prudential concerns for the safety and soundness of the banking system. Balancing different, and often conflicting, goals can be difficult at best. Differences in public policy are also embodied in perceptions concerning the proper role of bank supervisors. In many centrally planned economies, for example, supervisors have had to enforce compliance with credit quotas and targets under a national credit plan. Bank supervisors may also be called on to enforce tax compliance and foreign exchange control regulations, check reserve computations, and ensure compliance with directed credit programs.

Conflicting goals and the lack of a well-defined prudential role for bank supervision can only detract from its effectiveness in ensuring a safe and sound banking system. In most industrialized countries, public policy goals tend to be more clearly defined and better balanced. While desirable social objectives such as consumer protection may be embedded in public policy goals, emphasis is usually directed toward the protection of depositors, monetary stability, and an efficient and competitive financial system.

For banking supervision to be effective then, the role of bank supervision must be clearly defined and understood by public policy makers. In addition, supervisors must enjoy the support of government officials and the banking industry and political interference must be held to a minimum. When required, high ranking government officials may need to exhibit the courage and political will to undertake strong, and possibly radical, actions to preserve the integrity of the financial system. To achieve these ends, government officials need to understand clearly the linkages between macroeconomic performance and the health of the financial system. In addition, they will need to demonstrate the foresight to put aside short-term benefits for the long-term good. Banking supervision will not be effective unless government officials at the highest levels support a strong and active supervisory process and the public policy role of bank supervision is clearly defined. Assuming that these preconditions are met, actions can be taken to strengthen the institutional framework to achieve effective bank supervision and a healthy banking system.

Creating an Effective Framework of Prudential Regulation

A broad body of banking legislation is essential to ensure that bank supervisors can carry out and enforce their responsibilities. In most countries, the legal framework applicable to banks encompasses prudential laws and regulations, the laws governing commercial transactions and debt recovery, and bankruptcy laws. When an appropriate framework does not exist, it is a significant contributor to financial sector problems.

Prudential Regulation

Prudential regulations establish the outside limits and constraints placed on banks to ensure the safety and soundness of the banking system. They are the key elements to prevent, limit, or stop the damage caused by poor management. The establishment of an appropriate regulatory framework is essential to ensure that government supervisors can carry out and enforce their responsibilities. The absence or weakness of prudential regulation in critical areas could lead to banking failures and systemic instability.

The manner in which prudential regulations are implemented can have a profound effect on the financial marketplace, possibly leading to fragmentation of the financial markets. Care must be taken to implement a regulatory framework that is not distorted but that provides adequate protection to ensure a safe and sound financial system. For instance, it may be appropriate for all banking institutions in a country to be subject to the same banking laws and supervision in order to create a competitive market.[6] This is particularly important as a financial system develops and becomes more integrated with the international financial system. There is a need to harmonize regulation with international standards and create a level playing field so that domestic institutions can compete effectively and prosper both at home and abroad.

Broad authorities are needed to deal with troubled financial institutions, incompetent or abusive managements, insider or related company abuses, and concentrations of credit. Bank supervisors should have the ability to enact subsidiary regulations under broader powers granted by the legislative body in the country. In this way, the regulations can be easily amended to reflect changing conditions through regulatory action rather than new banking legislation.

Notwithstanding the necessity of an appropriate regulatory framework, it is important to recognize that regulation cannot preclude, nor should it attempt to preclude, every improper or ill-advised banking practice. Furthermore, it should be understood that, while economic deregulation and financial liberalization are important for a country to develop a viable and robust financial system, deregulation will remove the protections previously afforded the banking system. Increased competition, a changing price structure, new market entrants, and other factors will increase the risks banks assume. Regulation and supervision cannot prevent all bank failures. However, good regulation and supervision can serve to minimize the adverse impact of moral hazard and relative price shocks on the financial system, thus decreasing the likelihood of bank failures and financial system distress. This section reviews the principal types of regulations required to ensure the establishment of a sound financial system and the problems caused by their absence.

CRITERIA FOR ENTRY. Since newly licensed banks are particularly vulnerable to failure, the initial decision to grant a license is an important one. In making this decision, bank supervisors should have the

---

6. For example, regulations that impose restrictions on branching and bank mergers are often motivated by political considerations. In addition to fragmenting banking systems, such regulations limit the ability of banks to diversify their risks and thus increase the fragility of banking systems.

ability to screen access to ownership and management to prevent individuals lacking professional qualifications, experience, financial backing, and sound ethical standards from obtaining a banking license either through *de novo* entry or acquisition of an existing institution. Unfortunately, in many developing countries, licenses are granted by agencies of the government other than those with direct supervisory responsibility. Often the granting of licenses is politically motivated and a form of patronage or is designed to serve a special interest group, for example, agriculture or housing. Where this has occurred, problems and banking insolvency have often followed.

In many countries, commercial and industrial conglomerates attempt to establish banks to ensure their access to preferential or subsidized credit. In others, special purpose banks created outside the banking laws under various government ministries have led to distortions in the financial marketplace caused by credits granted to priority sectors at heavily subsidized interest rates. To eliminate or reduce these distortions and abuses, all decisions concerning licensing and other corporate activities, such as mergers and acquisitions, should require the satisfaction of specific criteria prior to approval by the supervisory authority. For example, for *de novo* entry, regulations should address the minimum amount of capital, the qualifications of management, the development of a reasonable business plan and projections, and the financial strength of the proposed owners. Failure to meet the minimum criteria or to present reasonable projections should result in the denial of a banking license. The establishment of specific criteria that must be met reduces the potential for political interference in the licensing process. The ease or difficulty of complying with such criteria can be used as a means of regulating new entrants into the marketplace. To further reduce political interference or the influence of special interest groups, decisions regarding licensing should be delegated to the supervisory unit as one of its normal operating functions.

CAPITAL ADEQUACY. Capital is necessary to absorb unusual losses. In most developing countries, financial institutions are significantly undercapitalized and in many cases stated capital is negative—even before portfolio and other losses are recognized. The regulatory framework often lacks meaningful minimum capital adequacy guidelines and the ability to impose restrictions on dividend payments when the bank is incurring losses. As a result, capital, as a cushion for unusual losses, is simply not sufficient for the risks that exist both on and off the balance sheet. Lacking adequate capital, the banks' potential for failure is greatly enhanced. Because banks are undercapitalized, management is often forced into hiding losses that would make insolvency apparent. Without appropriate action by bank managements, government officials, and bank supervisors, this unhealthy situation may continue until the banks face a liquidity crisis and the government is forced to act.

In some countries, government-owned banks operating with inadequate or negative capital are particularly vulnerable. Government officials and the public at large may believe that because of government ownership, there is no danger of failure. In such cases, management often lacks the discipline that would otherwise be required in managing a privately owned institution. A common result is that losses multiply at much higher rates than in privately owned banks, with the losses eventually absorbed by the fiscal budget. The ensuing distortions impact both economic development and financial intermediation.

To combat these problems, minimum capital adequacy guidelines should be established. In countries where banks' internal systems are weak, these guidelines may be more easily enforced when expressed as a simple percentage of total assets. A level not less than 5 to 8 percent should be the absolute floor. However, this percentage may need to be increased on a case-by-case basis due to a bank's particular risk profile or where substantial off-balance sheet risks exist. In countries where accounting and management information systems in banks are more sophisticated, it may be appropriate to adopt the risk-based capital adequacy guidelines formulated by the Basle Committee of Bank Supervisors. In either case, the components of what constitutes capital should be clearly defined. Dividends should not be permitted if the minimum capital percentage is not met. Given that the purpose of capital is to absorb unusual losses, the measurement of capital adequacy should be related to the areas of greatest risk, that is, assets and off-balance sheet contingencies. Therefore, a minimum capital adequacy guideline based on assets is to be preferred to one based on deposits.

ASSET DIVERSIFICATION. Banks can increase their returns or reduce their risks or generally achieve a better combination of risk and return by diversifying their operations. Restrictions on geographical expansion or on product diversification often increase the exposure of banks to particular risks. From the prudential point of view, such restrictions should not be condoned. However, lending limits, investment limits, and other exposure limits, which prevent the concentration of risk in a single borrower or a related group of borrowers, are necessary for prudential purposes. Such limits are normally expressed as a percentage of a bank's capital. In high income countries, credit to any one borrower cannot normally exceed 15 or 20 percent of capital. In some developing countries, lending limits do not exist. In others, the limits are established at imprudent levels, in some cases exceeding 100 percent of a bank's capital. In such instances, just one large problem borrower can render the bank insolvent if the borrower's loans become uncollectible. Fearing this eventuality, bank management loses control of the credit relationship to the borrower and may become involved in deception to avoid recognizing a problem situation.

While many developing countries have adopted lending limits, these limits are often circumvented by borrowers who borrow through nominees. Therefore, banking regulations should specify rules for combining loans to the ultimate user of credit. These rules would combine loans extended to a group of related borrowers, to borrowers exhibiting a common source of repayment, or in which the proceeds of loans can be shown to have been used by or for the benefit of one party.

A lending limit of 15 percent of the bank's capital is generally considered reasonable. In no event should the maximum lending limit exceed 25 percent of a bank's capital. To accommodate large borrowers, a mechanism should be in place to syndicate or sell participations in the credit. In such cases, the purchasing bank should conduct its own credit evaluation and must assume the full credit risk for its share. Lending limits should normally apply equally to both unsecured and secured credit, except where readily marketable collateral is obtained and properly pledged. Examples of such collateral include government securities and bank certificates of deposit.

Many argue that lending limits impose an unwarranted constraint on banks in capital-short economies or on indigenous banks in systems where foreign-owned banks are dominant. Notwithstanding these concerns, the failure to abide by reasonable prudential limits frequently results in banking insolvency and systemic distress. The costs of bank failures invariably outweigh the short-term constraints imposed by lending limits. By imposing a reasonable lending limit, bank supervisors will be sending a strong message that banks must have sufficient capital to attain a scale of operations that will permit them to compete effectively and serve their large customers.

LOANS TO INSIDERS AND CONNECTED PARTIES. A frequent cause of loan problems is credit granted to bank insiders and to individuals or firms connected through ownership or with the ability to exert control, whether direct or indirect. Examples of connected parties include a firm's parent, major shareholders, subsidiaries, affiliated companies, directors, and executive officers. Firms are also connected where they are controlled by the same family or group. Such credit may not meet the same standards as that extended to outside borrowers and the amount of credit often exceeds prudent levels. Frequently, the managerial attitudes of the related or subsidiary companies deteriorate because of the easy and systematic access to credit. In addition, banks tend to prop up or support connected companies that are in trouble rather than recognizing them as problem borrowers. Invariably, the close linkages result in losses.

To preclude the problems of connected lending, procedures should be established to ensure that loans to connected parties are granted at arm's length on terms not more favorable than those extended to similarly situated outside borrowers, that proper internal controls and credit limits are in place, and that concentrations of credit are avoided.

PERMISSIBLE OR PROHIBITED ACTIVITIES. Prudential regulations in some countries do not adequately define permissible or prohibited activities. As a result, banks may engage in commercial activities or enter lines of business that are unsuitable for financial institutions because of the risks involved and the specialized expertise required. Abuses can be as subtle as speculating in real estate by purchasing office buildings that far exceed actual banking needs. In other instances, banks engage in activities that are clearly nonfinancial, such as the ownership of manufacturing firms by many Latin American banks. The lack of clear definitions for permissible and prohibited activities increases the risks banks assume in their quest for profits and growth.

Regulations should detail, therefore, permissible and prohibited activities for banks. Such regulations should address whether banks can engage in commercial activities, own equity stakes in firms or enterprises, and participate in nonbanking financial activities.

ASSET CLASSIFICATION AND PROVISIONING. One of the most serious deficiencies in developing countries is the failure to recognize problem assets through classification, provisioning, write-off, and interest suspension. In a majority of cases, banks simply do not identify problem assets, establish realistic provisions for potential losses, write off or fully provide for actual losses, or suspend interest on nonperforming assets. As a result, the balance sheet does not reflect the bank's actual condition and the income statement overstates profits upon which dividends and taxes are paid. In many cases, if all losses were formally recognized, the banks would be insolvent.

Bank supervisors, in the course of their on-site examinations, may identify problem assets but are frequently powerless to require banks to make adequate provisions, direct the write-off of bad assets, and cause the suspension of interest on nonperforming assets for lack of the necessary legal powers. As a result, widespread abuses often continue unchecked and defer the recognition of financial system distress until the level of nonperforming assets gives way to liquidity crisis. Only then may the government be able to mobilize the political support and the resources necessary to deal with the problems that have been allowed to accumulate. If problem assets were appropriately identified and potential losses provided against in a timely manner, actions could be taken to strengthen or collect the problem assets, to prevent additional advances to problem borrowers, and to reflect upon and change lending policies leading to problems with the effect of containing actual losses at a controllable level.

There is a need, therefore, for banks to systematically and realistically identify their problem assets and provide adequate reserves for possible losses. One way to accomplish this is for developing countries to introduce regulations that require banks (1) to classify their assets as to quality according to specific criteria, (2) define nonperforming assets, (3) require the suspension of interest and reversal of previously accrued but uncollected interest on nonperforming assets, (4) preclude the refinancing or capitalization of interest, and (5) mandate minimum provisions to the reserve for possible losses based on the classification of assets.[7,8] The percentages established for provisions may in some sense be arbitrary. However, on balance, they will establish some discipline in the credit process and force the banks to more accurately reflect their actual state of affairs.

SCOPE, FREQUENCY, AND CONTENT OF THE AUDIT PROGRAM. External audits serve as a means to independently verify and disclose the financial condition of the bank or enterprise audited. However, in some countries, external audits of banks are not required. In others, audits are performed but there are no clear guidelines concerning the standards to be used, the scope and content of the audit program, nor the frequency of audit activities to be carried out. Where audit standards do exist, they may differ substantially from recognized international standards and practices. Frequently, audits are carried out in accordance with local customs, tradition, and practices. This leads to inadequate and misleading financial statements that fail to accurately portray the true condition of the institutions. In point of fact, there are many examples of banks having clean audits even though they are known to be technically insolvent.

The weaknesses in bank auditing standards and practices may require an active role on the part of bank supervisors to establish minimum standards for the scope, frequency, and content of the audit program as well as the form and content of financial disclosures based on such audits.

---

7. Many countries use categories called substandard, doubtful, and loss; however, the titles are not as important as the conceptual process of grading actual and potential risk.

8. A frequently used definition defines nonperforming assets as those that are 90 days or more past due and not well-secured and in the process of collection.

Regulations should empower bank supervisors to establish auditing standards and minimum disclosure requirements. Key elements of the audit program should include an examination of portfolio quality and standards for valuing assets, establishing reserves for losses, and treatment of interest on nonperforming assets. In addition, supervisors should have the power to appoint or dismiss auditors. Auditors should also be under an affirmative obligation to inform the supervisors of significant findings in a timely manner. This can be done in a manner that respects the bank's right to know, except where criminal acts are involved.

Depositors, investors, and creditors of a bank should have reliable and timely information to make informed decisions when transacting business with a bank. Well-informed investors, depositors, and creditors can be an efficient regulator in an age of technology, information, and free capital flows. Regulations governing the scope and content of financial statements provide a means for disseminating information that is complete, timely, and uniform, thus permitting comparison, informed decisionmaking, and market discipline. However, financial disclosure and market discipline may not be good ideas for developing countries whose financial systems are in disarray until appropriate safeguards are built into the system.

ENFORCEMENT POWERS. Bank supervisors can usually impose fines and penalties for criminal acts and violations of specific statutes. However, there may be very little they can do to address unsafe and unsound banking practices that are not specifically addressed by statute. In such instances, their options very often are to cancel the banking license or to do nothing—neither of which is acceptable. As the result, the lack of intermediate enforcement powers often leads not only to inaction on the part of bank supervisors but to a perpetuation of problems and abuses within a given institution.

In countries where the legal systems are more developed, there are a number of intermediate actions that can be taken. These include a full range of enforcement powers to deal with incompetent or abusive ownership and management, including: (1) the ability to remove management or directors; (2) monetary fines or penalties that can be assessed against individuals, as well as institutions, for criminal acts or violations of the banking regulations; (3) civil money penalties that can be assessed against individuals for engaging in unsound and unsafe banking practices; (4) the right to restrict or suspend dividend payments; (5) the ability to withhold branch or other corporate approvals; (6) cease and desist authority; and (7) the ability to impose financial liability against bank directors for losses incurred due to illegal acts carried out by the bank, for example, violations of the lending limit that result in loss.

Cease and desist orders put the power of the legal system behind the supervisors in requiring changes in unsafe, unsound, or abusive practices. Banking legislation does not need to limit or prohibit the specific activity that is the focus of supervisory concern. However, any willful violation of the cease and desist order is accorded the same legal status as a violation of a specific statute and is subject to civil or criminal remedies in the legal system. Supervisors should also have the authority to issue temporary orders to cease and desist, pending confirmation by the legal system, so that the bank will be forced to stop imprudent or abusive practices immediately.

The ability to impose joint and several personal financial liability upon directors for losses arising from illegal acts committed by the bank is designed to encourage greater involvement by a bank's board of directors in actively supervising the affairs of the bank and to guard against potential abuses committed by the directorate. Directors should take an active interest in the bank's affairs and insist on proper controls and reporting so that they may remain sufficiently informed to carry out their responsibilities in a prudent manner.

TREATMENT OF PROBLEM AND FAILED BANKS. In many developing countries, the laws and regulations governing banking are rooted in the legal systems inherited or borrowed from former colonial governments. One feature of these systems is that banks are incorporated under the provisions of a company's act, subjecting banks to the same bankruptcy proceedings that apply to other corporations. This has caused considerable problems for prudential supervisors since the power to quickly intervene in insolvent banks is lacking. The bank supervisors lack authority to close a bank, appoint a receiver, and liquidate or merge it. Instead, the bank must go through a normal bankruptcy process, initiated by a depositor or creditor. This process may take months or years to complete during which depositors may not have access to their monies. In addition, shareholders may retain an interest in their shares. This effectively prevents any attempt to re-capitalize the institution or transfer ownership to the government or new investors.

Legislation is necessary, therefore, to permit supervisors to declare banks insolvent, close banks, and place them in receivership outside the normal corporate bankruptcy process. This is necessary if supervisors are to protect depositors' interests and ensure public confidence in their ability to handle financial distress in an orderly and efficient manner. As part of this process, supervisors will also need broad powers to remove and replace management; eliminate the interests of shareholders; and purchase, sell, or transfer problem assets.

DEPOSIT INSURANCE. Many countries operate deposit insurance or deposit protection schemes as part of their prudential regulatory frameworks. Participation in such schemes is often compulsory. The primary objectives of deposit insurance schemes are to avert bank runs and protect the stability of the banking system. However, such schemes may also serve to protect small depositors, thus promoting competition by small banks. Under certain circumstances, deposit insurance schemes may act as catalysts for improving the system of prudential regulation, strengthening the effectiveness of bank supervision, and streamlining the machinery of bank restructuring.

However, deposit insurance may suffer from the problem of moral hazard affecting bank owners and depositors as well as bank supervisors. In countries with inadequate and ineffective supervision, deposit insurance may provide a false sense of security and lead to the taking of imprudent and unacceptable risks. Therefore, the establishment of deposit insurance schemes should be assessed on a case-by-case basis taking into account the administrative capabilities of different countries, the effectiveness of banking supervision, the structure of the banking system, and the sophistication of depositors.

Commercial Law, Debt Recovery, and Bankruptcy

In addition to prudential regulations designed to ensure the safety and soundness of the banking system, there is another important aspect of the legal framework that affects banks. This is the body of commercial laws and regulations governing a bank's contractual relationship with its customers. A key aspect of this legislation that often causes problems for the banks is that involving debt collection or recovery. In many countries, the commercial law dealing with debt collection and recovery overwhelmingly favors the banks' borrowers. Foreclosure and other legal actions involve a cumbersome legal process that may take years to complete at great expense to the banks. This cumbersome process is a disincentive to banks to take strong action to collect their problem debts. It may also encourage bankers to lend additional funds to carry the problem borrowers in the hope that the borrowers may recover and pay off their debts. All too often, though, the borrowers are unable to recover and the losses incurred by the banks multiply to even greater levels.

If banks are to remain viable, the legal system must be able to balance the rights of banks to foreclose on collateral with the rights of individuals and firms so that debts can be recovered in a timely manner. This may require changes in laws governing commercial transactions and bankruptcy and a wide range of actions to improve the effectiveness of the legal system, for example, hiring more judges and establishing courts specifically designed to hear commercial law and bankruptcy cases.

Building an Effective Framework for Bank Supervision

An ineffective legal framework may result in banking system distress but, more often than not, lack of enforcement and supervision are equally at fault. Supervisory problems may be rooted in conflicting public policy goals for supervision; political interference; a lack of political will to deal with problems; organizational weaknesses such as understaffing, inadequate compensation, poor leadership, and divided supervisory responsibilities; and the lack of a clear understanding on the role of supervision. Problems may also result from examination methodologies that focus on technical compliance with laws and regulations or that are diluted by responsibilities for nonprudential concerns such as tax compliance, foreign exchange controls, and special lending programs. In some cases, problems also occur because of the lack of an early warning system and off-site surveillance capabilities. More often than not, though, supervisory problems result from a combination of these factors.

Bank Supervision Models in the Industrialized Countries

Bank supervision in the industrialized countries developed in response to financial crises, economic events, and political phenomena. Very often, the form of bank supervision reflected philosophical and social differences in the role of government and in the organization of society, for example, the "clubby" approach in 19th century Britain, where the Bank of England exerted its moral authority and leadership through "nods and winks," versus the strongly populist and confrontational tradition of the United States, which was based on more or less detailed "rules of the game" and required a more elaborate mechanism for ensuring compliance with these rules. These differences were embodied in two principal models of bank regulation and supervision: an informal approach that relied on consultation and moral suasion; and a formalized approach that required active, "hands-on" verification through on-site inspection. In continental Europe, a legalistic approach was developed that was less "hands-on" than in the United States and delegated much of the verification and inspection of bank records to external auditors.

Bank Supervision in Britain

The informal approach to bank supervision is best exemplified by the approach taken by the Bank of England. In Britain, supervision was traditionally carried out by the Bank of England in consultation with banks. Moral suasion, discretion, and personal contact were the principal tools of bank supervisors. Each bank had an individual relationship with the Bank of England. Banks made prudential returns but, unlike other systems of supervision where examiners conduct on-site examinations to verify and extract information, the responsibility for passing on information to the Bank of England rested solely with the banks.[9] For many years this system worked relatively well in a highly concentrated banking industry. However, the system came under stress when the number of banks increased as a result of the creation of so-called secondary banks and the influx of foreign banks in the late 1960s and early 1970s.

The flaws of the informal system, which relied on information provided by management but without an independent assessment of the quality of bank portfolios and of the adequacy of provisions for possible loan losses, became apparent. Gradually, the British authorities adopted a more legalistic approach to bank regulation and supervision that brought British practice closer to continental European practice. Following the Johnson Matthey affair, which precipitated a reappraisal of the supervisory approach of the Bank of England, the British authorities effectively delegated on-site inspections to external auditors by strengthening the reporting requirements of banks' auditors to the Bank of England.[10] Steps were also taken to improve the off-site surveillance capability of the Bank of England.

For the informal approach to be effective, the U.K. experience would seem to suggest that several key conditions must exist: a small number of banks, a strong central authority, a tradition of close cooperation between government and industry as well as close personal relationships between bankers and supervisors, a highly skilled work force, effective management systems within the banks themselves, strong auditing and accounting practices, and full disclosure to ensure market discipline. Even then, dishonest or fraudulent management could deceive bank supervisors and cause irreparable damage to an institution. This system of informal supervision left a legacy of "hands-off" bank supervision in many former British colonies, which made them ill-prepared for the problems of banking in a developing environment. While this does not appear to have created difficulties in some countries, problems have emerged in many other Commonwealth countries in Africa and Asia where indigenous banks were promoted to compete against the hitherto dominant role of foreign banks.

---

9. See Blackhurst (1985).

10. For a discussion of the Johnson Matthey Bankers affair and the role of the Bank of England, see Ollard and Routledge (1985).

Bank Supervision in Continental Europe

The model of bank supervision found in continental European countries is based on a legalistic approach that stipulates various ratios that the banks must observe but delegates the on-site examination of banks and the verification of their records to external auditors. In Belgium, special auditors are appointed and paid by the authorities. In Switzerland, the auditors are licensed by the Federal Banking Commission and are subject to special statutory duties. In Germany, general auditors perform the examinations of banks and must inform the authorities if they discover facts that justify the qualification of an audit. However, supervisors retain the right to examine a bank's books and carry out examinations at any time. In each of these countries, the supervisors have established detailed rules concerning the form and content of the auditors' reports.

Delegating on-site bank examinations to external auditors effectively represents the privatization of the inspection process, although under strict government rules and guidelines. There are several advantages to this approach. Auditing firms may escape the resource and salary constraints that often prevent supervisory authorities, and governments generally, from employing and retaining highly skilled staff. Moreover, auditors may achieve operating economies by combining a prudential inspection with ordinary accounting audits.

However, this approach also raises some concerns. There are risks that if not properly structured and controlled, auditors may be placed in potentially conflicting roles with dual loyalties to both the banks and the government, particularly in cases where the auditors are permitted to undertake other work. In addition, there is a concern that, in their efforts to control costs and maximize profits, auditors may not devote sufficient resources to ensure proper performance of the audit.

The appropriate modality for on-site inspection, that is, supervisors or auditors, for any particular country ultimately depends on an evaluation of which group is best able to perform the on-site verification function. Factors to be evaluated include skills, competence, experience, and independence from political and other influence. This evaluation is best performed on a case-by-case basis.

Bank Supervision in the United States

Bank supervision in the United States exemplifies the formal approach to supervision that requires an active, on-site presence to verify conditions existing within banks. In the U.S. model, periodic on-site examinations have been the cornerstone of the supervisory process. The American approach is justified by the large number of small banks and on unit banking within particular states, both of which result from restrictions on geographic expansion. Whereas the concentrated banking systems of the European countries internalize most of the costs of policing branches and losses are dispersed at the branch level, in the American banking structure, policing costs are incurred to a much greater extent by the regulatory agencies, while bank losses are covered to a greater extent through formal deposit insurance schemes.[11] This creates greater social and political pressures for a hands-on approach to bank supervision.

Unlike countries where the authorities rely on outside experts, bank supervisors in the United States must themselves possess the skills to evaluate asset quality and other areas of a bank's activities. A major disadvantage of this approach is that it can be labor intensive and can be inhibited by budgetary constraints. U.S. supervisory agencies have responded to resource constraints in recent years by targeting on-site examinations, making greater use of off-site surveillance and early warning analysis, and taking advantage of advances in computer technology. These steps have permitted the supervisory agencies to hold the number of examining staff relatively constant despite the growth in assets and growing complexity of the financial system.

The more than 14,000 banks supervised by U.S. regulators is a major reason that a formal approach to supervision has been required. It also explains the adoption of the CAMEL rating system and the use of the Uniform Bank Performance Report. The CAMEL rating quantifies a supervised institution's condition in five critical areas and assigns an overall composite rating, while the Uniform Bank Performance Report (UBPR) is a statistical analysis of bank perfor-

---

11. See Vittas (1989).

mance that is based on data from quarterly prudential reports.[12] This report compares and ranks each bank against its peers. There are twenty-five peer groups, bringing together institutions with similar characteristics. These reports are publicly available and the computer tapes are made available to stock analysts and others. By using this technology, supervisors also have the ability to prepare ad hoc reports or to download data into microcomputer models where simulation or forecasting is performed. In the latest stage of technological advance, expert systems are being used to analyze prudential reports and generate written comments.

Harmonization and Convergence of Bank Supervision

Despite the differences in supervisory approaches, there is a growing consensus that bank supervision and regulation should be harmonized across national boundaries due to the ever-increasing global interdependence of financial markets. As developing countries grow and prosper, the integration of domestic financial markets with the larger international financial system will become more and more important so that distortions are minimized. In a world where financial transactions occur around the clock and banks enter into financial transactions with any number of foreign correspondents and counter-parties, the global financial system may only be as strong as its weakest links. Differences in regulation can distort the financial markets as well as increase the risks for banking activities performed beyond national borders. There is also a danger that domestic institutions operating abroad may escape supervision.

The failure of the West German *Bankhaus Herstatt* in 1974 due to foreign exchange and other losses had damaging effects on the international interbank market and focused attention on the need for greater international supervisory cooperation. This led to the formation of the Basle Committee later that year under the auspices of the Bank for International Settlements. This forum comprises banking supervisors from the Group of Ten countries plus Switzerland and

---

12. CAMEL is an acronym for Capital adequacy, Asset quality, Management, Earnings, and Liquidity, asset and liability management.

Luxembourg.[13] Following its creation, the committee addressed the issue of supervision of financial institutions operating abroad by developing broad guidelines to ensure that no institution escaped supervision. These guidelines are contained in the "Basle Concordat," which embodied the following key principles: (1) supervision of foreign banking establishments is the joint responsibility of parent and host authorities, (2) no foreign banking establishment should escape supervision, (3) supervision of liquidity should be the primary responsibility of the host authorities, (4) supervision of solvency is essentially a matter for the parent authority in the case of foreign branches and primarily the responsibility of the host authority in the case of foreign subsidiaries, and (5) practical cooperation should be promoted by the exchange of information between host and parent authorities and by the authorization of bank inspections by or on behalf of parent authorities on the territory of the host authority.[14]

Other important initiatives prompted by the work of the Basle Committee include recommendations that supervision of banks' international business be conducted on a consolidated basis, so that risks can be evaluated globally, and the adoption of risk-asset based capital adequacy standards. Continuing work focuses on banks' exposure to country risk, liquidity and interest rate risk, and off-balance sheet risk.[15]

Supervisory Methodologies

The growing integration of financial markets, especially among member states of the European Community, has led to a convergence of systems of bank supervision. It is now widely accepted that an adequate system of bank supervision should allow for both on-site examination and off-site surveillance and that nonprudential concerns, such as tax collection and compliance with currency controls and credit constraints, should be held to a minimum.

Supervisors' tools include on-site examinations of individual institutions and off-site surveillance from both macro and micro perspec-

---

13. The Group of Ten countries are Belgium, Canada, France, Germany, Italy, Japan, the Netherlands, Sweden, the United Kingdom, and the United States.

14. See Dale (1982).

15. See Committee on Banking Regulations and Supervisory Practices (1986).

tives. For most developing countries, on-site examinations are especially important. This is because problems of insolvency in developing countries usually occur due to credit losses, which are best determined while within an institution. Therefore, supervisors must concentrate on assessing asset quality and mandating provisions for bad debts and suspension of interest on nonperforming assets through on-site examination and verification. By determining asset quality and the condition of an institution, bank supervisors provide critical information to government policymakers on the health of the financial system.

ON-SITE EXAMINATIONS. Traditional on-site examination methodologies in many countries frequently focus on compliance with banking regulations and directives. As a result, prudential concerns for safety and soundness are often overlooked. Even in cases where supervisors attempt to address safety and soundness concerns, the examination process may only provide a "snapshot" of the institution's condition as of a given date without addressing potential risks and the management systems needed internally by the bank to control risk in a dynamic, changing environment. For example, examiners may determine the condition of a bank's loan portfolio but fail to evaluate the lending policies and practices that lead to loan problems or that may give rise to future loan problems. Indeed, in many cases, bank examiners fail to identify and quantify the extent and severity of problem assets—a major failure. Even when problems are identified, supervisors may lack the powers to require provisions and write-offs or other necessary actions.

To correct these weaknesses and improve the effectiveness of their on-site examination activities, supervisors need to move away from checking compliance with laws to assessing risk and assisting banks in managing risk. To accomplish this, bank supervisors should embrace a top-down approach that places emphasis on the direction and policies formulated by the board of directors and executive management. It is not enough to quantify problems—although this is certainly a necessary step. The causes of problems must also be understood and preventive action taken to reduce the likelihood of their recurrence.

As part of the examination process, on-site examiners should verify the accuracy of prudential reports submitted to the supervisory agency and analyze those aspects of a bank that cannot be adequately monitored by off-site surveillance. Examiners should focus on the banks' main activities and on the potential problems identified by off-site surveillance. In particular, they should assess the quality of assets, management, earnings, capital, and funds management, as well as the bank's internal control, audit, management information, and accounting systems. In evaluating asset quality, the examiner should review the bank's lending policies, written or implied, to determine whether they are reasonable and complete. Thereafter, he should examine the credit files of large borrowers, problem borrowers, and a sample of files belonging to smaller borrowers, to assess the quality of the loans, management's credit practices, and adherence to credit policies. Minutes of meetings of the credit committee and the board of directors should be reviewed. The examiner should also evaluate the bank's procedures for suspending the accrual of interest, writing off bad debts, and determining an adequate loan loss provision.

Bank supervisors should also review the business and strategic plans of individual banks and assess the capabilities of management to fulfill objectives. They should check that management systems in place are sufficient to ensure compliance with policies and proper functioning. Bank supervisors should also encourage banks to establish and strengthen their own internal management systems as the first lines of defense against unsound, unsafe, or illegal banking practices. Management systems should include written policies and procedures, formalized planning and budgeting, management information systems, internal loan review, compliance systems, internal and external audit activities, and internal controls. The development of management systems should be encouraged in both large and small banks, although their sophistication and complexity may differ.

Since the ongoing task of bank supervisors is typically to ensure the safety and soundness of the financial system—as opposed to individual banks—and to protect depositors, not the shareholders of banks, supervisory activities should focus on the areas of greatest risk to the system, for example, large financial institutions or banks whose activities may lead to contagion within the system. Within individual banks, efficient use of scarce supervisory resources should be made by targeting examination efforts to the areas of greatest risk, for example, asset quality, interest rate risk, foreign exchange activities, and so on. Examination activities should also avoid the examination of each and every branch office or operating subsidiary of an institution. Instead, the examination should focus on the condition of the consolidated institution by examining those units that have a significant impact on the institution's overall position. The remaining units should be evaluated on a sample basis.

The failure to follow up on problems and to enforce corrective action is a common weakness in the supervisory process. This occurs for many reasons including weak leadership, political influence, temerity in dealing with problems, organizational weaknesses, and a lack of appropriate enforcement tools. However, it also occurs because examination results and the type of corrective actions needed are not adequately communicated to the bank's board of directors and senior management. It is extremely important that examination results are clearly communicated to the bank through a written examination report and meetings with the board of directors and executive management. A transmittal letter attached to the written examination report and signed by the head of bank supervision or his designee should highlight the report's major conclusions and recommendations. In addition, the transmittal letter should require a formal response by the bank within a stated time frame. If progress reports concerning corrective actions to be taken by the bank are required, these should be outlined in the transmittal letter. Administrative procedures should be established for monitoring the bank's response and verifying corrective actions.

In most developing countries, written examination procedures are less than adequate, or lacking altogether, so that the examiner must rely totally on his or her experience, knowledge, and skills. This leads to a lack of uniformity and consistency in the conduct of on-site examinations from one examiner to the next. As a result, the head of bank supervision can never be sure which bank functions were reviewed and the manner in which the examination was performed. The lack of written examination procedures also deprives new staff of an essential training tool. Therefore, to ensure consistency and uniformity, and to provide a training tool for new examiners, written examination procedures and questionnaires should be developed for use in on-site examinations. These are not meant to supplant the examiner's judgment. However, they do provide a framework and support for the work to be carried out.

A complementary aspect to written examination procedures is the documentation of work performed and the maintenance of working papers. These are necessary to demonstrate that the actions recommended by the examiner are not arbitrary but are based on valid concerns and criticisms. This documentation may also be necessary to support legal enforcement actions proposed by the supervisors.

Over the long run, bank supervisors can use the on-site examination process as a catalyst for changing the fundamental ways in which banks operate by recommending actions for financial institutions to upgrade their operations. This usually involves the strengthening of management systems in banks, including written policies and procedures, formalized planning and budgeting, internal controls and audit procedures, management information, and loan review. The rationale for this approach is that supervisors will always face resource constraints. The banks themselves, therefore, must establish the first lines of defense against unsound or unsafe practices. Once management systems are in place, supervisors can determine that the systems are working by testing the systems. If the systems are inadequate, the scope of an examination should be expanded so that risks can be identified and quantified.

OFF-SITE SURVEILLANCE. An off-site surveillance capability provides an important complement to on-site examinations by providing early warning of actual or potential problems and a means for monitoring and comparing financial performance. However, off-site surveillance should not be viewed as a means to replace on-site examination as the primary form of supervision in a developing country. The quality of information and integrity of data provided by banks in all countries must be verified. In developing countries, the quality of information is frequently incomplete and inaccurate. Often, banks do not have the internal accounting and control systems to ensure timely and accurate preparation of information. Therefore, in most cases, it would be inappropriate to rely on off-site surveillance as more than a complement to on-site examinations.

In most developing countries, prudential reports, which form the basis for most off-site surveillance activities, are frequently limited to those concerning liquidity, reserve requirement computations, and credit guidelines. Analysis often consists of simply checking compliance with certain balance sheet ratios. Rarely is information gathered to meaningfully appraise risk.

For off-site surveillance and early warning analysis to be effective, prudential reports must move away from statistical inputs, liquidity and reserve requirement computations, and simple balance sheet calculations to inputs that permit the measurement of risk. This means that supervisors should collect data concerning a bank's loan portfolio, including delinquencies and problem assets, foreign exchange position, off-balance sheet commitments, and other risk areas, as well as balance sheet and profit and loss statements. To ensure uniformity, supervisors should have the ability to prescribe the timing, content, and format of the prudential returns so that comparative data can be prepared and used in a consistent fashion.

It is critical that the off-site surveillance function be fully integrated into the supervisory process so that weaknesses may be corrected. In some cases, it may be sufficient to contact the bank by phone or letter to discuss concerns identified off-site. However, in other cases, it may be necessary to send examiners into a bank to follow up on the weaknesses identified off-site. In any event, information and reports prepared off-site can provide important comparative data on areas of risk and efficiency and should be used by examiners during their on-site examinations.

Organizational Issues

Bank supervision is often placed under the umbrella of a country's central bank. Since the function of bank supervision is to ensure a safe and sound banking system and to prevent financial system instability, the central bank, as manager of a country's monetary policy and lender of last resort, is a logical place to house banking supervision. However, there is no compelling evidence to suggest that operating from within the central bank affords a distinct advantage over the creation of an autonomous supervisory agency provided that bank supervision is insulated from political influences, information derived in the supervisory process is shared with those managing monetary policy, and the agency is adequately funded through assessments or direct budget allocations. In fact, some argue that an agency that is solely responsible for bank supervision will devote greater attention to the fulfillment of its role than one that also has responsibilities for managing the nation's monetary policy. On the other hand, there is an argument that where supervisory responsibility is centered in a central bank, it is likely to be exercised with a wider degree of discretion than where the primary supervisory agency is autonomous and operates within defined statutory limits.[16]

In general, in countries that have strong central banks, it would seem inappropriate to dilute their influence and authority by assigning supervisory responsibilities to another institution. If the central bank is weak, then the case for an independent supervisory agency is stronger. In many high income countries, the division of responsibilities reflects historical factors.

Another alternative is to place the supervisory agency within the Ministry of Finance or Treasury. In most countries, this alternative is the least desirable since these ministries tend to be highly politicized and the coordination of policy with other government agencies tends to be problematic. Ultimately, it would seem, therefore, that the effectiveness of a bank supervisory body depends not so much on its organizational location but on its leadership and independence from political influence. If a particular institutional arrangement in a given country permits the bank supervision unit to operate free from inappropriate outside interference, that arrangement is probably the most desirable for the country.

Regardless of where supervision is located within government, there are important organizational steps that can be taken to enhance its effectiveness. The bank supervision unit should possess its own identity on at least a par with other important units within the central bank or ministry or as an independent agency. The director of bank supervision should be a high ranking government official and report directly to the central bank governor or deputy governor or the minister of finance or treasury. This is necessary to establish an appropriate degree

---

16. See Dale (1982).

of credibility with the banking industry so that directives issued by the supervisor will have effect.

Staffing and Compensation

In most developing countries, bank supervisors face resource and budget constraints. As a result, supervisory units are often under-staffed. This affects the supervisor's ability to conduct bank examina-tions and perform other supervisory duties. The most capable and qualified individuals are frequently employed in the private sector or in other activities where compensation is greater. In some cases, com-pensation for bank supervisors may not be as great as for other parts of government even though the responsibilities are greater. This af-fects the supervisor's ability to attract and retain qualified staff.

Needless to say, adequate staffing for bank supervision, both in terms of quantity and skill levels, is a must. To attract and retain qual-ified staff, compensation should be competitive within government and with the private sector. Governments frequently argue that they cannot afford additional staff or higher salaries. Nor can they justify differentiated salaries within government. However, there is an argu-ment to the contrary that governments cannot afford a banking crisis and its debilitating effects on economic growth and development. It should be noted that there are precedents for banking supervisors to be exempted from normal civil service guidelines and salary scales. The cost of even one bank failure may far exceed the costs incurred in employing and retaining competent staff, a situation clearly demon-strated by the U.S. savings and loan crisis when requests for additional staff were denied by the government administration then in power.

Career Path

In some countries, bank supervision is not viewed as a career, and employees are rotated in and out of the bank supervision unit in only a few years. This contrasts with countries where bank supervisors re-quire four to five years just to learn the skills necessary to examine small, well-managed institutions. If bank supervision is to be effective, it must be considered a full-time career option. Career paths and job descriptions should be developed to provide meaningful and challeng-ing responsibilities as well as upward mobility. This could include career milestones such as promotion from an assistant examiner to a full-fledged examiner to a senior examiner and, ultimately, into the ranks of management. Rotational assignments in other departments could be accommodated as a means of broadening an individual's knowledge and skills. However, it should not mean the end of a career as a bank supervisor.

Training

Training is often conducted solely on the job in a less than systematic manner so that skills are acquired in a hit-or-miss fashion. Inadequacies in training and development affect the supervisor's ability to build a skilled, knowledgeable, and competent staff. Training programs should ensure that each supervisor receives not less than two weeks training per year. This training should combine formal instruction, case study, and seminars. In addition, on-the-job training should be conducted in a systematic fashion. Senior staff should have the opportunity to mix with supervisors from other countries for cross-fertilization of ideas.

Inaction in Restructuring Banks

In the industrialized countries, bank supervisors attempt to minimize potential losses and liability to the government by closing banks near or at the point of reaching technical insolvency. However, in the developing countries, the absence of reliable information, an inadequate legal framework, and the lack of political will often permit banks to remain open and losses to multiply, even though the banks may have lost their reported book capital many times over. Inaction in dealing with insolvency may also occur because the institutional framework for dealing with insolvency is inadequate. Experience indicates that ad hoc approaches to dealing with insolvency generally do not succeed. Because banks are not closed, the effectiveness of bank supervision may be compromised. Bankers may know that supervisors are powerless to take appropriate action. To counter this, a systematic approach and mechanism for dealing with insolvency is necessary.[17]

---

17. For additional information on bank restructuring, see de Juan (1988).

Strengthening the Auditing and Accounting Framework

The development of a strong accounting profession can ensure the establishment of uniform accounting standards that accurately and properly reflect each financial institution's true condition. The rise of the accounting profession also gives way to the preparation of reliable financial information by which credit can be assessed. Auditors play an important role by providing a system of checks and balances, making recommendations to improve accounting and administrative controls, checking for compliance with laws and regulations as well as fraud, and certifying financial statements for public disclosure.

However, in many developing countries, an accounting and auditing tradition is lacking. There may be a shortage of skilled practitioners and, frequently, a professional accounting body does not exist. In addition, accounting and auditing systems and financial disclosure may be nonexistent. The effect is to hinder the development of a well-functioning financial system.

A major weakness in bank accounting and auditing for many developing countries is the absence of adequate accounting standards. Criteria for determining nonperforming assets is subjective, problem assets are not identified or properly valued, interest continues to accrue on nonperforming assets and in many cases it is capitalized or refinanced, and foreign exchange or other losses go unrecognized. These practices lead to inflated profits and overstated balance sheets, often hiding technical insolvency. Dividend payout often drives reported income, and banks manage their loan loss provisions and write-offs to achieve desired levels of profitability. Thus, the essential link between portfolio quality and the level of loan loss provisions is missing.

In some countries, banks may operate without the benefit of a uniform chart of accounts, consistent terminology, and standard accounting methodology. Charts of accounts often vary in structure and terminology, and the accounting principles used to determine account entries and classification are inconsistent from bank to bank. These weaknesses create distortions that make analysis and comparison difficult.

The absence of an accounting and auditing tradition extends beyond banking however. Credit is extended to borrowers without the benefit of current and reliable financial information. The lack of current and satisfactory financial information contributes to the perpetuation of collateral based lending since lenders are not able to appraise a borrower's ability to repay.

Financial disclosures made by banks and enterprises are often misleading and sometimes fraudulent. The lack of reliable financial information inhibits foreign investment and the growth of the capital markets. In the absence of reliable financial information, investors are simply reluctant to place their funds at risk.

To deal with these problems, accounting standards and the auditing profession must be strengthened. Standards that should be established include guidelines for asset classification, definitions for past dues and nonperforming assets, prohibitions against the capitalization or refinancing of interest that is due and unpaid, reversal of previously accrued but uncollected interest on nonperforming assets, adequate provisions for actual or potential loan losses, and guidelines for recognition of foreign exchange and other losses.

One way to accomplish this is to establish minimum standards as part of the legal framework. Another way is for the local professional accounting body to enact standards having the force of law. In countries where a local accounting body does not exist or where the local professional body is very weak, actions will be necessary to establish or enhance the role of a professional body and strengthen the profession by providing training courses at both the university and professional levels, encouraging university students to enter the field of accounting as a career, providing library and research facilities, establishing a professional advisory service and peer review, and imposing sanctions against auditors who consistently perform below acceptable standards. In addition, public policymakers must demonstrate a commitment to supporting the industry's efforts to strengthen its standards and performance.

Upgrading Banks at the Institutional Level

The primary line of defense against banking insolvency and financial system distress is neither bank supervision nor prudential regulation. It is the quality and character of management within the banks themselves. Therefore, efforts to strengthen the financial system must also focus on strengthening management and management systems through a process of institutional development. To begin this process, the initial step in most cases is to evaluate the bank's existing condition, for example, strengths, weaknesses, threats, and opportunities. Included in this step is the identification and quantification of problem assets and potential or unrecognized losses. Unfortunately, management information and other systems within many banks are relatively unsophisticated and the quality of information that is available may be inaccurate and incomplete. Further, management is frequently incapable of dealing with or unable or unwilling to recognize the bank's problems. It is simply more convenient to ignore problems than to face up to them. It may be necessary, therefore, to require the audit of the institution by qualified external auditors or an examination by supervisory authorities with a major goal of determining asset quality, the single factor most likely to erode capital and cause insolvency.

Once the full extent of problems and their causes are diagnosed, solutions can be developed. With portfolio quality problems, the necessary actions often involve changes in management, a reappraisal of implicit lending policies and practices, and strong efforts to collect or strengthen problem credits. Legal action is often necessary to foreclose or repossess assets or to pursue legal claims against guarantors. In extreme cases, where portfolio problems have led to or threaten insolvency, financial restructuring and recapitalization of the institution will be necessary.[18] These will normally require the replacement of management, elimination of shareholders' interests, and carving out of the bad assets.

After an institution has been returned to health, appropriate measures must be taken to ensure that it remains healthy. The deterioration in portfolio quality is apt to repeat unless the policies and practices leading to the decline in portfolio quality are reappraised and modified. Loan underwriting criteria must be reviewed. Repayment programs must be established at each loan's inception and enforced.

---

18. For the steps necessary to restructure banks, see de Juan (1988).

Credit should be predicated upon the borrower's ability to repay. Current and satisfactory financial information on each borrower should be obtained and analyzed on a timely basis. Concentrations of credit should be avoided. Adequate provisions should be set aside for loan losses, and loans should be written off when they are determined to be nonbankable. The accrual of interest should cease on nonperforming assets and previously accrued but uncollected interest should be reversed. Interest capitalization should normally be prohibited. Realistic past due and nonperforming criteria should be established.

It would be shortsighted, however, to evaluate policies and practices only in the context of past problems. Importantly, policies and procedures must be capable of guiding the institution in an ongoing, ever-changing environment. Therefore, one approach to upgrading at the institutional level starts at the top, with the policies and objectives established by the board of directors, and works its way down through the organization. This top-down approach places emphasis on the board of directors and executive management. Unless their full commitment to the process is obtained, the process of upgrading over the long term is likely to fall far short of success. The board of directors of any institution must be shown that it is in their own interests to prudently supervise the affairs of the institution.

The Role of Directors

The process of institution building should include a clear definition of the roles and responsibilities of the board of directors. These typically include the following responsibilities: (1) to select competent executive officers, (2) to effectively supervise the institution's affairs, (3) to adopt and follow sound policies and objectives, (4) to avoid self-serving practices, (5) to be informed of the bank's condition and management policies, (6) to maintain reasonable capitalization, (7) to observe laws, rules, and regulations, and (8) to ensure the bank has a beneficial influence on the economy.

Directors are placed in positions of trust and, though they may delegate the day-to-day routine of conducting the bank's business to their officers and directors, they should be held accountable for the consequences of unsound or imprudent policies and practices. Since the directors are responsible for safeguarding the interests of depositors and shareholders, it is advisable that a majority of the board is independent of political interests, active management, and the interests of major corporate shareholders.

Executive Management and Management Systems

A key responsibility of directors is to employ a competent chief executive officer. Thereafter, senior management assumes the responsibility to manage the day-to-day affairs of the bank, to implement and follow the framework of policies and objectives established by the board of directors, and to employ, maintain, and educate a qualified staff. Senior management conducts the operation and administration of the institution through various management systems. These include written policies and procedures, internal controls, loan review, compliance, planning, budgeting, internal and external auditing, and management information systems. Their effective implementation strengthens the quality of management decisionmaking and control.

WRITTEN POLICIES AND PROCEDURES. To ensure that management executes business plans and controls risks appropriately, written policies should be formulated for each major business activity or function the bank is engaged in. The policies and procedures should be comprehensive and should provide a clear framework within which management and staff can be expected to operate. Policies should be reviewed annually, or more often as needed, and should provide an appropriate mechanism for exceptions when warranted.

INTERNAL CONTROLS. A strong system of accounting and administrative controls is necessary to safeguard assets, check the accuracy and reliability of accounting data, promote operational efficiency, and encourage adherence to established policies. Such internal controls should include a plan of organization, procedures, and records that generate an accurate reporting system and accountability for assets and liabilities within the organization.

LOAN REVIEW. Since loans generally comprise the major component of bank assets, there should be an effective program of internal loan or asset quality review. Ideally, this analysis should be performed by an independent loan review department staffed by credit analysts who report directly to the board of directors, a board committee, or a senior officer not involved in lending. Its responsibilities are to identify problem loans based not only on performance but on financial statement analysis, prepare summations to substantiate credit ratings, determine compliance with lending policies, and ensure that corrective action is forthcoming to strengthen or collect problem credits. The results of the internal loan review program are used as a basis for determining the adequacy of the loan loss reserve. Loan officers should be required to identify their own problem loans at early stages of deterioration to supplement the loan review process.

COMPLIANCE. Compliance systems are necessary to ensure that the institution is operating within the constraints of law. Compliance systems may operate parallel to or as part of an institution's internal control and auditing program. However, the focus is on compliance with laws, rulings, and regulations rather than the safeguard of assets, reliability of information, operational efficiency, or adherence to policy.

PLANNING. Planning is fundamental for effective management. Changes in competitive conditions, volatility in the financial markets, technological advances, and deregulation increase the risks within the operating environment. Banks must continually reassess their activities and develop new ways of operating to adapt to those changes and control risk.

BUDGETING. Budgeting is important both as a planning device and as a means of control. Budgets are usually prepared for a period of one year. They translate operational activities into quantitative terms. The planning aspect involves the decisionmaking processes leading to the budget's preparation and/or subsequent revisions. The control aspect involves the comparison of budgeted expenditures and revenues versus actual results and the explanation of significant variations. As a planning and control device, a budget provides a benchmark to measure results and the adjustments necessary to meet performance objectives.

INTERNAL AND EXTERNAL AUDITING. Traditionally, the primary objectives of the internal audit function have been the detection of irregularities and the determination of adherence to the bank's policies and procedures. However, in recent years, the responsibilities of internal auditors have expanded to include the appraisal of accounting, operating, and administrative controls. This appraisal is intended to ensure that those controls provide for the prompt and accurate recording of transactions and the proper safeguarding of assets. In addition, internal auditors often have the responsibility of participating in the formulation of new or revised policies and procedures. Such participation ensures that adequate safeguards and controls are provided during the planning and implementation process. Additional responsibilities of internal auditors may include checking compliance with laws, evaluating the effectiveness of administrative controls and procedures, and evaluating the efficiency of operations, such as, operational auditing.[19]

The primary objective of external audits is generally aimed at enabling the auditor to express an opinion on financial statements. However, external auditors can also assist management in establishing strong internal controls, internal audit programs, and management information systems; help banks develop operating policies and methods of operations; provide greater assurance that financial reports to shareholders and the public are accurate and include all necessary disclosures; aid board members in fulfilling their fiduciary responsibilities; and assist management in conducting special studies (Office of the Comptroller of the Currency 1977).

Both internal and external auditors must demonstrate competence and independence. In this regard, internal auditors should report directly to the board of directors while external auditors should avoid any formal interest in the bank being audited.

MANAGEMENT INFORMATION SYSTEMS. To make informed decisions, management must have timely, accurate, and relevant information concerning the bank's loan portfolio, funding sources, foreign exchange risks, profit and loss position, off-balance sheet contingencies, interest rates, and so on. Balance sheets and profit and loss statements should be prepared at least monthly, if not more often.

---

19. See the Office of the Comptroller of the Currency, (1977).

Conclusion

To establish an effective program of banking supervision and prudential regulation, the public policy role of bank supervision must be clearly defined and understood. At the same time, actions to strengthen the legal framework, the supervisory process, accounting and auditing, and the institutions themselves should commence on parallel tracks. In most countries, it will take years to develop a truly effective institutional framework. But it is a framework that must be established if success in financial sector reform is to be achieved and preserved.

Bibliography

Bench, Robert R. (n.d.). *International Lending Supervision*. Washington, D.C.: Office of the Comptroller of Currency. Unpublished.

Blackhurst, Chris. (1985). "What Lurks Behind U.K. Bank Supervision?" *International Law Review* (February):4-10.

Committee on Banking Regulations and Supervisory Practices (1986). *Report on International Developments in Banking Supervision* 5. Basle, Switzerland: Bank for International Settlements. September.

Dale, Richard. (1982). "Issues in Bank Supervision Around the World." *The World of Banking* (September-October):14-24.

de Juan, Aristobulo. (1988). "Does Bank Insolvency Matter? And What to Do About It?" CEFCP. Processed.

Office of the Comptroller of the Currency. (1977). *Comptroller's Handbook for National Bank Examiners*. Washington, D.C.

Ollard, Will, and Nick Routledge. (1985). "How the Bank of England Failed the JMB Test." *Euromoney* (February):49-56.

Vittas, Dimitri. (1989). "The Complementary and Competitive Interaction of Financial Intermediaries and Markets." CECFP, The World Bank. September. Processed.

11

THE ROLE OF DEPOSIT INSURANCE

Samuel H. Talley and Ignacio Mas

Introduction

Banking instability can have serious adverse effects on a nation's economy because it can impair a nation's payments mechanism, reduce the nation's savings rate, diminish the financial intermediation process, and inflict serious harm on small savers. To prevent these adverse effects, many governments have created a variety of institutional arrangements designed to preserve banking stability. These arrangements typically include: (1) banking laws and regulations that set the ground rules for bank operations and attempt to constrain undue bank risk-taking, (2) the supervision and examination of banks to assure bank compliance with laws and regulations and to prevent banks from engaging in unsafe and unsound banking practices, and (3) lender of last resort facilities designed to prevent temporary bank illiquidity problems from turning into insolvencies.

In addition to these more traditional institutional arrangements, many governments, particularly during the 1970s and 1980s, have set up deposit insurance systems. These systems have been created to preserve public confidence in the banking system, provide the government with a formal mechanism for dealing with failing banks, and assure that small depositors are protected in the event of bank failures. At present, most of the major developed countries, including France, Germany, Japan, the United Kingdom, and the United States, have some form of deposit insurance system. Likewise, about a dozen developing countries have such systems, and several others are now considering the creation of a system. In many cases in both the developed and developing world, the establishment of a deposit insurance system was a direct outgrowth of a banking crisis.

This paper has two major purposes. The first is to analyze and evaluate the implications and desirability of creating a deposit insurance system in countries that do not already have such systems. In order to do this, it is first necessary to establish an analytical framework. In recent years, vast literature on deposit insurance has been produced. Most of this work has been done in the United States in response to widespread bank and thrift failures and the massive insolvency of the corporation that insured the deposits of thrift institutions. Without explicitly recognizing the fact, this deposit insurance literature has employed an analytical framework that compares a banking system with deposit insurance against a system where the government extends no protection to depositors in any form. This analytical framework is generally not appropriate because, in the absence of a deposit insurance system, governments in most countries typically *do* intervene to protect depositors in failing bank situations. Consequently, if an analysis and evaluation of deposit insurance is to be relevant and useful, it is necessary to evaluate these *explicit* deposit protection systems against the benchmark of *implicit* deposit protection schemes that are now widely employed in countries without deposit insurance. Using this analytical framework, the conclusions regarding deposit insurance in this paper differ significantly from those that have emerged from the existing deposit insurance literature.

The second objective of this paper is to identify the major features of deposit insurance systems, and then to review the pros and cons of alternative ways to structure each major feature. This analysis is relevant for countries that already have a deposit insurance system, as well as for those that might be contemplating the creation of such a system. The major features that will be discussed include whether the deposit insurance system should be public or private, the amount of insurance coverage that should be extended to depositors, how the system should be financed, how premiums should be set, and how the system should handle bank failures.

Analysis and Evaluation of Deposit Insurance

As indicated earlier, we believe that the most useful way to analyze and evaluate deposit insurance systems is to compare them with the implicit deposit protection schemes that typically are employed in countries without deposit insurance. In order to compare these two systems, it is necessary to specify the major features of implicit and explicit systems. It is important to emphasize that in actual practice implicit and explicit systems do not take the same form in every country. Consequently, it is necessary to *generalize* their basic features. Of course, in evaluating the two systems in a given country, policymakers should identify the specific features of the two systems in that country, and then use these features to compare the systems.

Nature of Implicit Deposit Protection Systems

In an implicit deposit protection system (IDPS), government protection of depositors is totally discretionary. The government offers such protection, not because it is obliged to do so by law, but because it believes that such action will achieve certain public policy goals, because it may feel at least partly responsible for the losses that must be absorbed, or because it may consider it to be cheaper in the long run to do so. Moreover, the determination of the amount and form of the protection is based on ad hoc decisionmaking within the government. No preexisting rules and procedures guide the decisionmaking process, although prior actions in similar circumstances may influence the outcome. Any protection offered depositors normally would be financed out of the government's current budget or through the Central Bank.

In an IDPS, the government can extend protection in three basic ways. First, when an insolvent bank is closed, the government can make direct payments to depositors or arrange for the failed bank's deposits to be assumed by another bank. Second, the government could arrange and financially support the merger of a problem bank into another bank. This initiative would prevent the failure of the bank, thereby protecting all depositors. Finally, the government can prevent the failure by rehabilitating the bank. This rehabilitation could take the form of a direct equity capital injection into the bank.

Alternatively, the government could acquire some or all of the failing bank's nonperforming assets at book value. This transaction would be tantamount to an equity injection, and also would have the advantage of giving the bank a fresh start with a clean portfolio. With both types of rehabilitation, the government is likely to emerge as the dominant shareholder, thereby effectively nationalizing the bank.

Nature of Deposit Insurance Systems

A formal deposit insurance system (DIS) is created by the passage of a deposit insurance statute, which sets forth the rules and procedures for the operation of the system. In particular, the act would specify the types of financial institutions and deposits that would be eligible for insurance, whether membership in the system would be voluntary or compulsory, the maximum amount of deposits that would be insured, how the system would be funded, the devices the insurer could employ to resolve failing bank situations, and so forth.

While deposit insurance systems can be financed in a variety of ways, by far the most common way is to create a deposit insurance fund and require insured banks to make periodic premium payments to the fund. The government often makes an initial equity capital contribution to the fund to give the DIS some degree of credibility at the beginning. In some DISs, the insurer has authority to borrow from the central bank or the treasury in order to meet its obligations. Also, the government may be authorized to contribute additional equity if the fund's capital should be depleted by losses.

The amount of protection that a DIS extends depositors depends on the maximum insurance coverage specified in the statute and whether the insurer has authority to resolve failing bank situations in ways that extend *de facto* protection to uninsured depositors. For purposes of this study, we will focus on three basic insurance coverage schemes. These three schemes cover quite well the range of deposit protection incorporated in DISs that already exist. The major features of these three schemes are presented in table 11.1, and can be compared with the major features of an IDPS and a system where the government does not intervene in failing bank situations.

The *limited coverage* scheme is designed primarily to protect small depositors when banks fail. Under this scheme, deposit accounts are

Table 11.1: Alternative Deposit Protection Schemes

		Nature of protection offered		Modality of operation	
Type of system	Prototype	Small depositors	Large depositors	Liquidation	Merger or rehabilitation
No intervention	U.S. before 1934	None	None	No	No
Implicit system	Thailand, Malaysia	Discretionary	Discretionary	Possible	Likely
Deposit insurance system:					
Limited coverage	Austria, France, Germany	Guaranteed	None	Yes	No
100% coverage	Argentina, 1946-71	Guaranteed	Guaranteed	Possible	Likely
Discretionary coverage	U.S., Spain	Guaranteed	Discretionary	Possible	Likely

insured up to a certain maximum amount. When a bank fails, the insurer is authorized to pay off insured depositors up to the maximum amount, or arrange for all of the failed bank's insured deposits to be transferred to another bank. With a limited coverage scheme, the surer is not authorized to rehabilitate banks or arrange financially assisted mergers, because to do so would extend *de facto* protection to uninsured depositors by preventing failures.

The *100 percent coverage* scheme is at the other end of the protection continuum. Under this scheme, all deposit accounts are fully insured. The insurer can employ a broad range of devices to resolve failing bank situations, including insured deposit payoffs or transfers, financially assisted mergers, and rehabilitations. It should be noted that 100 percent deposit insurance systems have been widely discussed in public policy circles and in the deposit insurance literature, but in practice have rarely been implemented.

Table 11.2: Major Differences Between Implicit Deposit Protection Systems and Deposit Insurance Systems

Feature	Implicit systems	Deposit insurance systems
Existence of rules and procedures governing deposit protection	No	Yes
Obligation to protect depositors	No legal obligation; protection is at the discretion of the government.	Legal obligation to protect depositors up to the insurance limit; insurer may have discretion to protect uninsured depositors.
Amount of protection extended to depositors	Can vary from no protection to total protection.	Can vary from limited protection to total protection.
Ex ante funding	None	Typically banks through premium payments; government may provide initial capitalization and possibly regular payments.
Funding in event of bank failure	Government	From fund; shortfalls may be covered by special assessments levied on banks or by loans or additional capital from government.

The *discretionary coverage* scheme lies between limited coverage and 100 percent insurance. Under this scheme, all deposit accounts are insured up to a certain amount. However, unlike a limited coverage system, the insurer is authorized *under certain circumstances* to extend *de facto* coverage to uninsured depositors by using a purchase and assumption transaction to resolve a failure, or by arranging a financially assisted merger or rehabilitation to prevent a failure.[1] The special circumstances that would have to prevail before the insurer could extend *de facto* protection to uninsured depositors would be: (1) the banking system is threatened by a loss of public confidence that might result in widespread bank runs, and (2) the need to protect against bank runs outweighs the erosion of market discipline that extending *de facto* protection to uninsured depositors would entail. In sum, a discretionary coverage scheme would function like a limited coverage arrangement when the banking system is not threatened, but could be converted into a de facto 100 percent insurance system if a threat is sufficiently serious to justify an erosion of market discipline. It should be noted that, given the instability and banking concentration often found in some banking systems, a discretionary coverage system might be used quite often to protect uninsured depositors. However, in this discussion we assume that the system would not degenerate into essentially *de facto* 100 percent coverage, as appears to have happened in some countries.

Comparison of the Two Systems

The goals of IDPSs and DISs are essentially the same—to promote banking stability and the development of the banking system and to contribute to social justice by protecting small depositors from losses when banks fail. At the same time, there are some important differences in the features of IDPSs and DISs. These differences are presented in table 11.2. The identification of these differences is crucial because they serve as the basis for evaluating the relative effects and desirability of these two alternative deposit protection systems. In the evaluation process, we will focus on the following six areas: (1) the failure resolution process, (2) the problem of moral hazard, (3) the prevention of bank runs, (4) the protection of small depositors, (5) the treatment of banks, and (6) the capacity to absorb large losses.

---

1. In a purchase and assumption transaction, the insurer arranges for another bank to assume *all* of a failing bank's deposits and acquire some or all of the failing bank's assets in return for a cash payment by the insurer. Such a transaction also could be used with 100 percent coverage or in an implicit system.

The Failure Resolution Process

In handling failing bank situations, IDPSs and DISs have certain similarities and dissimilarities. The two systems are alike in that both can employ the *same failure resolution devices*—closing and liquidating failing banks, merging the banks, or rehabilitating the banks to prevent their failure. However, as will be discussed below, the two systems are different regarding the *administrative process* involved in resolving failures.

The administrative process for handling failing banks and protecting depositors should be fast and smooth and produce outcomes that are relatively consistent over time. Based on these criteria, a DIS should produce better results than an IDPS. A DIS should result in faster and smoother resolutions because it operates on the basis of established rules and procedures spelled out in the deposit insurance statute. Moreover, a DIS is prefunded, thereby eliminating the need to determine the funding source for protecting depositors.

In marked contrast, the process of handling failing banks and protecting depositors with an IDPS will not necessarily be fast and smooth, and outcomes are likely to be unpredictable and inconsistent over time. An IDPS does not operate on the basis of predetermined rules and procedures. Rather, the entire process is discretionary and ad hoc, with only previous actions in somewhat similar circumstances serving as a possible guide. Moreover, because an IDPS is not prefunded, the government will have to determine a source of funding. If the source is the government budget, action by both the executive and legislative branches would likely be required. This required action may be slow and constitute a serious problem in a banking crisis when public confidence is eroding at a fast pace. Finally, an IDPS is apt to be subject to considerable political pressures, thereby making outcomes less predictable and consistent over time.

With an IDPS, however, the government has considerable degrees of freedom regarding the protection of depositors in failing bank situations. First, the government can control the *amount* of protection offered. At one extreme, the government can extend no protection at all. This decision is most likely to be made in the case of small banks where losses by depositors are least likely to lead to runs on other banks. At the other extreme, the government could fully protect all depositors—a result that is most likely in the case of large, prominent banks. The government also has the option of extending partial protection (for example, for half of outstanding deposit balances), thereby invoking the concept of co-insurance where depositors and the government share the losses from a bank failure.

In an IDPS, the government also has discretion to determine the *form* and *timing* of the protection offered depositors. For example, the government could pay off depositors of a failed bank in the form of either cash or government securities. Moreover, the total payment to depositors could be made very shortly after a bank failure, or could be in the form of installments stretched out over a considerable period, thereby lowering the present value of the total payment.

In contrast to an IDPS, the rules that govern a DIS tend to constrain the deposit protection options available to the insurer. For example, the insurer does not have the option of walking away from protecting insured depositors in individual cases. Likewise, with a DIS the insurer typically is required to pay off depositors in cash (rather than using some other types of assets), and the insurer cannot stretch out payments over time in order to reduce the present value of these payments.

In sum, the various constraints contained in the law governing a DIS can rule out cheaper options, thereby making a DIS a more expensive deposit protection device than an IDPS. On the other hand, in some cases the rules under which a DIS operates may give the insurer greater protection from political pressure to bail out all depositors than the government would have under an IDPS. If so, a DIS could turn out to be a cheaper device.

Moral Hazard

The problem of moral hazard arises from the distortion of incentives induced by deposit protection, whether implicit or explicit. The presence of protection affects the behavior of the economic agents involved, particularly their willingness to assume greater risk. Both bankers and depositors may be subject to moral hazard.

If deposit protection is achieved by bailing out banks and their shareholders, shareholders may be subject to moral hazard by their ability to bet on the government's or the insurer's money. In this case, banks can earn higher returns without facing the potential losses associated with higher risk strategies. However, it must be recognized that this danger can be present even without deposit protection because the existence of limited liability introduces an asymmetry in the risk/return tradeoff. Furthermore, if the deposit protection is structured so that shareholders and managers do not benefit from deposit protection, the introduction of this protection need not increase the moral hazard of bankers.

Depositors also experience moral hazard in that they no longer assume the risk associated with their choice of depository institution. If the investment decision is made without regard to the financial condition of the institution, the market fails to exert a disciplining effect on banks.

The issue of moral hazard has received a great deal of attention in the deposit insurance literature. While deposit insurance clearly involves moral hazard, the central role given to moral hazard is, in our opinion, misplaced. In evaluating the moral hazard associated with deposit insurance, the basis of comparison should be a world with implicit protection and limited liability, both of which already introduce a significant degree of moral hazard. Thus, the relevant measure should be the incremental amount of moral hazard introduced by switching to an explicit deposit insurance system, rather than focusing on the absolute amount of moral hazard associated with a DIS.

The degree of moral hazard induced by each type of scheme will depend directly on (1) whether protection is extended to bank management and shareholders, and (2) the feeling of safety imparted to depositors. Insofar as DISs operate through a set of established rules, they can completely eliminate the expectation of managers and shareholders that they will benefit from the insurer's actions. Because such options are not ruled out in IDPSs, these systems are likely to result in greater moral hazard on the part of bankers.

As to the feeling of safety enjoyed by depositors, this will depend on (1) the level of coverage offered, and (2) the public's confidence in the protection system. In our view, a DIS is likely to involve somewhat more moral hazard on the part of depositors than an equally credible IDPS.[2] The reason is that a DIS tends to extend more assured deposit protection. With a DIS, some depositors are given full protection and all depositors have at least some protection. By contrast, with an IDPS, no depositors are guaranteed protection. In the case of a DIS with a high coverage level, the system could involve considerably more moral hazard than an equally credible IDPS.

In conclusion, it is not possible to establish categorically how the conversion from an implicit protection scheme to an explicit scheme would affect the overall amount of moral hazard in the banking system. In general, however, it seems likely that the conversion would result in less moral hazard on the part of the bankers, but more moral hazard on the part of the depositors.

Bank Runs

The ability of deposit protection systems to stem bank runs depends on the extent that depositors feel protected from loss in the event of a bank failure. As indicated above, a DIS is likely to extend somewhat more assured deposit protection than an IDPS. Consequently, it follows that a DIS, as long as it is a credible system, is likely to be somewhat more effective than an IDPS in preventing bank runs. Moreover, the difference in the effectiveness of the two systems would tend to be greater the higher the coverage of the explicit system.

Small Depositor Protection

One of the traditional objectives of deposit protection systems is to protect small depositors. Both IDPSs and DISs are potentially capable of protecting small depositors. However, DISs appear to be better designed to accomplish this objective because the protection of small depositors is in the form of a legal obligation, and this legal obligation is backed up by a deposit insurance fund. By contrast, IDPSs involve no legal obligations to protect even small depositors.

---

2.   A priori, it is not clear whether a DIS or an IDPS would have more credibility.

Treatment of Banks

One of the more important differences between an IDPS and a DIS is the treatment of banks. An IDPS confers a subsidy on banks that increases their profits. By contrast, a DIS either could confer a subsidy on banks or impose a tax.

By extending some form of protection to depositors, an IDPS lowers the risk of deposits. This reduction in risk should result in portfolio adjustments by wealth holders that would lower the interest rate on deposits. This reduction in banks' cost of funds should increase bank profits.[3] With an IDPS, the losses incurred from protecting depositors are absorbed entirely by the government (taxpayers) or the central bank. Consequently, since banks derive benefits from an IDPS, but shoulder none of the costs, an IDPS confers a subsidy on banks.[4] By contrast, the effect of a DIS on banks is unclear. On the one hand, by protecting depositors, a DIS lowers banks' cost of funds. On the other hand, the costs of protecting depositors, while initially absorbed by the insurer, are ultimately passed on to banks in the form of premium payments.

Capacity to Absorb Losses

One of the key features of a deposit protection system is the ability to absorb losses when banks fail. If a system lacks the resources to absorb losses, bank supervisors may be forced to allow insolvent banks to continue to operate. Experience has shown that the failure to close insolvent banks is apt to compound the problem of banking instability because insolvent banks have an incentive to take high risks in an attempt to return to solvency.

With an IDPS, losses are absorbed either by the national government budget or the central bank. Both of these constitute potentially large funding sources, far exceeding the resources of even a well financed DIS. However, national government budgets typically have

---

3. Depending on competitive conditions in the banking industry, banks may pass on at least some of these profits to their customers in the form of more favorable prices on banking services.

4. This conclusion assumes that the government does not make an effort to offset this subsidy in some way—for example, by imposing some form of tax or regulatory requirement on banks that would have the effect of lowering bank profits.

strong contending demands, and governments may be reluctant to use central bank resources because of the inflationary implications. Therefore, the actual capacity of an IDPS to absorb losses may be significantly less than its considerable potential.

With most DISs, losses are absorbed by an insurance fund set up for that purpose. The ability of a DIS to meet its obligations depends on the fund's initial capitalization, the amount of premiums paid into the fund by insured banks over time, the size of the payments made to resolve failing bank situations, and the ability of the fund to borrow or receive additional capital injections when its resources are exhausted.

It is certainly possible for nations to establish financially sound DISs that are capable of dealing effectively with sizable losses. However, the historical record indicates that many countries, particularly in the developing world, do not create such systems. Rather, they tend to set up DISs that have relatively little capital and do not have strong government backup support that DISs may need to get through a difficult period. As a result, the systems often lack credibility and are frequently frozen into inaction during a banking crisis.

Summary and Conclusion

In this section, we have analyzed and evaluated DISs relative to IDPSs, which are used in most countries that do not have deposit insurance. We argued that a DIS has both advantages and disadvantages compared to an IDPS. First, a DIS constitutes a better administrative process for resolving failing bank situations and protecting depositors. It tends to be faster, smoother, and more predictable that an IDPS, and it tends to produce more consistent results over time. The reason is that a DIS operates on the basis of predetermined "rules of the game," whereas decisionmaking with an IDPS is discretionary and ad hoc. On the other hand, the inherent flexibility contained in an IDPS gives policymakers more degrees of freedom in fashioning deposit protection remedies. Consequently, policymakers should have more control over the amount, form, and timing of the protection offered. Second, a DIS is more effective in protecting small depositors because it is, in part, specifically designed to accomplish this result. By contrast, small depositors may not be protected in some cases with an IDPS, particularly in the case of the failure of a small bank. Third, a

DIS provides a vehicle for shifting some of the costs of deposit protection to the banking system. This seems appropriate because banks derive benefits from deposit protection in the form of a lower cost of funds. By contrast, with an IDPS banks derive the benefits of deposit protection, but incur none of the costs. As a result, an IDPS subsidizes banks at the expense of taxpayers.

It is widely argued in the deposit insurance literature that the primary problem with deposit insurance is moral hazard. We do not share this view. While there is no question that deposit insurance involves moral hazard, it is not clear that it involves any more moral hazard than an IDPS, which most countries use in the absence of a formal DIS. It is not the *absolute* amount of moral hazard that is important, but rather the *relative* amount.

Instead, we believe that the major problem with DISs is that they tend to be given weak financial structures. This is an especially serious problem in developing countries because they tend to have unstable banking systems that are likely to produce large losses. Given this situation, we believe that DISs should be considered only in those countries that: (1) have at least a fairly stable banking system, (2) have an effective prudential regulation and bank supervision system, and (3) exhibit a willingness to adequately fund a DIS and give it the necessary government backup support that may be required to get the system through a period of stress. In our judgment, there probably are relatively few developing countries that now meet these conditions.

For those countries that do not meet these conditions, the emphasis should be placed on trying to get the banking system under control. In many countries, this would require stabilizing the macroeconomic environment in which banks and business firms have to operate, strengthening the nation's banking laws and bank supervisory and examination systems, and continuing to rely on an IDPS to protect depositors and restructure banks.

Major Features of Deposit Insurance Systems

While deposit insurance is a relatively simple concept, deposit insurance systems are relatively complex mechanisms. In setting up a deposit insurance system, nations have to make a sizable number of decisions regarding the system's major features. This section identifies the major features, reviews the pros and cons of the alternative ways that each feature could be structured, and offers recommendations regarding the preferred options.

Public versus Private Systems

DISs can take a variety of forms with regard to their sponsorship, administration, and financing, ranging from pure public systems to pure private systems. The appropriate public sector-private sector mix for a DIS could vary significantly from country to country, depending on the unique characteristics and capabilities of the country involved. In general, however, a DIS is far more likely to achieve its objective of preserving public confidence, promoting the development of the financial sector, and protecting small deposits if it is either a public system or a quasi-public system (a system that is jointly managed by government and banking officials, but has some form of government financial backing). A private system that relies solely on the banking industry for financial support typically should be avoided because it is apt to break down during a banking crisis.

Losses incurred by a deposit insurance system are highly unpredictable and are likely to be large during a period of adversity. These large losses may well exceed the resources of the insurance fund, in which case a capital injection by the sponsors would be needed. A national government, which stands behind a public or quasi-public system, generally would have much greater capacity to provide capital than would the banking industry, which stands behind a private system. During a banking crisis, some banks are likely to suffer an erosion of capital. The need to transfer some of their remaining capital to the deposit insurance fund would further weaken their position. On the other hand, a refusal by some banks to provide capital might result in the insurer being unable to meet its obligations. This inability could produce a loss of confidence in the deposit insurance system and precipitate widespread runs on the banks. In sum, a private system where the banking industry, in effect, insures its own losses is inherently vulnerable and is unlikely to be successful over the long run.

A possible alternative way to design a private deposit insurance system is to have nonbanking organizations provide the insurance. The most likely provider would be the insurance industry. However, there are a number of reasons for doubting that such an arrangement would be feasible. First, in many countries the banking industry is far larger than the insurance industry and the insurance industry would not have the capacity to underwrite deposit insurance. Second, even if the insurance industry had the capacity, it is not clear that it would want to underwrite deposit insurance because of the risks involved— bank failures do not tend to be independent events. Third, insurance companies probably would be unwilling to insure deposits unless they could close insolvent banks—authority that the government almost surely would be unwilling to grant.[5] Likewise, insurance companies almost surely would want the power to cancel the insurance of individual banks. The act of canceling insurance, however, is likely to precipitate a large scale run on the bank involved and lead to its failure. It is doubtful that the government would be willing to give a private insurer that degree of control over the fate of individual banks.

Amount of Insurance Coverage

The amount of insurance protection extended to individual depositors probably has more to do with the basic character and the ultimate effects of the system than any other feature. As discussed earlier, insurance protection can take the form of *de jure* protection—the amount of protection that the insurer is legally obligated to extend to depositors in the event of a bank failure—and *de facto* protection— the protection that the insurer effectively extends to uninsured depositors by resolving a failure in a way that protects all depositors from losses.

POLICY IMPLICATIONS OF ALTERNATIVE SCHEMES. For purposes of analyzing the policy implications of different coverage schemes, we will return to the three coverage arrangements reviewed earlier in the paper—limited coverage, 100 percent insurance, and discretionary coverage. Most of the coverage schemes actually being used closely parallel one of these three arrangements.

---

5. Closing banks is a long-standing responsibility of the government. Moreover, to avoid losses, the insurer would have an incentive to close banks before they become insolvent.

A limited coverage scheme would fully protect small depositors because the coverage limit is expressly set to accomplish this result. However, limited coverage would give the banking system only partial protection against contagious bank runs because some depositors would not be fully insured and would have an incentive to start a run on banks perceived to be in trouble. Moreover, these large depositors are likely to be the most sophisticated and best informed depositors.

While limited coverage gives the banking system only partial protection against runs, it preserves a considerable degree of market discipline by depositors, thereby helping to constrain bank risk-taking. When banks fail and insurance coverage is limited, those depositors who are not fully protected become general creditors in the receivership. As general creditors, they will presumably sustain at least some loss, with the amount of the loss depending on the liquidation value of the assets in the receivership.

Limited coverage results in two types of inequities. First, small depositors obviously receive preferential treatment compared to large depositors. Second, some banks benefit from limited coverage more than others, depending on the percentage of their total deposits that are insured. Since insurance lowers the risk of deposits, the cost of insured deposits should be lower than for uninsured deposits, other things being equal. Consequently, banks with a high percentage of deposits that are insured would tend to have a lower cost of funds than banks with a low percentage. This funding advantage, however, could be offset if banks were required to pay insurance premiums based on the cost of funds savings.

With 100 percent insurance, all depositors, small and large, would be fully protected against loss. Moreover, full coverage would offer the banking system a high level of protection against contagious bank runs because depositors would have no incentive to start a run, so long as they retained faith in the ability of the insurer to meet its obligations in the event of bank failures. On the other hand, 100 percent insurance would eliminate market discipline because all depositors would be fully protected. As a result, banks would tend to take greater risks than they would with limited coverage or in the absence of deposit insurance.

A 100 percent insurance system would have no inequitable effects. All depositors and all banks would be treated equally because all deposits would be insured. No bank would gain a cost of funds advantage over another.

Like the other two forms of deposit insurance, the discretionary coverage system would fully protect small depositors. In addition, it would offer the banking system substantial protection against runs because the insurer could protect all depositors in a time of crisis. This protection, however, would not be as complete as with 100 percent insurance because the insurer might fail to recognize an emerging crisis and fail to extend the protection needed to preserve public confidence.

The discretionary coverage arrangement would have an adverse effect on market discipline that would lie somewhere between the other two coverage schemes. Small depositors would be totally protected and, therefore, would have no incentive to discipline banks. However, these depositors typically do not have sufficient knowledge to evaluate effectively the financial condition of individual banks. Consequently, the loss of market discipline from fully protecting these depositors would not be great. A more serious loss would result from extending potential protection to knowledgeable large depositors.

Discretionary coverage would produce inequities in the case of both depositors and banks. Small depositors would be protected in all failures, whereas large depositors would be protected only if a failure threatened the stability of the banking system. Extension of *de facto* protection would be more likely with large failing banks than with small failing banks. This would favor depositors in large banks and would tend to give large banks a cost of funds advantage over small banks in the market for large deposits.

In weighing the pros and cons of the three alternative coverage arrangements, policymakers should consider two important factors not previously discussed. The first is the extent that stepped up bank supervision could be substituted for the erosion of market discipline from extensive or full insurance coverage. For example, it is conceivable that supervisors could fully offset the erosion of market discipline by imposing higher capital standards for banks or by subjecting bank lending and investment practices to more stringent review.

Unfortunately, however, the quality of bank supervision (as measured by the thoroughness of the supervisory process and the willingness of supervisory authorities to take strong action) varies considerably from country to country, with many developing countries having very inadequate systems.

It is also possible that the loss of market discipline could be offset by imposing risk-adjusted insurance premiums. Such premiums would act as a disincentive for banks to take undue risks. However, as will be discussed later, there are major practical problems with implementing risk-adjusted premiums. Consequently, this method for offsetting the loss of market discipline may not be feasible.

The second consideration relates to bank runs and the lender of last resort. In recent years, a number of scholars, particularly in the United States, have argued that deposit insurance is not needed to prevent bank runs because an effective lender of last resort can handle such runs if they occur.[6] This view is based on the assumption that bank runs take the form of deposit transfers from weak banks to strong banks. These deposit transfers would result in no change in aggregate bank reserves and, therefore, would not produce a change in the money supply or interest rates. Consequently, the only action that the lender of last resort (presumably the central bank) has to take is to lend to any weak banks that become illiquid, and offset the resulting increase in bank reserves through open market sales or an increase in reserve requirements.

The problem with this argument is that things may not work out as smoothly as assumed. First, in some countries, particularly in the developing world, the bank run may take the form of a flight to currency or foreign exchange, rather than deposit transfers. If so, aggregate bank reserves would be reduced, and it would be up to the central bank to offset this loss promptly and effectively, or run the risk of a sharp decline in the money supply and the level of economic activity. Second, weak banks that experience large scale deposit withdrawals would have to borrow extensively from the central bank and might run out of collateral that is acceptable to the central bank before the run ceases.

---

6. For example, see Schwartz (1987), and Benston and Kaufman (1987).

The decision regarding the amount of insurance coverage is a crucial factor in constructing a DIS. The appropriate coverage arrangement depends on a number of institutional and policy considerations, and these considerations could vary significantly from one country to another. Of the three coverage arrangements considered in this study, we believe that one—100 percent insurance—should be avoided because it involves an untenable amount of moral hazard. This factor is undoubtedly the reason that almost all nations that have created DISs have opted for less than full deposit coverage. The real choice, therefore, is between limited coverage and discretionary coverage. The advantage of a discretionary system is that, if a contagious bank run begins, the nation has an institutional mechanism already in place to stem the bank run, assuming that the DIS has adequate financial resources to stem the run. With a limited coverage system, this mechanism is not in place. Consequently, a nation would have to resort to either of two alternatives: (1) trying to stop the run by quickly implementing an implicit protection system that would protect uninsured depositors, or (2) continuing to expose uninsured depositors to potential losses and relying on the lender of last resort mechanism to handle the run, irrespective of the size or form of the run.

Financing Deposit Insurance.

There are two major questions that must be resolved relating to the financing of deposit insurance. First, who should bear the costs of deposit insurance—that is, when depositors are protected from loss, who should absorb these losses? And second, how should the financing of deposit insurance be arranged? Should an insurance fund be set up and, if so, how large should the fund be?

ALLOCATING THE COSTS.   In most existing DISs, the costs of protection are absorbed ultimately by insured banks in the form of required premium payments into the insurance fund. The primary rationale for allocating the costs of deposit insurance to the banks is that they are the direct beneficiaries of the system. Deposit insurance lowers the risk of deposits and results in a decrease in banks' cost of funds. Some observers also would argue that banks should absorb the costs because banks produce the losses that must be covered.

However, there are two problems with requiring banks ultimately to absorb *all* the costs of deposit insurance. First, the deposit insurance system may experience very large losses during a banking crisis. If so, the costs passed on to the banks may seriously erode their capital and push some of them into insolvency. Second, the benefits accruing to banks from insurance may bear no close relationship to the costs. If the costs exceed the benefits, the deposit insurance system, in effect, would be imposing a "tax" on the banks.

In some deposit insurance systems, the government, in one form or another, has shared some of the cost burdens with the banks. For example, some governments made an initial capital contribution to the deposit insurance fund to help defray possible future losses. Using a different approach, the government in Spain regularly shares the cost burden by making periodic contributions to the insurance fund that match the aggregate contributions provided by the banking sector.

There are also a few deposit insurance systems (Yugoslavia is a good example) where the costs of the system are absorbed entirely by the government, thereby conferring a subsidy on banks.

SHOULD A FUND BE ESTABLISHED? There are two basic ways that deposit insurance is financed through bank contributions. The first is to set up a fund and require banks to make periodic premium payments into the fund. The other is to levy ex post premium assessments on banks. Most deposit insurance systems have used the fund approach, and this appears to be the better alternative.

One advantage of creating a fund is that it tends to promote depositor confidence because there is something tangible for insured depositors to look to for protection. Another advantage is that a fund is built up over time, and this has the important effect of spreading out the costs to banks over time.

Probably the major advantage of ex post assessments is that they avoid the very difficult problem of determining the appropriate size of the fund. With ex post assessments, there is no guesswork—the assessment is whatever is required to pay off insured depositors of a failed bank. Also, the ex post assessment approach avoids placing a burden on banks if, in fact, no bank failures occur.

On the other hand, ex post assessments have several major disadvantages that are responsible for their infrequent use. Most important, ex post assessments tend to concentrate costs rather than spreading them out over time. Moreover, because bank failures tend to occur during periods of adversity, these costs come at the worst time. Another problem is that the bank that fails and causes the assessment to be levied is the only bank that escapes the assessment. This result is obviously inequitable, especially in those countries where there are only a few banks to carry the burden. Ex post assessments also are likely to prove unworkable if the deposit insurance system is placed on a voluntary basis. During a period of adversity when failures are likely to occur, well-regarded banks would have an incentive to drop out of the system in order to avoid assessments. As more banks left the system, the potential burden of paying the assessments would fall disproportionately on the remaining banks in the system, thereby increasing their incentive to drop out. The end result could be the collapse of the deposit insurance system, just at the time that the system is most needed.

SIZE OF THE FUND. It is extremely difficult to determine the appropriate size of a deposit insurance fund because it is very hard to predict the number and the size of banks that will fail over a given period, or the extent that they will be insolvent. About all that policymakers can do is to use their best judgment and allow for a wide margin of error.

Traditionally, policymakers have used the ratio of capital and reserves to insured deposits as their measure to judge the adequacy of the fund. There is considerable variation in the capital ratios of deposit insurance systems in existence. Logically, this variation should reflect differences in the financial condition of banks in the system and their concentration of risks. However, it is apparent that other factors are at work, probably including differences in the capability of individual nations to fund their systems.

While there are many ways to arrange the funding of a deposit insurance system, the following would seem to be a reasonable approach. First, an initial capital contribution should be made to the fund, probably by the government. This contribution should place the capital ratio at a level that would give the fund initial credibility in the eyes of depositors. Also, the contribution should be sufficient to handle failures that might occur in a period of adversity during the system's first several years in operation.

In addition to setting an initial capital ratio, authorities should establish a range above this initial level in which the capital ratio would be allowed to fluctuate. Given the great uncertainty regarding future losses, it would be advisable to set a fairly wide range, thereby allowing the ratio to rise to a relatively high level before taking any action to prevent any further rise.

The "Achilles' heel" of a deposit insurance system is catastrophic losses—huge losses that cause the system to become illiquid and/or insolvent. If a system becomes illiquid and the insurer cannot pay off depositors of failed banks, depositors of other banks will lose confidence in the system and may start bank runs. Alternatively, primary supervisors of banks, knowing that the insurer would not be able to pay off depositors if they closed insolvent banks, might allow these banks to remain in operation. This is a very dangerous action because the management of an insolvent bank has a strong incentive to take high risks in search of large returns that might restore the bank to solvency. If these gambles turn out badly, the losses that the insurer will sustain when the bank is eventually closed will be even greater.

Catastrophic losses also may cause the insurer to become technically insolvent. It is possible for an insurer to operate with a negative net worth if it has adequate funding sources so that it can continue to meet its obligations. However, operating with a negative net worth always runs the risk of a loss of depositor confidence—a loss that might occur suddenly as the result of some development.

It is the prospect of catastrophic losses that requires that the government play at least a backup role in financing a deposit insurance system. First, the insurer should have the authority to borrow from the treasury or the central bank in order to be able to honor its obligations. This borrowing authority would allow supervisors to close insolvent banks without concern that their action might produce a crisis for the insurer, as well as the banking system. Second, the government should be authorized to inject additional capital into the insurer in order to preserve depositor confidence in the system and to move the capital ratio back into the target range if losses should push the ratio below the range.

Premium Assessment Policy

As indicated earlier, most countries place the cost burden of deposit insurance largely or entirely on the banking system in the form of periodic premium payments (and initial capital contributions in several countries such as Colombia and Japan). The following questions involving premium assessment policy must be addressed:

(1)   What should be the assessment base?
(2)   Should the assessment rate vary depending on the riskiness of individual insured banks?
(3)   What should be the level of the assessment rate?

ASSESSMENT BASE. The two measures that are the best candidates to be used as the assessment base are insured deposits and total deposits. Both measures have been used, with insured deposits now being employed in a substantial majority of deposit insurance systems.[7]

The major reason for using insured deposits as the assessment base is that it seems fair—the assessment base should be the same as the amount of protection being extended to depositors. By contrast, using total deposits as the assessment base does not seem fair because in many cases the assessment base would exceed (perhaps by a wide margin) the amount of protection.[8] The use of total deposits also would result in inequitable treatment of banks because some banks would have higher insured deposits to total deposits ratios than others and, therefore, would receive more protection relative to their assessment base.

The major reason for using total deposits is that banks always know the amount of their total deposits. Consequently, they can readily determine and report their assessment base. By contrast, banks find it difficult and costly to determine the amount of their insured deposits

---

7.   Those systems that do not use insured deposits include the United States, Colombia, and Germany (which use total deposits), and Norway (total assets).

8.   This argument against using total deposits as the assessment base may not apply if the deposit insurance system employs discretionary coverage and failures are frequently resolved in a way that protects all depositors, insured and uninsured alike.

because they may have to combine the accounts of individual depositors having more than one account at the bank.

FIXED VERSUS VARIABLE RATES. The assessment rate applied to the assessment base could be the same for all banks irrespective of a bank's financial condition, or could be made to depend on the bank's overall risk. This variable rate approach would mimic the way premium rates are typically set in the private sector—the greater the insurer's risk exposure, the higher the premium.

From a policy perspective, a good case can be made for implementing a variable premium rate structure. The major reason is that a variable rate system imposes costs on banks for taking risks, and hence creates an incentive for banks to limit their risk exposure. This result is particularly desirable because it offsets, at least in some degree, the erosion of market discipline that deposit insurance produces. A variable rate system also results in more equitable treatment of insured banks. It does not seem fair that low-risk banks should have to pay the same assessment rate as high-risk banks when the latter represent a greater threat to the deposit insurance fund.

The major problem with variable rates is that they must be based on some measure of overall bank risk. As policymakers are generally aware, the measurement of overall bank risk is very complex. First, there are many forms of bank risk and some of these forms, particularly credit risk and fraud risk, are very difficult to quantify on an ex ante basis. Second, even if each form of bank risk could be measured reasonably effectively, it would be difficult to weight these various risks in order to establish some sort of schedule of variable rates. It also should be noted that the types of risks to which banks are exposed tend to shift in importance over time.

In sum, the measurement problems associated with establishing a variable rate system, though not insurmountable, are nevertheless considerable. This fact undoubtedly explains why no deposit insurance systems employ variable rates, even though there are good reasons for doing so on policy grounds.

Beyond the measurement problems, the use of variable rates also tends to have a perverse effect on banking stability by increasing premium rates on those banks that get into trouble. Such premium increases would reduce the earnings of these banks, thereby eroding their capital at the worst possible time.

Finally, it should be noted that effective bank supervision can significantly reduce the shortcomings of fixed premium rates. This could be accomplished by varying the amount of capital that banks are required to hold in order to bring the overall risk profile of banks into greater balance than would otherwise be the case.

LEVEL OF ASSESSMENT RATE. As discussed earlier, one way to structure the financing of a deposit insurance system is to set a target range for the fund's capital ratio (capital plus reserves to insured deposits), and then maintain the fund's actual capital ratio within that range over time. Other than a capital injection, there are four major cash flows that affect the actual capital ratio—premium payments, investment income, claims payments, and administrative expenses. Of these four cash flows, the insurer has substantial control over only one-premium payments. Once the assessment base has been chosen, premium income is controlled over time by varying the assessment rate.

In order to keep the fund's actual capital ratio within the target range, the insurer could change the assessment rate periodically. Alternatively, the insurer could make premium rebates to banks when the actual ratio moves above the upper end of the target range, or require banks to make special assessment payments when the ratio moves below the lower end of the target range. As discussed earlier, catastrophic losses that wipe out the fund or seriously impair public confidence in the fund must be handled through a capital injection by the government, not through large scale special assessments on banks that could seriously erode their capital and force some banks into technical insolvency.

Handling Bank Failures

One of the major functions of an insurer is to resolve failing bank situations. Accordingly, it is important for the government to specify in the deposit insurance law what failure resolution devices the insurer can use and how these devices should be employed. In this section, we will identify several important failure resolution devices, describe how each device works and what its primary effects are, and suggest several criteria for choosing among alternative devices in individual failing bank situations.

FAILURE RESOLUTION DEVICES. For purposes of discussion, we will focus on the following four failure resolution devices: insured deposit payoffs or transfers, purchase and assumption transactions, financially assisted mergers, and the provision of financial assistance to a failing bank to prevent its closure. In practice, only relatively robust DISs, such as those in the United States or Spain, use most or all of these devices.

With an insured deposit payoff, the failing bank is closed and the insurer reimburses all depositors for the full amount of their deposits up to the coverage limit. Uninsured depositors and other general creditors receive no payments and become claimants in the receivership. The insurer also becomes a claimant in the receivership, taking the place of the insured depositors. All claimants in the receivership typically suffer some loss, as well as delays in receiving payment. In many respects, an insured deposit transfer is similar to an insured deposit payoff. The basic difference is that with an insured deposit transfer, the insurer arranges for all of the insured deposits of the closed bank to be assumed by another bank. In return for assuming these deposits, the assuming bank receives a cash payment from the insurer.[9] Typically, the deposits that the assuming bank acquires have an economic value, and the bank is willing to pay a modest premium over book value for these deposits. Consequently, the amount of cash that the acquiring bank receives is usually slightly less than the book value of the deposits assumed.

With a purchase and assumption transaction, the insurer arranges for *all* of the deposits of a closed bank to be transferred to another bank, along with some or all of the failed bank's assets. The insurer makes up for the difference between the book value of the deposits and the market value of the assets transferred by giving cash to the assuming bank, less any premium that the assuming bank is willing to pay for the deposits.

---

9. It also may be possible for the assuming bank to acquire some of the assets of the failing bank. If so, these assets reduce the amount of cash that the insurer pays the acquiring bank.

Having the assuming bank acquire at least some of the assets of the failing bank avoids having these assets end up in receivership, where they must be liquidated, often at unfavorable prices. The disadvantage of transferring assets to the assuming bank is that the bank will want to carefully evaluate these assets, particularly the loans. This evaluation process could delay the resolution of the failing bank. A key factor in a purchase and assumption transaction is that *all* depositors (both insured and uninsured) are fully protected from any losses. As a result, the transaction tends to preserve public confidence in the banking system, but erodes market discipline. A purchase and assumption transaction also may give the borrowers of the failing bank some comfort because they may be able to establish an ongoing relationship with the assuming bank if that bank acquires the borrowers' loans.

Rather than arrange a purchase and assumption transaction after a bank has failed, the insurer might arrange for the merger of the bank before it is closed. In arranging such a merger, the insurer and the acquiring bank would have to negotiate the terms of the deal, including the amount and form of the payment that the insurer would have to make to encourage the acquiring bank to take over an insolvent institution. The effects of a financially assisted merger are similar to a purchase and assumption transaction—all depositors are protected, thereby preserving public confidence, but market discipline is eroded. Also, the community involved would continue to receive banking services, because the offices of the failing bank typically would be converted into branches of the acquiring bank (as they usually are in the case of a purchase and assumption transaction). A major problem with trying to use financially assisted mergers (as well as purchase and assumption transactions) in some countries is that there may be no bank that is sufficiently sound to make the acquisition. Even if such banks exist, they may be unwilling to make the acquisition, at least on terms that are acceptable to the insurer. Moreover, as with a purchase and assumption transaction, the acquiring bank will want to carefully evaluate the failing bank. Indeed, the loss of time with a merger is likely to be significantly greater than for a purchase and assumption transaction. The reason is that in a merger the bank acquires *all* of the assets of the failing bank, whereas in a purchase and assumption transaction the assuming bank may acquire only relatively "clean" assets that do not require as careful an evaluation.

Finally, the insurer could address a failing situation by providing financial assistance to the bank in order to prevent its failure. This device is most likely to be used when all depositors must be protected to preserve public confidence, and a purchase and assumption transaction or financially assisted merger either is not feasible or is not authorized under the deposit insurance law. The financial assistance that the insurer provides can take a variety of forms, depending on circumstances. If the bank is merely experiencing a liquidity problem that cannot be resolved by borrowing from the central bank, the insurer could provide liquidity in the form of a loan or a deposit in the bank. More frequently, however, the bank will be experiencing an insolvency problem. In this event, the insurer might make an equity injection in the bank. Alternatively, the insurer could acquire some of the bank's nonperforming assets *at par*, giving the bank either cash or government securities. This transaction is tantamount to the injection of equity, and has the added advantage of giving the bank a fresh start by removing the bad assets that otherwise would have to be worked out. In providing support to an insolvent bank, the insurer typically would acquire an equity position that would make it the dominant shareholder. The insurer also would normally replace previous management that, at least in part, was responsible for the insolvency. From the perspective of the public, the effects of a financial assistance transaction are similar to the insurer arranging a purchase and assumption transaction or a merger—all depositors are protected (thereby preserving public confidence but eroding market discipline) and the community continues to be served (in this case by the same bank).

STATUTORY PROVISIONS. In creating a DIS, the government should include provisions in the deposit insurance law relating to failure resolution devices. Moreover, these provisions should assure that the devices used by the insurer are consistent with the objectives and form of the DIS. An example will illustrate this point. Suppose that a nation is establishing a limited coverage DIS, which is expressly designed to protect small depositors but expose large depositors to potential losses in order to maintain market discipline. In this event, the deposit insurance law should prevent the insurer from using failure resolution devices, such as purchase and assumption transactions, mergers, and financial assistance, that extend *de facto* protection to uninsured depositors.

There are two ways that failure resolution provisions can be specified in the deposit insurance law. One way is simply to list the devices that the insurer can use. The other way is to include general language that requires the insurer to use only those devices that are consistent with the objectives and form of the system. In general, the latter approach may be the better alternative because it would give the insurer the flexibility to employ new devices over time as business practices change and as innovations in handling failing bank situations are developed.

In addition, the deposit insurance law should specify the criteria that the insurer should consider in choosing among alternative authorized devices. In many DISs, the sole or dominant consideration is cost minimization. While cost minimization is important, it is not the only factor that should be considered in handling failing banks. In particular, there may be occasions when cost minimization may conflict with the objectives of a DIS to preserve banking stability. For example, if a nation has a discretionary coverage scheme, the insurer may feel compelled to extend *de facto* protection to uninsured depositors in order to avert contagious bank runs, but find that an insured deposit payoff or an insured deposit transfer (both of which do not protect uninsured depositors) would be the lowest cost option. In this event, it is important that the insurer pursue the objective of preserving banking stability, even if it means employing a higher short-run cost alternative.

Other public interest factors also might conflict with cost minimization. One possible factor is the convenience of the banking public. As indicated earlier, some failure resolution devices shield depositors and borrowers from the disruptions of a failure better than others. Consequently, since the function of the banking system is to serve the public, it would seem reasonable to allow the insurer to take public convenience into account in resolving failures. Second, while some failure resolution devices employ "private sector solutions" that transfer the assets and liabilities of the failing bank to other banks, one device—providing financial assistance to a failing bank—usually results in the insurer becoming the dominant shareholder of the failing bank. This result places the assets and liabilities of the bank under the control of the insurer (a government agency) and over time usually forces the insurer, however reluctantly, to become involved in credit allocation. In some countries, this outcome would not be looked upon favorably. Therefore, in these countries the insurer could be authorized to give weight to seeking private sector solutions, even though such solutions sometimes might be higher-cost alternatives.

Bibliography

Bentson, George J., and George G. Kaufman. (1987). *Risk and Solvency Regulation of Depository Institutions: Past Policies and Current Options.* American Enterprise Institute for Public Policy Research. November.

Schwartz, Anna J. (1987). *Financial Stability and the Federal Safety Net.* American Enterprise Institute for Public Policy Research. November.

12

LIFE INSURANCE REGULATION IN THE UNITED KINGDOM AND GERMANY

Thomas Rabe

Introduction

The objective of this paper is to describe and analyze the effects of life insurance regulation in the United Kingdom and Germany. The paper gives an overview of the rationale and the institutional framework of life insurance regulation in these two countries and addresses specific areas of regulation. The follow areas are covered: product design, premium rating, investments, financial position, marketing and selling, distribution, and insolvency. The final section outlines the EC Commission's internal market program for insurance and assesses its potential effects on the regulation, or deregulation, of European insurance markets.

Rationale of Life Insurance Regulation

It is a widely held view that the insurance business is of a special nature, so that if it was subjected to the rigors of free competition without any form of state control, the result would be a total failure of the market. To prevent market failure, governmental and state regulation, that is, constraints on competition, would be necessary.

One of the reasons given for the need to control competition is the high cost for the policyholders of collecting and analyzing information. First, private policyholders in particular are unable to conduct cost benefit comparisons for various insurance products. On the supply side, this could produce an incentive to offer so-called deceptive packages with inadequate insurance coverage.

Second, private policyholders in particular are not in a position to assess whether the current or future financial position of an insurance undertaking provides, or will provide, an adequate guarantee for the fulfillment of the insurer's contractual commitments. It has been argued that the supply side could be encouraged to calculate premiums carelessly, that is, to offer "dumping" prices that could jeopardize the insurer's solvency.

Another argument for the need for controls on competition is the high information costs on the part of the insurers. It is argued that insurers are unable to calculate the premiums independently and therefore have to cooperate, or to use common statistical evidence, and in order to arrive at common evidence, to apply standardized policy conditions.

Methods of Insurance Regulation

At first sight, the British life insurance market appears to be entirely free and competitive. The German market, on the other hand, appears to be highly regulated, conservative, and not particularly competitive. The situation is of course much more complex. Some argue that market operators in Britain have established a "functional equivalent" to the material approach in Germany, in the form of informal market agreements and self-regulation, especially of the marketing and selling of insurance products.

In Germany, insurance companies are subjected to government supervision in accordance with the Insurance Supervisory Law (VAG). The VAG covers the admission requirements, the qualifications required of managers and directors of an insurance company, the admissibility of assets to cover technical provisions, the methods of valuation for such assets, the solvency requirements, and the day-to-day supervision of insurance companies.

The day-to-day supervision is conducted by the Federal Supervisory Office for Insurance Companies (BAV) in Berlin. The BAV has wide-ranging powers to intervene in and examine every aspect of an insurer's activities. The BAV's primary functions cover the licensing of insurance companies, the supervision of their business operations, the monitoring of compliance with legal requirements, and the adherence to the terms of the business plan, as well as the issue of supervisory directives.

The system of supervision of life insurance business in the United Kingdom has often been described as "freedom with publicity"—and with a high degree of self-regulation. The principal statute governing insurance companies is the Insurance Companies Act of 1982. There are several supervisory bodies involved in the regulation and supervision of the insurance industry: the Department of Trade and Industry (DTI), the Council of Lloyd's, the Insurance Brokers Registration Council, and the Registrar of Friendly Societies.

The 1982 act gives wide powers of intervention to the DTI for policyholder protection. These powers include the authority to regulate the type of investments held, ensure that the companies maintain sufficient assets, perform an actuarial investigation of the company, or obtain information and documents at any time.

The Financial Services Act of 1986 has increased investor protection and restricted the carrying on of investment business to those authorized to do so. Authorization is normally obtained through membership of one of the Self-Regulatory Organizations (SROs) established by the act of 1986 and recognized by the Securities and Investment Board. Life insurance offices and life insurance departments of composites are regulated by various SROs: the Investment Management Regulatory Organization (IMRO) for the management of collective investment schemes, and the Life Assurance and Unit Trust Regulatory organization (LAUTRO) for the marketing and selling of insurance-linked investments.

In the life insurance business, a key person in the system of supervision is the appointed actuary. The appointed actuary has a wide range of responsibilities, especially for the determination of mathematical reserves, or, in more general terms, for ensuring the continuing financial viability of the company.

Regulation of Product Design

In Germany, general and special policy conditions are subject to approval by the supervisory authority. The philosophy lying behind this supervisory approach is the standardization of policy conditions as a means to ensure market transparency and to prevent product differentiations and so-called "deceptive" packages. The standardized policy conditions are usually elaborated by the insurers' association in cooperation with the BAV. Official standardization of policy conditions, which in effect means standardization of the products available on the market, leads to a paralysis in the dynamics of product innovation and a reduction of consumer choice.

In the United Kingdom, life insurers enjoy a high degree of freedom in designing policy conditions. The DTI does not approve, as such, individual contracts or products offered by life offices. Under the U.K. system, it is the responsibility of the appointed actuary to ensure that new products are soundly priced and that the company is able to finance satisfactorily the volume of business that it is writing.

The different levels of product regulation in the United Kingdom and Germany are reflected in the distribution of life insurance premiums, as listed in the following table. The figures reveal a significantly different level of product sophistication and development and the extent to which life insurance is used as a savings and investment medium.

Types of policies	Germany	United Kingdom
Permanent conventional life insurance	85	36
Unit-linked life insurance	1	22
Term life insurance	9	8
Pensions	5	36

Regulation of Premium Rating

There are marked differences between the United Kingdom and Germany in the degree of freedom life insurers possess to determine premium rates. In the United Kingdom, companies have considerable autonomy in matters of premium rating. Mortality and disability rates are usually derived from observations of insured lives. Life insurance offices cooperate in mortality and disability investigations, the results of which are published in the continuous mortality investigation report.

Life insurers (together with their actuaries) are largely free to choose their own mortality and disability rates. The same holds true for technical interest rates, which are usually selected with regard to the investment performance of a given life office.

In Germany, the basic elements of premium calculation—mortality, technical interest rate, and loadings—are subject to approval by the supervisory authority. The approved mortality rates are usually derived from population statistics, and the technical interest rate that all life insurance offices are required to use is 3.5 percent, which is excessively low in relation to long-term bond yields. It has been reported that the application by one insurer to the German supervisory authority to raise the prescribed interest rate from 3.5 percent to 4 percent was rejected. Apparently, it has been opposed by the German insurers on the grounds that to do so would be contrary to the interests of policyholders in that it would weaken the long-term guarantees relating to policyholders' benefits.

The result of German supervisory practice is that the premiums charged by most German life insurers are basically the same; any minor variations usually arise from different expense loadings. German premium rates are considerably higher than if insurers were competing in a competitive market free from such regulation. Another result is that only with-profits policies are available on the German market; all German policyholders have the right to participate in at least 90 percent of the mortality, interest, and loadings profits.

In the last few years, a great deal of research has been conducted on price differences for insurance products across European markets. One study carried out by Price Waterhouse in the framework of the EC commission report on the "Cost of Non-Europe" showed that, on average, British premium rates for term insurance were 30 percent lower than in Germany. These findings were supported by the results of a study conducted by the European Consumer Organization (BEUC) in six European countries. It concluded that for thirty-two possible combinations (capital, man, woman, age), premiums are lower in the United Kingdom than in all other countries (with the exception of the Netherlands).

Some claim that price differences between European countries are directly related to the degree of regulation. In a field study conducted by the Insurance Institute of the University of Cologne in 1989, insurance company managers were asked to classify EC-member states with respect to their regulatory intensity. The regulatory intensity was assessed at 2.35 for Germany and 1.4 for the United Kingdom. For all EC-member states taken together, the correlation of regulatory intensity and price levels amounts to 0.7, which is a fairly high figure and could be interpreted as a proof of the above thesis.

Regulation of Investments

The investment policy pursued by an insurance company affects both the potential return on the policyholders' funds and the degree of risks assumed. In Germany, regulations limit the freedom of investment by specifying the types of permitted assets, with limits on both particular classes of assets and individual items. In the United Kingdom, there are no rules governing the assets in which life insurance offices may invest. However, a large number of valuation rules affect the value that may be placed on the assets for the purpose of demonstrating that the technical reserves and the required solvency margin are covered. Valuation rules have a *de facto* effect on a company's investment policy, which is to place a nil value on all assets that are not covered by or that exceed the maximum percentages laid down in the Insurance Companies Regulation of 1982.

It is generally considered that U.K. offices enjoy a greater freedom of investment than German offices. To take one example: German insurance regulation requires life insurance offices to invest no more than 30 percent of the total amount of their funds in equity. On average, however, German life insurers invest a mere 3 percent of their funds in shares, which is due to the relatively narrow market in shares and a conservative investment approach rather than tight investment regulation.

In the United Kingdom, the average life insurance office invests a proportion of 36 percent of its funds in shares. It has been reported that for some life insurance offices, this figure is well above 60 percent.

On average, the investments of German and British life offices are as follows, in percent:

Investment assets	Germany	United Kingdom
Fixed-interest securities	62	36
Mortgages	22	6

Shares	3	36
Real estate	13	22

Not surprisingly, the average investment return of German life insurance offices amounts to 7 to 8 percent per annum, whereas U.K. offices achieve up to 15 to 20 percent per annum. It is clear that these

significant differences in the investment performance of life insurers have a direct effect on the price rating or, more precisely, in the level of premiums in the United Kingdom and Germany. Experience shows, however, that the differences between the real-term investment performance of U.K. and German life insurance offices decreases for longer-term contracts, an effect that is mainly due to considerable variations in the exchange rate of pounds sterling to deutschmarks.

Regulation of the Financial Position

Reserving

Adequate reserving is essential to ensure the solvency of life insurance offices and their ability to meet future contractual obligations. Both the DTI and the BAV conduct close supervision of the methods and bases underlying the calculation of technical provisions, especially mathematical provisions.

In Germany, these methods and bases have to be approved by the supervisory authority. Mortality tables, technical interest rates, and loadings are calculated in a similar, extremely prudent way as premium ratings.

In the United Kingdom, life insurance offices and their appointed actuaries have considerable freedom in the choice of methods and bases. However, both have to be reported to the government, which may, if necessary, take such action as it considers appropriate. This action can range from an advisory to a compulsory directive for one specific life insurer or even for all life insurers.

Valuation of Assets

The differences between Germany and the United Kingdom in the field of asset valuation lie mainly in the use of book or market values and the treatment of unrealized capital gains. Such differences are important not only in determining the solvency of a life insurer, but also in controlling the emergence and distribution of surplus on life funds.

In the United Kingdom, a variety of approaches are taken in the valuation of assets. Some life insurance offices show all assets at current value, some at historic cost, and some at a value between the two. In the statutory returns, it is a requirement for assets to be shown on a market value basis. The reason for this approach in the United Kingdom is the significant amount of equity investments within life insurance companies' funds.

It is common practice in the United Kingdom to show unrealized investment gains in the profit and loss account. It is the responsibility of the appointed actuary of a life insurance office to determine that portion of unrealized investment gains that can be distributed to the policyholders in the form of bonuses. Bonuses arising from unrealized investment gains are generally added to the face value of the policy, that is, the sum assured. Bonuses arising from unrealized investment appreciations may also be declared as permanent additions, but because of the uncertainties attached to unrealized gains and the potential negative effects of future value reductions, most U.K. life insurance offices distribute part of this in the form of terminal bonuses.

In Germany, assets must be valued at the lower of cost (less depreciation) and current value, if there is a permanent decline in value. For securities, the lower value must be used, even if the decline in value is not permanent. The lower value may be retained even when the reasons for the writing down have ceased to exist. Current values of investments do not have to be disclosed, and unrealized investment gains may not be taken into the profit and loss account, let alone be distributed. The result is that German life insurers hold considerable amounts of hidden reserves, which are sometimes considered as their hidden strength.

Regulation on the Marketing and Selling of Insurance Products

It was mentioned above that life insurance offices in the United Kingdom are regulated by several Self-Regulatory Organizations. For the selling and marketing of insurance, life insurers must abide by the standards set by LAUTRO. These standards cover, among other things, a general code of conduct, selling practices, product disclosure, and disclosure of commissions, as well as rules for advertising. However, it is generally agreed that the provisions are too onerous and revisions are therefore being considered by the U.K. government. In Germany, there is no regulation on the selling and marketing of life insurance other than those required by commercial law.

In the United Kingdom, all insurance brokers must register with the Insurance Brokers Registration Council (IBRC), which was established in 1977. The use of the title of "insurance broker" without such registration is not permitted. To be registered, an insurance broker must demonstrate the following: qualification by examination or experience, a minimum of £1,000 working capital, a minimum solvency margin of £1,000, a sufficient spread of business to guarantee independence, the required level of professional indemnity insurance, and an adequate system of client accounting.

To ensure that insurance brokers have adequate financial resources, the IBRC requires them to submit, on registration and annually thereafter, a set of audited accounts, together with a statement of particulars, which is a restatement of accounts in a standard format, reported on by the broker's auditors. In addition to registering with the IBRC, any broker doing life insurance business that constitutes more than 10 percent of his total business must either join the Financial Intermediaries, Managers and Brokers' Regulatory Association (FIMBRA), or become a tied agent or agent.

Both the IBRC and the FIMBRA maintain compensation schemes that may be used to assist policyholders in the event of the financial collapse of a broker or intermediary. Furthermore, professional indemnity coverage is compulsory for all insurance brokers.

One of the objectives of the Financial Services Act of 1986 (FSA) was the promotion of independent advice for investment and insurance purchasers. Among other things, the Financial Services Act requires independent brokers to give best advice to their clients. Independent brokers must provide information about the insurance products available on the market and must make sure that they recommend only such policies that are the best in view of the financial position and the needs of the client.

The effect of the Financial Services Act on the structure of insurance distribution was disastrous: 50 percent of the previously independent brokers (mostly the small brokers) decided to avoid the stringent standards for independent brokers by associating themselves with one company and thereby becoming a tied agent. In other words, the FSA, which had been intended to provide insurance purchasers with better information and advice, has had exactly the opposite effect.

In Germany, there is virtually no regulation on insurance intermediaries other than through normal commercial law. Insurance intermediaries are organized in different associations, which may issue nonbinding guidelines but do not exercise any form of self-regulation.

The structure of life insurance distribution in the United Kingdom and Germany is as follows, in percent:

Distribution networks	Germany	United Kingdom
Tied agents and part-time investment consultants	70	50
Brokers and investment consultants	37	48
Direct	3	2

An exclusive or "tied" agent only sells products of one life insurance office. He will promote these products, but will not give any information on its shortcomings or the advantages of other companies products. An exclusive agent is thus at best a limited source of information and at worst a source of disinformation.

In countries with strong restraints on competition based on the price and/or the nature of the product, tied agents are renowned for "hard-selling" techniques. Some claim that this in fact is a symptom of excessive non-price competition. Multiple agents and brokers provide information on more than one company (and those companies' products). In both cases, the consumer obtains a certain degree of independent advice.

When comparing the degrees of regulation with the market shares of the respective distribution channels, it is apparent that in highly regulated countries, such as Germany, tied advice dominates the market; and that in liberal countries, such as the United Kingdom, multiple advice dominates the market. The conclusion is therefore that countries that attempt to protect consumers by restricting price and/or product competition thereby promote distribution channels that provide consumers with limited advice.

On the other hand, countries that allow price and product competition promote multiple advice, which is essential if consumers are to make intelligent choices, or rather, be able to choose the product that best fits their personal circumstances.

From the viewpoint of international trade in insurance services, tied distribution channels constitute a *de facto* barrier to market entry for foreign insurers. In countries with a substantial insurance brokering market, a nonestablished foreign insurer is able to gain cheap and quick market access. This means that access to the German insurance market, where 81 percent of those selling life insurance are tied to one single company, is much more difficult, expensive, and risky than the access to the British market.

Regulation in the Event of Insolvency

In the United Kingdom, private policyholders that have effected United Kingdom policies with an authorized insurer enjoy the benefit of the Policyholder Protection Act of 1975 if that insurer becomes insolvent or is otherwise unable to meet its contractual commitments. In the case of private policyholders, the act provides for a transfer of 90 percent of the benefits of the insurance to another insurer, or if that proves impossible, the policyholder is entitled to the payment of the value of his or her policy. These guarantees are met by a levy on all insurers authorized to transact long-term insurance.

In Germany, guarantee funds to protect the policyholders in the event of a company's insolvency are thought to be unnecessary. This is because strict supervisory standards prevent such cases from arising. Life insurers are legally required to maintain trust funds (*Deckungsstock*) to cover the mathematical reserves. These can only be used with the approval of an independent trustee and—in the event of bankruptcy—are distributed to the policyholders.

Conclusion

It is clear from the foregoing that in both Germany and the United Kingdom, life insurers are highly regulated. In Germany, the so-called "system" of material state regulation is focused on the insurance company itself, that is, its financial position, the products it offers, and its premium rating. The probability of German life insurance offices going bankrupt is generally considered to be extremely low and the setting up of a guarantee or compensation scheme is therefore thought to be unnecessary. As the state itself approves the policies available to the market, it is considered to be rather unimportant who sells which product and how it is sold. It is therefore thought to be unnecessary to regulate insurance distribution and marketing.

The situation in the United Kingdom is rather different. State supervision is focused on the financial position, especially the solvency of life insurance offices, while product design and premium rating are left to the market operators. Besides the state supervision, a heavy load of responsibility is placed on the appointed actuary. Product diversity and different levels of life insurance premiums necessitate regulation on insurance distribution and selling. This task is largely left to the IBRC and Self-Regulatory Organizations. In the event of a life insurance office going bankrupt, the policyholders' protection fund compensates for 90 percent of the private policyholders' benefits.

In Germany, but also in several other European countries (for example, France), the current trend is toward deregulation of life insurance business. This trend forms part of a general trend toward deregulation of markets that was—at least partially—initiated by the European Commission's internal market program, launched in 1985.

In a speech Sir Leon Brittan, vice president of the EC Commission and responsible for EC competition policy and financial institutions, delivered last December to the European Insurance Association (CEA), he said:

"If my primary goal is to create a single market for insurance, this must be seen in conjunction with two parallel objectives which are every bit as important:

- The first is to maintain prudential standards and consumer protection ... ;
- The second, which must never be lost sight of in creating a single market, is the need to achieve the greatest possible flexibility and competition. For if the consumers have a right to protection, they also have a right to the widest possible choice

between different innovative and competitively priced insurance products. The single market would fail utterly in its purpose if it could only be achieved at the cost of unwarranted new restrictions in the market which are currently least regulated, yet where experience demonstrates that consumers are perfectly well protected."

In more concrete terms, it is the objective of the EC Commission to create an internal insurance market having the following characteristics: first, insurance companies established in any one member state of the European Community must be completely free to set up branches in any other member state (freedom of establishment, article 52 of the EEC Treaty). Second, insurance companies established in any one member state of community must be completely free to carry out insurance business in any other member state without having to use branches (freedom of services, article 59 of the EEC Treaty). Third, EC insurance companies would be subject to the same key supervisory rules ensuring that insurance companies are always able to meet their contractual commitments. These supervisory rules would cover the financial position of insurance companies (minimum guarantee fund, solvency, reserving, investments) and the product design (policy conditions, contract law). Fourth, there should be a certain degree of control over selling methods and insurance distribution.

The first objective, freedom of establishment, was achieved in 1973 and 1979 with the adoption of the Non-Life and Life Establishment Directives. In considering the effects of these "Establishment Directives," it must be recognized that their primary objective of improving access to separate national markets has been fully achieved. However, the second effect of these directives, the strengthening of insurance supervision within national markets, has probably increased their separation from each other.

It is clear that freedom of establishment alone only gives access to twelve national markets but does not create a true single insurance market. The EC Commission has therefore sought to develop freedom of services based on (the insurer's) home country supervisory control, but for a full decade, virtually no progress was made. In December 1986, however, the European Court of Justice delivered several important insurance rulings. In essence, the European Court upheld the principle of freedom of services, but recognized that insurance is a sensitive area and that the need for consumer protection is such that in the present state of community law, the member state where the service is being provided may impose on the insurer a requirement to be authorized and to respect large parts of its supervisory law.

Nevertheless, the court added that this need for consumer protection is not the same for all consumers and classes of insurance business; where this is so, there is no need for an authorization requirement and all that goes with it. From the regulatory point of view, the court's rulings are extremely interesting, as—for the first time—it was recognized that different types of consumers need different levels of protection and regulation. The main practical effects of the court's rulings were twofold: first, completion of the EC internal market for insurance for so-called large risks, which in non-life insurance are defined on the basis of the policyholder's balance sheet total, turnover, and the number of employees; and second, deregulation of EC insurance markets in the field of large risk business, which means, among other things, abolition of prior approval of policy conditions and premium rating.

The EC Commission is now working to build on the second crucial point emerging from the court's judgments. This is the confirmation that full freedom of services is the natural objective of the single insurance market and should come into being as soon as there is a sufficient community basis of recognition and prudential control.

In the course of the year, the EC Commission will table two further insurance directives: a Non-Life and a Life Framework Directive to take that crucial step. The aim of these two directives will be, quite simply, to complete the single European insurance market. In that market, the commission will be proposing that insurance companies should operate on a single insurance license. Companies will be free, that is, to sell the full range of their products throughout the European Community, either by way of establishment or by way of free provision of services, while being supervised by the member state of their head office.

In taking this very important, some may say, radical step, the main question is how much further regulatory coordination at the EC level is required. In essence, the commission's approach is to coordinate the financial position of EC insurers by setting prudential standards on companies' solvency, reserving, and investments. On product design and premium rating, it is the commission's objective to give insurers the widest possible freedom to adapt to consumer demand. Any form of state regulation in this area will therefore be abolished. It is generally recognized that the EC Commission's approach will considerably affect insurance regulation in Europe, especially in countries that currently favor a system of material state control. Some claim that with the abolition of state control on policy conditions and premium rating, insurance supervision in Germany would be more liberal than in the United Kingdom. Not surprisingly, therefore, alternative systems of insurance supervision and regulation are already being discussed.

In its report to the German government in 1987, the so-called monopoly commission suggested the following:

- The Federal Insurance Supervisory Authority should discontinue the standardization of policy conditions. The BAV should, however, retain the right to stipulate individual clauses as part of the policy conditions, but only to the extent that such clauses are absolutely essential. The BAV should establish noncompulsory specimen standard terms of insurance policies, which insurers should then hand over to the policyholders as a means of orientation and as a basis for comparison.
- Official authorization for premium rating should be abolished.
- The risk of insolvency should be identified within the framework of existing solvency control.
- In the rare cases of insurers going bankrupt, a state-organized guarantee fund should pay the bill for private and small industrial policyholders.

The outcome of the ongoing discussions on deregulation of insurance markets at both the European and national levels is uncertain. The coming years will therefore be interesting, at least in this respect.

Bibliography

Brittan, Leon (1989). *The Single Insurance Market—Prospects for 1992.* Brussels, Belgium: European Community Commission.

Finsinger, Jorg, et al. (1985). *Insurance Competition or Regulation—A Comparative Study of the Insurance Markets in the United Kingdom and the* (former) *Federal Republic of Germany.* Institute of Fiscal Studies Report Series No. 19, London, England.

Finsinger, Jorg, and Mark Pauly (eds.) (1986). *The Economics of Insurance Regulation.* Hong Kong: Macmillan.

13

UNIVERSAL BANKING:
THE CANADIAN VIEW[1]

Charles Freedman[2]

Introduction

It would be highly recommendable to introduce the topic of universal banking, its importance and relevance in today's financial systems, and its relation with Canada. Why is Canada able to talk about universal banking? Universal banking is an issue that does not generate any wide consensus today. There are many different ways of approaching it; many different historic experiences that determine a country's position toward it: love or hate. Canada today is heading toward a universal banking system and has reflected on some of the questions resulting from this system.

The second section of this paper lays out the structure of the Canadian financial system in the 1970s and 1980s. It discusses the factors motivating legislative change, and summarizes the overall structure that has been proposed by the government.[3] The third and most important part of the paper deals with the developments that led

---

1. Revised version of notes used for presentation to the Seminar on Financial Sector Liberalization, Cambridge, Massachusetts, June 14, 1990.
2. Deputy Governor, Bank of Canada. This paper was written while the author was on leave to the Department of Finance as Clifford Clark Visiting Economist. The views expressed are those of the author and do not necessarily reflect those of the Bank of Canada or the Department of Finance.
3 . *Note by the editor*: This paper was completed before the adoption in December 1991 of four new acts that govern the operations of financial institutions. For some details on the new legislation, see chapter 1.

banks and other deposit-taking financial institutions into the securities business and the debate surrounding these changes. This section also discusses corporate structure, in particular the issues surrounding the question of whether the authorities should require the securities business to be done in a downstream subsidiary of the financial institution (as in Canada), or a subsidiary of the holding company (as proposed in the United States), or whether the financial institution should be permitted to engage in such transactions in its own name and on its own books (as in the United Kingdom and Germany). It then briefly updates the developments since the 1987 legislative changes that permitted banks to enter the securities business.

Some Definitions

There are two principal uses of the term "universal banking." Within the context of these broad meanings there are also a number of further distinctions that can usefully be made.

One definition of universal banking refers to the ability of a bank (used in this paper as a generic term for all deposit taking financial institutions) to engage in a wide range of financial activities, and in particular the securities business. A second definition (which relates, for example, to the situation in Germany) refers to the ability of a bank to own and control nonfinancial entities, in addition to engaging in a broad range of financial activities. Discussions of the second definition often include references to commercial-financial linkages. It is important to recognize that there are two quite distinct types of such linkages: upstream linkages (the ownership of financial institutions by commercial concerns) and downstream linkages (the ownership of commercial institutions by financial institutions). It is worthy of note that the arguments regarding the advantages and disadvantages of upstream linkages are quite different from those regarding downstream linkages.

In addition to the two basic definitions of universal banking, reference is sometimes made to the Japanese *keiretsu* model, in which financial institutions and nonfinancial entities have a variety of affiliations or linkages that may not include direct ownership.

The analysis in this paper deals primarily with the first, or narrower, definition of universal banking, and focuses primarily on the integration of banking and securities activities. In this context it is worth making two further distinctions: one on the structure of the bank-securities dealer link, and the second on the range of activities permitted to the group.

As far as structure is concerned there are three polar cases:

- Banks are permitted to engage in securities business on their own books.
- Banks are permitted to engage in securities business via a downstream subsidiary.
- The organization of which the bank is a part is permitted to engage in securities business via a subsidiary of the holding company of the bank.

As far as the range of business is concerned, the meaning of the term securities business is not very precise. It can include retail and wholesale trading operations, involvement in a wide variety of ways of financing corporations (for example, underwriting bonds and equities, short-term paper issues, swaps of different types, etc.), the provision of expert advice (e.g., on mergers and acquisitions), the sale and administration of mutual funds, temporary or bridge financing of takeover deals, and venture capital financing; and may go all the way to temporary or permanent involvement in the ownership and management of nonfinancial corporations. If banks were permitted to engage directly or indirectly in the full gamut of merchant banking activities without any restriction on magnitude, the narrow definition of universal banking would merge into the broader definition. In Canada, the interest of the banks in obtaining a securities dealer was originally focused primarily on the opportunity to engage in underwriting corporate debt and equity, so the narrow definition is appropriate.

The Canadian Financial System[4]

The System Before Restructuring

The Canadian financial markets are among the most highly developed in the world. For many years, there have been no restrictions on

---

4. The discussion in this section is based to a considerable extent on the author's own paper, "Financial Restructuring: The Canadian Experience" (1987).

who has access to these markets and very few restrictions on who could enter these markets to offer financial services—with the exception of the restrictions on financial institutions that were already active in one financial area or another. The 1967 Bank Act revisions removed interest rate ceilings on bank loans, and interest rates since that time on both loans and deposits have tended to move with market rates. Since there were no foreign exchange controls or credit controls in Canada, domestic borrowers were free to seek out the best deal possible in either domestic or foreign markets.

One can describe Canadian financial institutions of the 1970s and early 1980s in broad-brush fashion as having the following characteristics:

- Compartmentalization by function, but with the compartmentalization increasingly breaking down.
- Widely held ownership of major deposit taking financial institutions but with a tendency for some large nonbank deposit taking financial institutions to come under closely held, commercially linked ownership.
- Division of regulatory responsibility among the federal and provincial governments, with the federal government having sole responsibility for banking; both levels of government incorporating and regulating trust/companies and insurance companies; the provincial governments having predominant responsibility for the cooperative sector (credit unions and *caisses populaires*) and for regulating the securities industry.
- A tripartite supervisory system that includes internal auditors, external auditors, and supervisors.

Historically, the Canadian financial system was based on five principal groupings (commonly referred to as the "four pillars"): chartered banks, trust and mortgage companies, cooperative credit movements, life insurance companies, and securities dealers. The chartered banks, all of which are chartered and supervised by the federal government, were always involved in commercial lending and deposit taking. In the past three decades, they have become significant sources of personal loan and residential mortgage credit.

Trust and mortgage loan companies have tended to specialize in residential mortgage lending, but within the past 10 to 15 years they have aggressively moved into the consumer lending area and into certain types of commercial loans. Most of these institutions (as measured by assets) are federally incorporated and supervised, but some operate under provincial charters. The cooperative credit movement (credit unions and *caisses populaires,* operating under provincial jurisdiction) has primarily made mortgage and consumer loans to the personal sector, but recently these institutions have also been moving into the commercial loan area. Chartered banks, trust and mortgage loan companies, and cooperative credit institutions have competed strongly for personal deposits, and recently the latter two groups of institutions have begun to compete more actively for government and business deposits.

Life insurance companies have moved from their traditional business of selling life insurance and investing the proceeds in a mix of mortgages and bond and stock investments to a business that now generates significant amounts of funds from the sale of single premium deferred annuities—which closely resemble fixed-term deposits at other institutions—and investing the proceeds in a more diversified range of assets. Indeed in a number of companies the inflow of funds from the sale of annuities now exceeds the premium income from the sale of insurance. The vast majority of this group is federally incorporated and supervised, although some companies are provincially incorporated and supervised.

Finally, the securities dealers have been principally involved with the underwriting and selling of bond and stock issues under a legislative framework established by provincial governments. Over time the separation between banking and the securities business came under increasing pressure, as did the distinction between the various types of financial institutions, a process that seems to have been driven by the desire of such institutions to offer a greater array of services and products to meet the shifting preferences of their customers.

In short, while the Canadian financial system was historically characterized by a separation of functions among the different institutions, the separation has been blurring over the past 25 years or more, with the penetration by each group into the others' primary areas of business accelerating over the recent period.

The other useful piece of background information is that the Canadian financial system traditionally was marked by a separation of financial companies from nonfinancial companies and by widely held ownership of the major deposit taking financial institutions. However, more recently, there has been a dramatic change with respect to upstream commercial linkages in the trust industry, with all the major widely held companies having been taken over by commercial concerns. In many cases, these same purchasers have bought or established life insurance and property and casualty insurance companies, merchant banks, and other types of financial companies to create a diversified financial conglomerate.

Factors Motivating Restructuring

While the evolving structure described above provided the background for the impetus for major legislative restructuring, various other factors also came to play an important role both in intensifying the pressure for change and in determining the types of changes needed. Thus, the factors that have had an important influence on the process of restructuring are:

- The need to modernize near-bank legislation;
- The pressure and the need to define the appropriate range of business powers that would be available to each type of financial institution;
- Given the development of closely held ownership, commercial-financial links, and common ownership of different types of financial institutions, the need to deal with the concerns raised by the increased potential for self-dealing, conflicts of interest, and concentration of ownership;
- The failure during the 1980s of a number of trust and mortgage loan companies and two small western banks, which raised questions about the structure of the deposit insurance system and about the adequacy of the supervisory structure;
- The introduction by provincial governments of new legislation governing the nonbank financial institutions under their jurisdiction, creating the need for the reharmonization of federal and provincial policies;

- The increasing recognition of the importance of internationalization and securitization as the process of legislative change moved forward.

The first three factors were mainly responsible for initiating the process for change, while the last three added to the impetus and changed its direction. The section of this paper on banking-securities linkages will go into more detail on the aspects of these pressures that impinged directly on the legislative changes permitting banks to engage in the securities business.

The Nature of the Proposed Restructuring

There have been a large number of studies and proposals by both governments and industry as well as a discussion draft of proposed legislation that sets out the direction in which the federal government has been proposing to move. Moreover, some legislation has already been passed by the federal government (including that permitting bank-securities linkages) and by provincial governments. This section sketches out some elements of the structure that has been proposed by the federal government.[5]

POWERS. The proposed changes included a very considerable expansion of the business powers granted to financial institutions, both in the form of in-house powers and in the ability to invest downstream in other types of financial institutions. All trust and mortgage loan companies and life insurance companies would have the right to make consumer loans without limit, and companies above a certain minimum size, which receive supervisory approval, would have the right to make commercial loans without specific quantitative limits. In addition, regulated financial institutions would, to an important extent, be permitted to invest in, purchase, or start up institutions in other financial sectors, including the securities industry. (The legislation permitting the latter has already been passed.) Institutions would also be permitted to engage in the networking of one another's products (with the exception of the retailing of insurance products by banks and trust

---

5. See, in particular, the so-called Blue Paper entitled "New Directions for the Financial Sector" (December 18, 1986), and the discussion draft of the proposed legislation for trust and mortgage loan companies issued in December 1987.

companies through their deposit taking branch network) and to engage in a number of ancillary activities that were prohibited in the past.

As a result of the proposed changes, the differences between the various types of financial institutions would be smaller than in the past. And there would likely be a spread of the groupings that provide virtually every kind of financial service to business customers, or to personal customers, or to both. Institutions that chose to stand alone would also be able to offer, if they chose, many kinds of financial services, either directly or as an agent. Of course, some institutions might continue to specialize in one or more areas, offering a boutique-type service in their area of special expertise.

OWNERSHIP. This has probably been the most contentious area in the debate on the proposed legislation because of the desire to reconcile concerns regarding financial-commercial linkages with a recognition of the present reality. Currently banks are required by law to be widely held, while many nonbank financial institutions are closely held and commercially linked. The government's position at present is "that there is no clear cut conclusion that would suggest that we cannot continue to be well served by the forms of ownership that have developed in Canada."

SELF-DEALING. There would be strong controls placed on transactions between financial institutions and related parties (i.e., those persons or companies who are in positions to influence the behavior of the financial institution). Of primary importance as related parties are significant shareholders (owning more than 10 percent of the shares of an institution), the directors and officers of the institution, and their significant business interests. Most asset transactions between the financial institution and nonfinancial related parties would be banned. Transactions between affiliated regulated financial institutions would be permitted, but only on a restricted basis, subject to approval by the institution's board of directors or a subcommittee thereof, and a supervisory approval in special circumstances. Furthermore, consideration is being given to placing transactions between parent and subsidiary, where both are federally regulated financial institutions, under a less restrictive regime.

CONFLICTS OF INTERESTS. Directors of a financial institution would be required to establish procedures to provide disclosure of prescribed information to customers. They would also be required to establish and monitor procedures to resolve conflicts of interest, including techniques for the identification of potential conflict situations and for restricting the flow of confidential information. It must also be recognized that financial institutions themselves have a strong interest in handling conflict of interest situations appropriately in order to maintain a reputation for fair dealing with their customers. These types of situations are not new, but the potential for them under the current proposals would be considerably increased. More attention would therefore have to be paid to resolving these conflicts than has been the case in the past.

CORPORATE GOVERNANCE. Some changes with respect to the role of the external auditors and directors would be put in place. External auditors would continue to play their role in the tripartite supervisory system (which includes internal auditors, external auditors, and supervisors), and measures have been proposed to improve the quality of the information flowing to them, to bolster their independence from the management of the institution, and to improve communication between the auditors and the board of directors and the supervisor.

It is proposed to improve the functioning of the board of directors by ensuring that the board has access to the views and judgment of directors that do not have a significant association with the institution. Thus, one-third of the directors would be required to be unaffiliated, and these directors would be given important roles in reviewing the corporate practices with respect to self-dealing transactions and any other transaction or practice that might have a material effect on the health of the financial institution.

SUPERVISION AND DEPOSIT INSURANCE. There have been a number of important changes to the supervisory and deposit insurance structure, but these are not of an especially radical character. The two federal supervisory bodies, the Office of the Inspector-General of Banks and the Department of Insurance (which was responsible for supervising federal trust and mortgage loan companies as well as federal insurance companies) have been merged into a new Office of the Superintendent of Financial Institutions. This change is particularly appropriate given the proposed changes in the powers of the various financial institutions that would make them much more similar than in the past. Other possible changes to the structure of the supervisory body for which there are models in other jurisdictions, such as a merger with the deposit insurer or shifting supervisory responsibilities to the central bank, were not pursued. The supervisor was also given new powers, of which the power to make "cease and desist" orders is the most important. In addition, a new interagency committee has been established, consisting of the heads of the supervisory office, the central bank, and the deposit insurance agency, as well as the deputy minister of finance. The committee ensures exchange of information and consultation on supervisory matters that have implications for solvency, last resort lending, and risk of deposit insurance payout. Also, by ensuring that the concerns of the deposit insurer and the lender of last resort are given full weight in decisions on troubled institutions, the new committee will strengthen the supervisor's "will to act" in these situations.

On the deposit insurance front, neither coinsurance nor risk-related premiums were introduced in the 1987 legislative package. However, the Canada Deposit Insurance Corporation (CDIC) has been given increased powers in the issuance and termination of insurance coverage, and it has been given the power to levy a premium surcharge on member institutions that are following unacceptable practices (as specified by CDIC bylaws).

Universal Banking: The Link between Banks and Securities Dealers

Historical Background

Until the recent changes in legislation, a combination of custom and law limited the involvement of banks in the securities business.[6] Thus, the Bank Act prohibited banks from acquiring more than 10 percent of the voting shares of nonbanking companies (subject to certain exceptions). And at the provincial level there were measures in

---

6. For an interesting and insightful analysis of some of the issues covered in this section of the paper, see Dale (1988).

a number of provinces, most notably Ontario, that prevented any non-industry investor (including banks) from holding more than 10 percent of the voting shares of a securities firm. There were, thus, tight restrictions on both upstream and downstream linkages between banks and securities dealers. It is worth noting that provincial laws also restricted foreign access to domestic securities markets. For example, the Ontario Securities Act limited the holdings of nonresidents in the aggregate to a maximum of 25 percent of the shares of a securities firm, while no single nonresident investor could hold more than 10 percent. Thus (with some grandfathered exceptions), Canadian securities dealers were owned by individual Canadian residents.

Until 1980, custom and tradition had led banks to remain out of the business of underwriting corporate bonds and equities, although there was no legal restriction on their involvement in this field. The 1980 Bank Act established precise rules specifying which securities activities the banks were permitted to engage in and which they were excluded from.

Thus, under the 1980 act, banks are permitted to invest in corporate securities (both debt and equity) for portfolio purposes, although they are subject to a 10 percent voting share limitation on holdings in any one company. They are also permitted to underwrite and distribute government bonds, to buy and sell securities generally on an agency basis, and to distribute corporate securities as members of a selling group. However, until the 1987 amendment to the Bank Act, they were prohibited from underwriting corporate securities (subject to the selling group exception) and a bank could not hold itself out as engaging in portfolio management or investment counseling in Canada.[7] As these restrictions applied only to securities business carried out by banks through their domestic offices, Canadian banks have been able to conduct investment banking operations through their overseas subsidiaries.

---

7. As a historical footnote, it is of interest to note that the banks were the first underwriters in Canada.

Rationale

It is perhaps worth speculating at this point on the rationale for the type of compartmentalization by function that has limited the banks' involvement in the securities business. From today's vantage point one can see perhaps three types of rationale for separating banks and securities dealers. The first is the alleged excessive risk of permitting banks to engage in the underwriting business.[8] A sophisticated variant of this argument is concerned with the extension of the safety net (comprising government supervision and access to deposit insurance and lender of last resort facilities) to riskier activities.

The second line of argument relates to the concern that a bank's role as lender and its role as underwriter of securities might lead directly to conflict of interest situations. For example, a bank with a doubtful loan to a client might try to extricate itself by underwriting and selling shares in that company to its investment clients. A similar concern with potential conflicts of interest probably accounts for the fact that in Canada banks are not permitted to handle trust accounts. The potential conflict of interest in this case arises from the possible use of such trust accounts to purchase bonds or shares in a company in difficulty to which the bank has a loan outstanding. The combination of trust business and underwriting could raise similar problems, that is, an underwriting that was not successful could be salvaged by selling the securities to the trust under the control of the underwriting company or its parent. Similar kinds of problems could arise with the combination of corporate investment banking and trust business, for example, the question of deciding whether to sell shares held by the trusts in a takeover bid organized by the investment banker. Different jurisdictions have taken different attitudes to combinations of business that potentially can give rise to conflicts of interest. For example, in virtually all countries securities dealers function both as underwriters and as brokers, although this was not permitted until recently in the United Kingdom. And in the United States banks are permitted to carry on a trust business. It is not entirely clear whether these differences across jurisdictions are simply accidents of history, whether they

---

8.   This appears also to have been the main rationale for the Glass-Steagall legislation in the United States.

reflect a view that the costs of these types of financial conflicts of interest are sufficiently small relative to the gains from permitting the combination of the various activities that they can be ignored, or whether they indicate a reliance on other techniques to minimize the problems.

A third type of argument for separation of banks and securities dealers is related to the concerns about increased concentration in the financial industry. Sometimes this was expressed in terms of reduced competition (since banks and dealers both compete for the business of lending to corporations). At other times the emphasis seems rather to have been on the political notion of concentration of power.

Some observers have attached considerable responsibility for the compartmentalization to the division of regulatory power between the federal and provincial governments. Dale has argued that "the fact that the federal government has sole jurisdiction over banks and banking, while the provinces claim exclusive regulatory responsibility for the securities markets (a matter of some controversy) has strengthened the separatist tendencies within the system."[9] More generally, Kane has suggested that regulators face bureaucratic and political incentives that will be an important influence on the nature of the regulatory regime, along with policy concerns about the efficiency and stability of the financial structure.[10]

Factors Motivating Change

In addition to the broad motivations for change discussed earlier, there were a number of factors specific to the securities area that were important in motivating the change in legislation that permitted the banks to purchase securities dealers. These include most notably securitization and globalization, but other factors also played a role.

As in other areas, there had been increased interpenetration of banks and securities dealers into each other's core business areas. Thus the payment of interest on credit balances by dealers brought them into competition with bank deposits. And banks made syndicated loans that competed directly with bond issues. More importantly,

---

9. See Dale (1988, p. 119).
10. See Kane (1990).

the separation of banking and securities business had come under increasing pressure as banks entered the discount brokerage business and as a growing share of the short-term financing business of the corporate sector was done in the form of commercial paper and bankers' acceptances. Indeed, the increasing use of securities markets by corporate borrowers was probably the single most important factor driving the integration of the banking and securities industries. As the traditional bank loan lost ground to the bond, equity, and, especially, the paper market (including bankers' acceptances), as well as to Euro-Canadian dollar and foreign currency issues, the banks became increasingly concerned about their ability to operate profitably and to compete effectively with both domestic securities dealers and with foreign banks and securities dealers. Some observers in the mid-1980s went so far as to argue that there was no future for the traditional bank with its focus on corporate loans, and that the future would belong to institutions that could offer their clients the widest possible range of financing options. Another way of expressing this point is to argue that there are considerable synergies to be had from being able to service all the financing needs of the corporate borrower in one institution. The banks also argued that it was essential that they have the ability to underwrite securities in the domestic market in order to develop the expertise that would enable them to compete with universal banks and investment banks in a world of increasing securitization, globalization, and integration of functions.

At the same time there was growing debate about the capacity of securities dealers, as they were then constituted in Canada, to compete in an increasingly globalized market. This debate reflected an increasing concern about the performance of the Canadian securities industry, comprised of relatively small firms in a rather protected environment, at a time of increasing competition in and from other major world securities markets.[11]

A principal argument of those who supported change was that dealers needed a larger capital base, particularly in a world of "bought deals" with greater than traditional risks and the associated

---

11. A detailed discussion of the issues in this debate can be found in T. J. Courchene (1984).

need for more capital. Recall that the structure of the industry with its reliance on individual investors limited the amount of capital that could be invested in the industry. There was also concern that the Canadian securities market would become a backwater if it did not open up to the rest of the world and that more competition was necessary to ensure that the Canadian securities industry did not fall behind in a very innovative world environment. This concern was exacerbated by the fear that developments in communications, by reducing transaction costs, would permit an increasing share of Canadian lending and borrowing to be conducted outside the country if the Canadian securities industry was insufficiently efficient or innovative.

In summary, the combination of concerns regarding the need for lenders to corporations to be able to be involved in both direct lending and market intermediation and the importance to Canada of having an innovative and competitive securities industry at a time of increasing pressures from globalization were probably the two most important factors leading to the breakdown of the barriers between the banking and securities industries.

Legislative Developments

The pressures for change resulted in the introduction of new legislation by both the federal government and Ontario, which had the effect of opening up the Ontario securities industry to outsiders. Thus, from June 30, 1987, there was to be no limit on investments in securities firms by Canadian financial institutions. Nonresidents were to be permitted to own up to 50 percent of an existing securities firm from June 30, 1987, and up to 100 percent from June 30, 1988. Also, direct entry into the Ontario market by foreign securities firms was to be permitted from June 10, 1987, without limit.

Although there was broad agreement between Ontario and the federal government on the question of the timing and scale of outside entry into the securities markets, there remained the sensitive jurisdictional question of how regulatory responsibilities were to be divided between provincial and federal authorities. The Office of the Superintendent of Financial Institutions (OSFI), the federal regulatory agency for banks, had to be satisfied that banks were not exposing themselves to unacceptable risks through the operations of their securities subsidiaries. And the Ontario government wished to maintain its longstanding jurisdiction over securities firms. In April 1987 the Ontario government and the federal government reached agreement on which securities activities could be carried out directly by federal financial institutions (and would therefore be regulated directly by the OSFI) and which could only be carried on in a subsidiary or affiliate (and would accordingly be regulated at the provincial level). The "in house" activities included all transactions in government debt, money market activities, secondary market trading in corporate debt securities, capital market activities in syndicated or consortium loans, unsolicited participation in secondary trading of equity securities, and, once these were permitted under the Bank Act, portfolio management and investment advice. Securities activities that could only be carried on through a subsidiary or affiliate included all activities relating to the primary distribution of equity and corporate debt securities and secondary market trading in equity securities.

In spite of this agreement and passage of legislation by the federal government and Ontario, the provincial-federal jurisdiction issue was not finally settled. There were problems with the implementation of the accord, and the other nine Canadian provinces declined to participate. In 1988, agreements were concluded between the federal government and the provinces of Ontario, Quebec, and British Columbia that involved the exchange of memorandums of understanding between the OSFI and their provincial securities commissions. These set out the ways in which the regulation of dealers by the securities commissions and of financial institutions by the OSFI would be coordinated. Among other things, they recognized the legitimate policy concerns of OSFI regarding the scope of business carried on by dealers associated with banks, and committed the provincial securities regulators not to amend the capital adequacy rules for the dealers before consulting with the OSFI. They also dealt with the sharing of information between the federal and provincial authorities in relation to federal financial institutions and their affiliated securities firms. The agreements were intended to give the OSFI the ability to ensure that the financial condition of a bank was not jeopardized by its securities subsidiary, while the securities commissions maintained their role as primary regulators of participants in the securities markets.

Some Implications of the Changes

CONFLICTS OF INTEREST. It is intended that conflicts of interest be dealt with in the forthcoming legislation. The policy would require the establishment of procedures to resolve conflicts of interest, including techniques for the identification of potential conflict situations and for restricting the flow of confidential information. One would also expect that the importance of reputational considerations to the financial institution and the cost in lost business of acquiring a reputation for unfair treatment of customers would play an important role in ensuring that institutions do not use inside information to take unfair advantage of their customers. Indeed, a number of banks that have entered into the securities business have already established rules and procedures to deal with potential conflicts of interest and set up compliance offices to monitor these arrangements.

In addition, the Canadian Securities Administrators (comprising representatives of the provincial and territorial securities commissions) have issued two sets of principles of regulation applying to dealers related to financial institutions. In the case of dealers that conduct securities activities within branches of their related financial institutions, these principles deal with such matters as separation of premises and activities, disclosure, solicitation of clients, and the question of dual employment of an individual by both the financial institution and the securities dealer. The other set of principles deals with selling arrangements between a dealer and its related financial institution, the transfer of confidential client information by the dealer to its related financial institution, and the settling of transactions through a client's accounts at the related financial institution.

THE STRUCTURE AND RISKS OF BANK-SECURITIES LINKAGES. Should excessive risk to the bank be a concern in allowing the banks to engage in the securities business? Is there a consequent problem with expansion of the safety net (including deposit insurance, lender of last resort facilities, and government supervision)? What are the arguments for and against the various ways of requiring the bank to structure its securities business?

Does the entry of commercial banks into investment banking make them riskier as a whole? Does it increase the likelihood that banks will require access to the safety net? These are complex issues over which there has been considerable debate. As far as risk is concerned, because of increased diversification it may well be that total risk can actually be reduced as a result of integrating the two types of operation (where risk is defined in terms of variability of returns). That is, because the nature of the principal risks faced is different: commercial banks primarily face credit risk by holding relatively low risk diversified assets for a long period of time, while in the traditional securities business, institutions primarily face price risk by holding relatively undiversified assets for very short periods. The merging of the two types of activities may actually reduce the variability of returns of a bank. However, this conclusion is probably dependent on the extent and range of securities activities in which the banking group is permitted to engage. Generally speaking, the more restricted the bank is in its ability to engage in the riskiest types of activities, either by outright exclusion or in terms of the magnitude of its permissible involvement relative to its capital, the less of a problem such activities would probably pose for the health of the overall operation. Of course, any firm conclusion in this context would depend also on the covariance of returns of the different kinds of securities activities *vis-á-vis* the other operations of the group.

If it were argued that permitting a bank to enter into the securities business increased overall risk, there would be a clear further concern that this would lead banks to make more use of the safety net than otherwise, unless the corporate structure segregated the securities business from the banking business in such a way as to prevent the securities business from having access to the safety net. However, even if one accepted the view that permitting a bank to enter the securities business did not increase overall risk, there would still be a concern about expansion of the safety net, since a wider range of activities would now be associated with the safety net. A particular further concern, some would argue, is the subsidization of these activities, which results from the inappropriate pricing of deposit insurance.

The appropriate response to these concerns is to ensure that suitable incentives are established with respect to the safety net, and in particular deposit insurance, and that overly rigid limitations on the ability of banks to engage in the securities business should not be set up. In practice, given the difficulties of establishing risk-related pre-mia on deposit insurance or credible co-insurance (especially because of the so-called implicit guarantee of large institutions), this might in-volve a combination of limiting or preventing banks from entering into the riskiest types of securities activities and setting stringent re-quirements for banks to have a capital base that is appropriate to the size and nature of their banking and securities activities. By ensuring through careful supervision that banks are not permitted to operate with insufficient capital, one can reduce or eliminate the incentive for an institution to engage in "plunger" behavior, that is, to risk every-thing on, say, an extremely risky, high return, underwriting venture because it is near failure.

The argument thus far suggests that there need not be strong con-cerns about increased use of the safety net, provided three conditions are met. First, the addition of securities powers leads to diversification benefits to deposit-taking institutions (i.e., a reduction or no great in-crease in risk); second, there are limitations on the banks' involvement in the riskiest types of activities; and third and most important, capital standards are maintained. In this context it is worth examining the ra-tionale for the structure of the corporate relationships between banks and securities dealers that have been imposed or are being proposed in various countries.

Among the objectives of the financial restructuring that is going on worldwide, perhaps the most important are "to secure the efficiency and competitive benefits of financial diversification, while imposing sufficient regulatory safeguards to ensure financial stability."[12] From this perspective one might caricature the British and American view-points on corporate structure as follows. The British, who permit the banks to engage in securities activities on their own balance sheets, are prepared to accept some potential increase in risk for the financial system (which they presumably deem to be relatively small) from this change in structure in return for the improved synergies. The Americans, who are considering requiring the securities activities to be carried out in a subsidiary of the bank holding company, aim at

---

12. See Dale (1988, p. 124). Dale goes on to discuss in some detail the U.K. and U.S. aproaches to the linkages between the banking and securities industries.

minimizing the perceived risks, while accepting that their institutions will get far less in the way of synergies. In his discussion of the various options, Dale argued that:

> "Canada, by way of contrast, has rejected both the risk segregation model proposed in the U.S. Senate Bill, and the U.K. model based on functional integration. Instead, the new Canadian regulatory framework for financial conglomerates combines risk-pooling with regulatory separation and various constraints on intergroup financial transactions. The difficulty with this approach is that it could result in the worst of all worlds, by denying to financial institutions the full economic benefits of diversification, but nevertheless exposing the banking sector to securities markets risks."[13]

In fact, the principal rationale for the current Canadian model of requiring certain securities activities to be situated in a subsidiary is that it reflects the federal provincial structure of regulation and supervision and the desire to continue to make use of the traditional expertise regarding banking and securities supervision, which is lodged in the OSFI and the securities commissions, respectively.[14] Except for the differences in the locus of regulation and supervision there is not very much difference between Canadian and British models, particularly since the constraints on parent-subsidiary transactions are not very restrictive. Although the Canadian approach allows for the theoretical possibility that the securities subsidiary could fail without the parent bank failing, in practice this would not be a likely occurrence. As described earlier, the riskiness of the securities activities would be limited by relying on a combination of constraints on the scope and extent of the riskier activities, appropriately stringent capital requirements, and a regulatory/supervisory apparatus that has had long experience in dealing with bank activities on the one hand (OSFI), and securities dealers activities on the other (OSC/QSC).

Moreover, concerns would be tempered by the belief that the traditional securities activities are not inherently excessively risky. Nonetheless, one might expect that the increase in the complexity of the activities of the bank securities groupings and the greater dependence of regulators on other regulators' actions would make regulation somewhat more difficult in the future than in the past.

---

13. Dale (1988, p. 126).
14. Note the difference in approach in the United Kingdom, with its emphasis on a lead regulator.

Recent Developments

As a result of the new legislation, all the large Canadian banks have entered the securities business, most by purchasing an existing Canadian dealer. All large dealers are now part of a broader financial services group, while some medium-sized Canadian dealers do continue to exist as independent entities, in some cases with minority foreign ownership. Also, there has been a significant influx of foreign dealers (about twenty new entrants), although not as many as might have been expected before the 1987 stock market crash. The elimination of barriers to entry to the securities industry in 1987 appears to have had beneficial results—increasing competition, lowering the level of fees, and increasing the capitalization of the securities dealers. It is also of interest to note that many trust companies and insurance companies have chosen not to enter the securities business directly, apparently because of the concern about potential conflicts of interest between fiduciary and underwriting activities.

Some of the bank-dealer combinations have chosen to transact as much of the securities business as they legally can on the books of the parent bank, while others have used the securities dealer subsidiary as the locus of their securities operations. This suggests that the difference in capital requirements between booking such transactions upstream and downstream is not very great and that administrative considerations have probably played an important role in the decision whether to use the parent or subsidiary as the primary operational center for the securities business. Also, in some instances, the parent bank is becoming increasingly involved in funding the securities part of the operation, and hence there has been some overall reduction in the use of the call loan market for financing purposes by the securities industry.

Although it is probably too early to reach definitive conclusions, it appears likely that the securities market of the future will be composed of three principal groupings: large Canadian and foreign banks with their dealer subsidiaries, the foreign dealer community, and several independent mid-sized Canadian dealers. This structure, and the potential competition from foreign markets, should ensure that in the long run strong and healthy competition prevails in Canadian securities markets. It is the purchasers of financial services that will decide whether supermarket-type providers of the full range of services will tend to dominate the market at the expense of the specialized boutique-type operations, or whether, as is more likely, both types of operation will coexist indefinitely.

Bibliography

Courchene, T. J. (1984). "A Really Secure Industry or a Real Securities Industry." Centre for the Analysis of National Economic Policy (CANEP), Working Paper 84-01, Department of Economics, University of Western Ontario, London, Ontario.

Dale, R. S. (1988). "The New Regulatory Framework in Canada." *Journal of International Banking Law*:117-126.

Freedman, Charles (1987). "Financial Restructuring: The Canadian Experience." In *Restructuring the Financial System*. Federal Reserve Bank of Kansas City, pp. 63-79.

Government of Canada (1986). "New Directions for the Financial Sector." Blue Paper, December 18.

Kane, E. J. (1990). "Incentive Conflict in the International Regulatory Agreement on Risk-Based Capital." Paper presented at the 26th Conference on Bank Structure and Competition, sponsored by the Federal Reserve Bank of Chicago, May 9-11.

14

THE CASE FOR AND AGAINST FINANCIAL CONGLOMERATE GROUPS: THE ITALIAN DEBATE ON THE EVE OF THE EUROPEAN BANKING INTEGRATION

Mario Draghi

Introduction

This paper is made up of four parts.[1] In the first, a short history of the Italian banking system provides the background for the presentation of the current bank versus industry debate which is described in the second part. The major legislative developments in this area are presented in the third section, and the main policy conclusions are discussed in the fourth part of the paper.

Although the first two sections are primarily directed at foreign readers unacquainted with the Italian banking structure, the intent of the paper is not merely descriptive but normative as well. Not in the sense of suggesting new rules, but rather in its case for harmonizing the existing national legislation with the community directives. This is argued in the last two sections—through several examples of "reverse discrimination"—as a most compelling course of action for the Italian legislature, which in its most recent deliberations and in some others still under discussion in the Italian Parliament imposes upon the Italian

1. This is a substantially revised version of the address given by the author at the Seminar on "Financial Sector Liberalization and Regulation" held at the Harvard Law School in June 1990 within the Program on International Financial Systems. Helpful comments and suggestions by Messrs. G. Amato, P. Ciocca, E. Granata, T. Padoa-Schioppa, and G. Visentini are gratefully acknowledged. The views and conclusions set forth are those of the author and do not represent expression of the position of Bank of Italy on the issues discussed in the paper.

banking system more restrictive standards than the ones that banks of other European Economic Community (EEC) member states will be asked to follow when operating in Italy.

Historical Background

The current structure of the Italian banking system is deeply rooted in a series of laws enacted during the 1930s following the worst of the several banking crises that had plagued Italy since its birth as a unified state. Until then the prevailing banking model was the German universal bank, free to operate over the entire spectrum of maturities and financial assets. At that time capital markets were still largely undeveloped in Italy, and poor asset-liability management created serious problems for the major banks' balance sheets. Most bank liabilities were in the form of short-term deposits, while bank lending was heavily concentrated into a few large industries, which ten years after the end of World War I still had trouble in returning to profitability. Banks had gradually been acquiring an increasing share of these industries' capital, and bank officials were on many of their boards, where they often had, at least nominally, supervisory capacity. Given the low profitability of these companies and the fragility of the stock market, which was unfit to assess their real value and to absorb any sizable liquidation, these positions were highly illiquid and a potential source of instability.

One should also remember that in 1920, for a somewhat similar case of mismatching in maturities, one of the largest banks had gone into bankruptcy without any intervention by the monetary authorities. This episode, disastrous for several thousands of small depositors, had a major macroeconomic consequence: the share of savings intermediated by the banking system dropped dramatically for almost twenty years. Therefore, in the face of the new crisis, the monetary authorities decided to intervene drastically into what was rightly perceived as a threat to the financial stability of the whole economy.

IRI (Istituto Per La Ricostruzione Industriale), a financial holding, was created with public capital drawn upon the government finances; it bought up Banca Commerciale Italiana, Banco di Roma, and Credito Italiano; it relieved them from all their industrial participations, which were in the most important sectors of the Italian economy; and proceeded to an industrial restructuring of gigantic proportions that lasted with great success throughout the 1950s.

In 1936 the government enacted the banking law upon which the present banking system is still largely based; its fundamental principles took origin from what were perceived the main causes of the crisis:[2]

- Maturity mismatching: borrowing short and lending long
- Asset risk mismatching: investment in industrial stocks with an uncertain yield, while liabilities were both liquid and with certain cash outflow
- Poor care and monitoring of these investments: simple presence of bank officials in the board of the industries entangled the banks but with little positive impact on the profitability of their investments
- Overall lack of independence of the banks in relation to the industrial concerns.

It was also recognized that those controls that are typical of a capitalistic economy had not worked.[3] Neither markets nor institutional surveillance had effectively signaled the massive, although gradual, deterioration of bank balance sheets. The authorities' reaction was to enhance surveillance, while hopes to have a well-developed capital market capable of signaling crises and absorbing them were abandoned for several years, and little action to this extent followed.

Consequences of the 1936 Banking Act

Among the consequences brought either directly or indirectly by the 1936 Banking Act, the following are relevant in our context:

- Ample discretionary powers of surveillance over the banking industry were assigned to the Bank of Italy.
- Commercial banks having deposits were forbidden to hold participations in nonbank institutions. This principle of strict separation between bank and industry was not explicitly stated by the law, but became one of the cornerstones in the interpretation and the application given to the law by the Bank of Italy.

---

2. R.D.L. 12 marzo 1936, n. 375, converted into law with L. 7/3/1938 n. 141.
3. Ciocca and Frasca (1987).

- Bank bylaws were mandated to contain provisions relative to specialization of banking activity into either short-term or long-term intermediation, with strict observance of maturity matching.
- The banking industry was considered predominantly to be of public interest and most banks, either because they were absorbed by IRI or because they were created as public institutions, were recognized to be subject to the public law.

Since all the banks that were involved in the crisis had their borrowing in the form of short-term, or time, deposits, it became necessary to accompany the increased specialization of the new system through the enhancement of the institution specialized into medium- and long-term lending: this is IMI (Istituto Mobiliare Italiano), which performs such a function issuing long-term bonds. It is interesting to note that IMI, differently from commercial banks, was authorized by the law to hold securities; however, this capacity never developed itself to any sizable extent.

In conclusion, the 1936 Banking Act laid the foundations of a modern banking sector. It was quite a prophetic act of law as its application introduced in the Italian banking system the principles of specialization, corporate separateness, and discretionary surveillance. However, the resulting system was not based on the markets, but on a few large banks, and any form of equity financing was severely constrained. As a consequence of this lack of reliance on the markets, and on their monitoring function, there was growing dependence of the system on the supervisory authority of the Bank of Italy. It is not coincidental that the timid growth of the financial markets in the last few years was accompanied by a growing debate on the discretionary powers of the Bank of Italy surveillance and on the scope of its coverage.

Regulatory Protection

Before developing this theme any further, it is worthwhile explaining the affection of our legislature to the present system as it came to be designed by the events of the 1930s. IRI, the financial holding, was meant to be a hospital for the temporarily ill, but became a permanent feature of our economy: it had a key role during the period of reconstruction in the 1950s and the buildup of infrastructures in the 1960s when large dimensions were necessary to exploit the economies of scale and of scope that a large and a well-managed conglomerate could benefit from. IMI, the medium-term credit institution, provided financing of large projects, both private and public, which were undertaken in that period.

The few large commercial banks, most of which, though not all, were under IRI control, had a quiet life in a highly protected environment, as they were shielded from both external competition by the scarce internationalization of the banking sector and from internal competition as well. Both new entrants, which were only rarely allowed, and domestic expansion of operations through the opening of new branches or subsidiaries had to receive specific authorizations by the Bank of Italy, and they were sparingly given.

A similar, though less welcome, kind of protection was given to the Italian banking system during the 1970s and the first part of the 1980s. Following the repeated oil shocks to which the Italian economy did not adjust very fast, the process of credit creation became highly controlled through ceilings on credit expansion, subsidies of various kinds, and a strict control on international capital movements. This protection certainly delayed the introduction of modern technologies and the development of managerial skills, which were taking place abroad during those years. The granting of large economic rents increased the profitability of the banking system as a whole and strengthened the capital position of several banks.[4]

The second part of the 1980s saw the progressive and continuous dismantling of controls, first radically reducing the role of interest rate subsidies and abandoning the credit ceilings, then relaxing limitations to capital movements, and finally liberalizing them completely. During 1990 the authorization system limiting the opening of new branches was relaxed as well. At the same time, international financial integration was enhanced by giving certainty to the lira as a medium of payment, through the adoption of the narrow band of fluctuation within the European Monetary System (EMS). This wave of liberal-

---

4. For a description of the Italian banking system until the early 1980s, see Cesarini, et al, (1988).

izations marked for the Italian banking system the beginning of an era of restructuring and was accompanied by a still continuing debate on whether the necessary changes could be achieved by the banking sector alone or whether they needed the participation of the industrial sector, which had already restructured itself with astonishing success.

The Current Debate

Many of the arguments in favor of strict separation between bank and industry, public ownership of the major banks so as to guarantee their independence, and the specialization of the banking activity draw their strength from the events of the 1930s. In order to assess their robustness today one should ask whether those events could take place in our world with fairly developed capital markets and with the well-developed and highly effective surveillance of our authorities. Judged from this perspective, these arguments lose a lot of their power: unprofitable participations are routinely liquidated or merged in many countries' financial systems, without problems for the stability of their economies. The built-in controls of the markets and the institutional control of the monetary authorities' surveillance would quickly point out any serious distortion before it could turn into a threat for the system. At the same time, the largest, most developed, and most specialized banking system in the world has to cope with very serious problems, simply because of the poor quality of its traditional lending. Doubts about the benefits of universal banking must be based on arguments other than its potential threat to the stability of the banking system. It is true that some corporate structures are more easily monitorable than others, and the universal bank is not one of them. But convenience of the regulators has rarely been a winning argument in the long run.

Arguments for Industrial Participation

On the other side of the debate the most frequently cited reasons in favor of industrial participation in the banks' capital in the form of a controlling interest include:

- The banks need capital to comply with the ratios set by the Bank of Italy.

- They also need managerial skills that are best provided by the industrial sector, given its recent experience.
- Italian banks should be freed from the pervading and harmful political interference.
- Public ownership is simply overextended everywhere and in particular in the banking sector, where the state owns roughly 65 percent of the whole system; therefore, privatization is badly needed.

All these arguments have some intrinsic value, but by themselves they do not grant the conclusion that the Italian financial system should turn into the world's possibly unique example to have industries controlling the banking system.

Let us briefly examine these points. First, the banking system as a whole is not undercapitalized; there are some banks—some public banks—that need capital and, as it will be seen later in this paper, their owners have laid down the foundations necessary to solve this problem. Capital can be raised through several channels: mergers with existing banks, recourse to the market, use of the taxpayer funds to fill the gap since we are dealing with public banks, or sale of the banking concerns to the private sector and more specifically to nonbanks. In principle these are all feasible routes and, in the textbook competitive world, they are also equivalent from a resource allocation viewpoint. Therefore, while economic theory should help to indicate the clearly suboptimal solutions, the final choice will likely depend more on institutional, historical, and political factors. At the present time the first three routes are actively being pursued by Italy's legislature, which has also set precise limits to the feasibility of the fourth.

Second, the needed transfer of managerial skills does not imply a transfer of ownership as well: in fact, to claim the opposite sounds ominous for the kind of relationship between ownership and management of the bank that is implied, and by itself justifies the resistances to any such move.

This last consideration is relevant to the issue of public interference in bank management. What matters is not the identity of the owner, but the existence of rules defining with precision and rigor the borderline between the area of competence of the ownership and that of the management.

Finally, the necessity to limit the area of public ownership in the banking sector by itself does not imply transfer of control power to nonbanks. The same goal could be achieved through greater participation of foreign private banks into Italy's banking and financial companies.

The current debate does not point to any decisive reason in favor of either course of action. Some light on criteria other than economic theory or managerial convenience may come from the analysis of other countries' experiences where a more defined banking model has a long history of continuity.

The successful German experience is often referred to as the example to follow and is in fact used as the main powerful argument for suggesting the desirability of interlocking the interests of bank and industry.[5] This is a somewhat confused reasoning since it points out to a form of control of banks over industries, which is the opposite of the one that is the object of debate in Italy these days; nonetheless, it is relevant from a different angle: for a country where universal banking does not exist yet and where it is to be decided which organization the financial markets should have, it may be important to choose whether to lay grounds for the development of a wide-ranging securities market or to give such a task to the banking sector.

Before we give a cursory look to either course of action, we wish to remind ourselves that comparisons and ordering of systems is a temptation that should be resisted: being the result of historical processes, these systems have become self-justified; so, the universal banking system originated from the need to have long-term financing in a situation of undeveloped capital markets; today capital markets in Germany are less developed than in some other countries, and the universal banking system has become indispensable, and probably optimal, given the weakness of other sources of financing. For the same reason, it is likely that, transplanted in other contexts, it would not yield the benefits for which it became famous. They are:[6]

---

5.   For a comparative analysis of the credit markets in Germany, France, and Italy, see Nardozzi (1983).

6.   See Steinherr and Huveneers (1989).

- Economies of scope coming from bundling several services, and therefore reducing the fixed cost element in each client relationship
- Minimization of information and monitoring costs
- Accumulation of knowledge about the borrower that is more valuable than any material guarantee.

If these benefits—some of which are intimately linked to large dimensions, a point on which we shall come back later—were transferred to the customer, one should observe greater differentiation of risk premia, longer maturities, or riskier firms being financed. However, there is no evidence that this is actually occurring.[7]

But suppose that these benefits do indeed exist in the German case: Would they persist in a different reality where markets are not undeveloped, or where it is a goal of economic policy that they should grow? The answer is likely to be negative. On one hand, the economies of scope would have to be compared with the ones coming from a higher specialization, and there are no priors on which one is the larger. On the other hand, the risk premia differentiation would probably be better appreciated by the markets that, either directly or through securitization, could ensure transparent pricing of risky projects. Finally and most important, the same large investment made by the universal bank in developing a bank-client relationship, where privileged information is the dominant element, would become valueless if the same information were to be supplied to the markets. This would be the case with a mixed system where corporations would draw their financing from both banks and the markets, and where loan securitization has become a permanent feature of the financial landscape.

Arguments Against Industrial Participation

The main counter arguments to developing a universal banking system deal with the issues of conflict of interest and of concentration of power. These arguments are also valid in the case of industries controlling the banking system, and are at the core of the Italian

---

7. Ibid.

Antitrust Law that has been recently approved by the Italian Parliament.[8]

Some of the main examples of conflict of interest are:[9]

- Since universal banks conduct deposit business and stock exchange transactions they may not uphold the interests of their customers in investing in securities.
- There is a danger that banks could withhold information obtained in the credit business from their customers in the securities business.
- Banks could be inclined to build up participations without transacting on the stock exchange.
- Universal banks could be more interested in the credit business than in their borrowers' capital issues.
- Banks may use information from the credit business that gives them an advantage over other stock exchange operators.
- Banks could press upon their investment funds own stocks or issues of their customers.
- Because banks own participations, exercise proxy votes, and are represented on supervisory boards they accumulate inside information that they may use as investment advisers of their clients.

It is often argued that the corporate separateness required by a system based on holding companies would not be a sufficient barrier against these conflicts of interest. The answer clearly depends on how powerful are the incentives and penalties for the management of the controlled companies to achieve maximum profitability, even when this entails independent behavior from the holding company.

However, there is no doubt that, *prima facie,* the universal bank is more exposed to these perversions than the specialized intermediary. The case of banks controlled by industries is even worse because, while not immune from the above anomalies, it is open to the possible use by the controlling industry of information on competitors released by them as clients of the bank.

---

8.   L. 10 ottobre 1990 n. 287 "Norme per la tutela della concorrenza e del mercato."

9.   Ibid, p. 21. For other examples of conflict of interest related to self-lending or connected lending, see Ciocca (1983).

But what our public opinion and our Parliament fear most are the gigantic dimensions to which the fortunes and the successes of the universal bank are unavoidably linked. In the Italian reality where industrial conglomerates are already extended—certainly overextended for the standards of a Tocquevillian democracy—over a plurality of sensitive sectors, concentration of power, so difficult to describe in analytical terms yet so tangible in its consequences, is still largely unregulated. Until this is done, the case for letting industries control banks, especially if it stays confined within the national boundaries, is unlikely to prevail, as it is intertwined with privatization of public banks. Such privatization, needed but difficult to enact, would have to go hand in hand, with a widening of those conglomerates, the power of which already worries so many who would certainly reject any further increase, particularly if perceived to take place at the "expense" of the state. The regulatory provisions of the Antitrust Law certainly reflect this conviction and strongly limit the presence of industry in the banking system.

The necessity to avoid concentrations of power too large in relation to the size of the economy is hardly disputable. To use national legislation for this purpose in an open and expanding financial space may be ineffective and under certain circumstances counterproductive. Possible developments toward a greater variety of ownership structures may stem from the widening of our financial market to the rest of Europe—where concentration of power will acquire a different meaning—and from the necessity to reach a unified set of rules common to all EEC member states.

Legislative Developments

The debate over the restructuring of the banking sector in Italy has extended to the whole financial system and has taken the specific form of two laws[10], recently approved, and some other projects of law, which at this writing were still under discussion in the Italian

---

10. Legge 30/7/1990 n. 219 "Disposizioni in materia di ristrutturazione e integrazione patrimoniale degli istituti di credito di diritto pubblico"; Legge 10/10/1990 n. 287 "Norme per la tutela della concorrenza e del mercato."

Parliament.[11] While these laws were taking shape, the second EEC directive was elaborated.[12] It came out at the end of 1989, and some of its differences with the main thrust of the national legislation undoubtedly come from the simultaneity of the two legislative processes.

The Second EEC Directive

The second EEC directive on banking activity coordinates banking legislation at the European level and reflects the increasing integration that is leading to a unified European market by 1992.[13] The directive is based on two principles: minimal harmonization of national legislations, and mutual recognition of banking activity. By this second principle, the authorization given by the authorities of one country to an institution to carry on banking activity is valid and recognized in all the other countries of the European Community. The second EEC directive concerns harmonization of:

- Conditions for authorization to exercise the banking activity
- Relationships with third countries
- Conditions for the exercise of the banking activity
- Freedom of establishment.

Although the directive is wide in its scope and definition so that a plurality of national regimes can be accommodated within it, a specific view of what is a bank and what it can do is clearly defined as the basis, common to all member states, for the granting of such authorization. We shall briefly overview the directive for its implications on the range of permissible activities for a bank, for its perspective on the relationship between bank and industry, for its stance on the issue of specialization and corporate separateness, and for its prescriptions in the realm of surveillance.

"Credit institutions" (CI) are defined as those concerns that borrow from the public deposits and other reimbursable funds, and give credit. The restrictive character of this definition is tempered by the provision that an institution, if authorized as a CI by the authorities of

---

11. D.d.l. "Disciplina delle attivita' di intermediazione immobiliare e disposizioni sull'organizzazione dei mercati mobiliari" (C 3870); D.d.l. "Disciplina sulle offerte pubbliche di azioni e di obbligazioni" (C2889).

12. Second Council Directive of December 15, 1989, 89/646/EEC.

13. See Steinherr and Gilibert (1989).

the country where it is based, can carry on an extensive list of activities that will be mutually recognized by all the other member countries.

The following activities, if supplied by a CI or by its subsidiaries, will be mutually recognized over the entire European Community:

- Acceptance of deposits and other repayable funds from the public
- Lending
- Financial leasing
- Money transmission services
- Issuing and administering means of payments
- Guarantees and commitments
- Trading for own account or for account of customers in:
  - money market instruments
  - foreign exchange
  - financial futures and options
  - exchange and interest rate instruments
  - transferable securities
- Participation in share issues and the provision of services related to such issues
- Advice to undertakings on capital structure, industrial strategy, and advice and services relating to mergers and the purchase of undertakings
- Money broking
- Portfolio management and advice
- Safekeeping and administration of securities
- Credit reference services
- Safe custody services

The directive does not preclude nonbanks from having controlling interests in banks, with the only proviso that communication be given to the surveillance authorities that maintain the right of not granting authorization, but only in case of dissatisfaction about the shareholders as persons; communication should also be given in case of relevant bank assets sales, but again no distinction is being made between banks and nonbanks.

The directive does introduce a limitation on the participations that a bank can acquire in nonbank institutions. Individually these should not exceed 15 percent and globally 60 percent of the bank's equity capital (own funds), with exceptions possibly being made for insurance companies. These limitations clearly have only the purpose of keeping the banks' capital adequately diversified and potentially liquid, not of establishing any serious barriers between banks and nonbanks.

The activities described in the list can be carried out by branches or subsidiaries anywhere in the European Community provided they have in their bylaws that: (1) their holding company has been authorized as a bank in their home country, (2) their holding company owns at least 90 percent of the branch's capital, (3) their holding company is jointly liable with the branch for all its commitments, and (4) such a liability should be deemed satisfactory by the home country's authorities.

The directive becomes rather tight on the harmonization of the activity of surveillance: the home country authorities are responsible for the surveillance regarding solvency and financial solidity; the host country authorities supervise liquidity and the response of the banks to their actions pertaining to the realm of monetary policy; they are jointly responsible for surveillance concerning market risk; and it is also envisaged that surveillance be carried at a consolidated level.

At the cost of a little repetition, a summary of the main points of the second EEC directive from our perspective is worthwhile. The directive:

- Nowhere requires that financial intermediaries be specialized by their activity
- Does not erect significant barriers to reciprocal controlling influence between banks and nonbanks
- Establishes the principle of full liability of the mother company versus its subsidiaries, as a precondition for their mutual recognition by all the member states
- Requires surveillance to be carried on at a consolidated level.

Finally, it is important to stress a point inherent to the nature of the second EEC directive. This states that "the Member States must ensure that there are no obstacles to carrying on activities receiving mutual recognition in the same manner as in the home Member State, as long as the latter do not conflict with legal provisions protecting the general good in the host Member State." Therefore, the directive strongly limits the possibility of applying to other EEC members' CI rules that are stricter than the directive. At the same time it foresees for the member states the option to adopt more restrictive rules for their own national CI. This provision is explicitly stated for the areas pertaining to articles: 4 (capital requirements), 5 (information requirements on the identity and suitability of the shareholders), 11 (treatment of qualified holdings in CI), 12 (treatment of qualified holdings in non-CI), and 16 (use and disclosure of confidential information)—of which only the provisions relative to articles 11 and 12 are relevant in our context.

Of course the incentive by member states to do so is greatly diminished by the danger that more restrictive rules could reduce the competitiveness of their own banks without yielding the possible institutional benefits of their greater severity. An example will be useful to clarify this point that is crucial for defining the scope of national legislations in this area. Consider the case of a country's authorities that deem the principle of corporate separateness essential to limit the danger of diffusion of instability and to discipline potential conflicts of interest. Suppose they require this principle to be enforced in the sense of having some of the activities listed by the second directive carried on by separate corporations that would be subsidiaries of a CI. In taking this course of action, the authorities would on one hand penalize their country's CI, since the other countries' CI operating on their national market cannot be asked to comply with the requirement of corporate separateness. On the other hand, they would not immunize their market from the contagion of instability, or proceed to a better regulation of conflicts of interest since full joint liability of the mother company and its subsidiaries is required by the directive for access to mutual recognition by all the member states.

Therefore, the scope of the national legislations is in practice greatly restricted by the second directive. The two aims of assuring that national priorities are reflected in the legislation and that the domestic banking system remains competitive in the new European market are not always compatible.

The Amato Law

Of the first three laws regarding financial markets, which are being discussed in the Italian Parliament, the most directly connected to the banking sector is the Amato Law, named after the treasury minister who originally drafted it two years ago.[14] The law addresses the following areas:

- Mergers, transformations, capital increases
- Recapitalization of public banks
- Surveillance
- Taxation
- Labor relations.

We shall discuss in some detail as relevant to the present context only the first three points. As far as taxation is concerned, it suffices to say that the aim of the law is to make the processes regulated under the first point easier to implement than they would have been otherwise.

The major purpose of the law is to build the foundations of the ownership restructuring necessary for public banks to reach a size and a capital basis adequate for the increased competition originating from the process of financial liberalization, as described above. To this extent the law authorizes public banks to convert themselves into corporations. As such the intent of the law is not to privatize but to make it easier to form new and larger entities. In fact any transformation, sales of relevant portion of the stock, and mergers have to be authorized by the treasury, the Committee for Credit and Saving, and the Bank of Italy.

The terms at which quotas of the banks to be incorporated are exchanged with shares have to be supervised and approved by the same institutions and by the Consob (the Italian equivalent of the Securities and Exchange Commission). The government remains the majority owner of the banks: this is guaranteed by statutory clauses, and by various layers of authorizations. More specifically, government control in the form of 50.1 percent of the voting rights is preserved in the majority of the cases.

---

14. L. 30/7/1990 n. 218 "Disposizioni in materia di ristrutturazione e integrazione patrimoniale degli istituti di credito di diritto pubblico."

However, exception to this provision may be made in some specific instances. When privatization of credit institutions satisfies one of the following criteria:

- It is instrumental in strengthening the Italian banking system.
- It would enhance its international presence.
- It increases its net worth.
- It develops its size so as to increase its competitiveness.
- It satisfies public interest goals.

It may be authorized, although subject to the following conditions:

- The bylaws of the concerned credit institutions should contain provisions excluding the possibility of control being acquired by nonbanks or by individuals.
- Agreement by the Bank of Italy is required.
- The Council of Ministers should approve the operation.

To read this list as the legislature's official blueprint for privatization would certainly be unfair to the law, the aim of which is not, as said before, to give a discipline in this area. However, such reading could be informative as to the currently prevailing views in the Italian Parliament on the issue of privatization. Which conclusions would one draw from the list presented above? First, that these guidelines, being a combination of loosely defined criteria and a strikingly tight authorization process, are designed to preserve the maximum discretionary power in the hands of the government. Second, that by requiring the bylaws of the newly privatized banks to contain provisions to this extent, they confirm that in general public ownership is deemed necessary so as to avoid the danger that nonbanking concerns might acquire control of these banks.

In line with the other existing legislation, the Amato Law reaffirms the principle of corporate separateness between short- and medium-term borrowing activity. It does not forbid mergers and acquisitions of banks with different specializations, but it states that the resulting entity should keep the two borrowing activities separate in the sense of establishing separate corporations for each of them. This is the only instance when corporate separateness is explicitly required by this law.

The definition of a bank upon which the Amato Law is based is the same as the one provided by the first EEC directive.[15] The resulting banking system is one based on holding companies, where the various corporations can operate over the whole spectrum of banking and financial activities respecting the principle of specialization, as stated above. However, this law also defines for the first time the banking group. There may be two possibilities: in the first, where the controlling holding is itself a bank, the group does not need other prerequisites to be defined as a banking group. In the second, where the controlling holding company is not a bank, the law requires that certain preconditions be satisfied for the group to be authorized as a banking group:

- The holding company should have a financial character, and it should be established in Italy.
- The participations in the controlled companies carrying on banking or financial activities should be predominant with respect to the participations in companies having other purposes.
- A banking group is one where the controlled companies have a share of the nationwide deposits or lending equal or greater than 1 percent, or if at least half of the group's assets is formed by assets owned by banks controlled by the holding company.

This definition is wider than the one given in the second EEC directive, as it allows for the possibility of a financial company being the controlling holding. This law, to the extent that it does not change the discipline of the 1936 law on the issue of nonbanking participations by banks or by banking groups, is also less restrictive than the second EEC directive but only as far as the qualified—that is, 10 percent or more—holdings are concerned. The two are equivalent with respect to the discipline concerning the amount of nonqualified holdings that a bank can have in its assets.

These differences between the definition of a banking group in the Amato Law and that one implicit in the second directive raise a more general point: whenever the national legislation is wider than the directive, there is a problem of harmonization that needs to be solved if the national banks are to benefit from the mutual recognition. On the

---

15. First Council Directive, 17/12/77 n.77/780/EEC.

other hand, when the national rules are stricter than the directive, there is the possibility of discrimination against the national C.I. It is likely that many of these differences will disappear when the EEC directive on financial services will be officially approved. But the possibility of "reverse discrimination" could still arise with respect to the separation between long-term and short-term borrowing, along the lines previously discussed.

The second observation concerns the power of the third prerequisite, which in its first part is reminiscent of the definition of bank given by the first EEC directive, while in its second part accepts entirely the second EEC directive: the requirement that the amount of the assets of the banking component of the group may theoretically be satisfied with assets relative to all the activities, other than lending, which are listed in the second EEC directive.

On the issue of recapitalization, the law states that public banks that are undercapitalized according to the ratios set by the Bank of Italy, will get from their owner, and out of the public budget $1.5 billion over the next four years.

The law foresees extensive prudential surveillance through request of information on a consolidated basis, precise directions concerning observance of risk and capital ratios, nature and quantity of the participations in the banks' portfolio, and handling of crisis situations. Since, as far as it concerns the first two items, the law does not introduce elements of novelty with respect to the standards of most regulatory systems, it is worth focusing on the third aspect of the surveillance, the handling of crisis, because the way it has been regulated is symptomatic of the extreme caution of the legislature's approach to changes in the legal structure of the banking system. The law states that when one of the corporations of the group is in a state of crisis of relevant proportions relative to the whole group, the holding company itself may be subject to the procedures of extraordinary administration by itself. While this does not entail increased liability for the holding it does entail dispossession of management prerogatives in favor of a special administrator appointed by the government upon advice of the Bank of Italy. It is interesting to note that in such a way the principle of corporate separateness is overcome, as far as management responsibilities are concerned. This reflects the conviction that regardless of corporate separateness, the various units of a bank holding company tend to act in an integrated fashion.

Beyond the points mentioned before in support of a closer relationship between banks and industries, critics of this law observe that it does little to help our banks to raise capital on the markets, since maintaining control in public hands removes the main reason for the interest that private investors might have in these shares. In any event, they propose that to ease the raising of capital on the markets, transformation into corporations should not be left optional and, for the same reason, private control should be made more accessible than proposed by the Amato Law. They finally view the proposed powers of surveillance as excessive since they exceed the traditional tasks of orientation, guarantee, and prudential control. In particular, it is observed that there is a potential inconsistency between the limited liability regime by which the administrators of the holding company have limited responsibility for the management of the controlled subsidiaries, and the surveillance regime in crisis situations.

Overall this law introduces two profound innovations with respect to the philosophy of the 1936 banking act:

- The incorporation of public banks that brings them into the realm of the private law
- The adoption, as the basis of the banking system, of the holding company where the controlled corporations operate as different legal persons over the whole spectrum of banking and financial activities.

At the same time, this law retains from the existing regulatory system the principle of specialization between short- and medium-term borrowing, with the possibility of ad hoc deviations, and the reliance on the discretionary powers of the Bank of Italy on this and other matters, and on its advice as far as changes in ownership and control are concerned.

The Antitrust Law

The issue of private versus public ownership, although not intended to be a primary aim of the law, has been the one to elicit the most controversy, especially for the extreme caution with which it deals with possible bank privatizations. The question of participation into banks by private nonbanks or nonfinancial companies is answered by the Antitrust Law, one section of which is dedicated to the discipline of private participations in Italian banks.[16] The law regulates:

- Acquisitions of participations in the banking sector
- Definition of controlling shareholding
- Reciprocity relationships with other countries
- Conflict of interest.

Any acquisition by which the share of a bank's capital owned by a single individual or an institution would exceed 5 percent of the bank's total capital must be authorized by the Bank of Italy. Such authorization is always needed when, regardless of this limit, the change in shareholding affects the control of the company, also defined as a situation where one or more shareholders linked by a control pact, or through any other channel, own more than 25 percent of the bank stock, or more than 10 percent, if the bank shares are traded on the stock market.

For concerns other than banks or financial institutions, the maximum allowable ceiling is 15 percent: in these cases no authorization will be granted for acquisitions beyond this limit, or whenever control is implied by such an acquisition. The terms nonbank or nonfinancial institution mean not only an entity that does not carry out credit or financial activities; the terms also refer to financial institutions with a controlling interest in a nonfinancial company. This would also apply to those banks or financial institutions being controlled by nonbanks.

Relationships with other countries in this area are dealt with by the article stating that the prime minister, upon advice of the treasury minister, may deny the authorization to purchase or to underwrite relevant banking stocks to those banks or financial companies established in countries where the independence of credit institutions is not preserved by laws having the same effect as the Italian Antitrust Law.

A discussion of this law within the newly integrated European market would suggest the following. Its content is substantially stricter than the second EEC directive's article 11 regulating acquisitions of qualified holdings in credit institutions by natural or legal persons. As it was discussed above, the second EEC directive foresees that in this

---

16. L. 10/10/90 n. 287 "Norme per la tutela della concorrenza e del mercato."

and certain other matters, member states may establish rules that are stricter than the directive's, but that would apply only to their own authorized institutions. In light of this consideration, the provision of the Italian Antitrust Law conditioning the authorization for acquisitions of controlling holdings of credit institutions to the prerequisites illustrated above would not be applicable to foreign banks beyond the limits stated by the second EEC directive. Consequently, the provision of the Antitrust Law, requiring a sort of extension to other countries of the rules governing the independence of credit institutions in Italy, has no practical value.

The Italian Antitrust Law cannot restrict a bank that has been authorized by another member state to carry on the activities listed in the annex of the second directive—and more specifically, trading for own account in transferable securities—from acquiring a controlling holding of an Italian bank, whether or not the foreign bank is controlled by or controls a nonbank.

The other, this time deliberate, exception to the principle of separateness between bank and industry excludes from the application of the law the state industrial conglomerate IRI, which owns more than 60 percent of the Banca Commerciale Italiana, Credito Italiano, and Banco di Roma.

In conclusion, the Antitrust Law does not prevent the existence of a mixed banking system with banks and industries having reciprocal controlling holdings. It restricts such possibility only to foreign banks and discriminates against Italian banks and nonbanking concerns.

When dealing with conflicts of interest relative to self-lending or to connected lending, this law delegates the Bank of Italy to set the relevant limits only with reference to the credit institution's own assets and to the shareholding of the potential borrower. It also mandates a Ministerial Committee (Comitato Interministeriale per il Credito e il Risparmio) to issue directives in the area of conflicts of interest. At the present time shareholders having 5 percent or more of a bank's stock cannot borrow more than one-fifth of this bank's own assets and two-fifths of that portion of its assets corresponding to their shareholding.

Other Legislation

The other law of interest in this context regulates public offers of stocks.[17] For changes in ownership it states that whenever a natural or legal person owns 25 percent of the capital stock of a company, he or she is allowed to purchase on the market only another 5 percent, and is required to give communication to CONSOB before undertaking the transaction. Beyond the ceiling of 30 percent any further purchase must take the form of a public bid. This procedure does not apply to cases where more than 50 percent of a company's stock is already owned. In this case any further purchase can take place even without public offer.

Another recently approved law regulates the banking activity in the securities intermediation industry.[18] It authorizes banks to undertake a list of activities ranging from underwriting of securities to their management, custody, and administration for account of customers.

On one hand this law does not increase the scope of the banking activity, since banks were not prevented by any of the existing laws from carrying on these activities, and had already been doing so for quite a time. On the other hand the combined application of this law and of the second EEC directive introduces the possibility of "reverse discrimination" against the financial intermediation carried on by Italian banks.

An example of such discrimination is provided by this law's mandate that banks cannot trade for their own account or for account of customers in tradable securities. Since this activity is also contained in the second EEC directive's list, this limitation would not apply to foreign banks. It is true that Italian banks could easily overcome it by establishing separate corporations that could satisfy the requirements of this law, and would be authorized to undertake this activity, but it would be a roundabout route that the banks established in other member states could not be asked to follow.

This law foresees that all transactions should be executed on the "regulated markets." The currently prevailing interpretation restricts

---

17. D.d.l. "Disciplina sulle offerte pubbliche di azioni e di obbligazioni" (C2889).

18. D.d.l. "Disciplina delle attivita' di intermediazione immobiliare e disposizioni sull'organizzazione dei mercati mobiliari" (C3870).

them to be the Italian ones. On the other hand the second EEC directive states that banks, authorized according to the directive, can carry on "activities in the same manner as in the home member state, as long as the latter do not conflict with legal provisions protecting the general good in the host member state." While it may be conceivable that execution of trading operations on account of customers could be subject to the limitation of the "general good" and therefore to the provisions of the host member state, certainly one sees no reason why such limitation should apply to execution of trading operations on own account. This more restrictive provision will apply only to securities firms that are subsidiaries of Italian banks and that will have to execute all securities transactions in Italy, while other member states' banks or their securities firms subsidiaries, while trading on their own account, will be free to execute their transactions according to the rules of their home countries.

Future Legislative and Regulatory Changes

In spite of the recent modifications, it is foreseeable that over the next few years the Italian banking legislation will undergo further substantial changes. These will concern not only rules regarding the banking system as far as specialization by activity and ownership control are concerned, but also the monetary authorities in their functions of surveillance and of lender of last resort. Several facts suggest that such revision is unavoidable and that it cannot be postponed without great cost to the Italian banking system.

First, the letter of the 1936 banking law allowed banks to be run as universal banks and did not mandate any separation between the short- and the medium-term provisioning activities. Furthermore, it did not limit in any way the holding of banking stocks by nonbanks as well as the participation by banks into nonbanking concerns.[19] However, the monetary authorities interpreted the spirit of the law as requiring the observance of specialization by activity, and the separation between bank and industry. Consequently they introduced several limitations and restrictions, usually in the form of administrative regulations. These were frequently adapted to the changing times, and

---

19. See Costi (1990).

produced a system regulated by the pragmatic discretion of the authorities, where banks are free to carry on some of the activities listed by the second directive, though not all of them. The recent legislation gives the status of law to these regulations just in the areas where the second EEC directive is much less restrictive than the Italian regulatory system: the separation between short- and medium-term borrowing, the distinction between banking activity and securities trading for account of customers, and the control holding of banks by nonbanks. The dynamics of our banking legislation becomes asymmetric with respect to the EEC's one, which our authorities, among others, have contributed to shape.

Second, the application of national rules that are more restrictive than the second EEC directive's, in the areas addressed by the articles 4, 5, 11, 12, and 16 of the directive and relatively to national credit institutions only, will remain possible. However, such possibility will imply a tradeoff between consistency at the national level and *de facto* discrimination against Italian banks, without in many cases necessarily achieving the ultimate purposes of the legislation.[20] It is foreseeable that the objective of not discriminating against national banks will prevail in the legislature's aim, entailing a revision of Italian laws along the lines of the second directive.

Third, the concept of "excessive" concentration of power, which is at the heart of Italy's Antitrust Law and of the prohibition for industries to acquire banks, will have to be assessed in relation to the dimensions of the European market. In other words, what is "excessive" for the size of the Italian market may not be so when its frontiers expand and become the edges of the European Community's single market.

Fourth, the next few years will also see substantial changes in the action of the monetary authorities. More specifically, their functions of surveillance and of lender of last resort will have to enlarge their scope, and reflect the new market conditions.

The definition of banking activities provided by the second EEC directive widens considerably the number and the type of institutions

---

20. For a view stressing this competition among legal systems and the need to redesign the national economic policies in the unified European market, see Padoa-Schioppa (1990).

that are subject to surveillance by the monetary authorities. Several important issues concerning the function of lender of last resort will also be raised by the new developments:

- First, to the extent that the universal bank will become the prevailing model, this function will *de facto* be extended to a spectrum of activities that goes well beyond that of short-term borrowing from the public.
- Second, from this viewpoint the choice between the bank holding group and the universal bank is not only a choice of organizational convenience, but could become the dividing line between a system, where the lender of last resort is only reserved to banks, in the traditional sense, with the other activities carried on by separate and specialized corporations, and a system where the counterpart of the lender of last resort is the universal bank, where all the activities, including securities trading and holding of participations into nonbanks, are carried on indistinctly within the same corporate organization.
- Third, in both cases the range of instruments by which the function of lender of last resort is performed today by the monetary authorities will need to be enlarged. On the one hand, such updating of a law that is more than 80 years old is necessary in order to reflect the changed composition of the banks' balance sheets.[21] But, on the other hand, this change will also have to put Italian banks on an equal footing with the other member states' competitors.

The next few years will tell us how successful our legislature will be in bringing together all these instances and viewpoints into a consistent framework from which a banking system ready for the challenges of the European financial integration will emerge.

Bibliography

Cesarini, F., M. Grillo, M. Monti, and M. Onado (eds.) (1988). "Banco E Mercato." Part 3. Bologna: Il Mulino, pp. 469-655.

---

21. See Ciocca (1990).

Ciocca, P. (1983). "La Valutazione Dell'Affidamento Della Clientela Da Parte Delle Banche: Criteri E Prassi Operative." *Bancaria* (10).

Ciocca, P. (1990). "Ancora Sul Credito Di Ultima Istanza." *Moneta E Credito* (giugno, no. 170).

Ciocca, P., and F. Frasca. (1987). "I Rapporti Tra Industria E Finanza: Problemi E Prospettive." *Politica Economica* (4):29-50.

Costi, R. (1990). *Due Modelli Per Il Credito*. Il Sole-24 Ore 15/11.

Nardozzi, G. (1983). "Tre Sistemi Creditizi." Bologna: Il Mulino.

Padoa-Schioppa, T. (1990). Politica Economica Nazionale E Concorrenza Tra Sistemi. Banca d'Italia, Bollettino Economico, no. 15,10.

Steinherr, A. and P. L. Gilibert. (1989) *The Impact of Financial Market Integration on the European Banking Industry*. Center for European Policy Studies, No. 1.

Steinherr, A., and C. Huveneers (1989). "Universal Banking: A View Inspired by German Experience." Paper presented at the Conference on the Separation of Industry and Finance, and the Specialization of Financial Intermediaries, Milan, March 1989.

15

BANK HOLDING COMPANIES: A BETTER STRUCTURE FOR CONDUCTING UNIVERSAL BANKING?

Samuel H. Talley

Introduction

In recent years, banking systems in many countries have been experiencing increasing instability. At the same time, market forces have been pushing banks to expand into various universal banking activities, some of which appear to involve greater risks than traditional banking activities. The combination of these two developments has raised the question whether it might be possible to *restructure* banking organizations in order to permit them to pursue universal banking activities without impairing the stability of the banking system.

Organizationally, there are three alternative ways in which banking organizations can participate in universal banking activities. First, they can conduct these activities directly in the bank. This appears to be the arrangement that is most widely used. Second, they can conduct these activities in subsidiaries of the bank, an arrangement that appears to be increasing in use. Third, they can conduct these activities in bank holding companies (either in the parent company or in nonbank subsidiaries of the parent). To date, this organizational arrangement has not been widely used, but is being increasingly discussed in banking and public policy circles.

Proponents of bank holding companies argue that conducting universal banking activities in holding company affiliates is clearly superior to conducting these activities either directly in the bank or in subsidiaries of the bank. These advantages include shielding the bank against the risks that universal banking activities may entail, avoiding the spread of bank-type regulation, and promoting a level playing field between banking and nonbanking competitors.

The objective of this paper is to evaluate the bank holding company device as a vehicle for conducting universal banking activities. The paper identifies the major issues involved, reviews the empirical evidence on the use of the holding company structure, and discusses several proposals to make the use of the holding company device more effective from a public policy perspective.

The paper is divided into eight sections. Following this introductory section, the paper briefly reviews the pros and cons of universal banking. In the third section, the basic features of the bank holding company proposal are presented and explained. In the next two sections, the alleged advantages of the bank holding company proposal are presented, followed by various challenges to these alleged advantages. In the sixth section, the empirical evidence on the use of the holding company device for conducting universal banking activities is reviewed. Unfortunately, this empirical evidence is very limited because only one country, the United States, has expressly employed the holding company device on a wide scale to conduct universal banking activities. In the next section, two variants of the basic bank holding company proposal—the fail-proof bank proposal and the fail-proof parent proposal—are presented and evaluated. The major conclusions of the paper are presented in the final section.

Universal Banking

The term "universal banking" does not appear to have a precise definition. In general, however, the term implies that banking organizations have powers to engage in activities that go significantly beyond traditional banking activities. These broader activities might include lending and investing that involve substantial term transformation, engaging in securities underwriting and dealing, and, in some countries, even holding equity positions in commercial and industrial companies.

As indicated earlier, there has been considerable controversy regarding the merits of universal banking.[1] The proponents of universal banking argue that this form of banking will promote economic growth by making available much needed long-term financing to commerce and industry. Universal banking also will promote efficiency by allowing banks to achieve economies of scale and scope. Moreover, universal banking will foster competition by opening up various areas of finance for entry by banks.

Opponents of universal banking argue that it will distort credit allocation because of an increase in connected lending. Also, universal banking inevitably will lead to a greater concentration of economic resources and political power. Further, universal banking is bound to lead to conflicts of interest—for example, a bank underwriting securities for a troubled firm where the proceeds of the issue would be used to pay off the bank's own loan to the company. Finally, and perhaps most important, universal banking could involve banks engaging in risky activities that could jeopardize the stability of the banking system.

The difference of views regarding the merits of universal banking is reflected in several World Bank reports over the last decade or so. In the late 1970s, the Bank staff recommended the implementation of universal banking in the Philippines. Shortly thereafter, the staff turned around and argued against universal banking for Brazil and Mexico.[2] The staff's apparent inconsistent approach may simply reflect Maxwell Fry's comment: "There is, therefore, no universal case for or against universal banking."[3]

The Basic Bank Holding Company Proposal

The proposal to use bank holding companies to engage in universal banking activities could take various forms. The form used in this paper is the one that seems to appear most frequently in public policy discussions. This proposal, which will be referred to as the *basic* bank holding company proposal, contains three major elements.

---

1. For a detailed review of the pros and cons of universal banking, see Khatkhate and Riechel, (1980, pp. 478-516).
2. See Long, (1983, p. 40).
3. See Fry (1988, p. 283).

First, any bank that wants to operate as a universal bank would be required to form a holding company and then conduct all riskier activities in holding company units, rather than directly in the bank. These riskier activities could be conducted either in the holding company itself, or nonbank subsidiaries of the parent company. The bank would continue to engage in traditional banking activities that involve "bankable" risks.

Second, the government would develop laws and regulations designed to insulate the bank from any financial problems that might occur in holding company affiliates of the bank. At a minimum, these "firewall" provisions would include: (1) strict quantitative limitations on bank loans or other extensions of credit to holding company affiliates, as well as tight limits on bank purchases of securities or other assets from these affiliates; (2) requirements that all bank transactions with affiliates be on "market terms"—that is, on terms and conditions that are substantially the same as those on bank transactions with non-affiliated parties; and (3) provisions that would prevent the holding company from extracting excessive dividends from the bank that would unduly deplete the bank's capital.

Third, holding company units would be subject to little or no supervision by bank regulatory authorities.[4] Instead, the financial affairs of these affiliates would be disciplined largely or entirely by the marketplace. The rationale for not subjecting holding company affiliates to bank-type regulation is that it is not needed if the bank can be effectively insulated from holding company financial problems.

Alleged Advantages of the Proposal

Proponents of the basic bank holding company proposal argue that the proposal would produce substantial public benefits. Most important, the proposal would allow the public to derive the benefits of universal banking without placing the stability of the banking system in jeopardy. The bank holding company proposal also would minimize the spread of bank-type regulation. By conducting risky universal

---

4. Holding company affiliates participating in certain nonbanking activities might be subject to regulation by other government agencies. For example, if an affiliate engages in securities underwriting and dealing, this activity might be supervised by a securities regulatory authority.

banking activities in holding company affiliates, it would not be necessary to subject these activities to bank-type regulation because the bank is protected by firewalls. By contrast, if these risky activities were conducted directly in the bank, or even subsidiaries of the bank, these activities almost surely would be subject to bank-type regulation. As a result, the movement to universal banking probably would result over time in the spread of bank-type regulation throughout much of the financial system. Moreover, it would tend to result in regulatory duplication in those financial industries (such as securities and insurance) that are probably already subject to regulation by "functional" regulators.

Another advantage of the bank holding company proposal is that it would place banking and nonbanking competitors on a level playing field. First, both banking and nonbanking rivals would be subject to essentially the same amount of regulation. By contrast, if universal banking activities were conducted directly in the bank, or in subsidiaries of the banks, the bank would be subject to bank-type regulation, whereas its nonbanking rivals would not. Second, the bank holding company proposal would promote competitive equality in the funding of universal banking activities. If these activities were conducted directly in the bank, banks would tend to have a lower cost of funds because banks are protected by the government through such devices as deposit insurance and access to a lender of last resort. Under the bank holding company proposal, however, activities would have to be conducted in holding company affiliates. These affiliates would have to do their own funding in the marketplace or, alternatively, if funded by the bank, would be required to pay market rates. Consequently, holding company affiliates could not gain a funding advantage over their nonbank rivals.

Challenges to the Alleged Advantages

On first view, the basic bank holding company proposal seems to represent an extremely attractive way to allow banking organizations to engage in universal banking. The proposal holds out the promise that universal banking can be conducted without jeopardizing banking stability or spreading bank-type regulation throughout the financial sector, and also would place banking and nonbanking competitors on a level playing field.

However, these alleged advantages of the bank holding company proposal have been subject to serious challenges. The most important of these challenges is that, in fact, it may not be possible to insulate banks from holding company problems. If the firewalls develop cracks, most of the alleged advantages of the proposal would disappear. There are three ways that holding company problems might spill over onto banks.

First, if a holding company affiliate fails, creditors of the affiliate might successfully sue the bank to honor the debts of its affiliate. Such a court ruling is referred to as "piercing the corporate veil" and effectively nullifies the technical legal separation of affiliated corporations.

The willingness of courts to pierce the corporate veil could vary considerably from country to country, depending on the laws of the various countries and how courts have chosen to interpret these laws over time. What can be said, however, is that courts in many countries have been willing to pierce the corporate veil under certain circumstances. In particular, courts have permitted piercing in cases where the business affairs of affiliates have been extensively commingled, the affiliates have operated or held themselves out to the public as a single entity, or the policies of the failed affiliate were directed to the interest of surviving affiliates rather than to its own interests.

Second, holding company problems may be transmitted to banks in the form of adverse transactions. Even with laws designed to prevent such transactions, banking authorities may not be able to prevent them in all cases. One reason is that examiners who would monitor these transactions cannot be entirely sure whether some transactions are on terms that are entirely fair to the bank. For example, it is difficult for an examiner to determine whether the amount of management fees that the bank pays the holding company is appropriate for the services rendered to the bank. Likewise, within a certain range, it is difficult for an examiner to judge whether the tax payment that the bank makes to the holding company to cover the bank's share of the consolidated organization's tax liability is appropriate, or whether the bank's operations have been manipulated in various ways to maximize this tax payment.

In addition to the problems of effectively monitoring intercompany transactions, it is possible that desperate holding company management will knowingly violate banking laws by forcing the bank to bail out a failing holding company affiliate. In banking, the pressures to avoid a failure are great because banking is preeminently a reputation business.

The third way that holding company financial problems could be transmitted to the bank is through a loss of market confidence in the bank. This loss of confidence might occur because depositors closely identify the bank with the holding company. In other words, depositors view the entire bank holding company organization as a single entity, ignoring the fact that the organization actually is composed of a number of legally separate corporate entities.

There are a number of reasons why market participants may view the entire holding company organization as a single entity. One reason is that holding companies often try to project a single entity image through such devices as giving similar names to their various units. This device could capitalize on name recognition and the organization's favorable reputation in the marketplace. Another reason is that holding companies usually operate their organization as a single entity, rather than as a group of unrelated units. Market participants perceive this managerial approach and are influenced by it. Finally, holding companies are likely to do most or all of their financial reporting on a consolidated basis. This practice tends to foster a single entity perception in the marketplace. It also makes it difficult for market participants to evaluate the financial condition of individual units in the holding company, including the bank.

Even if market participants were not conditioned to view bank holding companies as a single entity, they still might commence a run on the bank if an important holding company unit failed. One reason is that major units of holding companies usually are managed by essentially the same group of people. Consequently, if one holding company affiliate has been seriously mismanaged, it is not unreasonable for market participants to assume that other units in the organization, including the bank, may be in trouble too. Moreover, market participants might fear that the bank may be abused in a desperate attempt by holding company management to bail out the troubled affiliate.

As discussed earlier, one of the alleged advantages of the holding company proposal is that it would avoid spreading bank-type regulation throughout much of the financial system. This contention rests on the assumption that banks, in fact, can be effectively insulated. If it is subsequently discovered that insulation does not work, it is probable that the government would subject holding companies to bank-type regulation, thereby spreading this type of regulation to other areas of finance. In addition, if holding companies were subsequently subjected to bank-type regulation, another alleged advantage of the proposal—the equal regulatory treatment of banking and nonbanking competitors—would be eliminated.

Finally, it is alleged that the holding company proposal would promote competitive equality by removing banking organization's inherent funding advantage over nonbanking firms. It appears that this contention has been almost universally accepted in public policy discussions. In fact, the argument is seriously flawed. As discussed earlier, the funding advantage would presumably be eliminated because any bank funding of holding company affiliates would have to be on market terms. The crucial implicit assumption in the argument is that these affiliates would then use this regulatory mandated cost of funds as the basis for setting prices for services offered to the public. In fact, it is unlikely that the affiliate would use its *own* cost of funds because this cost merely represents an *internal* transaction between two units in the same organization. Consequently, this cost figure would have no implications for the consolidated organization and would not be used by a profit maximizing organization to set prices. Instead, the organization would use the bank's "subsidized" cost of funds, because this represents the consolidated organization's *external* borrowing cost. In the final analysis, the only way that a banking organization's funding advantage can be removed is to *prohibit* the bank from funding affiliates, thereby forcing these affiliates to do their own funding in the marketplace, presumably at "nonsubsidized" market rates.

Empirical Evidence on Insulation

Whether banks can be effectively insulated from financial problems in holding companies is ultimately an empirical question. Unfortunately, there is at present only very limited empirical evidence on this crucial issue. First, there appears to be only one country—the United States—where banks have made a concerted effort to convert to the holding company form of organization in order to engage in a broader range of activities than existing laws permit banks to conduct. Second, even though the holding company form of organization is pervasive in the American banking system, there have been very few real tests of the firewall concept. One reason is that policymakers have placed fairly strict limitations on the universal banking activities of holding companies. Consequently, these nonbank activities often are not large enough to cause serious problems for the consolidated organization. In addition, since the mid 1970s, holding company nonbanking activities have been subjected to close supervision by the Federal Reserve. This supervision has tended to constrain risk-taking, and probably has led to fewer financial problems than otherwise would have occurred.

However, there have been two cases in the United States that clearly have tested the insulation concept. The first occurred in 1973 and involved a small bank holding company in California named Beverly Hills Bancorp. This holding company owned Beverly Hills National Bank, but also was involved in making commercial real estate loans that were funded by commercial paper. When one of the holding company's large borrowers defaulted, the holding company was unable to pay off its maturing commercial paper and was placed in bankruptcy. The adverse publicity that accompanied the bankruptcy, and the close public identification of the bank with the holding company, resulted in large-scale runs on Beverly Hills National Bank. These runs required bank supervisors to merge this illiquid, but solvent, bank into another bank.

The second, and far more important, test occurred in 1975 and involved Hamilton Bankshares. This holding company owned Hamilton National Bank, one of the largest banks in the state of Tennessee. In the early 1970s under new, aggressive management, the holding company set up a mortgage banking company and proceeded to expand the company's operations very rapidly. Within a short period of time, the mortgage company had a large amount of nonperforming loans and was experiencing funding problems. In order to save the mortgage company, management arranged for Hamilton National Bank to buy a large amount of the troubled mortgages. These transactions, which were in clear violation of existing banking laws, subsequently caused the bank to fail. At the time of the failure, Hamilton National Bank was the third largest bank failure in American history.

The Beverly Hills and Hamilton cases understandably have raised some degree of skepticism in the United States regarding the ability to insulate banks from holding company financial problems. Yet, it is important to recognize that both of these cases occurred about 15 years ago, and one involved a relatively insignificant bank. Consequently, while these cases lend some weight against the firewall concept, they definitely do not constitute conclusive evidence.

There are several other aspects of the American experience with bank holding companies that are worth noting. First, in the two cases where the firewalls cracked, they cracked for different reasons. In the Beverly Hills case, the spillover effect took the form of a loss of market confidence in the bank. In the Hamilton case, the spillover effect involved massive adverse transactions. So far, there have been no cases where American banks have been "pierced" and forced to honor the debts of holding company affiliates. Moreover, there is almost universal agreement among lawyers, bank regulators, and academics that courts in the United States are unlikely to pierce the corporate veil, except in extraordinary cases involving gross commingling of the business affairs of separately incorporated entities.

Second, it is instructive to note how the Federal Reserve, the supervisor of bank holding companies in the United States, reacted to the Beverly Hills and Hamilton failures. Prior to these failures, the Federal Reserve had relied largely on the market to discipline the financial affairs of bank holding companies and their nonbanking affiliates. Shortly after the failures, however, the Federal Reserve changed its policy and began to subject holding companies and their nonbank affiliates to bank-type regulation, including on-site examinations, off-site surveillance, and extensive financial reporting (including reports on a wide variety of transactions between holding company units and the bank). Moreover, it appears that the Federal Reserve still does not have great faith in the firewall concept, because the Federal Reserve has continued to subject bank holding companies to strict bank-type regulation, even though there have been no known spillover problems since the mid 1970s.

Finally, there may be some marginal benefit in reflecting on the following statement relating to the insulation question that was made a few years ago by Walter Wriston, the former Chairman of Citicorp:

> "It is inconceivable that any major bank would walk away from any subsidiary of its holding company. If your name is on the door, all of your capital funds are going to be behind it in the real world. Lawyers can say you have separation, but the marketplace is persuasive, and it would not see it that way."[5]

Other Proposals

While the basic bank holding company proposal holds out great promise, the benefits are crucially dependent on the ability to insulate banks from holding company financial problems. As indicated in the last two sections, there are certain reasons, as well as some limited empirical evidence, for doubting that insulation will actually work. Given this skepticism, two other proposals—both variants of the basic proposal—have been developed. The better known variant is usually referred to as the fail-proof bank (or narrow bank) proposal. The other variant is known as the fail-proof parent proposal. Both proposals are designed to make insulation more effective than it would be in the basic bank holding company proposal.

Fail-Proof Bank Proposal

The fail-proof bank proposal is essentially an extreme form of the basic bank holding company previously discussed.[6] The fail-proof bank proposal would force banks to separate their traditional deposit

---

5. *Financial Institutions Restructuring and Services Act of 1981*, Hearings before the Senate Committee on Banking, Housing and Urban Affairs, Congress of the United States, 1981, pp. 589-90.

6. The fail-proof bank proposal was originally developed by Robert J. Lawrence, and was subsequently elaborated on by Robert Litan in a Brookings Institution study. See Lawrence (1985, pp. 22-31) and Litan (1987).

issuing and lending functions. Once the proposal is implemented, banks would be confined to issuing deposits and investing in virtually risk-free assets, such as short-term government securities or perhaps high quality commercial paper. All previous bank activities that involved any meaningful degree of risk would be transferred to holding company affiliates. These affiliates also would do all the future lending for the banking organization.

Under the proposal, banks would be required to closely match their asset and liability maturities to virtually eliminate interest rate risk. Moreover, banks would be prohibited from engaging in bond trading, foreign exchange trading, or conducting various off-balance sheet activities. Banks also would be required to have a small amount of capital that would be sufficient to absorb any remaining, unavoidable risks. Any transactions between a fail-proof bank and its holding company affiliates would have to be on market terms, and examiners would closely monitor all intercompany transactions to make sure that the bank was not abused.

Because fail-proof banks would be virtually risk free, the government could fully insure all bank deposits without exposing the government to any significant risk. From a depositor's perspective, this insurance would constitute a strong second line of defense behind a virtually risk-free bank.

A final feature of the proposal is that holding company affiliates would not be subject to bank-type regulation. Instead, these affiliates would be disciplined solely by the market.

The great virtue of the fail-proof bank proposal is that it would give banks almost perfect insulation against holding company financial problems. First, the proposal would essentially eliminate any possibility that the bank would be pierced. The reason is that the severe restrictions imposed on fail-proof banks would make it virtually impossible for them to commingle their business affairs with those of their affiliates. Second, fail-proof banks would be exposed to only minimal risks of adverse transactions because the banks could not lend to affiliates and could purchase only virtually risk-free assets from affiliates. These two types of transactions are potentially the most dangerous ones that banks can have with affiliates. Third, and most important, fail-proof banks would not be threatened by a loss of market confidence if a holding company affiliate failed. The reason is that depositors would know that the bank was virtually risk free and that they were fully insured by the government. Moreover, in the extremely unlikely event that depositors ignored these protections, the bank would be in an excellent position to withstand a run. The bank's portfolio would be composed entirely of short-term assets that either would mature within a very short period, or could be sold at very little or no loss. Further, the bank would have access to the lender of last resort and would have a large portfolio of acceptable collateral.

The fail-proof bank proposal would minimize the amount of regulation of the banking system. As stated above, there would be no need to regulate holding company affiliates because banks would be almost perfectly insulated from holding company problems. In addition, the proposal would permit a substantial cutback in the existing regulation of banks. For example, the banking agencies would no longer have to review banks' loan portfolios, a particularly time-consuming and expensive affair. Instead, the examination of fail-proof banks would be limited largely to determining whether the banks were in compliance with the special requirements for fail-proof banks, whether any bank transactions with holding company affiliates were on market terms, and whether there had been any misappropriation of bank funds.

The fail-proof bank proposal also would get high marks in promoting competitive equality between banking organizations and their nonbanking rivals. First, by prohibiting banks from lending to affiliates and forcing these affiliates to do their own funding, the proposal would prevent banks from transferring their inherent funding advantage to their affiliates. Second, the proposal would subject holding company affiliates and nonbanking firms to the same degree of regulation. Under the proposal, holding company affiliates would not be subject to bank-type regulation. As a result, in those nonbanking activities that are regulated, these affiliates would be supervised only by the traditional functional regulator, as would their nonbanking rivals. In those nonbanking activities that are not regulated, both holding company affiliates and their nonbanking rivals would be subject only to the discipline of the marketplace.

From the perspective of achieving public benefits from the transfer of risk within a banking organization, the fail-proof bank proposal is clearly superior to the basic bank holding company proposal. The reason is that with the fail-proof bank proposal, public benefits are virtually assured because the effective insulation of banks is virtually assured. By contrast, with the basic bank holding company proposal, public benefits are problematic because the effective insulation of banks is in question.

If the fail-proof bank proposal can produce virtually assured, major public benefits, why hasn't it been used? The answer is that its implementation might not be feasible.[7] First, the proposal would require a wrenching change in the structure and operation of the banking and financial system. Under the proposal, banks could continue to hold only a small portion of their existing assets. Consequently, banks either would have to sell most of their assets in the open market or sell them internally to holding company affiliates. Both types of asset sales would produce major problems, particularly since the entire banking system presumably would be selling assets at about the same time. Large asset sales in the open market would drive down market prices, thereby causing banks to incur capital losses. Large asset sales to holding company affiliates would require these affiliates to do a large amount of financing, thereby driving up their cost of funds.

Another problem is that there might not be enough virtually risk-free assets in existence for banks to hold. Indeed, there are probably few, if any, financial systems in the world where the amount of virtually risk-free assets exceeds the amount of bank deposits. In this case, the only way that the proposal could be implemented would be to relax the requirement that banks hold virtually risk-free assets. If this were done, however, the basic character of the proposal changes from a fail-proof bank proposal to a "somewhat less than fail-proof bank" proposal. And with this change, the assurance that banks will be totally insulated and that public benefits will be achieved begins to slip. In sum, the fail-proof bank proposal involves an inevitable tradeoff between achieving public benefits and the feasibility of implementing the proposal.

---

7. For a detailed discussion of why the fail-proof bank proposal may not be feasible in the United States, see Lawrence and Talley (1988, pp. 344-59).

Fail-Proof Parent Proposal

The fail-proof parent proposal is another variant of the basic bank holding company proposal, although a considerably less extreme one than the fail-proof bank proposal.[8] Like the basic proposal, the fail-proof parent proposal would require banking organizations to transfer relatively risky activities (but not all activities involving risk) from the bank to the holding company. However, unlike the basic proposal, which would allow these riskier activities to be conducted either in the parent company or nonbank subsidiaries of the parent, the fail-proof parent proposal would require these activities to be conducted only in nonbank affiliates. The reason is to assure that the parent company would not fail as the result of sustaining large operating losses. Another major feature of the proposal is to prohibit the parent company from issuing debt. This provision would assure that the parent would not fail because it could not service its debt obligations.

The proposal also would prohibit banks from engaging in most types of transactions with holding company affiliates, such as lending or the purchase of assets. Only transactions that are essential, such as paying dividends and making tax payments to the parent, would be permitted, and these would be subject to close oversight by bank supervisors to prevent any abuse of the bank.

It should be noted that under the fail-proof parent proposal, nonbank affiliates probably would do most of their own funding. However, the parent company could issue stock and use dividend income to fund these affiliates. Also, the holding company could set up a financing subsidiary that could raise funds for the nonbank affiliates. This procedure could centralize funding for the entire nonbanking part of the holding company organization, thereby exploiting any economies of scale that might be involved.

Under the fail-proof parent proposal, nonbank affiliates would not be regulated and supervised by banking authorities. Instead, these affiliates would be subject only to the discipline of the marketplace.

---

8. The fail-proof parent proposal was originally developed by staff of the Federal Reserve Board in the mid-1970s. The proposal was presented for consideration by the Board in 1975, but was not implemented. For a discussion of the proposal, see Lawrence and Talley (1978, pp. 1-10). For a more recent discussion, see Lawrence (1983, pp. 39-52).

The crucial assumptions underlying the fail-proof parent proposal are: (1) it makes a difference where risky activities are conducted in the holding company structure; and (2) it is better for these activities to be conducted in nonbank subsidiaries of the parent than in the parent company itself. The reason is that the failure of a nonbank affiliate is likely to have a significantly less adverse effect on market psychology, and would be less likely to cause a loss of public confidence in the bank, than would the failure of the parent. In a holding company organization, the parent is a particularly important entity. It is the top tier of the organization and, even more important, it is the entity whose stock is held by the public. Given these factors, it is hard to imagine that the failure of the parent would not inflict severe reputation damage on the bank. By contrast, a nonbank affiliate is only a branch in the holding company structure, and its stock is not held by the public. Consequently, the failure of a nonbank affiliate probably would not inflict as much reputation damage on the bank. Moreover, if the parent company is debt free, the failure of a nonbank affiliate would not cause the failure of the parent, and the continued existence of the highly visible parent should help to sustain public confidence in the bank.

In addition to giving banks greater insulation, the fail-proof parent proposal has several other desirable features. First, by not subjecting holding company affiliates to regulation by the banking authorities, it would not spread bank-type regulation throughout the financial sector or result in regulatory duplication. Second, the proposal would promote competitive equality between banking and nonbanking rivals: (1) by subjecting them to similar regulation; and (2) by removing the inherent funding advantage of banking organizations by prohibiting banks from lending to their nonbank affiliates.

Conclusion

This paper has dealt with the question of whether it would be desirable to conduct universal banking activities (or at least those that are relatively risky) in bank holding companies, rather than directly in banks. Stated differently, from a public policy perspective, does it make any sense to encourage or force the transfer of risk among units of a banking organization? The major conclusions of the study are as follows.

First, the use of the bank holding company device for conducting universal banking activities holds out the promise of important public benefits. These benefits include: (1) a sounder commercial banking system, (2) a reduction in banking regulation, and (3) greater competitive equality between banking and nonbanking units. However, these benefits are critically dependent on the ability to insulate banks from future problems that might arise in holding company affiliates. There are three basic ways that holding company problems could be transmitted to banks: (1) through piercing the corporate veil, (2) through adverse transactions, and (3) through a loss of market confidence in the bank. The first two spillover effects would inflict losses on the bank and erode the bank's capital. The third would result in the bank experiencing liquidity problems that might force the bank to sell assets at a loss.

Second, at present there is no conclusive empirical evidence on whether banks can be effectively insulated from holding company financial problems. Bank holding companies have been used extensively as a device for conducting universal banking activities in only one country, the United States, and the evidence from that country is very limited. In those two cases where holding company affiliates experienced major financial trouble, the problems did spill over onto the bank and caused the bank to fail.

Third, public policymakers can do much to prevent banks from being pierced by requiring banks not to commingle their business affairs with holding company affiliates. Likewise, policymakers can minimize the likelihood of banks being forced into adverse transactions by prohibiting all bank transactions with affiliates except those that are essential (such as paying dividends and taxes to the parent company), having bank supervisors closely monitor these essential transactions to assure that the bank is not abused, and imposing stiff penalties for violating rules governing bank transactions with affiliates.

Fourth, it is much harder to prevent a loss of market confidence in a bank if holding company affiliates get into trouble. In this event, depositors are likely to commence a run on the bank because they typically do not have detailed information on the condition of the bank, and they are aware that essentially the same people usually manage both the holding company and the bank. Consequently, depositors are likely to play it safe and assume that if the holding company is in trouble, the bank may be in trouble too.

Fifth, one way to virtually eliminate the possibility that holding company problems would lead to bank runs is to require banks to be fail proof. However, the process of converting banks into fail-proof institutions would probably result in unacceptable shocks to the financial system. A less extreme proposal that would reduce, but not eliminate, the prospect of bank runs would require: (1) universal banking activities to be conducted in nonbank subsidiaries of the parent company, rather than directly in the parent; and (2) the parent company to be debt-free (or at least lowly leveraged). With these requirements, bank runs would be less likely because the highly visible parent company would survive.

Sixth, while a major objective of having universal banking activities conducted in holding companies is to preserve banking stability, it is possible that it could have the opposite effect. The major risk is that policymakers will assume that the firewalls protecting banks are impregnable and allow holding companies to engage in highly risky activities that policymakers would never consider permitting banks to conduct. If holding company affiliates subsequently encountered serious problems and it turns out that the firewalls have cracks, banks could be seriously harmed. It also should be recognized that having universal banking activities in holding companies could concentrate specific types of risks in a number of individual holding company affiliates, rather than having a wide diversification of risks in one unit, the bank.

Bibliography

Black, Fischer, Merton H. Miller and Richard A. Posner, (1978). "An Approach to the Regulation of Bank Holding Companies," *The Journal of Business*, July, pp. 395-98.

Chase, Samuel B., (1972). "The Bank Holding Company—A Superior Device for Expanding Activities?" *Policies for a More Competitive Financial System*, Federal Reserve Bank of Boston, pp. 77-87. Also see the discussion of the Chase paper by Phillip E. Areeda, pp. 88-93.

_____ and Donn L. Waage, (1983). *Corporate Separateness as a Tool of Bank Regulation*, Study prepared for the American Bankers Association.

Chase, Samuel B., (1988). "Insulating Banks from Risks Run by Nonbank Affiliates," *Proceedings of a Conference on Bank Structure and Competition*, Federal Reserve Bank of Chicago, pp. 291-324.

Cornyn, Anthony G. and Samuel H. Talley, (1983). "Activity Deregulation and Bank Soundness," *Proceedings from a Conference on Bank Structure and Competition*, Federal Reserve Bank of Chicago, pp. 28-38.

_____, Stephen Rhoades and John Rose, (1986). "An Analysis of the Concept of Corporate Separation in BHC Regulation from an Economic Perspective," *Proceedings from a Conference on Bank Structure and Competition*, Federal Reserve Bank of Chicago, pp. 174-212.

Corrigan, E. Gerald, (1986). "Financial Market Structure: A Longer View," *Annual Report*, Federal Reserve Bank of New York.

Eisenbeis, Robert A., (1983). "How Should Bank Holding Companies Be Regulated?," *Economic Review*, Federal Reserve Bank of Atlanta, January pp. 42-47.

_____, (1983). "Bank Holding Companies and Public Policy," in *Financial Services: The Changing Institutions and Government Policy*, Prentice Hall, pp. 127-55.

Flannery, Mark J., (1986). "Contagious Bank Runs, Financial Structure and Corporate Separateness Within a Bank Holding Company," *Proceedings of a Conference on Bank Structure and Competition*, Federal Reserve Bank of Chicago, pp. 213-30.

Fry, Maxwell J. (1988). *Money, Interest and Banking in Economic Development*. Johns Hopkins University Press.

General Accounting Office, (1987). Bank Powers: Insulating Banks from the Potential Risks of Expanded Activities, Report to the Chairman of the House and Senate Banking Committees, April.

Khatkhate, Deena R. and Klaus-Walter Riechel, (1980). "Multipurpose Banking: Its Nature, Scope, and Relevance for Less Developed Countries," Staff Papers, International Monetary Fund, September, pp. 478-516.

Lawrence, Robert J., (1983). "Holding Companies and Deregulation," *Proceedings of a Conference on Bank Structure and Regulation*. Federal Reserve Bank of Chicago, pp. 39-52.

_____, (1985). "Minimizing Regulation of the Financial Services Industry," Issues in Bank Regulation, Summer, pp. 21-31.

_____, and Samuel H. Talley, (1978). "An Alternative Approach to Regulating Bank Holding Companies," *Proceedings of a Conference on Bank Structure and Competition.* Federal Reserve Bank of Chicago, pp. 1-10.

_____, and Samuel H. Talley, (1988). "Fail-Proof Banking: Severing the Risk-Taking and Deposit Functions of Banks." *Issues in Bank Regulation* (Fall) pp. 20-24.

_____, and Samuel H. Talley, (1988). "Implementing a Fail-Proof Banking System," Proceedings of a Conference on Bank Structure and Competition, Federal Reserve Bank of Chicago, pp. 344-59.

Litan, Robert E., (1986). "How to Take the Dangers Out of Bank Deregulation," The Brookings Review (Fall) pp. 3-12.

_____, (1987). *What Should Banks Do?* Brookings Institution.

Long, Millard (1983). "Review of Financial Sector Work." World Bank Financial Development Unit, Industry Department. October.

Rose, John T. and Samuel H. Talley, (1984). "Financial Transactions within Bank Holding Companies," *The Journal of Financial Research* (Fall) pp. 209-17.

_____, (1978). "Bank Holding Companies as Operational Single Entities," in *The Bank Holding Company Movement to 1978: A Compendium,* Board of Governors of the Federal Reserve System, pp. 69-93.

Talley, Samuel H., (1985). "Activity Deregulation and Banking Stability," *Issues in Bank Regulation*, Summer, pp. 32-38.

_____, (1986). "An Evaluation of Bank Holding Companies," *Issues in Bank Regulation*, Summer, pp. 37-45.

Wall, Larry D., (1984). "Insulating Banks from Nonbank Affiliates," *Economic Review*, Federal Reserve Bank of Atlanta, September, pp. 18-28.

INDEX

(Page numbers in italics indicate material in tables or figures.)